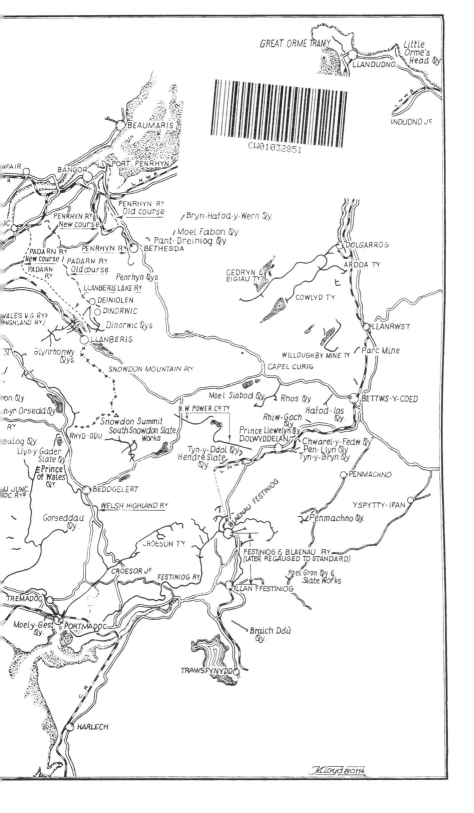

NARROW GAUGE RAILWAYS IN SOUTH CAERNARVONSHIRE

VOLUME 1

© Oakwood Press & J. I. C. Boyd

British Library Cataloguing in Publication Data
A Record for this book is available from the British Library
ISBN 0 85361 365 6

First Edition 1972
Enlarged Revised Edition in two volumes 1988
Reprinted 2000

Printed by Oakdale Printing Co., Poole, Dorset

To the Memory of Tom Davies
Last Engineman of the Old Order on the Festiniog Railway;
sometime on the Welsh Highland Railway,
A patient teacher and devoted Railwayman
whose enthusiasm inspired this book.

Published by The Oakwood Press, P.O. Box 13, Usk, Mon., NP15 1YS.
E-mail: oakwood-press@dial.pipex.com
Website: http://ds.dial.pipex.com/oakwood-press

NARROW GAUGE RAILWAYS IN SOUTH CAERNARVONSHIRE

(2nd Edition) Enlarged and Revised

VOLUME 1

THE EMBANKMENT TRAMWAY, THE GORSEDDAU TRAMWAY, THE FESTINIOG & BLAENAU RAILWAY, THE MERIONETHSHIRE RAILWAY, THE CROESOR TRAMWAY, THE BETTWS-Y-COED & FESTINIOG RAILWAY, THE NORTH WALES NARROW GAUGE RAILWAYS and THE PORTMADOC BEDDGELERT & SOUTH SNOWDON RAILWAY

by

JAMES I. C. BOYD

THE OAKWOOD PRESS

* ***Out of Print***

CONTENTS   *Page*

Note on track diagrams and signalling arrangements

These have been compiled by the Author using field work, photographic and a limited quantity of official material. The latter is frequently misleading, as it usually denotes 'intent' rather than accomplishment. All drawings are original and based on these sources; this is brought to notice as most drawings in this Series are not copies from official sources open for public inspection.

Note on place-names

The spelling of place-names is based on that commonly used in Bradshaw's Timetable, allowing for changes in Bradshaw's spelling and alterations in the names of stations etc. Where railway systems had no passenger service and Bradshaw cannot be quoted, the customary spelling used by railway historians has been adopted. Early maps frequently mis-spelt Welsh names, and official documents (usually of English origin) are disastrous in this particular. Official changes from Anglicised to more Welsh forms of spelling have occurred over the period covered in the book, e.g. Carnarvon to Caernarvon etc. and more recently, Port Madoc to Porth Madog etc., etc., and care is necessary in identifying some smaller places, especially as names are often duplicated within a comparatively small area. Caernarvonshire now forms part of Gwynedd.

(A few minor changes in the form of names have been introduced into this Second Edition, and may be slightly at variance with the maps which have been taken from the First Edition without alteration.)

AUTHOR'S NOTE TO THE FIRST EDITION

Railway history has traditionally been presented in the form of Company History. This is convenient for the chronicler and tidy for the reader, but it is basically misleading and makes for insipid reading. There is more to be said for presenting railway history as a regional study and not to confine it by artificial commercial boundaries.

There is a certain danger that the history of the Festiniog Railway (which forms a part of this Series), will be read in isolation because of its prominent position but in reality it was but one thread in a tangled skein, the more interesting because it was one of the oldest and strongest strands of that skein.

The other strands, some even older and often much smaller, are also full of legend and interest; in fact in many respects they are more so. Without their existence – or threat of existence – the Festiniog would have become lazy and lifeless. So now the opportunity is taken to study the remainder of the pattern in greater detail, avoiding, it is hoped, over-emphasis on each individual undertaking, but showing how it stood up both against and alongside its contemporaries.

Unfortunately the regional boundary method does not permit a convenient assemblage and has not been too rigidly applied in consequence. Thus the volume dealing with South Caernarvonshire, takes in also a part of North Merionethshire. In this will be the railways with which the Festiniog had to live. The northern part of Caernarvon is covered by the second part, dealing with some railways without whose earlier existence the Festiniog Railway would not have come into being.

Colwall, Herefordshire.   James I.C. Boyd
December, 1971.

AUTHOR'S NOTE TO THE SECOND EDITION

This Note enjoys a background which to date, other Notes to books in this Series – covering the Isle of Man and Wales in their content – could not possess . . . the knowledge that the Series is complete. Spread over almost forty years it is natural that some of the titles have gone out of print, so it seemed, for all time. However, the deep-seated interest in our past has continued to grow and the number of railway-orientated publications has multiplied to meet what in most instances is simply a form of nostalgia.

This Series is not for such dilettante approach: it seeks to inform (and dare I say, amuse?) rather than entertain, believing that the pace of change not only on the face of the ground but in society itself is erasing memory of even the recent past.

A revised and enlarged edition of this title (many years out of print) is overdue. Knowledge of these matters never ceases to increase, it is very satisfying to be able to re-publish in two volumes rather than one, and so give effective coverage to railways (in what is now known as a part of Gwynedd) which were born and died within the lifetime of an average man.

Colwall, Herefordshire.   James I.C. Boyd
March, 1988.

INTRODUCTION

For many people, the railways of Caernarvonshire (a county title which is so much more definitive than the modern usage of "Gwynedd"!) simply consist of that line which clings to the north coast connecting Conway and Holyhead as part of the route of the 'Irish Mail'. Some others knew about the standard gauge lines from north to south and along part of the county's south coast, and that was about all. For the esoteric there was a bonus of fascinating little railways – most now a memory – which mapmakers seldom drew, because the system appeared and disappeared between Editions! And being non-passenger-carrying lines, railway timetables ignored them. Many were private, some were pioneer, and all are part of an age which has disappeared very quickly since the Second War.

The origins of these railways lay in the mineral resources of the county. These are so prodigious that more narrow gauge railways were built in Caernarvonshire than any other county in the Kingdom. For the terrain and the job, the small-gauge tramway was ideally suited. The most important of these resources was slate; in some places it had been worked for over 300 years before the coming of railways. Of the lesser railway-users, certain minerals were carried by rail, but often they were mined erratically over the years by successive owners or lease-holders, so that there was no continuity. For instance, one landowning family is said to have simply 'poured money down holes in the ground' in the expectancy of fortunes from below the earth's surface. Some of the more barefaced promotions which were publicly financed, made great promise of their potential and sometimes built railways to carry it away; all too often they went into liquidation within the next decade. The problem with minerals and their associated tramways was that they went through intensely profitable periods (usually the result of political and economic pressures of the times), but they were highly sensitive to slump. The tramways connecting these speculative ventures are among the most ephemeral in the country. Only human memory recorded them, and those who dared record these memories in print were often contradicted by the next raconteur.

The predecessors of rail transport in this part of Wales included the horse or mule carrying a pannier along a specially built path over the rough mountainside. A later development was to enlarge the path into a very rough road and use the traditional Welsh farm sledge. This was widely used in all places and seasons where wheeled transport was impracticable. The next development, if required, was the building of a macadam road, and the landed proprietors were foremost in providing good roads through the mountains, mainly for their own promotions. These same proprietors followed their road-making activities by building 'Iron Railways' (as they were often termed in these parts) when it became clear that whilst a horse might haul a road wagon along a new road quite easily, that same horse could haul a greater tonnage over iron rails and moreover, right out of the workings and down to the sea coast and a ship's side.

It is possible that certain early tramways were initially laid out as sledge-ways and were used as such, probably having rails laid on them at a later stage. This was certainly true in some quarries, notably Dinorwic, where man-carrying sledges descended the inclines in formidable fashion.

An account of sledging in the Llangynog slate quarry in the early 19th century is revealing: '. . . slates . . . are brought down the steep declivity of rock in sledges containing about 5 cwt. each, with extreme danger to the persons engaged in this arduous task. When the sledge is loaded, and drawn to the edge of the declivity, a conductor sits upon it, passing over his shoulders a rope which is fastened at each extremity to the front, and also being assisted with a pole. Then raising his feet from the ground, he begins his descent by a narrow winding path, guiding the sledge by opposing his feet to the projecting points of the rock . . . governing its velocity by pressing firmly with his feet upon the ground and sustaining the weight of the carriage by the rope which passes over his shoulders . . . sometimes the guide . . . instead of sitting on the front of the sledge, descends backwards . . . when in danger of being overpowered . . . by the sledge, slipping the rope over his head, detaches himself from the carriage and throws it sideways over the precipice, regarding only his own preservation.' For this work, the guide received twopence per run.

All of which suggests that the advent of balanced-incline tramways, even with all their attendant risks of cable breakages etc., must have been welcomed by such 'guides' (as the account calls them) 'who expose themselves to inevitable destruction'.

Every user of mineral workings faced the problem of transport. Little of his products was used locally and most had to be shipped. Slate went to many overseas markets as well as England and Ireland, and copper and other metal ores to South Wales for smelting. Water was the cheapest form of transport and even inland waters would be used for part of a load's journey if available, the cost of trans-shipment being considered unimportant. The coming of the tramway, with its flexibility, cheapness and penetrating capability soon opened up workings which hitherto had lacked development for their inaccessibility, and some remote tramways came into being.

The county had only one important port, Caernarvon. Pwllheli was also used, but was not so convenient. Artificial ports came into existence during the railway period, among them Portmadoc, Port Dinorwic and Port Penrhyn, all within twenty years of each other. Later the coast was to be dotted with shipping points where quarries on the hilltops along the coast ran tramways onto jetties and ships could load at most stages of the tide. Indeed, in neighbouring Denbighshire a jetty with tramway from the Llandulas Lime Quarry on it, had been built as early as 1822. In the context of this book, Caernarvonshire looked to the sea and the railway or tramway formed an integral part of the route.

The railway systems which resulted from this demand were very personal and parochial. Those which did not develop until the age of the steam locomotive were often too late for the trade they intended to serve. The slate industry was already declining in the 1880s and generally continued so from that time onward. Other minerals enjoyed intermittently good times. Usually, it was the oldest-established lines which had the longest lives and lasted until the nineteen-sixties. There were cases where a line which had been faithful to horse-power remained so to the end of its days.

The original narrow gauge railways of Caernarvonshire have almost passed into memory. Walking along their mountainy courses today, it is hard to imagine the intrigue, high hopes and lost causes which surrounded most of them. Money was made and lost in a big way in this still very unpopulated region. After the Second War there came a time when hopes were high, but the expected boom in slate and tourists never came. Ultimately the remaining slate lines closed down and more recently, some of the largest slate quarries in the world have gone under the hammer.

Caernarvonshire has some of the finest scenery in the world and yet – at least at the time these lines are written – no narrow gauge railway of the type which flourishes under 'preservation' auspices, runs entirely within the county. This is not to make out a case for the establishment of one, but in a county which did more for the birth of narrow gauge railways and their establishment throughout the world than any other, it is ironic that the few passenger lines struggled hard and died early. Certainly at the present time when expansion in narrow gauge tourist railways is manifest, some native Welsh are still recalling the Welsh Highland Railway débâcle, so it seems that, even today, authority in Caernarvonshire is divided on the merits of passenger narrow gauge railways. Which, considering all that has passed within its boundaries, is a pity.

In an effort to make the sequence of events more easily followed (a pattern which even the staff of the Board of Trade found almost impossible to discern . . . witness the correspondence which accompanies the official documents!!) additional preface material has been added to this Second Edition.

Certain chapters have, where relevant, been grouped into Sections. Each Section has now been given a Historical Summary in date order so as to emphasise the ambition and intent of the promoters. The complex period of Section IV is 1900–1911 and 1921–23 at which last date the Welsh Highland Railway received its last Order; affairs of that Company are covered in *Volume 2*. The concerns involved in Section IV have been abbreviated in the Summary as follows:

Portmadoc, Croesor & Beddgelert Tram Railway Co.	Portmadoc Co.
North Wales Narrow Gauge Railways Co.	Railways Co.
Portmadoc, Beddgelert & South Snowdon Railway Co.	Snowdon Co.

Snowdon & Bettws-y-Coed Railway   Bettws Co.

North Wales Power & Traction Co.   Power Co.

These abbreviations agree with those used in Board of Trade documentation, and have been used throughout the text following the Summaries.

THE EMBANKMENT TRAMWAY 1808–c.1830
(Gauge 3 ft)

Used in the construction of the Embankment or Cob at Traeth Mawr, between 1808 and 1811, and retained thereafter for maintenance purposes. Disposed of before building of the Festiniog Railway over the Embankment and materials possibly disposed of to local users, including the Tremadoc Tramway.

Length: app. 1 mile as completed; double track.

The story of the Great Embankment (or 'Cob') and its place in the history of North Wales has already been fully told. In dealing with its designer and builder, W.A. Madocks, Elizabeth Beazley's 'MADOCKS AND THE WONDER OF WALES' concentrates on its conception, construction and aftermath. The Tramway in relation to the Festiniog Railway and other railways which entered Portmadoc, is adequately covered in 'The Festiniog Railway' and it is therefore unnecessary to repeat the background save that for good order's sake the Tramway should be mentioned here as being the second to be built in South Caernarvonshire.

The danger of consulting the above-mentioned works is that having regard to Madocks' remarkable genius and buoyant enthusiasm for everything he did (which is fully brought out) it might be concluded that he was engaged in some pioneer effort. The work, and the Tramway used to build it, was truly remarkable but not unique; it was more difficult as being done in a then very isolated part of North Wales.

Reclamation work had been done in the Dee Estuary by Nathaniel Kenderley & Co., following an Act of 1734 for improving the navigation of the river to Chester, and passing through Saltney Marsh. This was completed in 1737. A new canal was formed and 800 acres of new land was appropriated by the Company for their own use on the north side of it. Between 1754 and 1790 further land was reclaimed which ultimately became Sealand. Another 2,000 acres was added under another Act of 1778. At Golvtyn (Golftyn) the Irish Coal Co. erected a large quay and pier at the mouth of the New Dee Channel.* Here in fact, was the immediate predecessor of Madocks' schemes for reclamation, canal, town and port, not more than 50 miles from his Penmorfa Estate, purchased in 1798.

Madocks' first experience in reclamation came with two dykes he built to enclose parts of this estate from river and tidal flood; the second dyke, the James Creassy Embankment of 1800, is said to have had the assistance of a wooden railway to bring the soil etc. with which it was built, from the hills surrounding, but the source of information is somewhat open to doubt. This sea wall was lightly made, not using rock or solid material at all.

Madocks' ambition was far greater than this; he proposed in 1770 to enclose the estuary of the river Glaslyn by building a barrage between the shores of Caernarvonshire and Merionethshire, and build a road along it to connect England and Ireland. His first interest was in

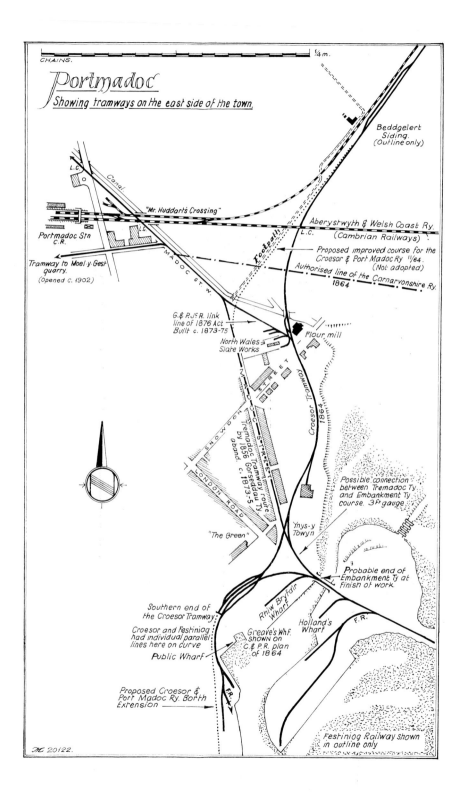

CHAINS. ¼ m.

Portmadoc
Showing tramways on the east side of the town.

L.C.

Canal

Beddgelert
Siding.
(Outline only)

"Mr. Huddart's Crossing"

L.C.

Aberystwyth & Welsh Coast Ry.
(Cambrian Railways)
L.C.

Portmadoc Stn
C.R.

MADOC ST. W.

Tramway to Moel-y-Gest
quarry.
(Opened c. 1902)

Footpath

Proposed improved course for the
Croesor & Port Madoc Ry. ¹¹/₆₄
(Not adopted)
Authorised line of the Carnarvonshire Ry.
1864

G. & P.Jⁿᴿ. link
line of 1876 Act
Built c. 1873-75

North Wales Slate Works

Flour mill

Croesor Tramway
1864

NOSSON STREET

LONDON ROAD

Tremadoc Tramway route
by 1856 Gorseddau Ty.
aband. c. 1873-5

Possible connection
between Tremadoc Ty.
and Embankment Ty.
course. 3 ft. gauge

"The Green"

Ynys-y-
Towyn

Probable end of
Embankment Ty. at
finish of work

Southern end of
the Croesor Tramway.

Croesor and Festiniog
had individual parallel
lines here on curve.

Public Wharf

Rhiw Bryfdir
Wharf

Greave's Whf.
shown on
C. & P.R. plan
of 1864

Holland's
Wharf

F.R.

F.R.

Proposed Croesor &
Port Madoc Ry. Borth
Extension

Festiniog Railway shown
in outline only

JIC 20122.

communications; the reclaimed land was a secondary matter. He was anxious to promote Porth Dinllaen (he had given £600 towards the cost of a pier there) as the seaport for Dublin, and such a road would lie on the direct London–Porth Dinllaen–Dublin route; more importantly for him, his new town of Tre Madoc would lie on it too. He acquired the right to build the Embankment at his own expense under an Act of 1807 (47 Geo. III Cap. 36) which vested any sands reclaimed in him and gave him an annual rent of 1/5th of the marshlands reclaimed. With only the first few hundred yards on the west bank in Caernarvonshire, he proposed to extend the bank from the rocky outcrop of Ynys-y-Towyn to a point near Penrhyn Isa farm on the Merioneth shore, nearest to where rock might be found for infilling. To carry materials from quarries at Ynys and Penrhyn, he built a double tracked Tramway which ultimately extended the full length of the work and into the stables, yards and workshops and quarries at each end. The idea for such a Tramway may have originated with the 1800 embankment (if such a Tramway had in fact been used there) and possibly that on the Embankment was influenced by his friend, Benjamin Wyatt, agent to Lord Penrhyn.

Madocks' first mentions the Tramway in correspondence of January 1808; it was at work in the following March. The stone quarried from opposite shores was tipped from horse-drawn wagons into the rapacious sands. The track was carried beyond the stonework on 'stilts' (piles) covered by a wooden platform; as the arms of the great bastion gradually closed together, so the Tramway crept forward and its use intensified to frenzied proportions as time and money ran out, and the gap between the solid matter grew less and less, while the force of water grew greater and swept away all the materials thrown into it. At this time 600 wagon loads of stone were discharged into the breach on a good day, and there might have been more but for a chronic shortage of horses. The gap was closed in July 1811 and an official opening took place on 17th September, 1811.

The vast cost, met from Madocks' own pocket, bankrupted him. Inventories of the site were prepared by his creditors and vary in their content. It seems there was about a mile of track (2 miles double line) valued by one at only £370. The number of 'small waggons' on the site varies between 20 and 40, but all agree there were both old and new to be found. One list included a 'caravan' and a Bathing Machine.

With the work done, part of the Tramway was taken up, possibly sold to meet creditors' demands. Evidence suggests it saw further service locally. Then in the following February a storm broke down the Cob and a great hole resulted. So appalling was this tragedy to all in the neighbourhood that there seems to have been an extraordinary effort by all concerned to repair it. The Tramway was replaced with some difficulty, but was probably never completely put back. When the Cob had been repaired in late 1814 the track was, despite pressure from Madocks' creditors, allowed to lie undisturbed in case an emergency should require its use again. Possibly its materials ultimately found their way into the Tremadoc Tramway which, allowing for part-disposal in the 1811–14 period, would just about account for what was available when the track was hurriedly relaid. What had been Penrhyn Cottage on the Merioneth side, was enlarged into workshops, stables and offices and in May 1811 took the name of Boston Lodge after Madocks' Parliamentary constituency. The premises later became the Festiniog Railway's Works.

Of the permanent way materials, little is known: they may have been of the same pattern of 'Round Rails' invented by Benjamin Wyatt (they were in fact, more elliptical than round) and used on the Penrhyn Railway which had opened in July 1801. On the other hand it may equally have come through an idea put forward by Richard L. Edgeworth of Co. Longford for reclaiming Irish bogland in 1787, and which Edgeworth admitted in 1810 to having been adopted on the Penrhyn Railway. By 'Round Rails', oval rails were meant, and to suit them, wheels with a concave rim were provided. If the Embankment Tramway track is likely to have been very similar to that on the Penrhyn in 1801 (and there is good reason for suggesting it) then it had oval rails of cast iron, laid crudely into cast-iron chairs which were bolted through slate or slab sleepers. This was not an efficient track; the Penrhyn pioneer rail was soon replaced by a different section in lengths of 4 ft 6 in. which did not wear the wheel treads hollow – a state of affairs which would have affected the Embankment wagons with their intensive usage. The simple chairs had no means of securing the oval rails either; the rail rested in a form of plain saddle and stayed there by its own weight.

The rails and chairs must have been removed ultimately from the Embankment when the Festiniog Railway was laid on the site in due course. If the Tramway was laid with slab sleepers they would have been available for re-use and this would predetermine the gauge of the purchaser's track. The Tremadoc Tramway is known to have been of 3 ft gauge and, when extended to serve the Gorseddau⋆ Quarry, continued in that gauge. (It was not converted to 2 ft until the Gorseddau Junction and Portmadoc Railways Act sanctioned the conversion.) If the Tremadoc Tramway used Embankment Tramway redundant materials including stone sleepers, then the Embankment Tramway would have been to 3 ft gauge. If however, Penrhyn experience was followed in the matter of gauge, a nominal 2 ft gauge would have existed; this would logically suggest that (as distinct from individual blocks) some of the numerous slab sleepers used under the early Festiniog track might have had their origins in the Tramway. All this is speculation.

The rails and some of the wagon wheels came from Jones of Wrexham, perhaps from a foundry of Edward Jones of Tuttle Street in that town and to provide ready-to-run wagons, some were purchased from South Wales. However, Beazley maintains the rails were cast at

⋆*Gorseddau* – 'a place where on a great copped heap of stones, sat the Druid whilst he instructs the people'.

'the famous Brymbo works near Wrexham' in which Madocks had a holding. They went by road and canal to Chester, thence by sea. Madocks records that the wagon bodies were mainly built by local carpenters; perhaps this was before the day of the sheet-iron sided wagon or the ability of local industry to build them.

The Embankment under construction, with a scene of the Tramway at work, was incorporated in a drawing 'The Embankment, Traeth Mawer . . . In the autumn of 1810', by H.W. Billington. Though proportionately inaccurate, the detail of the wagons is probably fairly accurate and shows how little contractors' stock has changed in 150 years. The wagon shown has inside bearings for the axles (the wheels are likely to have been loose on them anyway, and secured by a wedge holding a collar in place at the axle-end), a wooden frame and body, and has a drop side door. Other detail in the picture suggests the wagons could swivel round on the frame.

TREMADOC TRAMWAY
(Gauge 3 ft)

Incorporated by Act: None.
Opened: Mineral traffic; before 1845.
Closed: Absorbed by and became a portion of, the Gorseddau Tramway 1855.
Length: app. 1 m. 30 ch.

GORSEDDAU TRAMWAY
(Gauge 3 ft)

Incorporated by Act: None.
Opened: 1856–7. Used existing portion of Tremadoc Tramway between Portmadoc and Tremadoc.
   Absorbed by and became part of Gorseddau Junction & Portmadoc Railways under Act 35/6. Vic. Cap. 155 25th July, 1872.
Length: 8 m. 5 ch.
Capital: None; constructed privately.

GORSEDDAU JUNCTION & PORTMADOC RAILWAYS COMPANY
(Gauge 2 ft)

Incorporated by Act: 35/6 Vic. Cap. 155 of 25th July, 1872.
   39/40 Vic. Cap. 137 of 13th July, 1876, increase of capital etc.
   55/6 Vic. Cap. 44 of 20th June, 1892, rates and charges.
Opened: Goods and minerals; official opening 2nd June, 1875; actual 2nd September, 1875.
Closed: Braich-y-Bib to Gorseddau Quarry about 1875, Cwm Trwsgl to Cwm Dwyfor by 1884. Remainder by 1892.

Registered Office: St. Clement's House, London, E.C.

Length: Gorseddau Tramway section: 8 m. 1 fur. 1½ ch.
   Cwm Pennant extension: Braich-y-Bib (Old Junction) to
   Mine: 5 m. 1 fur. 1½ ch.
   Total: 13 m. 2 fur. 3 ch. (Only 11 m. used from 1875.)

Maximum Gradient: 1 in 25.

Minimum Curve: 2 chains.

Capital: 1872 Act. £20,000 in £10 Ordinary shares. £6,666 in Debentures (= ⅓ capital).
   1876 Act. £10,000 additional capital in Ordinary. £3,333 additional Debentures (issued as £800 Loan @ 6% + £5,800 Loan
   @ 8%). Meeting of 22 September 1876 sanctions issue of
   1,000 First Perpetual Preference Shares (5%) @ £10 each –
   £1,400 issued December 1876 + £1,650 in 1877 + £2,100 in
   1885 = £5,150 @ 5%.

Cost per Mile: £2,750 to 1876.

Historical Summary

1845	By this date there was already in existence a 3 ft gauge tramway (The Tremadoc Tramway) between Tremadoc and Portmadoc Harbour.
1856	By this date The Tremadoc Tramway had been extended to reach the Gorseddau Quarry, and was now The Gorseddau Tramway.
1872	By Act of Parliament the section of The Gorseddau Tramway between Portmadoc Harbour and Braich-y-Bib was converted to 2 ft gauge, and extended from thence to Cwm Trwsgl, the whole statutory undertaking named The Gorseddau Junction & Portmadoc Railways. Doubts exist if the section Braich-y-Bib to Gorseddau became 2 ft gauge, or was in use at any time after the passing of the Act.
1875	Gorseddau Junction & Portmadoc Railways opened for goods and mineral traffic (only).
mid-1880s	Railway out of use by this date (*see text for detail*).

History

   The origins of what was ultimately to become the Gorseddau Junction & Portmadoc Railways lay firstly in a canal and secondly in two
earlier tramways. The canal would have remained a mere land drain
had it not been for the imagination of one who 'canalised' the drain in
order to landscape his creation of Tremadoc, and the tramways came
into being because of the existence of nearby Embankment Tramway
materials which were no longer required for their original purpose.

   William Alexander Madocks has already come to notice in a previous chapter on the Cob Tramway. He had come into the district in 1798 after purchasing the Penmorfa Estate, (Penmorfa was described in 1800 as a 'wretched village') and lived at nearby Tan-yr-Allt, overlooking the then sea-washed Glaslyn Estuary. He conceived a model village to enhance his own importance, to satisfy his whims and improve the view from his residence! The name Tre Madoc or Tremadoc was given to it and building began in 1805. It stood 3 ft below low water mark. A large woollen mill, finished in 1800, lay within the town, and with 60 looms, was larger than anything similar in North Wales. Madocks conceived boldly . . . as with the Mill, so later with the Cob. One of his characteristics is still perpetuated in the district at Port Meirion by Clough Williams-Ellis; he too was fond of architectural whimsy and decorated Tremadoc with follies and other romanticisms, even the Public Convenience. Madocks had a weakness for having ships within his vision, and to improve the appearance and businesslike atmosphere of the town, built a short branch from the main land-drain nearby, right into the town. This drain, known as Y Cyt (or The Cut – the Lancashire vernacular for a canal is apparent) was the fruit of an earlier land reclamation scheme and its water passed through the 1800 embankment by means of the Great Sluice and so into the Glaslyn. Madocks formed a 'Bason' at the top of his new branch, alongside London Street (now Church Street) and arranged for it to be filled with boats so as to impress his London and Dublin friends when passing through. The drain thus became a canal. It was easy on the eye as well as having a limited commercial application.

The Bron-y-Gadair Copper Mine, owned by Samuel Holland Senr. of Liverpool used it, as water transport was the only means of getting the ore out to sea-going vessels. The mines in this district however, were very prone to flooding and in 1836 Holland sold out to the Cambrian Mining Co. who, though they installed a 12 h.p. steam engine to pump out the workings, had to cease when they were drowned out in 1844.

West of the town at Llidiart Yspytty, was a small ironstone mine which had been worked from at least the 1820s; records of its tonnages through Portmadoc Harbour in the 1839–40 period have survived. Clearly the canal was of limited value to this mine for, at an unknown date, (but before 1845 as it is shown on Portmadoc Harbour Improvement Plans of that date) a tramway (shown on the Tithe Map of 1842) was laid down on the west bank of Y Cyt to connect the mine and Portmadoc Harbour. Materials formerly used by Madocks in the Tramway built for the construction of the Cob may have been utilised for a second time for this line; these had been partly disposed of after the work was finished thought it is on record that part of the Tramway was kept for maintenance purposes at least. We have seen that the Cob Tramway may have been of 3 ft gauge; the new Tramway certainly was of that gauge and was owned by Martin Williams, Manager of the Tremadoc Estate, of Bryn Gwyn, Denbighshire. The lessee was John Williams, agent to Martin Williams, and the occupier John Haywood (or Heywood).

A lease dated 28th March, 1840 from "John Williams of Brecon Place in the County of Caernarvon to Henry Cooper of Aberglaslyn and James Robins Croft of Liverpool of Llidart-y-Spytty and Penysyflog" gives the right "to make and continue a railway or railways from the demised premises or any part thereof to any wharf, key or shipping place at Port Madoc aforeso". There is also a covenant by John Williams within twelve months subject to Act of God etc., to lay down an iron railroad to the Port and provide a weighbridge. There is provision for a reduction of the royalties payable by 8d. per ton until the railway is built and when built the reduction is to be 4d. a ton out of a total royalty of 2/- per ton.

On 2nd February, 1841 a further lease was granted by "John Williams then of Plas Tanyrallt to Henry Prichard of Llidarty-y-Spytty and Penysyflog". The terms are the same as in the lease of 20th March, 1840 save that the railway is expressed to be in the progress of being made. There is also a lease date 10th November, 1846 by "John Williams to John Heywood of the Llidart-y-Spytty Iron Mines" and this lease states that the railroad to Port Madoc had been built.[1]

[It is known that Madocks indulged in some ingenious manoeuvres to outwit his creditors; one of them may have been to mortgage the Tremadoc Estate. For instance, in 1845 the Llidiartyspytty Railway (sic) was stated to be owned by "Martin Williams of Bryngwyn in the County of Montgomery surviving trustee of Sydney Madocks of Glanywern in the County of Denbigh widow . . .". In short, Madocks' intention was by mortgaging the Estate to Trustees for his nephew's wife so as to secure money to pay off his creditors; the Trustees then took whole possession to keep out the other creditors! The ploy is only a part of the complications of this matter.]

Despite the building of the tramway, the town continued to provide the canal with some traffic. In its heyday, the waterway could accommodate vessels of up to 120 tons and astonishingly, despatched a steamboat for New York in 1830! Ultimately it fell into disuse and today has reverted to the drain it was designed to be. Inspiration for building it is said to have come from Madocks' visits to Talgarth, and seeing the Brecon Canal nearby.

The Tremadoc Tramway – as it is convenient to call the Llidiart Yspytty line – is recorded on the Portmadoc Harbour Plans of 1846 as making its way southwards along Madoc Street, Portmadoc, crossing London Road on the level and curving round the west bank of the Glaslyn to the Outer Harbour. It is presently impossible to say if the 2 ft gauge Festiniog Railway, opened in 1836, or the Tremadoc Tramway was first on the scene, but if the latter was the case, then there must have been mixed gauge lines on the west bank of the river. Being almost level for its entire length, the Tremadoc line is likely to have been horse-worked in either direction throughout its life. Its wagon stock may have been supplied locally and may not have differed much from 3 ft 6 in. gauge wagons on the nearby Nantlle Railway. This is conjec-

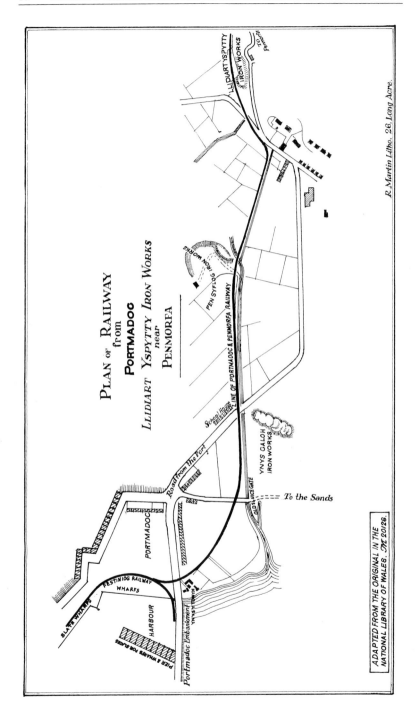

PLAN OF RAILWAY
from
PORTMADOC
to
LLIDIART YSPYTTY IRON WORKS
near
PENMORFA

R. Martin Litho. 26, Long Acre.

ADAPTED FROM THE ORIGINAL IN THE
NATIONAL LIBRARY OF WALES. JM 20/26.

ture, as is the nature of the track materials; perhaps both track and wagons came from the Embankment Tramway and perhaps in the surviving Nantlle material we may have much of the character and features of this early system.

The Carnarvon Turnpike Trustees made an Agreement for the Tremadoc line to cross the Turnpike, dated January 1842.

With the fortunes of the iron mining ventures running out, the Tremadoc line became less well used and without Parliamentary authority the Bangor & Portmadoc Slate & Slate Slab Co. Ltd. approached the owners and arranged to extend the line by means of wayleave and a reversing neck and junction beside the Llidiart Yspytty Mine.

The Bangor & Portmadoc Slate & Slate Slab Co. Ltd. (hereinafter called the Bangor Co.) came into being because Richard Morris Griffith of Bangor had intended to lease the distant slate quarry at Gorseddau to Henry Van Uster in 1853. (He was later connected with the nearby Hendre-ddu slate and slab quarry near Dolbenmaen, 1861).

A draft was drawn up by a Bangor solicitor whose name (though less well known than C.E. Spooner as a promoter of narrow gauge railways), crops up continually at this time in South Caernarvonshire railway and quarry matters. He was Hugh Beaver Roberts, then of Plas Llandoget, Llanrwst. The proposal fell through, but Robert Gill of Mansfield and John Harris of Darlington took up a lease for 63 years: Edwin Dixon was appointed Quarry Manager. In May 1855 they planned a tramway to Portmadoc. On 12th April, 1856 the following appeared in 'THE NORTH WALES CHRONICLE':

To Contractors

The Bangor & Portmadoc Slate Company are prepared to receive tenders for the execution of the works on that part of their railway extending from the Turnpike Road at Tremadoc to the Old Turnpike Road at Glan Bwll being a distance of 2¼ miles. The drawings, specifications and quantities may be had from E.J.J. Dixon Esqr., Glanhelen Villa, Carnarvon or at the office of James Brunlees Esqr. C.E., Essex Street, Manchester.

Tenders must be sent in before 16th of April.

In the same month the 'CARNARVON & DENBIGH HERALD' had:

To Builders

The Bangor & Portmadoc Slate Co. are prepared to contract for building a Fore man's House at Gorsedda Quarry, near Portmdoc (etc.).

There are other scanty pieces of evidence that work was beginning. The Carnarvon Old Turnpike Trust Minutes:

order that the B.&P.S. Co. be allowed to continue their railway under the Turnpike roads near Pencaenewydd . . .

(this on 19th October, 1855). Then on 4th July, 1856:

On the application of James Dixon Esqr. on behalf of the Gorsedda Slate Co. to raise the Turnpike road over an arch at Tynllan near Penmorfa to take a railway under it. It was ordered that they be allowed . . . and pay the costs . . .

So, whatever style the newspapers may have accorded to the concern working the Gorseddau Quarry, using the Tremadoc Tramway as its vital link with Portmadoc shipping, the quarry was at last reached by rail, construction covering a period 1856–8 when the average output of the workings was '1338 tons of roofing slate'. In terms of rail traffic, this meant about 4–5 one ton loaded wagons passed down the line each working day. It is important to distinguish the quarries around Penmorfa from others in those parts, as the rock hereabouts was suited less to slate than making slabs, flagstones and paving setts. One reason for the failure of the quarries served by the line (and its later extension) was not only the low output and skeletal transport method, but the fall in demand due to a better quality product at a cheaper price being available in other parts of the county.

The 'CARNARVON & DENBIGH HERALD' for January 1857 records:

An accident which might have terminated fatally, occurred last week on the line of railway between the Gorsedda Slate Quarry and Port Madoc, which is now nearly completed, and the fences of which are in course of construction. Wagons loaded with stone are running down for this purpose. The incline on the railway being very great, the utmost caution is required in breaking (sic) the wagons. Some slight obstruction occurring on the road, the run was nearly stopped, and during this time the hooks connecting the wagons together became unfastened; the two first wagons got detached and then the speed was enormous. Happily no human being stood in its way, but the constructor's horses were working lower down the road, and could not be reached . . .

(and one was killed).

Above Tremadoc it served other concerns, and to keep gradients to a minimum, it reached Gorseddau by a circuitous route through Hen-efail. Even so, west of Tremadoc severe inclinations of 1 in 23 and 1 in 25 were involved. Luckily this was mainly against empty wagons returning to the quarry and horse-working was used over the whole system which was open by May.

The 3 ft gauge of the Tremadoc line was also retained, though the materials used for the track of the extension are not known. Slate wagons and a 'Passenger Carriage' were supplied by Boston Lodge and there was an exchange of letters between C.E. Spooner of the Festiniog Railway and the Bangor Co.'s Manager, Dixon, concerning wagons, sizes and design, in April 1857. Since the line had no Parliamentary authority and no public service was envisaged, presumably the Carriage was for the private use of the management. The correspondence includes a letter from Boston Lodge (31st March, 1857):

. . . we could undertake to make your Company Waggons to fit your 3 foot gauge and on the same principal as those made by Thomas & de Winton but of a greater length by one foot, with Wrought Iron tyres, first quality iron with the timber work of Foreign Oak, for £17 5s. each.

(Spooner was clearly a little confused between principle and principal!)

Under an arrangement with John Priestley of Ty-uchaf-Cwmystradllyn dated 31st December, 1857 regarding a lease of his land for the tramway, it was agreed that Priestley's servants and agents be given:

> full and free liberty at all seasonable times on one day in every week at his or their option and on the days of holding horse and cattle fairs at Portmadoc, Tremadoc and Penmorfa, after the construction of the said tramway or railway, or using so much of the same as shall be in and upon the hereby demised premises with his and their own trucks for the conveyance thereby of corn and other crops, stock and produce of the said farm . . . and of timber, coals, lime, bricks, tiles and other materials . . . for the purposes of the same farm and for rebuilding and repairing . . . etc.

The land was to be rented from Priestley for 63 years from 15th March, 1858 at an annual rental of £2; the tenants agreed to fence the land alongside the line and to provide within six months of opening the track, at their own expense 'a siding extending at a proper and convenient angle from the said tramway or railway'. At a level crossing on the same premises, gates were to be provided and a pencilled note has been added in the margin of the draft lease, 'I think it would be a hardship upon the lessees to be bound to watch the gates constantly by night'!

In consequence Priestley seems to have come out of it very well; not only was he permitted to use the tramway which crossed his own lands, but one day a week he could use the whole line to Portmadoc (or elsewhere) with his own 'trucks'

> . . . with full power to make use of the horse or other locomotive power for the time being employed in conveying slates or other minerals or goods by the said Robert Gill and John Harris etc.'

Lease of the line would terminate if Richard M. Griffith re-entered the Gorseddau Quarry. The lease was again drawn up by H. Beaver Roberts now of Bangor, (formerly of Llanrwst).

It should be added that Priestley did not sign the lease which gave him his once-weekly right until at least early 1858; he would not commit himself to any one day saying he was 'requiring full and free liberty' to use the line. The actual lease has not survived, but presumably traffic could not use the full length until reconciliation, on which Priestley agreed to use it on a 'Horse and Cattle fair days' basis, was achieved. Priestley seems to have been astute enough to believe his land could be surrended on his own terms. He had already prevented the building of another railway to Portmadoc because he set his sights too high.

It is unlikely that sufficient track material from the Embankment Tramway was available for the extension to Gorseddau, but perhaps ex-Festiniog Railway discarded track materials were used beyond Tremadoc whilst the original equipment in 3 ft gauge survived below. By the 1850s, they must have been becoming somewhat careworn. The provision of new slate wagons suggests the existing stock was probably too old and unsuited to the new traffic. It is evident that the tramway

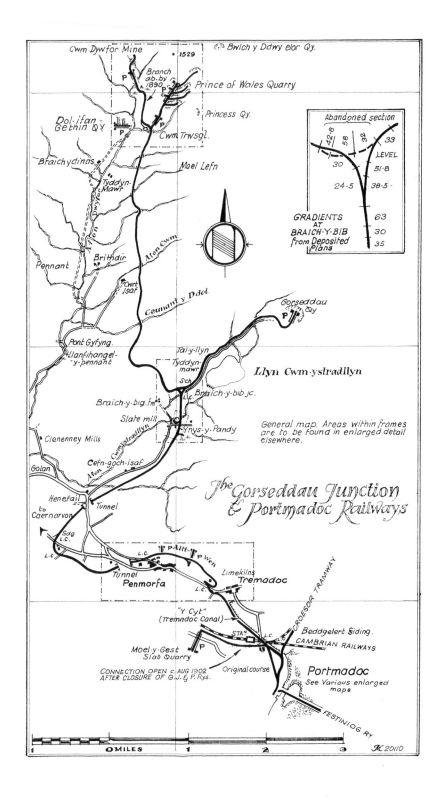

Cwm Dwyfor Mine
Bwlch y Ddwy elor Qy.
• 1529
Branch ab. by 1890
Prince of Wales Quarry
Dol-ifan-Gethin Qy.
Princess Qy.
P
Cwm Trwsgl.
Braichydinas
Maes Lefn
Tyddyn-Mawr
Afon Dwyfor
Pennant
Brithdir
Cwnt Isaf
Ceunant y Ddol
Afon Cwm
Pont Gyfyng
Tal-y-llyn
Gorseddau Qy.
Llanfihongel-y-pennant
Tyddyn-mawr
Sch
Llyn Cwm-ystradllyn
Braich-y-big.fm
L.C. Braich-y-bib jc.
Slate mill
Afon Cwmystradllyn
Ynys-y-Pandy
L.C.
Glenenney Mills
Cefn-goch-isaf
Golan
Afon
Henefail
to Caernarvon
Tunnel
Sdg L.C.
L.C.
L.C.
P Allt
P Wen
Tunnel
Penmorfa
L.C.
Limekilns
Tremadoc
Croefor Tramway

Abandoned section
42·8
58
32
33
LEVEL
30
51·8
24·5
38·5
GRADIENTS
AT
BRAICH·Y·BIB
from Deposited Plans
63
30
35

General map. Areas within frames are to be found in enlarged detail elsewhere.

The Gorseddau Junction & Portmadoc Railways

"Y Cyt"
(Tremadoc Canal)
Moel-y-Gest Slab Quarry
P
STA.
L.C.
Beddgelert Siding.
CAMBRIAN RAILWAYS
CONNECTION OPEN c. AUG 1902 AFTER CLOSURE OF G.J.& P. Rys.
Original course
Portmadoc
See various enlarged maps
FESTINIOG RY.

1
0 MILES
1
2
3
JC 20110

was to become a slate carrier and its former mineral traffic had dwindled away.

[D.E. Bick, the authority on Welsh Metal Mining, gives locations for iron ore mining in the Tremadoc district as: a. 1⅓ m. northwest (Tyn-y-Llon), b. 500 yds. west (Llidiart Yspytty), c. ½ m. south (Pen-Syflog), d. ¾ m. southwest of the town (no rail connection). The second location was the most important and lay within the curve formed by the later tramway to Gorseddau Quarry. The junction at this mine, shown on the First Edition O.S. Map of 1888, is marked 'Gorseddau Junction' and the line beyond as 'Gorseddau Railway'. In all these locations the iron ore was largely obtained by open quarrying but work had ceased by 1860. The site at Yspytty is still comparatively clear, together with traces of an adit. Tyn-y-Llon and Pen-Syflog are also easily found. Lead too was being mined at Gêst, Penmorfa, in the 1850s.]

A small modification was made to arrangements in Portmadoc; by 1863 a slate wharf had been built for the use of the Gorseddau Slate Co. (sic) on a wharf on the north corner of the Sluice Bridge (near the present Glaslyn Foundry) so giving the Madoc Street route direct access to it at the south end of the street. By this means the Gorseddau owners had independent wharfage at Portmadoc without passing over or alongside Festiniog metals on the south side of London Road. It could be suggested that this line was on the site of a link between Cob Tramway and Tremadoc Tramway, but this is pure conjecture.

A second tramway now came on the scene, making the third railed access to Portmadoc, all for similar purpose. The Croesor Tramway was building in 1863 and like the Gorseddau line had been built without statutory consent; it was opened in August 1864 and came into the town from the north-east, using the Creassy land-reclamation embankment for the latter part of its route. Being of the '24 inch gauge' it had no physical connection with the Gorseddau, but it made an acute angle crossing on the level with it on the north side of London Road (later High Street) before making for those same west bank wharves to which both the Tremadoc and Festiniog lines had at first aspired!

The construction of the Tremadoc line, its extension and then change of gauge all makes for unusual reading; the involvement of one no less than James Brunlees (later Sir James) in this metemorphosis is even more remarkable. [James Brunlees (1816–1892): became an assistant to Sir John Hawkshaw on the Lancashire & Yorkshire Railway. From 1856 he was involved in the construction of railways in Brazil, and later the Mersey Railway, Avonmouth Docks etc., etc.] He spent much of his formative years in Manchester in practice as a Civil Engineer and during the middle fifties "he constructed a line between Portmadoc and Gorseddau to a gauge of 3 ft." so the Proceedings of the Institute of Civil Engineers for 11th April, 1865 advises. The cost was but £2,000 per mile, including the land. (In due course Sir James would become President of that Institution.)

Working with Brunlees as a pupil was Daniel Makinson Fox (then in his mid-twenties) who had much to do with planning the route of the later and spectacular Sao Paulo Railway: "he assisted among other enterprises, in laying out and constructing a narrow gauge line in North Wales". It is a comment on those times that railway engineers of potential might be involved in a Welsh quarry line and, well within the next decade, leading in Brazil, a railway enterprise of such stupendous problems as the Sao Paulo!

Brunlees had not grown so famous as to forget his building of the Gorseddau line in later life; on 11th April, 1865, in discussion at The Institution of Civil Engineers following a paper on the Festiniog Railway by Captain H.W. Tyler, he said 'he did not question the success of working locomotives on so narrow a gauge mechanically (but) he much doubted their success commercially. On the other hand, he believed that beyond a certain limit, the wider the gauge the less would be the dividend . . . some years ago he constructed a narrow gauge line from Portmadoc to Gorsedda . . . a gauge of 3 feet . . . length 8 miles . . . total rise was 900 ft . . . The sharpest curve had a radius of 200 feet and the down loads were worked entirely by gravitation; but passengers were not carried on the line, and although he had advised this line to be made on the narrow gauge, he was not prepared to recommend its further adoption, unless for exceptional purposes . . .' So Brunlees was recorded in the Proceedings.

The Portmadoc railway scene was not to remain in this form for long. Already there were plans for various lines of standard gauge in the district, mainly linking points along the coast. These plans took shape when the Aberystwyth & Welsh Coast Railway opened between Barmouth and Portmadoc and on to Pwllheli on 10th October, 1867.

This Company, although under the terms of its Act to have working arrangements with the Festiniog, Croesor & Port Madoc Railway (as the Croesor Tramway had become dubbed), and the Gorseddau Tramway, was faced with an arrangement at Portmadoc which it had also faced between Machynlleth and Dovey Junction . . . it was obliged to cross a rail tramway of earlier date by means of a crossing on the level – a state of affairs quite unacceptable to A. & W.C. Board. The position at Portmadoc was doubly frustrating! Here the incomer faced crossing two tramways on the level within a matter of 330 yards and in physical circumstances where it was impossible for anyone to build a bridge without going to an expense which was quite unjustified. The Cambrian Railways (as the A. & W.C.R. soon became) was in no doubt of its liability to provide sufficient safeguards to its trains at these crossings, at its own expense. Nor was it in doubt as to which of the three lines was the senior, and does not appear to have questioned the elderly status of the Gorseddau line. With the Croesor, which had preceded the Cambrian by only a matter of a few years, the position was different and the Cambrian attempted to blackmail the Croesor into accepting some liability for safety expenditure at the crossing. As neither of the tramways enjoyed legal substance at the time, there are no plans of the actual arrangements at each crossing when the Coast Line opened; to judge from evidence available, the Cambrian put trap blades into each side of the tramways' crossings and interlocked them with signals on its own line only. A hut was provided for a signalman at each railway's point of intersection. These arrangements were to last for the full period of the Croesor as a horse-worked line – and were little improved when the Croesor became the Welsh Highland Railway and took on the status of a Light Railway. The Gorseddau crossing was short-lived in this form.

On 8th November, 1871 public notice was given of intention to apply to Parliament for an Act for a new railway of length 5 m. 11 ch. 'on a gauge of 2 feet' and also to purchase the 8 m. 11 ch. tramway of the Bangor Co., 'from Gorseddau Slate Quarry . . . to a certain slate yard in Portmadoc . . .' (then being voluntarily wound up and to relay it 'with new rails').

The Bangor Co. was in voluntary liquidation by April 1870 and under supervision of the Court in July 1870. It was reported in November 1873 that the quarry had had £130,000 spent on it (including the tramway) and was then abandoned as not worth working . . .' a costly Mill and Machinery were erected for working slabs (flags).'

The Bangor Co. did not have legal entitlement to all lands passed over by the tramway and the Act would remedy this. On 22nd February, 1872 the Cambrian petitioned against the Bill and was followed by Mr. E. Breese and the Ynyscynhaiarn Board of Health the day after; however, on 23rd April the owners of property along the proposed route petitioned in favour of the line. Certain copies of the plans had 1871 Edition O.S. maps correctly attached to them, and these had been carefully overprinted to show the railway as if already in existence. The implication of this might be sinister, but at least showed strength of purpose! The title was to be the Gorseddau Junction & Portmadoc Railways. The spelling of Gorseddau had reverted to that used locally for the slate quarry of that name, and the locally fashionable habit of putting 'Railways' in the plural may be noted.

A Prospectus appeared in 'THE TIMES' for 18th September, 1872 and read:

Issue of 1,126 shares of £10 each being the balance of the 2,000 shares of £10 each constituting the share capital of the Gorsedda Junction and Portmadoc Railways Company. Incorporated by Act of Parliament 35 & 36 Victoria. Royal Assent 28 July 1872.

Directors

Charles James Fox Esq.	James Maw Esq.
James Stewart Esq.	Thomas Harvey Esq.

Bankers – The Alliance Bank (limited) Bartholomew Lane, London E.C.

Secretary

G.J. Gray Esq.

Offices – 84 St Clements House, Clements Lane, London, E.C.

The Directors of the Gorsedda Junction and Portmadoc Railways Company are prepared to receive applications at par for 1,126 shares of £10 each being the balance of the 2,000 shares of £10 each constituting the share capital of the Company authorised by its Act of Parliament. Payment will be accepted as follows:

£2 10s. on application and
£2 10s. on allotment

The remainder by calls not exceeding £2 per share at intervals of not less than two months.

The object of the Company as sanctioned by the Act of Parliament is to maintain a line of railway from the Gorsedda Slate Quarry in the county of Carnarvon to Portmadoc, already constructed under arrangements with land-owners and others and also to make a railway from certain mines and quarries to join said existing railway – both lines are shown on the map annexed to the prospectus.

The unprecedented success of the Festiniog Railway constructed on a two foot gauge which has paid the original shareholders upwards of 30 per cent on their outlay has now become a matter of history.

The Company purchased the existing line which is eight miles in length. They will at present utilise 6½ miles thereof and have the advantage of all the surplus materials. Beyond a point on this line where a junction is to be effected the company propose to construct a line of about five miles to the Prince of Wales Quarry and the Cwm Dwyfor Mines. These works are singularly inexpensive and the estimated cost as certified by the Engineer to Parliament including the purchase of land is under £7,000. The whole of the works are mere surface works and the total sums for cutting and banking does not exceed £550.

The length of the Festiniog line is 14 miles the first cost of which was about £36,000 – about £12,571 per mile. The length of the Gorsedda Junction and Portmadoc Railways is 13 miles and the total cost of the line will only be about £15,000 or £1,154 per mile.

Although the cost of these lines will not be one half that of the Festiniog Railway which has paid 30 per cent on the original capital the prospects of profitable return on working are even greater than on that line.

There is a slate district at and beyond the terminus of the proposed line of several square miles in extent producing some of the finest slate in the world besides an inexhaustible supply of slabs. There are also several copper mines and silver lead mines of great richness and a large part of the district traversed by these railways abounds in slate and metallic minerals.

Overtures have already been received from quarry owners and others near the route for the transit of their produce down and supplies from the port upwards. Within a mile from the intended railway on a parallel line for four or five miles are quarries and mines the whole of the traffic of which must naturally come upon these lines.

In addition to such undoubted advantages the mills and agricultural necessities of the district will it is expected produce a large addition to the traffic and consequently a great increase of revenue. Both lines will be on a two foot gauge and under the Act traffic arrangements are sanctioned with the Cambrian and the Croesor and Portmadoc Railway Companies whose lines intersect at Portmadoc. By means of these railways slates and other traffic can be forwarded direct to any part of the Kingdom and by vessels from Portmadoc to any part of the world.

The proposed railway will thoroughly develop the slate and mineral traffic of one of the largest and most important districts of North Wales where at present there are scarcely any facilities for the transit of such traffic or of agricultural products or manures or building materials. The actual tonnage of slate conveyed by the Festiniog Railway in 1860 was 46,694 tons and in 1869 112,402 tons showing the enormous increase of over 150 per cent in nine years.

The small amount of capital necessary for the completion of these extra-ordinarily useful lines and the large amount of traffic of all descriptions which they must undoubtedly appropriate leave no room for question as to the profit on the working being probably greater than that upon any railway yet constructed in the United Kingdom.

The line will no doubt be opened for traffic within six months from commencement of works.

On 25th July, 1872 (35 and 36 Vic. Cap. 155) an Act authorised the adoption and subsequent maintenance of the existing railway from the Gorsedda (sic) Slate Quarry to Portmadoc and for the building of an extension from the existing line at Braich-y-Bib to Blaen-y-Pennant. The gauge was to be 24 inches. Three years were allowed for the building: 3d. per ton mile would be charged for private wagons plus 1d. if the Company's wagons were used for slate or copper ore carriage. Permission was granted to use the Croesor Tramway between Portmadoc Gas Works and the end of that line on the wharves, and a junction was duly made with the Tramway opposite the Portmadoc Flour Mill, for which the Croesor charged tolls for the length of track run over.

There were to be working arrangements with the Portmadoc Croesor & Beddgelert Tram Railway Co. Ltd. and Cambrian Company. The promoters were the New Prince of Wales Slate Co. Ltd. formed in 1868, and their Engineer was Richard James Davids of Caernarvon. James Stewart, later a director of the Railway, was Chairman of the New Prince of Wales Company and also connected with the Cloddfarlon or Penbryn Quarry, Nantlle; (a locomotive at the latter quarry carried his name). J. Maw, another director, was also on the board of the Dorothea Quarry there. The title of 'New' was adopted by the promoters as they intended to buy both the Prince of Wales and the Bangor quarries. (The Prince of Wales quarry up at Cwm Trwsgl had not of course, at the time, any railway connection, and the original Prince of Wales venture was hopelessly insolvent and in voluntary liquidation by early 1868. It was established in 1863 with £50,000 capital of which £45,000 was paid up, and with Thomas Harvey as Manager.)[2]

The matter of the existing Gorseddau Tramway's course down Madoc Street had been the subject of a letter to Edward Breese (solicitor to the Tremadoc Estate) and Thomas Harvey, solicitor who was to become the Chairman of the G.J. & P. Rlys. Harvey, writing on 23rd November, 1871, says he had commissioned Davids the Engineer to point out that they intended to purchase the line exactly as laid down and they must therefore prepare notices and plans on the subject as it existed and not add in any alternative lines. He adds 'we have no intention whatever to use Madock Street but to arrange with you for a

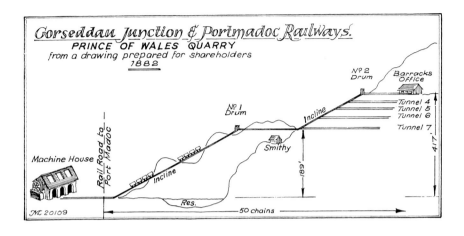

Gorseddau Junction & Portmadoc Railways.
PRINCE OF WALES QUARRY
from a drawing prepared for shareholders
1882

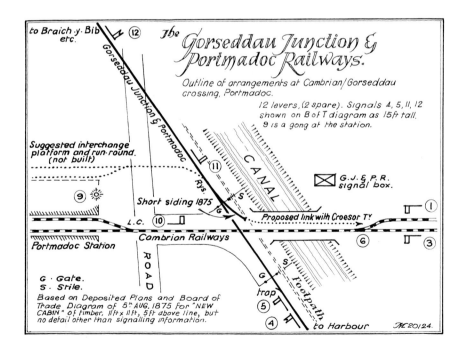

The Gorseddau Junction & Portmadoc Railways.

Outline of arrangements at Cambrian/Gorseddau crossing, Portmadoc.

12 levers, (2 spare). Signals 4, 5, 11, 12 shown on B of T diagram as 15 ft tall.
9 is a gong at the station.

Suggested interchange platform and run-round. (not built)

G . Gate.
S . Stile.
Based on Deposited Plans and Board of Trade Diagram of 5ᵗʰ AUG. 1875 for "NEW CABIN" of timber, 11 ft x 11 ft, 5 ft above line, but no detail other than signalling information.

junction with the Croesor in the manner suggested . . . we can only show what we apply to purchase and we can only purchase what the Gorseddau possess *or use* . . .' This clearly did not satisfy the Estate as they petitioned against the Bill.

The Act was a sequel to an Agreement of 20th April, 1872 between the New Prince of Wales Co. and the G.J. & P. Rlys. Co. This sold the Slate Co. to the Railways Co. for £5,000 in cash, a deposit of £500 to be paid on the incorporation of the Railways Co. and the balance six months afterwards. If however, the Railways Co. put down £2,000 after depositing the £500, they might commence rebuilding their line at once, regardless of incorporation. An Estimate of £6,756 6s. 8d. was given for the work. George Gray, Secretary of the Railways Co. was also Agent for the Slate Co. A maximum number of 25 men was employed in the quarry in 1885, so the concern was not a large one.

The position of the original Tramway, built partly by wayleave, was regularised by the Act; at Blaen-y-Pennant the new line was to divide into two branches, the westerly leading on a falling gradient for one mile to the foot of an incline serving the Cwm Dwyfor Copper & Silverlead Mine. The easterly branch rose up an incline to the existing Prince of Wales slate quarry. According to the Returns of 1875, only 11 miles of the line was by then being operated, which confirms that the old tramway between Braich-y-Bib and Gorseddau quarry was not being worked.

The junction for the extension at Braich-y-Bib entailed yet another reversal in order to gain the new line, and there must have been a loop line to enable the engine to run round its train. This procedure would have to be done twice in a journey from Portmadoc. The Act provided for locomotives, passengers and goods traffic, and anticipation of the latter, mainly in agricultural produce, was very keen.

On 19th September, 1872 'THE TIMES' reported that subscriptions had been invited for the balance of 2,000 shares in the Railways Co., 1,126 at £10 each being offered.

The existing permanent way was lifted, and the whole line relaid in more robust materials which were clearly purchased from the same source (and were much of the same pattern) as had been used for the Croesor track. Local foundries were the suppliers of chairs. The new 1867 crossing over the Cambrian was re-furbished, the traps in the Gorseddau line being extended on the north side into a siding, the narrow gauge gated and both gauges signalled. Oddly, the signal box controlling the crossing was on the east side of Y Cyt and not beside the tramway. It was the property of the Gorseddau.

Among other working arrangements was one with the Hafod-y-Llan Slate Co. whose office and wharf was in front of the Festiniog Railway's Harbour station.

In view of the reduction of rail gauge sanctioned by Section 4 of the Act, running powers were given between the other railway users of Portmadoc Harbour, and the old 3 ft gauge Gorseddau Quarry wharf was abandoned.

Apparently construction, reconstruction and re-equipping was a somewhat slow business. Between the Act of 1872 and the running of a special opening train, (reported in 'THE MINING JOURNAL') on 2nd June, 1875 over three years were taken for the changeover.

'THE MINING JOURNAL' for 12th June, 1875 heads its article 'A New Narrow Gauge Railway' and says it is the latest addition to the miniature-gauge system inaugurated by the now well-known and justly-celebrated Festiniog Railway, totally ignoring the fact that the new railway had its roots in a local railway which pre-dated the Festiniog . . . The JOURNAL also believed 'the gradients to be the most severe of any locomotive line in existence'. Thomas Harvey is given credit for conceiving the transformation of the old Tramway, and the extension of the original line and reduction in gauge; the period of dis-use of the old Gorseddau Tramway following the collapse of the quarry undertaking is stressed and the cost of taking goods *up* the line by horsepower was considerable.

The Special Train on 2nd June must have been a jolly sight; headed by the de Winton-built vertical-boilered engine,

> the train consisted of two carriages (kindly lent for the occasion by Mr. Spooner of the Festiniog Railway) and six mineral wagons, and the working of the Company's engine was found to be very satisfactory.

At Cwm-Dwyfor Mines

> large piles of lead and copper are lying, waiting to be crushed and sent down over the railway . . . and at Prince of Wales Quarry considerable quantities of slates and slabs are ready to be transmitted.

The intention of the New Prince of Wales Company to acquire the assets of the Gorseddau quarries had been carried into effect, for that same day

> the extensive machine house at Ynyspandy, belonging to the Prince of Wales Quarry . . . recently put in order for the manufacture of slabs.

A little tragi-comedy was enacted over the land of one G.H. Owen (owner of the Ymwlch Estate) whose property to the extent of 1 acre 16 poles was on the route of the new Pennant line. Owen did not wish to sell his land to the Company; they offered to treat on 16th July, 1873. Correspondence dragged on until February 1874, but meanwhile the contractors entered his land in the autumn of 1873 and started work. The Company, getting no further with Owen, applied to the Board of Trade for a valuation; Owen wanted £80 for the land and the Railway had refused to pay it. A Bond for £51 12s. 0d. was then paid into Court by directors Thomas Harvey (Solicitor) and James Stewart (Wine Merchant) to secure the purchase money. The matter dragged on, not for months but for years, the land ultimately being conveyed on 24th November, 1888, by which time the railway had almost ceased business; in fact on 8th July, 1887 Owen's solicitors wrote to him: 'We

A reproduction of H.W. Billington's drawing of the Embankment Tramway "as it appeared in the autumn of 1810", showing quarrying and stone wagons, and the incomplete 'Cob' with Ynys-y-towyn at its far end.
(From a copy in Gwynedd Archives)

Above. Civil engineering works on the South Snowdon Quarry Tramway, between the top incline and the Quarry, west of Snowdon. This Quarry, seen here in 1970, though unconnected with the Croesor, used that Tramway for deliveries to the Beddgelert Siding. *J.I.C. Boyd*

Left. Llyn-y-gader Quarry Tramway, South Snowdon, looking towards Rhyd-ddu in 1968 when the Tramway was partially intact.

J.I.C. Boyd

In the years immediately after the First War, the diminutive *Tryfan* and *Cadfan* with 'tenders', posed in the Moel Tryfan Quarry. They were built by the Hunslet Engine Co. in 1902 and 1904 respectively for working through the small bore tunnel connecting with the Alexandra Quarry.

Collection: M. South

Side by side, both engines stand in the cutting leading to the tunnel. Note the re-railing jack and spare coupling chains on *Tryfan*.

Collection: *M. South*

Junction of Gorseddau line (*left*) and Croesor line (*foreground*) in Portmadoc seen here in October 1948. Both lines had been laid in heavy rail and the nearer had been used for Welsh Highland trains; the former Gorseddau line led only to a monumental mason's yard.

J.I.C. Boyd

Site of 'Mr. Huddart's Crossing' looking northwest in October 1948 up the Gorseddau course, and over the G.W.R. towards Tremadoc. This was once the course of the Llidiart Yspytty Tramway.

J.I.C. Boyd

Top. 'Railway Terrace' with the site of the Gorseddau line passing eastwards towards the foot of Penmorfa escarpment photographed in February 1971

J.I.C. Boyd

Middle. Hen-efail road overbridge looking northwards, March 1946.

J.I.C. Boyd

Bottom. Ynysypandy Slate Mill, February 1971 from the southeast, showing the high level line into the first floor of the Mill and the low level line beneath the retaining embankment wall to the left. *J.I.C. Boyd*

The cutting north of Ynyspandy Mill, with river bridge in foreground. Braich-y-Bin Junction lies one quarter mile to the north, February 1971. *J.I.C. Boyd*

Cwm Trwsgl Slate Mill with single slab pillar standing, once used to support troughs to carry water to the Mill wheel. The Gorseddau embankment is in the foreground: the line swung round and passed through the cutting in the distance, September 1970. *J.I.C. Boyd*

Left. Cwm Dwyfor Copper Mine branch seen in September 1970; the 33 ft deep cutting west of Cwm Trwsgl Mill. *J.I.C. Boyd*

Below. Cwm Trwsgl with Mill (*to left*) aqueduct pillars crossing course of line and Prince of Wales Quarry Incline rising ahead to the right, September 1970. *J.I.C. Boyd*

understand the company have ceased working and have now no funds and fear that there is but little prospect of the Bills you refer to being paid'. In 1888 he received the £51 12s. 0d. paid into the Court fourteen years earlier . . . and nothing more.

The deviations from the authorised 1872 course were at Braich-y-Bib Junction and in the streets of Portmadoc. At the former place the north side of the triangle was officially abandoned when a junction of 9 chains 5 links was put in to give direct access to Blaen-y-Pennant. At the latter the route along Madoc Street was abandoned and a new line of 9 chains 45 links from the south side of the Cambrian crossing to meet the Croesor near the Gas Works, was put in. To give some idea of the traffic using this second section, 295 tons passed over Croesor metals on its way to the wharves in October 1875 and in ensuing years, hundreds of tons of flour for Watkins & Williams of Clenenny Mills at Brynkir went back up the Gorseddau from the Flour Mill.

The Cambrian was much inconvenienced by having two level crossings in the vicinity and intended to rid itself of both if possible. It proposed a junction between the Gorseddau and Croesor lines north (instead of south) of its metals, and though the Act provided for such a connection, nothing was done. It would have entailed a third reversal for Gorseddau wagons to reach the Harbour. A trans-shipment siding was built instead (Section 14) which passed over Y Cyt bridge alongside the Cambrian, but on its north side and eastwards in front of the Gorseddau signal box to terminate a few yards further on at a stop block. At a later date it was extended to make an end-on junction with the Croesor's spur from the Beddgelert Siding, so nominally at least, meeting Cambrian wishes for a junction north of its line. This by no means spelt the end of usage of the Gorseddau's own crossing; it had been agreed that if the Gorseddau would provide the land for the above-mentioned exchange siding free of cost to the Cambrian, the Cambrian would make no toll over the crossing. Free use of the crossing thus continued, but the exchange siding took more and more traffic as the Cambrian enjoyed a dominant role at the crossing and it was operated to suit their convenience. Their legal right to do this was established when, for the purposes of the 1872 Gorseddau Act, the existence of the old Gorseddau Tramway was officially ignored. There thus existed the curious state of affairs whereby the Cambrian, the incoming railway on the scene, was given priority of traffic and forced the original railway to provide a signal box and man it for traffic which was subordinate to the Cambrian's!

This was not the end of the affair. Under a later scheme of 1879 it was suggested that by means of a trailing junction in the Gorseddau line Portmadoc-bound trains would terminate north of the crossing and reverse over the street into the north side of the Cambrian Portmadoc station. Here a new standard/narrow gauge platform would be built with sidings and locomotive run-round, the latter terminating behind the Cambrian engine shed.

(In the fullness of time, the Cambrian would be relieved of the Gorseddau without any effort on its own part.)

It would be a pity to pass over this crossing, so to speak, without further mention as it was a situation which in terms of the present day would not be tolerated but which in those times, was typical of the problems which incoming and often London-based standard gauge trunk routes had to face all round the coasts of Britain where near-coastal projects found themselves obliged to cross elderly horse-worked tramroads of more ancient vintage, *and on the level!* Naturally the Board of Trade hated such locations. On 19th August, 1875 the Cambrian reported to the Board of Trade that Colonel Rich had passed the (signalling) 'work as constructed by the Cambrian Railways Company but required two "catch points" to be put in by the Gorseddau Railway Company, these to be ultimately connected with the junction box'. One can almost sense the delight of the Cambrian's Engineer at scoring off the little Gorseddau!

It has been noted that a reverse of the customary obligations has taken place here and the Cambrian was given certain rights over the Gorseddau. This may have been sound and watertight in the plush offices of solicitors and the like, but out on the ground it carried little weight with those who quarried and those who transported. In due course the Cambrian made claim against the G.J. & P.R. for the payment of £708 10s. 10d. being £379 8s. 10d. for the cost of erecting a signal box, locking apparatus etc. and the balance of working the junction 26th January, 1875 to 31st December, 1882. Way back on 29th June, 1876 judgement had been obtained for the first-incurred item but no payment had been made by 1883 and working costs of the box had been estimated at 'fully £40 per annum'. The Cambrian Board instructed their solicitor to apply for the appointment of a Receiver to the Gorseddau undertaking; this was done on 23rd January that year according to one source, but a search of such appointments does not support the application. Two reasons may account for this a) that no business was being done by the Gorseddau concern or, that b) since a Receiver is entitled to be paid as priority over the debt due to the Petitioner, there may have been insufficient income from traffic receipts to make the whole exercise worthwhile.

'THE TIMES' of 17th December, 1875 made mention of the Directors' Report stating that 'the line was fully opened for goods traffic on 2nd September last'. Up to 30th June the land and works had cost considerably more than was estimated and it was necessary to apply to Parliament in the ensuing session for further capital powers. 'New properties were being developed along the line of route and new sources of traffic had been discovered'.

By arrangement between the two companies, Gorseddau trains began to use Festiniog tracks in the Harbour area during 1875.

The Act forecast in the 1875 Report was duly obtained (39 and 40 Vic. Cap. 137 of 13th July, 1876), the principal features being:

1. It regularised the position of two lengths of line where the Engineer had diverted outside the limitations of the 1872 Act.
2. Authority was given to construct a siding at a cost of £81 15s. 7d. in the parish of Ynyscynhaiarn (namely the Cambrian exchange siding already noted) and to use a portion of the Festiniog Railway giving access to the west bank of the Glaslyn (namely, between its termination on the Public Wharf and the Sluice Bridge).
3. Permission was given to raise additional finance.

There was some alteration to the awkward junction at Tremadoc where the original steep extension connection was 'improved', leaving a reversing neck with a 2½ chain curve on a gradient of 1 in 23! The Act gave powers of abandonment to the sections superseded by these alterations, which were just about sufficient to take it from the horse power era into the steam age. So it was that on 10th July, 1874, the Cambrian Railways' goods train delivered a steam locomotive to the Beddgelert Siding, and this load, together with a quantity of chairs, was taken up the line. At this late stage, the new engine must have been a useful asset in completing the railway, but it might have been a shock to the promoters if they could have foreseen that its useful life would not exceed the next four years! It is difficult to see just why a locomotive was obtained at all; if the traffic was to be all that was promised, it was too small for such a heavily graded line. Its water capacity would have meant frequent stops if it was intended to work the whole route in one journey. Perhaps it was intended that horses should do the work, the engine being used as a stand-by when business was brisk. This was exactly how events turned out.

At the Board Meeting on 22nd September, 1876 it was said that since opening

A fair amount of traffic had been obtained. The Directors however believed arrangements were now about to be made for the more vigorous working of some of the undertakings on the line of route by which the traffic would be very much increased . . . believed the line would be the means of speedily developing the whole of the district through which it runs. They regretted they had to apply for further capital . . . for these purposes for the complete equipment of the line and the construction of the mile and a half branch railway not yet made it would be necessary to raise £6,000 or £7,000.

A shareholder asked why the prospectus had said the line could be made for £15,000 and it had already cost £29,000. Now they asked for more. The Chairman said the money was for a further extension of the line not contemplated when the prospectus was issued. Great miscalculations had been made, particularly as to the price paid for land. ('THE TIMES' 23rd September, 1876).

The next half yearly meeting to be reported in the press was mentioned in 'THE TIMES' on 22nd October, 1877. 'The non-completion of arrangements referred to in the last report' was brought up. The quarries had provided unfavourable traffic returns; the Company could not declare an Ordinary Dividend and had been compelled to postpone payment of the Debenture Interest. The usual glib hopes were expressed by the Chairman, who added that £31,583 had been spent on the railway, being a rate of 'only £2,746 per mile'.

Certainly the westerly arm of the line at the head of Cwm Pennant was a futile scheme. This farthest reach of the track was described in the preamble:

> . . . To commence at Blaen-y-Pennant in a field called Llanfawr the property of G.A. Huddart and 23 chains south of the Cwm Dwyfor Copper & Silverlead Mines Company Limited's Blacksmith's Shop and terminating at Braich-y-Bib at a junction with the existing tramway in a field called Gors-uchaf, 42 chains north of the Weighing Machine House of the Gorseddau Company.

This Weigh House stood at the junction of the branch into the Gorseddau's slate mill.

The mine at Cwm-Dwyfor which had opened some time after 1840 and before the railway was conceived, rejoiced in the name of the Dinas Great Consols Mine. Names of such ventures were frequently changed as the financial collapse of one undertaking was succeeded by another under a new title, all with the intention of attracting fresh public money in the speculation. In the year mentioned, the mine amalgamated with the nearby Moel Hebog Mine, one mile off the new railway's course near Cwrt-Isaf. Dinas Great Consols was useless from the start and Hebog was equally so! Though the ore struck was very rich, it turned out to be iron and not copper as expected and was accidently discovered whilst digging a leat to bring water to a waterwheel. It became the Cwm Dwyfor Mining Co. to meet this unforeseen event, but on 4th November, 1868 changed to the Cwm Dwyfor Copper & Silverlead Mining Co. Ltd., the title given in describing the approach of the new railway to serve it. 'THE TIMES', 2nd August, 1871: 'A prospectus has been issued by the Cwm Dwyfor Copper & Silver Lead Mines Co. Ltd. with a capital of £12,500 in shares of £1 to develop a mining property in North Wales.' No sooner had rail connection been achieved, than the concern got into difficulties. A visit to the workings will show how incomplete were mine, incline and railway works even when final abandonment took place. A little mining was done in 1877 when thirteen men below and four men above ground produced five tons of *lead* ore. Work was suspended again, but carried on in a small way between 1883 and 1887.

The C.D.C. & S.M. Co. Ltd. worked on land leased from the New Prince of Wales Co. The latter was the dominant feature of the Pennant valley within the context of this study, being linked with the Railways Co. and, in the absence of other users of the line, providing the railway with almost all its mineral traffic. When the Slate Company failed, the railway fortunes fell to zero. The Railways Co., as has been seen, were ever hopeful that fresh sources of mineral traffic might develop. They never did. The C.D.C. & S.M. Co. Ltd. liquidated in 1876, its assets being bought by a concern of the former title, the Cwm Dwyfor Mining Co. Ltd. in 1877. Our old friend James Stewart was on the Board and the faithful G.J. Gray was Secretary. Formed with a capital of £10,005 (a peculiar sum) the investing public had already been persuaded by 1878 to part with 18s. 9d. for every 20s. share they had taken up. Not surprisingly there were insufficient funds for this venture too, and it sold out such equipment as it had to the Cwm Dwyfor & Brynarian Mines Co. Ltd. in 1882. During all these changes of ownership, the railway traffic continued to dwindle throughout the period, and evidence of work around either mine or slate quarry was on a very limited scale.

The highest train mileage is recorded in 1876 (3,533 miles) and assuming the full outward and return journey of approximately 20 miles is taken as a measure of distance, this made the equivalent of about 180 return workings in (say) 265 working days of the year, assuming full journeys were not made on Saturdays. On this day and mileage basis a full journey would operate on two days out of three, but when mileages fell significantly in later years, once a week was sufficient.

The New Prince of Wales Company succumbed in 1880, having no further capital available to exploit the works. A last appeal for finance was accompanied by the innuendo that if only their probings in the Trial Shaft would strike the 'Glanrafon Vein' – that same vein which was worked by the Glanrafon Quarry over the mountain and to the east, and served by the North Wales Narrow Gauge Railways – all would be well. A new company, reverting to the title Prince of Wales Slate Co. Ltd. took over the remnants in 1881; Charles Baron of the Railways Co. was on the board, but Stewart had disappeared. Gray, inevitably it seems, was appointed Secretary. The prospects of the quarry were highlighted in a report by Thomas Williams of Bryn Croesor and Manager of the Croesor New Slate Co. Ltd. in 1882. The new concern, with a pitiful output over the railway, was soon appealing to shareholders over Gray's name, to take up the balance of 10% 3-year secured shares in order to drive a horizontal adit and prove the slate by means of cross-tunnelling recommended by Williams. It was no use, and even the Railways Co. 'went to ground' in 1882–4 and no Returns were made. In fact, from 1881 slate traffic over the line virtually ceased. The Company ceased to render financial reports in 1886.

Under the Railway Rates & Charges No. 6 (Festiniog Railway & Etc.) Order of 1893 (55 & 56 Vic. Cap. 44) 20th June, 1892, new rates and charges for the Gorseddau were brought into force as from 1st January, 1893: the Portmadoc Crosesor & Beddgelert Tram Railway Co. Ltd., North Wales Narrow Gauge Railways and Festiniog Railway were included also. It was of little help to the Gorseddau whose last mileages had already been recorded. The Prince of Wales Slate Company was wound up in 1899 and removed from the Stock Exchange Register.

'BRADSHAW'S MANUAL' for 1902 states simply 'No recent returns have been received' and the Stock Exchange Year Book for the same year says 'Debenture is in arrear and working of the line suspended. No figures have been furnished for Board of Trade returns of 1897 onward'. In truth, no Returns were made for 1894, or subsequently. Even in 1920 the title of the Company still appeared in the latter publications reading 'Not working and no returns available'!

The last full Returns issued 1893 show:

> Expenditure on Capital Account £31,560
> Issued: £19,995 Ordinary Shares
> £ 2,100 5% Preference Shares
> £   800 in Loan @ 6%
> £ 5,800 in Loan @ 8%
>   Debentures = ⅓ capital

It would seem that at the rebuilding period, the section between Braich-y-Bib and the Gorseddau Quarry was not rebuilt – at least a descriptive article of June 1875 stated that the branch had not then been tackled, and it is quite possible that with the lessening traffic over it, the most economical way would have been to retain the old materials and gauge, and trans-ship at Braich-y-Bib. The line seems to have escaped attention during its lifetime and only one contemporary article exists; with the Gorseddau there is ample material for the imaginative mind!

A brief article was published in 'ENGINEERING' (11th June, 1875) but without illustration. It differs from the evidence which survives in a few particulars, and it could have been supplied by the Bangor Co. rather than have been a first-hand account. At this time the line had just opened for public traffic and was awaiting inspection of signals at the Cambrian crossing. The gauge is given as 1 ft 11½ in. From the port the line was level to Tremadoc and then rose to 810 ft in just under 6 miles. The ruling grade of 1 in 25 pertained for considerable lengths, but eased to 1 in 152 elsewhere. There was a summit level of nearly two miles, followed by a fall of 1 in 70. At the topmost end the line was almost level. The sharpest curve was 2 chains radius. In addition to developing the mines and quarries already named, agriculture and adjacent peat works were to benefit; there were no alternative roads. Details of the right of way, track and motive power followed. Gravity working was carried on one way, with locomotive power the other – this seems unlikely over much of the line, which was unfavourable for this type of working. Reference is also made to locomotives in the plural, but the concern only owned the one and this featured in all the Returns. No assistance or co-operation was received from the local landowners when building the line, which cost '£2,500 per mile'. The Engineer for the railway construction had been George Wilson M.I.C.E., 22 Parliament Street, Westminster.

No dividend was ever paid: in the 'STOCK EXCHANGE YEAR BOOK' for 1881 it stated, 'In 1877 the payment of the debenture interest had to be postponed. Nothing further has transpired . . .' It never did. Occasional references do nothing to throw any bright light onto what happened to the railway or its owners thereafter. A late-in-the-day reference to warn tourists that it was of little use to them appeared in 'THE GOSSIPPING GUIDE' for 1881

> . . . there is now a 1 ft 11½ in. gauge line the Gorseddau Railway running from Portmadoc up among the hills between Moel Hebog and the sea, but it is only used for goods traffic . . .

The brief injection of new capital by a further issue of 5% Preference Shares in 1885 was simply to throw good money after bad – working restarted under the Cwm Dwyfor & Brynarian Mines umbrella and there seems to have been fitful traffic for a year or so, but the mine had closed in 1887. On 31st December, 1889 'THE LONDON GAZETTE' refers to an action and Order made 14th November, 1887, Priestley v. G.J. & P. Rlys Co. to sell 'Certain freehold land . . . more or less now used as and forming part of the said railway'. The words 'more or less now used' speak for themselves! In November 1897 the land which included Gorseddau Quarry, the Cwm-Ystradllyn Estate, was put up for sale. The 'STOCK EXCHANGE INTELLIGENCE' for 1899 which contains particulars of certain non-quoted companies (such as this one) had

> Gross receipts for 1890 were £3 and working expenses £32, leaving a deficiency of £29
> . . . the Company appears to have ceased working the line.

The same entry had appeared in previous years.

It is suggested that if the Prince of Wales Quarry was the Railway Company's principal creditor, it might not have bothered with a Receiver but sold the railway equipment for scrap along with the quarry machinery. There seems to have been no attempt to dispose legally (or illegally) of the land and none of the Company's creditors seems to have taken any steps to realise its assets: a list of shareholders has not materialised. Money was still being paid into the Chancery Court in 1896 but in 1899 there is no record of it. So the mystery remains!

A summary of sites and their operators including information available shows how the railway fell victim to the closure of its customers; only the main sites north of Penmorfa are valid enough for inclusion:

Site & Operators	Registered	Ceased
CWM DWYFOR MINE		
(or Dinas Great Consols) working copper & lead		
Cwm Dwyfor Mining Co. Ltd.	c. 1845	1868
Cwm Dwyfor Copper & Silver Lead Mines Co. Ltd.	1868	by 1876
Cwm Dwyfor Mining Co. Ltd.	1877	1882
Cwm Dwyfor & Brynarian Mines Co. Ltd.	1882	1887

GORSEDDAU QUARRY working slate, slab & flagstones

Bangor & Portmadoc Slate & Slate Slab Co. Ltd.	c. 1853	1870
Prince of Wales Co. Ltd. – see Prince of Wales Quarry		

PRINCE OF WALES QUARRY working slate & slab

Prince of Wales Co. Ltd.	1863	1868
New Prince of Wales Co. Ltd.	1868	1880
Prince of Wales Co. Ltd.	1881	?

TY CERRIG QUARRY working slab & flagstones

Tremadoc & Ralltwen Slab Co. Ltd.	1865	1867

PENMORFA QUARRY working slabs, setts & flagstones

Penmorfa Slate & Slab Co. Ltd.	?	by 1883

The Route described: Portmadoc to Gorseddau Quarry

(Field Survey of Railway made in 1943–46 and ensuing account is based on this.)

Because of the uncertainty of the extent of the Gorseddau line in times past, it is easier to describe the line's course from its wharf at the north-east corner of the Sluice Bridge, Portmadoc. There would have been only limited accommodation here as the site was small. Immediately behind it the tramway would have been crossed, after 1864, by the Croesor Tramway. Originally, as the two lines were of differing gauge, this meant a simple acute crossing of rails in the roadway. The Gorseddau line, virtually level within the town, then made its way up the east side of Madoc Street, which at the time of the tramway's building, would certainly not have been skirted with housing as it is today. At the top of the street the track turned north-westward and made a straight course behind the town along what is still a piece of undeveloped and uninteresting ground. The route is now a footpath, and within the past ten years has been excavated by the writer at various points between the standard gauge crossing to the west and the later site of junction with the Cambrian to the east. This proved that this section of line was never properly lifted; almost all sleepers and chairs were intact though rails had gone. At the time of inspection, the track had been buried about nine inches by the footway. The north-east edge of the site is bounded by the erstwhile Canal and beyond this were allotment gardens.

From about 1902 there was retained a section just short of the Cambrian Crossing. A branch tramway led westwards along Cambrian Street, over the main road and then beside the Cambrian goods yard to the Moel-y-Gest Quarry who owned and worked it, latterly with their own locomotive. (The Gorseddau line from this concern's junction, along Madoc Street West to the junction with the Croesor at the Flour Mill, remained in use for Moel-y-Gest purposes after abandonment of the Gorseddau proper.)

The former Cambrian Railways' crossing is now reached and today is crossed with the aid of stiles in the boundary fences, and a foot crossing on the site of the old line. Within a few yards, still using the west bank of the canal, the line crossed what is now Avenue Road, with the standard gauge level crossing at hand to the south, and the Queens Hotel on the left hand. The tramway passed between the Hotel and the canal bank. Thirty-three chains from the Cambrian crossing was a short branch to the west to serve the Pen-Syflog Ironstone Mine – still a prominent rock outcrop. This was followed by a stone bridge over the Afon Oer. Continuing in flat country of little note, and still on the canal side until within a few yards south of Dublin Street, 15 chains west of the Tremadoc town centre and 1 m. 20 ch. from the Sluice Bridge it curved into the southern edge of Dublin Street and ran beside it for two chains. Turning slowly right it crossed the road on the level at the point of a fork between Criccieth and Caernarvon roads, and ran in behind a wall bordering the north edge of the Caernarvon road. Some indication of the lowness of the land may be gained from a nearby Bench Mark showing slightly under 13 feet.

The terminus of the original tramway to Llidiart Yspytty Mine was now reached. Though clearly marked with the earthworks of former rail access, it is now too overgrown to pick out all the detail. From the Deposited Plans it is shown that the new railway, extended from here, did not use the full length of the first tramway as a reversing neck, and that the layout at the mine was probably unchanged despite the coming of the extension. Access to the mine was made by a back shunt from the end of the old tramway, up a steep incline still visible from the nearby road. Thus there were, in effect, two reversing junctions from the line running beside the Penmorfa road; the more easterly route climbed up a shelf at 1 in 23, and turning anticlockwise, completed rather more than a 180 degree turn by means of this 2½ chain curve – a formidable obstacle to train working! By the time the line had rounded the bend, it was several feet above the level at which it had crossed Dublin Street, and below it to the left hand, lay the site of the mine. One spur of the mine tramway passed under the new line to reach the workings; the adit entrance has been filled in. Ahead now stretches the Gorseddau Railway, as the O.S. 1884 map labels this length. It is interesting to note two features still visible at this site; firstly as to how the line carried itself up through a cutting behind the school, and secondly, how use of it could have been made for the nearby limekilns, both of which existed here before the extension was built; though a difficult piece of line to operate, it is ingeniously surveyed and built. The route ahead was not easy. Now with the flat lands behind it, the course was forced to run between the foot of a craggy escarpment, Allt Wen, and the Penmorfa road and village below. The road, in fact, climbs to a point where, at the west end of Penmorfa village, it can pass over the tramway. Allt Wen is one of several similar ridges in the neighbourhood, and seen from afar, they resemble waves of hills with their crests in the breaking position. The face of Allt Wen was in fact broken with scree in many places so the tramway was part-built on an embankment through the debris at the bottom of the ridge. In parts the foundations of the line were boulders which had fallen years before; since the closing of the line, sections have been covered by later rock falls. The wooded climb is still severe, 1 in 25 continuing for this section.

Signs of early inclines and workings into the face of Allt Wen will be seen at Cae-Crwn and, a few yards further west, where the Penmorfa Quarry – formerly the Ty Cerrig Quarry – worked by the Tremadoc & Ralltwen Slate Co. Ltd. of 1865, was served. Both quarries had spur connections to the tramway: Tremadoc & Ralltwen was in liquidation within two years and sold out to the neighbouring Penmorfa Slate & Slab Co., a company which itself was dissolved before 1883. One by one the quarries which the Gorseddau served were to close down, leaving the railway with but little to do.

Here (2 m. 10 ch.) there is a small row of cottages still named 'Railway Terrace', a title they seem to have acquired at the time more of the closure of the tramway than whilst it was working! The tramway is now running almost westward and leaves the foot of Allt Wen for the upland meadows beyond Penmorfa. It crossed a minor road on the level and then came back to the main Caernarvon road beside its northern edge, a quarter of a mile west of Penmorfa. Gradually the road climbs above the level of the tramway which dropped into a cutting beside the highway. About here both are 164 feet above sea level and at this site was Tyn-y-Llon Mine, the most distant quarry of the local group which mined for iron ore.

The County Council made use of the available railway route to widen the road here in 1966–7, and in doing so destroyed the east mouth of the stone tunnel which took the line under it. The west mouth may still be partly discerned, but the blocking of the bore took place over thirty years ago. The bore dimensions are: height 9 ft 6 in., width 10 ft, and length approx. 25 yd.

The course now runs parallel but to the south of the road, much of it along a tree-lined embankment which takes it to Glan-Byl Farm and to cross a minor road on the level immediately beforehand. There is now a short run of a few yards before the Caernarvon road is crossed on the level once more, but between the last two road crossings, farming has partly obliterated the site; on this length too, the tramway has changed direction from westward and now faces north-east. There follows another straight section of about half a mile – an unusual feature in this sinuous line – mainly over a low embankment. At the beginning of this earthwork, and alongside the Caernarvonshire road crossing was Glan-Byl, an agricultural siding 20 yards long (3 m. 50 ch.).

The land each side now is marshy and the ordered fields begin to change their style into upland sheep-farming country. The straight length ends with a deep cutting and a well-preserved stone-built tunnel (bore: height 9 ft 6 in., width 9 ft, and length approx. 26 yd.) at

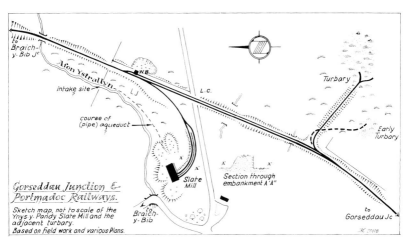

Gorseddau Junction & Portmadoc Railways.

Sketch map, not to scale of the Ynys-y-Pandy Slate Mill and the adjacent turbary.
Based on field work and various Plans.

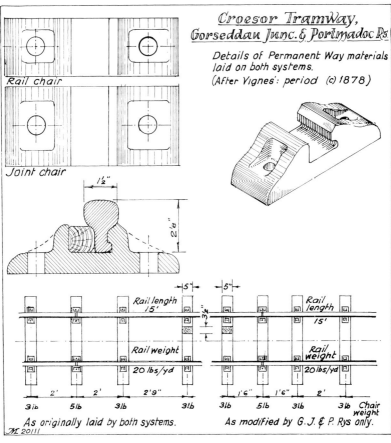

Croesor Tramway, Gorseddau Junc. & Portmadoc Rs.

Details of Permanent Way materials laid on both systems.
(After Vignes': period (c) 1878)

Rail chair

Joint chair

As originally laid by both systems.

As modified by G.J. & P. Rys only.

Hen-efail under the old Caernarvon road. The railway is now at a height of 459 ft and 4 m. 20 ch. from the Sluice Bridge.

Climbing out of the bridge cutting, the scenery changes immediately. Ahead stand the bare uplands of Caernarvonshire, the rounded foothills near at hand and more spectacular peaks rising to 2,000 and more feet beyond. On a sunny day this cycloramic sweep has a colourful beauty which is never forgotten, but all too frequently the uplands are blanketed down in a wet mist off the sea and the magic of this view is so completely lost that it cannot be imagined. So up into this bleak country, with the surrounding land becoming more wet and scrubby, pressed the railway to the Gorseddau Quarry, now on the western flank of the foothills. On this length, the route is wet and gorsey until at about 5 miles the ancient Meini Hirion standing stones are passed on the right hand.[3] The cutting here then widens and for the first time, the line doubled. The track on the east side then branched off at a junction and its route over the mountainside can easily be followed as it cuts its way through the rough moorland in a straight line and through an ever-deepening cutting. In about a quarter of a mile the branch ends in a shallow depression of considerable extent, the remaining vestiges of the turbary which featured in early descriptions of the line.[4] Owing to the natural tendency of peat to be unstable, the levels have obviously filled up with new growth and the original arrangements have lost their definition: there is little doubt that at least a portion of this area was that worked by the Portmadoc Brick Clay & Peat Works Ltd., incorporated in 1879. ('THE MINING JOURNAL' 1879 pp. 146 & 207.) This undertaking was probably successor to The Ereiniog Peat Fuel & Firebrick Works, mentioned in the 'JOURNAL' during 1876.

At the beginning of this branch, and almost immediately after its junction with the main line, may be traced the route of a still earlier line to the south of the later one. This track passes through the cutting of the newer line at its west end and may be followed for a short distance to a depression in the ground where there were once the original turbary workings. The impressions of sleepers in the soft ground along this long-abandoned course, are remarkably clear.

Returning to the main line again, the double track extends over an embankment carrying a large culvert beneath, passes through walls where once was a level road crossing and continues as a double line past what was formerly the slate yard of Ynys-y-Pandy with its weighing machine, rubbish sidings etc., all now hardly traceable (630 ft). Double line becomes single again beyond the yard's precincts. To the left a remarkable ruin dominates the scene. This is the old slate mill of the Gorseddau Quarry.

The Gorseddau Quarry was unusual. Instead of work being carried out on the stone within the quarry precincts, it was brought here to be sawn and split. This building, with its water power and suitability, was clearly considered preferable to anything the company might build near the workings. The junction into it faces the quarry and a branch line curves away to the west, and supported by a high stone wall on its southern flank, enters the building by the first floor, so to speak. A second line, outside the wall, entered at a lower floor. The machinery was driven by two wheels at different levels, one at right angles to the other. Both are within the building and the water for the larger one falls down a vertical shaft below the access tramway to drive the undershot wheel which lay 'athwart' the structure. After passing under the wheel, the water was led out through a tunnel mouth on the lower side of the mill, and so into a valley alongside to rejoin the Afon Cwm-Ystradllyn. The building itself is of considerable interest to the industrial historian, and is ornamented in a style rare in a slate mill! The roof was taken off in 1905 and is said to have been the finest in the district.

The north end of the yard outside the mill is marked by the site of the Weighing Machine House, a building used as a reference point in the Plans of 1875. After passing northwards through a cutting, another short straight length ensues and the Cwm-Ystradllyn river is crossed by a stone-piered bridge with 15 in. square timber spans. A short run brings it to the site of the 'New Junction of 1875' or Braich-y-Bib (also known as Braich-y-Big). The line is now 690 feet above the sea, and having entered a section where the gradients are subject to Statutory Plans, it is known that the rise from Hen-efail tunnel has involved an almost continuous pull of 1 in 67/51/38/27/38/52, luckily only against empty slate workings. The junction is 6 m. 10 ch. from the Sluice Bridge.

Ignoring the new line to the head of the Pennant Valley for the time being, the course of the older Gorseddau line may be followed over a road crossing and sweeping eastwards above a minor road, as it climbs up behind the now derelict schoolroom and chapel (Capel Saron). The initial gradient of this section is known: 1 in 21½/32/34, and so on almost as steep as far as the quarry. Of course, this line was always worked by horses and as has been stated, is unlikely to have been reduced from its original gauge of 3 ft, laid in what may have been Cob Tramway materials. (A piece of fish-bellied rail in use as fencing along here, and found by the writer in 1946, does nothing to confirm that any fish-bellied track of Nantlle or similar type was used up here. There is widespread use of rails in fencing, roofing etc. and it may not be indigenous to the district.) The vista is now wild and bleak; below is the former Llyn Cwm-Ystradllyn, now a reservoir. Ahead is the re-entrant at the top of which the extensive working of the Gorseddau Quarry dominates the view; behind and above climb the rocky sides of Moel Hebog (2,568 ft) whose summit is out of sight. The tramway has now had a slab-built ledge constructed for it, and there being no other route, has become a roadway of sorts. For the last mile the ledge curves eastwards and then south-eastwards before, at the eight-mile point, describing a half circle to end its journey at the foot of the long incline which divides the workings almost into two equal parts and takes the upper galleries, served by the tramway, along ledges over 1,000 feet high in the slopes of Fridd Uchaf. The O.S. 1 in./1 m. Second Edition Map (surveyed 1874–1888) whilst showing the line to Cwm Trwsgl, does not show the original track to Gorseddau at all.

The Route described: Braich-y-Bib to Cwm-Dwyfor Copper Mine

The area of the triangular junction at Braich-y-Bib is clearly marked in the patch of ground bounded by stone walls to the south of the road to the Gorseddau Quarry. Although more overgrown than it was, the three sides of rails may be followed. The southern junction of 1875 is the last one; the first access to the Pennant valley extension (The Gorseddau Junction and Portmadoc Railway proper) of 1871 was by means of a line which trailed into the Gorseddau Tramway and which would oblige a short section at least to be regauged for use as a headshunt. The section off the new line, and down to the 1871 junction, fell at 1 in 34/42/58/32 before becoming level for a short stabling length. The newest (west) side of the triangle was empowered by the 1875 G.J. & P.R. Act and this short section inclined upward from Braich-y-Bib at 1 in 24/30/108/42/34. Beyond the north-west junction there was a level crossing★ and the line climbed upward at 1 in 34, passing over the flank of Braich-y-Cornel and through the 700 ft contour. The sharpest section of curve from the new junction was 3 chains 50 links. Mileages were now officially measured from Cwm Trwsgl; the new junction was 4 m. 20 ch. from there.

As the shoulder of land is crossed, the line takes a long slow bend to the north and falls at 1 in 50 for a furlong. Between the four-mile point and 1 m. 6 ch., the course is level, being a somewhat monotonous contour-hugging northward drive towards the valley head at about 825 ft. The route is mainly a levelling of the hillside which here is not steep. Here and there are shallow cuttings, and where streams are crossed, embankments are used with small stone culverts in the bottom. The Pennant valley below, is entered high on its eastern flank near Caer-Fadog. In the valley below to the south-east lay the estate of Brynkir, with its tower-topped hill. Here between 1809 and 1910 lived the Huddart family, closely linked with the narrow gauge railways of the district from the time of Madocks at Tan-yr-Allt. Nearer lies the hamlet of Llanfihangel-y-Pennant, and beyond both, there are glimpses of golden sands and the sea. It would have been a wonderful vista had a passenger service ever operated. Instead, the line passes an occasional derelict farmstead and there are numerous slate tips on the far side of the valley marking Dol-ifan-Gethin, Chwarel-y-Plas, Hendre-Ddu and Moelfre Slate Quarries. The spoil tips of Gilfach Copper Mine lie

---

★Col. Yolland, inspecting for the Board of Trade, was in favour of the level crossing being replaced, but was overruled by the House of Lords' Standing Orders Committee (6th July, 1876).

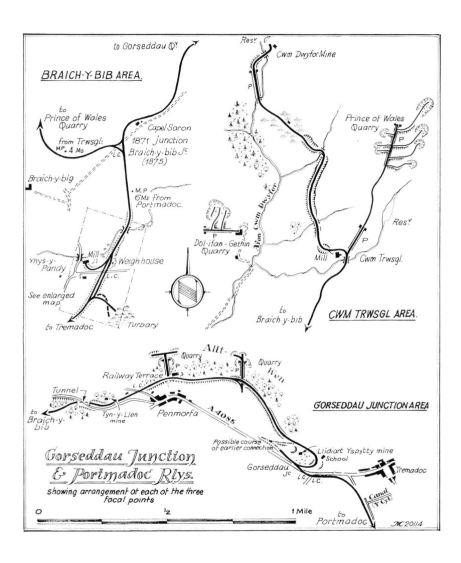

to Gorseddau Qy.

Resy

Cwm Dwyfor Mine

BRAICH-Y-BIB AREA.

P

to
Prince of Wales
Quarry

Capel Saron

from Trwsgl:
MP. 4 Ms

1871 junction
Braich-y-bib Jc
(1875)

L.C.

Braich-y-big

• M.P
6 Ms from
Portmadoc.

Prince of Wales
Quarry

P

Afon Cwm Dwyfor

Resy

P

Dol-ifan - Gethin
Quarry

Mill

Cwm Trwsgl.

Ynys-y-
Pandy

Mill
Weigh house

L.C.

See enlarged
map

to Tremadoc   Turbary

to
Braich-y-bib

CWM TRWSGL AREA.

Allt-

Quarry

P

Railway Terrace

L.C.

Quarry

Llen

GORSEDDAU JUNCTION AREA

Tunnel

to
Braich-y-
bib

Tyn-y-Llen
mine

Penmorfa

A4085

Possible course
of earlier connection

Llidiart Yspytty mine
School

Gorseddau Junction
& Portmadoc Rlys.

showing arrangement of each of the three
focal points

Gorseddau
Jc   L.C./L.C.

Tremadoc

Canal
Y Cyt

0   ½   1 Mile

to
Portmadoc

JMC 20114

below. All these had internal tramways, but all are now abandoned. Gilfach's large water wheel was a feature of the district. Above Cwrt-Isaf, the Afon Cwm-Llefrith is crossed. This was once bridged and the approach embankments are the largest on this section. One mile to the east, nearly 1,500 feet up in the rocks of Moel Hebog, was the Moel Hebog Mine, an offshoot of the Cwm-Dwyfor Mine and if anything, even less lucky! Apart from a rough path, there was no connection with the outer world in general or the G.J.&P.R. in particular. Above Brithdir Mawr another stream is crossed and beyond here the level section at 810 ft above sea level ends, the line falling the rest of the way to Cwm Trwsgl at 1 in 76, a very unhelpful arrangement. There are a few shallow cuttings as Cwm Trwsgl is approached, and in certain sections the marks of where the sleepers have lain would suggest the line has only recently been lifted. There is a stone embankment and culvert over the Afon Cwm Trwsgl and short level section to the route.

To the left stands the roofless building of the Prince of Wales slate mill, with its wheelpit alongside the Trwsgl stream. Ahead, though somewhat obliterated due to the instability and wetness of the ground, climbs the lower incline to the Prince of Wales Quarry. The exact layout here is impossible to trace, but the plans show a level crossing between the main tramway as it swings west behind the slate mill en route for Cwm-Dwyfor, and the foot of the line coming off the lower Prince of Wales incline as it made its way into the mill. If the Prince of Wales line is followed, there are remains of the drum at the head of the lower incline. There is then a quarter of a mile of near level tramway and a second incline is entered. From this spine-like incline, fingers extend on either side; these were tramways, their boundaries flanked by piled rubbish as each made its way to levels in the mountainside. There is abundant evidence that although extensive, the quarry did not produce much slate throughout its life. Its situation is impressive; that is about all. Looking south, the rock-strewn slopes on the left sweep up to Moel Hebog directly ahead; the shallow bowl of the Pennant valley falls slowly to the hills which prevent a direct view of the mouth of the Glaslyn estuary, but allow glimpses of light on mountain and horizon down the length of Cardigan Bay. To the right the Pennant valley has narrowed considerably and a prominent feature is the Dol-ifan-Gethin slate quarry opposite with its steep incline and three parallel tramways near the summit. At the foot of the incline nestle the remains of the slate mill, barracks and workshops.

Returning now to the main line at Cwm Trwsgl slate mill; the railway curves to the left and passes behind the end of the mill building. Within this curve may be seen the site of three tracks each entering the mill building by its own separate arched entrance. The water wheel would have driven a shaft running the length of the mill, at right angles to the tramways entering the building. The three lines were carried right through it to tips on the west side. To the south and east of the mill

stand five of six slab pillars which carried an aqueduct with water for
the overshot wheel. The spent water was conducted by a short sluice
back into the Trwsgl. The Plans show a connection from the west side
of the mill back onto the main line again, but earthworks do not
confirm the building of the connection. The railway now has to pierce a
rocky bluff by means of a curved cutting, 33 ft deep and with 9 ft width
clearance at track level. At its further end the line is running due north
along an 8 ft 6 in. formation ledge, as here the mountainside is steeper
than formerly. Cwm Trwsgl farm lies immediately below the line and
was the most northerly habitation on this side of the valley. The Plans
give this section of line a 'Level' indication but in fact the course
continues to fall to the foot of the Cwm-Dwyfor mine incline. The
valley is now quite narrow, but more attractive, and is wooded on the
other side. An immense amphitheatre of mountain, its summit rounded
and uniformly shaped, cradles the end of the valley. There is no
footpath to the north; exit from the valley is from the end which the
railway entered only! Over this northern ridge whose highest point is
2,408 ft, lies the Drws-y-Coed valley which runs due east and west, and
from whose western end the Nantlle Railway emanated. From this
position on the Gorseddau Junction line, there is and never has been
reason for communication over this impressive barrier, there being no
col to make it practicable. Ahead, the line can be seen clinging to the
eastern slopes, disappearing for a short stretch into a re-entrant to the
right, and then proceeding along its ledge to the bottom of the clearly-
defined final incline. There are three fillings where streams are crossed,
and the largest of these in the re-entrant has been almost entirely swept
away by a spectacular landslide of water and rock. Traces of the permanent way are not so clear and the ground is more marshy; chairs and
pins have been found here so confirming that the same track materials
were provided throughout the system. Shortly before the incline a
remote stone building is passed though its connection with the railway
is unclear. The final double-tracked incline is not steep and the drumhouse is curious having separate passages for each track.

   The incline lifts the track from 740 to 915 feet, its foot being almost
exactly a mile from Cwm Trwsgl. At the incline top, it leads ahead
towards the smooth bowl at the top of the valley. In front lie spoil tips
in disarray, the remains of wheelpit, engine house, processing floors
and barracks. The track curves eastward over a low embankment and
after crossing the infant Dwyfawr (the correct spelling of the corrupted
Dwyfor) it forks; a very short spur runs into the blacksmith's shop and
the other, hardly longer, disappears into what must have been a loading
bank. On a higher level and beyond stand various heaps of variegated
rock spoil, their composition and colour revealing the complex geological variety of these rocks. Clearly the mine was built with adequate
capital, its buildings and tramway works being soundly constructed of a
dark grey stone which must have been brought here for the purpose. As
at Cwm Trwsgl, there are the remains of stone piers to carry water to

the overshot wheel. Once more, and as with the Croesor Tramway, the lasting impression is of the immense amount of labour and money which was poured into a railway to connect this lonely spot with the sea. In the case of the Croesor, the subsequent output of slate probably justified the effort . . . in the present example, the result must have been quite disastrous.

It was likely to have been this mile from Cwm Trwsgl which showed weaknesses in the new permanent way provided by the G.J. & P.R.; at first the sleepers were spaced at 2 ft 9 in. intervals; from impressions along the foundations of the Cwm-Dwyfor branch, the sleepers have been reduced to 2 ft intervals. Had copper or iron ore been carried in any quantity, insufficient support on this boggy length would soon be evident. What is not known is whether it was the output which was destructive – which seems unlikely – or simply the provision of heavy stone for the erection of the mine's buildings.

Permanent Way

Such information as is available or conjectured concerning the track of the Llidiart Yspytty Ironstone Mine Tramway, and the extension of this line from Tremadoc to the Gorseddau slate quarry at Ffridd Uchaf, has already been given. The first precise description of Croesor and Gorseddau permanent way is that given by Vignes in 1878. The ancestry of the T-section rail carried in chairs as used by the Croesor when building in 1862–3, is still an open question, but Vignes confirms that Croesor and Gorseddau materials were identical in the mid-1870s. The original supplier of rail and chairs was probably a Portmadoc foundry.

[The T-section rail with bulb on one side of the foot was not confined to North Wales. Specimens of an almost identical section were found in autumn 1971 on the site of a tramway on Congleton Edge, Cheshire, stated to have closed after about 1809.]

It is convenient to repeat the material dimensions for the opening of the Croesor Tramway in August 1864 and the Gorseddau Junction & Portmadoc Railways in September 1875. Despite the eleven years intervening, the Railways Company had not seen fit to introduce a heavier specification, even though the Croesor line was built for horse haulage and the G.J. & P.R. had powers to work with locomotives and carry goods and passengers from the start. This was because there was already a surfeit of this material available locally and "the Company already possessed a quantity of that weight". The gradients and curves of the new railway suggest a speculative element in the whole undertaking: so the new Gorseddau Railway came to be laid in 15 ft length wrought-iron T rails weighing 20 lbs. per yard which were carried in supporting cast-iron chairs of 3 lbs. and butt-jointed in larger chairs weighing 5 lbs.* having 4 in. length plain fixing pins. At first, iron wedges keyed the rail in the chair; later wood was used. The wooden

---

*'ENGINEERING', 11th June, 1875 gives 5 lbs. and 7 lbs.

sleepers were nominally 4 ft long and the formation 8 ft wide but in practice sleepers of any suitable length were used and the formation was wider in places. Sleepers were 5 in. wide × 3½ in. deep and spaced at 2 ft 9 in. centres except at joints where the adjoining spacing was 2 ft. The gauge was precisely as the Croesor, 24 in.

Despite the generous bearing surface and weight of rails compared with any standard gauge line, as soon as the locomotive started work the track became distorted in several locations, the engine 'ironing-out' some of the sharper curves. The light rails were badly affected by expansion on hot days, and the butted rail joints misaligned so to overcome this much of the sleepering was reduced to 2 ft centres, with 1 ft 6 in. at joints.

At the time of Vignes' visit, all the old tramway had been converted to the narrower gauge in this material: all, that is, save '3 Km.' which on 1st January, 1877, 'remained to be converted' and this was presumably the section between Braich-y-Bib and the Gorseddau quarry.

Clearly, the new trackwork with its evidence of thrift, was not satisfactory. The costs involved in maintenance of works and way for the years 1875–78 support this. The rails were found to be too light for many of the sharp curves, which though few in number, were very restrictive. Some were actually under 2 chains radius as reported. There were also problems of holding the rails in gauge during summer when the butt-joints did not take kindly to the expanding rails. When the sleepers were closed in, each rail was supported in nine places. Vignes emphasises the additional problems and cost of this revision and states the track is still only suitable for light traffic, which apparently, was all that the railway carried, fortunately!

Ballast was obtained by blasting rock, taken from the line of construction, into small pieces which gives it the appearance of slate shale. It was laid about 6 in. deep.

Civil Engineering

The line was built through a difficult terrain. Between Penmorfa and Braich-y-Bib where no official gradients have been documented, the average rise was 1 in 152. Having regard to the difficult country, heavy engineering works were avoided and construction costs reduced. Operating costs were much enhanced, of course. Embankment sides were sloped to 45 degrees and cuttings in rock were given vertical faces. Bridges and aqueducts were built up in rough stone blasted from the site. Some were laid loose, and others part-mortared.

Train Working

The sources of traffic were stated to include *lead* from Cwm-Dwyfor, peat and slates from Gorseddau and Prince of Wales quarries. Slab tombstones were a particular feature of it! Vignes commented that certain traffic came Down to Tremadoc by gravity and that men, pushing a single wagon, was not unknown. 'The locomotive was only used to bring back the empties or to take loads to areas served by the railway.' It would seem that the locomotive was used only when and where necessary, and only until 1878. Thereafter it was stored. Croesor accounts show flour and corn traffic between Portmadoc and Clenenney Mills, near Hen-efail.

Local tradition maintains that quite a brisk passenger traffic was carried unofficially. A Brynkir Mill owner's grandmother took mill products to the nearby short tunnel at Hen-efail where the train would pick her up and take her to Tremadoc for the market there. Another woman walked to and from Caernarvon for provisions for the quarrymen and caught Up trains to the quarry from the same point. She would sell groceries to the quarrymen at Ystradllyn. It is also said that on the Down journey, the horses rode in a Dandy at the rear of the train, Festiniog Railway-fashion. This cannot be confirmed.

Locomotive and Rolling Stock

There is the evidence from Festiniog records concerning the supply of slate wagons and a passenger carriage from Boston Lodge. As this took place before the G.J.&P.R. Act, they would be for 3 ft gauge and possibly such stock was not suitable for conversion to narrow gauge. On 1st January, 1878 Vignes gives the stock returns as: One Locomotive; 15 Wagons suitable for slate or goods – by 1885 reduced to 7 Wagons – together with additional wagons owned by the quarries and some hired from the Festiniog Railway: 'THE MINING JOURNAL' gives de Winton & Co. Union Works, Caernarvon as the wagon-builders, all 'having powerful brakes, the wheels being made of chilled iron which has proved to be even more lasting than steel'.

There was one locomotive, a vertical boilered four-wheeler also built by de Winton & Co. A contemporary source gives its dimensions as 20 in. diameter driving wheels, 4 ft wheelbase, 6 in. × 12 in. cylinders, and boiler 5 ft 6 in. × 2 ft 9 in. diameter (these would be the measurements over cladding; heating surface 100 sq. ft. 'The boiler was pressed to work at 130 lbs. but would be capable of carrying a higher pressure'; ¾ ton of fuel was carried and 180 gallons of water. Tanks on such engines varied in size. The Weight in Working Order was 4½ tons and Tractive Effort 2,150 lbs.

The engine rejoiced in the name of *Pert* and was supplied new to the Prince of Wales Slate Quarry Company. The Portmadoc Croesor & Beddgelert Tram Railway Company's accounts contain a debit entry for the Gorseddau on 10th July, 1874. 'To use of siding in unloading loco engine 10s.'. (This was the Beddgelert Siding). When traffic ceased after 1894, it was placed out of service 'near Tremadoc' (probably on the Ironstone Mine spur) before going to Messrs. Owen, Isaac & Owen, (dealers) of the Vulcan Foundry, Portmadoc. It is possible that it became the second of three similar engines which worked at the

Coedmadoc Slate Company's quarry, Glodd-fa'r-Glai, Nantlle, when that quarry re-opened in 1896. This undertaking liquidated at the end of December 1908 and the equipment was auctioned at the end of the following March.

Whatever may have been its fate, *Pert* can hardly have been much worn when her duties on the Gorseddau line were over. A contemporary account of working on the line said the engine was quite suitable for negotiating the sharp curves, light enough to treat the track gently and sufficiently powerful for the steep gradients. Clearly, it was not overloaded! On test the engine would haul 20 tons including its own weight, or 20 loaded wagons up 1 in 25. (Braked wagons were 15 cwt. and unbraked 13 cwt. tare.)

Signalling

The only signalling on the whole system was in G.J.&P.R. days at the Cambrian Railway's crossing. There had been two crossings here on the same spot. The original was replaced and inspected by Col. F.H. Rich for the B.O.T. who reported on 18th August, 1875 that no traps had been put into the Gorseddau line to protect the Cambrian. Rich refers to the 'Cambrian signalman's permission' (to use the crossing) as if the adjacent box was their property. Unfortunately, Cambrian records do not enlighten, but the signal box was intended to be Gorseddau property. It cannot be proven that all features on the Deposited Plans were carried out, but the diagram included shows the full arrangements, to which have been added the 1879 proposal for the interchange platform and run-round at the Cambrian station. The Plans do not show the Down Home Cambrian signal, but one would have been provided. In Cambrian records the crossing is known as 'Mr. Huddart's'. [The Huddart family bought the Brynkir estate in 1809 and held it for about 100 years. The Hall was demolished after the First War and held German P.O.W. during that war. Purchase was made by Captain Joseph Huddart, Elder Brother of Trinity House who, after siting the South Stack Light, reported on Holyhead Harbour and surveyed the maritime side for an Irish Mail route via Holyhead. His son, also Joseph, became High Sheriff for the county and was knighted at the opening of Telford's Menai Bridge by George IV in 1826. The family played a great part in South Caernarvonshire and North Merionethshire during the Industrial Revolution. Brynkir passed from Sir Joseph to George Augustus who died in 1885; he was co-patentee with Spooner of the rail fishplate device which bears their names. His eldest son was the Rev. Dr. G.A.W. Huddart, prominent in Festiniog Railway affairs and anxious to find management for that line which would develop the tourist trade at a time when the standard gauge was siphoning off the slate trade. The family was a large holder of Festiniog stock etc. and may be said to have financed the line in a liberal way from its earliest days. The estate's lands included parts of Criccieth, Penygroes, Penrhyn, Portmadoc etc.]

The Gorseddau's trap point on the north side of the crossing was extended to form a short siding, and had the Gorseddau-Croesor link been built, this siding would have extended alongside and over the Cambrian bridge to cross the Canal and run up into the Beddgelert Siding, Croesor tramway. According to Cambrian records, Mr. Huddart's crossing had been lifted by 1892. The Gorseddau trans-shipped some slate traffic to the Cambrian *north of the crossing* by means of the short siding already mentioned, and presumably a Cambrian siding would have been built for loading. Of this there is no trace today.

Vignes has some supplementary information about this railway crossing: the operating of it was to conform to Clauses 9–12 of the Railway Clauses Act 1863; and there were to be mutual trans-shipment arrangements at a Goods Station by the crossing – probably by means of the short siding just mentioned – and the operation of the crossing was to be controlled by the Cambrian.

REFERENCES

1. Harrison Deeds. Box 65. Parcel 4. National Library of Wales.
2. Prince of Wales Quarry: see 'LAW TIMES' Report Vol. XVIII: 21st March, 1868.
3. 'Meini Hirion' or 'Menhirs' is the accepted Welsh for Long Stones, either a single standing stone or more, e.g. a stone circle. This example is thought to be pre-Bronze Age and was probably the traditional way of honouring the dead. There is a collection of stones with an identical name near Penmaenmawr.
4. At this time coal was expensive and not commonly used, having to be imported from Flintshire or Lancashire. Consequently most homesteads had access to a turbary.

GORSEDDAU JUNCTION & PORTMADOC RAILWAYS
(& GORSEDDAU TRAMWAY) Mileages

Miles Chains from Sluice Bridge		Location	Gorseddau Tramway	G.J.&P. Rlys.
0	0	Tramway Wharf	Zero Point	–
0	40	Portmadoc	Crossing with Cambrian Rlys.	–
1	50	Tremadoc	Reversing neck	–
5	53	Ynys-y-pandy	Slate Mill	–
8	10	Gorseddau	Slate Quarry	–

Miles Chains from Cwm Trwsgl		(including variations on official distances due to different points of origin.)		
4	53	Ynys-y-pandy	–	Slate Mill
4	20	Braich-y-Bib	–	New 1875 Junction
0	0	Cwm Trwsgl	–	Slate Mill
0	30	Prince of Wales Qy.	–	Foot of second incline
1	14	Cwm-Dwyfor Mine	–	End of line at Mine.

	1875	1876	1877	1878	1879	1880	1881	1885	1886	1887	1888	1889	1890	1891	1892	1893	1894
Cost Works and Way	£186	88	65	16	4	–	9	5	2	4	5	6	4	4	–	–	–
Cost Loco power	65	24	40	15													
Cost Carr/Wag maint.	2	3															
Traffic expenses	44	111	203	82	96	96	96										
Legal expenses	–	100	–	–	13												
Loss on working	414	512	545	404	354	232	255	48	47	43	45	51	49	29	28	28	?
Merchandise Tons	324	1042	1270	856	649	443	329	–	39	–	4						
Minerals Tons	381	733	318	345	371	157	184	–	–	46	93	31	21	20	–	–	
Train mileage	2050	3533	2701	1658	2239	1347	1350	–	60	440	221	248	80	60			

Locos — Returned as One throughout period

Wagons — 15 1875–81   7 1886–93

Comment on the above:

Cost of Works and Way	Figures suggest track etc. incomplete when traffic began.
Loco costs	Loco used for four years only; thereafter stored as it was returned throughout the above period.
	Returns state 'Freighters using own horses' after 1880.
Carr/Wagon costs	Presumably charged in Quarry Accounts after first two years?
Traffic expenses	Little reduction after horses replaced locomotive. Possibly charged to Quarry Account after 1885?
Loss on working	These much reduced in second period. Mineral traffic possibly charged to Quarry Account?
Tonnage carried	Merchandise exceeds mineral traffic in first period, but falls to nothing in second (or is not returned). Zenith in 1876, thereafter line appears to have been only used occasionally.
Wagon Returns	Figures suggest 15 wagons of first period were for merchandise traffic and half were disposed of in second period. Quarries' own wagons used for mineral traffic.
No Returns made 1882–4	(Railways Company under threat of proceedings for not furnishing same.)

Directors (Quorum 3 Directors)

1873 Charles James FOX   James STEWART of London (Wine Merchant)   James
MAW   Thomas HARVEY of Brixton (Solicitor).

1876 Herbert C. MAUDSLAY   James STEWART   Rev. Logan LOGAN   Thomas
HARVEY.

1883 James STEWART of London E.C.   Charles BARTON of Wincanton   Rev.
Logan LOGAN of Bournemouth.

1896 Charles BARTON of Wincanton.   Rev. Logan LOGAN of Bournemouth   (One
seat unfilled).

No director other than Barton had any other railway directorships; he was of the
Gloucester & Dean Forest Rly.

Secretary throughout above period: George Joseph GRAY, St. Clement's House,
London, E.C.

The Seal of the Company shows the strong influence of Robert Fairlie's double
engine but does not imply the Company's commitment!

FESTINIOG & BLAENAU
RAILWAY CO. LTD.
(Gauge 1 ft 11¾ in.)

Registered as a Company under the Limited Liability Act of 1862: 7th August, 1862.

Absorbed by standard-gauge Bala & Festiniog Railway 13th April, 1883 under powers given to Bala & Festiniog Railway by Great Western Railway Act 43/4 Vic. Cap. 141 Sections 63–6 of 6th August, 1880.

Opened to all traffic: 29th May, 1868.

Converted to standard gauge: April–September 1883★

Standard gauge opened: 1st November, 1882: Bala–Llan Ffestiniog (except sidings). Llan Ffestiniog–Blaenau Ffestiniog: 10th September, 1883.

Standard gauge closed: Passengers 4th January, 1960; Freight 27th January, 1961.

Registered Office: Melbourne House, Llan Ffestiniog. From June 1868 Duffws Blaenau Festiniog (later, a second office in Portmadoc).

Length: 3 m. 40 ch.

Maximum Gradient: 1 in 58.

Minimum Curve: 6 chains.

Maximum Speed: 12 m.p.h. – under Sealed Undertaking.

Capital: £20,000 in £10 Ordinary Shares.

★After gauge conversion, the L.N.W.R. was to be permitted to use the line under Section 65 of the G.W.R. Act 1880, but such powers not to be granted until L.N.W.R. physically connected with F. & B.R. ('The Blaenau Railway') which it never was, as the Festiniog Railway owned the connecting and intervening land!

Horse omnibuses ran between Llan Ffestiniog & Bala 1868–1871 'three months each time'.

Historical Summary

1862 Company formed under Limited Liability Act 7th August, 1862 largely by the anti-Festiniog Railway interest of quarries owned by Samuel Holland and Turner & Casson.

1868 Line opened for all traffic (29th May). [Board of Trade inspection 26th May.] (G.W.R. working Ruabon – Dolgelley with effect from 4th August).

1876 Agreement that F. & B.R. should be purchased by B. & F.R. for £14,000 etc. (15th July) following an earlier arrangement to raise £190,000 by subscription.

1882 B. & F.R. reaches Llan Ffestiniog (1st November).

1883 Gauge conversion of F. & B.R. (April–September). Open as standard gauge 10th September.

History

The original quarries which opened in the neighbourhood of Blaenau Festiniog were, so far as the important ones were concerned, all connected to the Festiniog Railway by 1860. Slate quarrying had developed however, to the east and south of the town, extending southwards as far as Llan Ffestiniog, a large village some three miles away from its industrial namesake, Blaenau Festiniog. Llan Ffestiniog remains today quite unchanged by a century and a half of slate quarrying in the neighbourhood. It was the most southward point of the extent of the 'catchment area' from which the quarries drew their labour, and though having itself no connections with the slate industry, it marked the boundary, so to speak, of the quarrying 'dormitory' area which surrounded Blaenau to east and north.

Quarries east and south of Blaenau had no direct rail access to the Festiniog, at that time the only railway in the vicinity. Whilst the advantages of having a rail outlet to Portmadoc and the sea and, from 1872, an interchange connection at Minffordd with the standard gauge Cambrian Railways, were undeniable, the reality was greatly diminished by the then hopelessly overburdened state of the Festiniog Railway. This line still displayed most of the shortcomings of its 1836 horse tramway origins. Its track was primitive, its course was winding, and though the gradient favoured loaded trains, these were still worked by horse-and-gravity system over the single line of rails. The proprietors of the line were keenly aware of the wrath of the quarry owners, the bottlenecks on their system and the delays to traffic at the collection points in Blaenau (of which there were two, one at Dinas and the other at Duffws), and at the quayside at Portmadoc. To be fair to them, slate output had grown to such an extent that they had been unable to meet its transport. They were actively engaged in laying more robust permanent way, in eliminating the more unsatisfactory sections

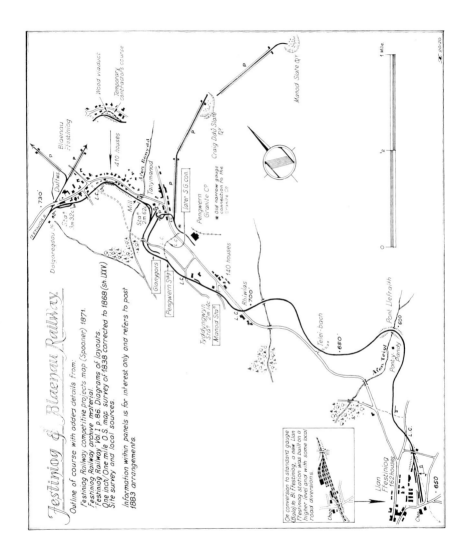

Festiniog & Blaenau Railway

Outline of course with added details from:
Festiniog Railway competitive project's map (Spooner) 1871.
Festiniog Railway archive material.
'Festiniog Railway' Vol I p. 86 Diagrams of layouts.
One inch/One mile O.S. map survey of 1838 corrected to 1868 (sh. LXV)
Site survey and local sources

Information within panels is for interest only and refers to post 1883 arrangements.

On conversion to standard gauge (Bala) to Bl. Festiniog, a new Llan Festiniog station was built on a higher level and with some local road diversions of the tramway period, in finding a successor to the rustic horsepower and building more and larger slate wagons. But they were at full stretch. As if to make the position worse, a railway which was to be in essence an extension of the Festiniog, was incorporated under the Company's Act on 7th August, 1862, to link Blaenau and Llan Ffestiniog! It lay just outside the Caernarvonshire boundary and shortly it will be recorded as having aspirations with a projected Merionethshire Railway: these systems find a place under the current title in view of their relations with the Festiniog Railway's south Caernarvonshire Portmadoc outlet.

It should be stressed that appearances proved to be deceptive. The Festiniog & Blaenau Railway was designed, it was true, to make a physical junction with the Festiniog's terminal at Duffws and then extend as a continuation but under an independent concern for the 3½ miles (officially quoted as 4 miles of single line) to Llan Ffestiniog. It must have been abundantly clear from those foremost promoting it, (who had not been on the best of terms with the Festiniog) that there was more to it than first appeared. It is significant that it was not until 1860 did Turner & Casson's slate quarry, operating under the name 'Wm. Turner & Co.' start to do business with the overburdened Festiniog Railway, having declined to do so ever since the Railway had opened in 1836. Even then, it had to wait until 1865 before a direct rail link with the F.R. (the Duffws Incline) was completed – by which date the Festiniog & Blaenau Railway was already under construction and Turner was ready to throw in his lot with the new railway. Possibly these intentions were upset by the death of George Casson in the following year, and the subsequent sale of the quarry to the newly-incorporated Diphwys Casson Slate Co. Ltd. of 1863; at this time the quarry had to cart slate to the head of Rhiwbach No. 3 Incline where D.C.-marked wagons were available for them on the Festiniog. No member of the Board of the new quarry company had any local allegiances, though C.E. Spooner was its Engineer: the eventual promise of an outlet for their products which would meet what would become the Great Western Railway near Bala, would relieve them of reliance on the Festiniog. [The Corwen & Bala Railway reached Bala in April 1868.][1] The local landowners were to donate the land where the line was to pass through their property. All major civil engineering works were to be built in anticipation of conversion to 4 ft 8½ in. gauge as and when necessary. Great care would be taken when laying out reverse curves to make these transitional and avoid any straight connecting sections; the minimum curve would be 6 chains against the 2 chains on the Festiniog. (It was intended that the steepest grade should be 1 in 100, but compulsory deviations almost doubled the steepness).

The prospectus issued in September 1866 stated:

Capital £10,000 in 1,000 shares of £10 each. Deposit £1 per share. The calls after the first to be made at intervals as required.

'This Company has been formed for the purpose of making a railway from

Festiniog to the Quarry District at Blaenau and there forming a junction with the existing railway to Portmadoc.

The Promoters of the Company are the land-owners, quarry proprietors and other persons interested in the prosperity of the neighbourhood.

The length of the proposed railway is about 3½ miles and the estimated cost is £10,000. A survey has been made and a line selected which combines good gradients with facilities and cheapness of construction. It commences by the village of Festiniog, passes by Cornel-y-wal and Bethania and terminates by a junction with the existing railway at a point a little to the West of the Dol-y-garreg-ddu Station.

Enquiries have been made as to the existing goods traffic between Festiniog and Portmadoc by the different routes and the result has satisfied the Promoters that the proposed railway will when opened command a very large traffic in goods.

The passenger traffic will also be very great. A railway is now in course of construction from Llanrwst to Bettws-y-coed and active steps are being taken to make a new turnpike road from there to Blaenau for which purpose an Act of Parliament has recently been obtained. When these improvements have been carried out and the proposed railway made to Festiniog a line of country unrivalled in its beauties will be opened out to Summer Visitors and the number of Tourists passing along the route will be immense. The local passenger traffic will also necessarily be very great as it is intended to run cheap morning and evening trains for the convenience of workmen.

The traffic between Portmadoc and Trawsfynydd and the upper portion of the parish of Maentwrog will be secured to the proposed railway by improvements in the turnpike roads leading to those districts from Festiniog.

Looking at the cheapness of the line and the traffic that may be calculated upon the Directors anticipate that the capital to be expended will yield a high rate of dividend to the shareholders.

A large proportion of the capital has been already subscribed by the Promoters and the balance is now offered to the people of Festiniog and the neighbourhood generally. It is intended that the line shall be made by and for the benefit of the inhabitants of the district.

Applications for shares may be made on the following form and addressed to the Secretary, Robert Griffith at Melbourne House, Festiniog or to the Bankers, Casson & Co., Festiniog.

Applications for shares must be sent in before 20th October, 1866.'

There followed a simple Application Form which was also printed in Welsh.

A resolution of 11th January, 1868 increased the capital to £20,000, shares to be offered to existing holders in relation to their holdings. The Directors were authorised to borrow up to £1,000. On 22nd March, 1868 the Board was permitted to borrow up to £2,500 for buying rolling stock.

A glance at the list of promoters showed that they contained the principal complainants regarding the Festiniog Railway's monopoly of coast-bound slate traffic and that they were among the biggest users of that line. As in later years in South Wales, when dissatisfaction and monopoly produced the strikingly militant Barry Railway, so here, sixteen years earlier, industrialists were tired of the shortcomings of the Festiniog route, and a line to connect Blaenau and Llan Festiniog was a cunningly contrived scheme; at this distant date, it is impossible to guess if the Festiniog board really appreciated what was in the wind. In any case, the Festiniog Company was fully engaged with its own problems, and in view of the fact that they hoped to introduce steam locomotives (and passenger working) very shortly – the former came about in October 1863 – they probably thought little more than that this new extension to their line was an event they could willingly accommodate if steam power lived up to its promise.

Samuel Holland of Maentwrog and London was the moving spirit in the F. & B.R. venture. He was later to become Member of Parliament for Merionethshire, and at the time his quarry's tonnages over the Festiniog were excelled by no other owner. His brother Charles of Liverpool, another active railway director, had a son, Charles Menzies Holland, who also joined the board. C.M. Holland was a civil engineer living in Wallasey, Cheshire. Other initial directors were quarry owners William Davies, Capt. T.H. Wynne, George and John Casson and Robert Roberts. Morgan Lloyd, Q.C., M.P., of Beaumaris and London and owner of an extensive estate on the south side of the Vale of Ffestiniog completed an influential picture. The official description was 'for a line from Diphwys on the Festiniog Railway to Festiniog, Merioneth'. It was to be of single line and to 1 ft 11¾ in. gauge, a quarter of an inch more than the Festiniog figure. Capital was eventually £80,000 in £10 shares. The offices of the Company were at first in Melbourne House, Llan Ffestiniog, where the Manager and Secretary were housed; these offices as well as that of auditor were all filled by persons named Davies! In June 1868 it moved to Duffws terminus and there was also an office in Portmadoc.

C.M. Holland, though not termed Engineer to the undertaking, was given the task of building the line and equipping it. During the early 1860s he seems to have had something of a roving commission as he was engaged in superintending the building of a line from London to Croydon, during which he occasionally went over to Messrs. George England & Co's works to review progress on the new locomotives for the Festiniog Railway, then building there. When the first locomotive trials took place at Portmadoc, he was in charge of one of the two engines. Holland had recently taken full credit for the Festiniog engine design, by letter to the editor of 'ENGINEERING' from Essex Chambers, Manchester. Perhaps this is one reason, among others, why progress in building the new line was somewhat tardy.

Whilst the Festiniog was busily occupied firstly in introducing new motive power and, on 6th January, 1865, starting a passenger service, the F. & B. bided its time patiently until the F.R. was in a position to cater for extra traffic and to see how the new power behaved over a period. Even with the slow progress of the works, and the problems of a viaduct at Tan-y-Manod, locomotives for the new line were not ready for the opening on 29th May, 1868. Between then and 31st August following trains were worked by the Festiniog Railway under contract.

C.M. Holland had advised the Board of Trade as early as 13th

November, 1867 that the line was ready for inspection, but nothing was then done. On 28th May, 1868 he wrote asking the B.O.T. to write to him at his London address asking for the line to be inspected by Friday of that week (its own locos presumably even then not being available for the service) 'as it is all-important to so small a concern to open their line before the close of this week and avail of the Whit Monday traffic'. They replied that they could only reply to the Secretary of the Company.

At a meeting with the B.O.T. Holland discussed the position of a Railway Company not incorporated by Act of Parliament, and it was concluded that for B.O.T. purposes the Company should be treated as though it had been.

This letter conflicts strangely in date with the Official Inspection date and one must conclude it was made without Holland being aware of it, for Captain H.W. Tyler inspected and reported to the Board of Trade on 26th May, 1868:

> This railway has been constructed for about 3½ miles, between the town of Festiniog and a junction near Blaenau with the existing line to Portmadoc, on a gauge of Two Feet or, more accurately, 1 ft 11¼ in. in the clear. It has been made without Act of Parliament, but consent of the landowners, and it will be largely used by quarry workmen and others interested in the slate quarries. It is intended to run cheap trains morning and evening for the workmen. A considerable traffic in goods is also expected.
>
> The steepest gradient is 1 in 58. The sharpest curves have a radii of six chains.
>
> The permanent way is laid with rails of (here is denoted flat-bottomed section) section weighing about 38 lbs. to the lineal yard and secured by dog spikes to transverse sleepers. The sleepers are of larch averaging 4 ft 9 in. long, by 8 in. × 4 in. and are 2 ft 4 in. apart at the joints and 2 ft 7 in. at the intermediate spaces, from centre to centre.
>
> There are nine bridges over or under the railway, which appear to be standing well, and which are constructed of masonry, brickwork and timber. Certain symptoms of movement are however, visible in a cattle creep 2 m. 65 ch. from Festiniog, and in some of the retaining walls. These points should be carefully watched. There is a viaduct at three miles from Festiniog, originally constructed with four spans of 80 ft each, covered by lattice girders of timber, resting on masonry piers and abutments. The girders having been constructed without camber, and applied to the viaduct in curved form, considerable deflection showed itself when they were erected, which has been partially obviated by the addition of intermediate trestles, reducing the spans to 40 feet. Halving the spans, and reducing also the load by half, these intermediate piers have quadrupled the relative strength of the girders. But the viaduct is not even now, with a view to permanent stability, in a satisfactory condition. I have therefore recommended that the intermediate trestles should be strengthened, that corbels should be added over them, and that covers should be added on the joints of the timbers forming the lower booms of the girders. The weight, however, to pass over the viaduct will be comparatively slight, the engines weighing only about eight tons each, and the trucks when loaded about 2½ tons each.
>
> I inclose a certificate signed by the chairman, under the seal of the company, stating that these works will be carried out, as well as that some improvements, which I have also recommended, will be made at the junction near Blaenau; and I am of the opinion

that the sanction of the Board of Trade may, upon these conditions, be given to the opening of the line for public traffic.

A certificate should, however, also be given in regard to the working of the single line which is, I understand, to be conducted upon the train-staff system; and I have requested that this should be forwarded to the Board of Trade. This portion of line is, I am informed, to be worked under agreement by the Festiniog (to Portmadoc) Company, pending the completion of certain rolling stock which has been ordered for the Festiniog and Blaenau Railway.

Before closing this report, I think it only right to remark, as I have already done to some of the directors personally upon the spot, upon the question of speed, as connected with lines of this description, because I have observed a tendency to run undue risk in this respect.

I only consented to recommend the Board of Trade to sanction the opening of the railway to Portmadoc on the express condition that the same restriction should be borne in mind on the present occasion. These little railways, on a very narrow gauge, and neither constructed nor maintained with the same degree of perfection as a first-class passenger railway, may be worked with safety at slow but are not at present fitted for a speed of more than 10 or 12 miles an hour; and it is necessary, not only that such a rule should be laid down, but that the directors should by watchfulness and by a series of fines prevent their officers and servants from employing them at higher speed. Those who work them from day to day, finding how great a degree of safety is attainable upon them, are too apt to increase the speed of the trains; and they may do this for a time with impunity; but they will in doing so meet sooner or later with very disastrous consequences, unless they are checked in this respect, and prevented by the exercise of authority from exceeding the strict bounds of prudence; and they will thus also bring discredit upon a system which is very convenient in this particular district, and which may under proper control be worked with safety and efficiency.

The conditions imposed by the Captain included:

1. The removal of certain facing points near the Blaenau terminus of the line, and also opposite the main junction signal box at that point.
2. The removal of the main junction semaphore signal and to reposition it at or nearly opposite the junction between the Festiniog and F. & B Railways.
3. The said junction points be fitted with locking apparatus and until this is done, to be locked between the passage of trains and subjected to a speed of 3 miles an hour.
4. The viaduct at 3 miles to be strengthened as suggested.

On 5th June, 1868 the Board informed the Company that there was no objection to opening for public traffic; nevertheless, the passenger service appears to have commenced already on 29th May!

At the start, the new line was worked so closely in conjunction with the Festiniog that 'it would almost have seemed to be a branch line of that concern'. Later, the opposite was true; it had become a fierce competitor. During 1870 the Festiniog closed its Dinas terminal to passenger services and all trains ran to Duffws.

One of the causes of friction between Festiniog and F. & B. Railways was the slate rates. In 1864 the Festiniog offered lower rates to quarry

This scene has been variously described, but the title on the original print says "Dinas, Festiniog". The train is posed with engine No. 2, (with the humps of the Manods rising behind the train) on an afternoon working from Llan Ffestiniog. The heavy shadow on the right suggests a building, perhaps the station – out of sight?

F. Frith & Co.

This damaged print was discovered by the author behind a photograph of the local football team in the G.W.R. station waiting room at Blaenau. Said then to be a train at Duffws (or 'Dinas' as the previous picture would describe it), it may actually be at Llan Ffestiniog, with perhaps the engine shed behind.

Collection J.I.C. Boyd

A view looking northwards towards Blaenau Festiniog from Manod, in the late 1860s, showing the newly-completed railway with the small Tyddyngwyn station and signal, (*central left*). The main road between Llan and Blaenau Festiniog runs between the terrace houses in the foreground. Slate quarries to the west of Blaenau are just visible.

Caernarvonshire Record Office

The just-completed wooden viaduct immediately north of Tan-y-Manod leads the railway into Blaenau Festiniog, where much of the housing is clearly new. The course of the bridge may still be seen today.

Caernarvonshire Record Office

Tan-y-Manod station (looking towards Duffws) with double-arm signal. Probably photographed in the 1870s, the scene was still much the same in the 1970s.
Collection J.I.C. Boyd

Tan-y-Manod photographed a century after the previous picture: many of the civil engineering features of the narrow gauge line were retained after gauge conversion.   *J.I.C. Boyd*

This scene in November 1947, incorporates the area shown in the two previous pictures: it is the Tan-y-Manod yard of the G.W.R., with former engine shed and loading platforms from which narrow gauge slate wagons were carried away 'pick-a-back' on standard gauge transporters. These travelled in both directions according to customer demand. (The narrow gauge station was to the left of centre.)   *J.I.C. Boyd*

A Llan Ffestiniog train stops on the wooden viaduct approaching Tan-y-Manod. Was it an important occasion, for all types of people are to be seen? If the photograph was taken at the same time as the other similar pictures of the Festiniog Railway around Duffws, then the date is about 1876. The rails are still flat-bottomed and the scene confirms that over the years, engines were used facing either direction. Note that rain strips have been added to the carriage roofs.

National Library of Wales

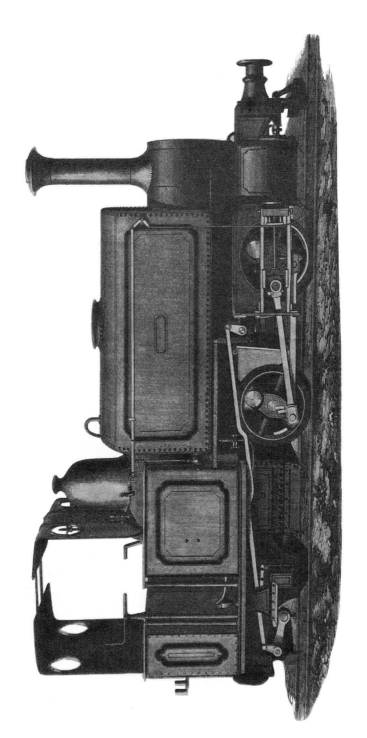

An engraving from ENGINEERING 15th April, 1870 of Manning, Wardle's engine for the Festiniog & Blaenau Railway.

owners in exchange for an agreement to use their line exclusively for the next fourteen years. Holland's and Greaves' quarries were among others which contracted to pay 2s. 6d. per ton. In 1871 the Festiniog made a contract with the Welsh Slate, Copper & Lead Mining Co. at 2s. 1½d. a ton but over an increased period of thirty years. When these terms were offered to the other quarry owners, they refused to accept them, pointing out that under the Regulation of Railways Act 1873, railway companies could not make unfair contracts between customers. Holland and Greaves took out an injunction against the Festiniog, claiming parity with other contract holders whom they maintained were being better treated. In February 1876 the Railway Commissioners granted an injunction against the Festiniog Railway. By the date of opening of the F. & B., the 2s. 6d. per ton contract had only run for four years out of fourteen. Even by that time, the motives of the Festiniog had become suspect.

First public evidence of plans afoot for yet another new railway appeared in 'THE NORTH WALES CHRONICLE' for Saturday 28th January, 1871 and was almost a word-for-word copy of the prospectus for a new railway:

> We understand that Standing Orders have been complied with as regards railway communication between Festiniog village and Talsarnau . . . it is proposed that the railway shall be constructed on the same gauge as the Cambrian and form a junction with the Festiniog & Blaenau Railway at about 300 yards distant from Festiniog village and then run to Hendre mur . . . through the valley of Felenrhydd-fawr and just above the waterfall down to within about 600 yards of the Pile Bridge over Waeth Bach estuary on the Talsarnau side, and form a double junction with the Cambrian Company's line.

'THE NORTH WALES CHRONICLE' of 29th April, 1871 also refers to a public meeting in the Market Hall, Blaenau Festiniog, to support a new railway to the town. This plan to tap the slate quarries and quit the Festiniog area (not the only one in which the Hollands were interested) received Parliamentary approval on 29th June, 1871 as the Merionethshire Railway. The scheme was not only to rob the Festiniog Railway of traffic from Blaenau almost completely, but in part to give it to the Cambrian Railways, not at Minffordd – for which purpose the Festiniog Railway had to be traversed – but at Talsarnau, farther south along the Cambrian coast line.

This was not all of Samuel Holland's interests. He was also urging extension of the standard gauge westwards from Ruabon on the Shrewsbury – Chester section of the G.W.R. This had reached Corwen by May 1865 by means of the Llangollen & Corwen Railway; Bala by April 1868 (the Corwen & Bala Railway); and was being extended westward again by the Bala & Dolgelley Railway Act of 30th June, 1862, the latter having suspended plans to thrust southwards by means of a line via Machynlleth to Aberystwyth. In this district it was Holland the Member of Parliament for the county at work, rather than Holland the quarry proprietor!

He now became associated with the formation of the Bala & Festiniog Railway, nominally independent but like all the foregoing lines, to all practical purposes under the Great Western umbrella. The B. & F.R. was to build a standard gauge line from a point short of the original Corwen & Bala Railway terminus south of Bala town, and extend up through the mountains on a spectacular route to make an end-on junction with the tiny but now strategic Festiniog & Blaenau Railway at Llan Ffestiniog. South of where Maentwrog Road station was later to be sited, there was to be another triangular junction with the Merionethshire Railway's line. The completion of these lines would have given slate an outlet from Blaenau to the south east; Holland had thrown in his hand with Paddington. As an alternative, it might be worked to the coast at Talsarnau, and taken by the Cambrian Railways thereafter. In the event, the standard gauge connection to Llan Ffestiniog was completed and the Merionethshire Railway proved to be unnecessary; powers to build lapsed in 1885 when it was allowed to die a natural death. The threat of it had played its part.

The period of the F. & B.R.'s narrow gauge existence, and the constant threat that a Merionethshire Railway would materialise, was evidently a source of concern to the Festiniog Company. Among Festiniog records, unfortunately undated, are drawings for a mixed standard and narrow gauge railway from Llan Ffestiniog into Blaenau with plans for a mixed gauge station on the site of the F. & B.R. Duffws terminal. Here the Festiniog would have entered from the west and the mixed gauge led off from the east. The mixed gauge line was shown on the site of the later standard gauge run-round loop and the narrow gauge only at the platform face, suggesting through working of minerals but passenger services worked by the Festiniog and F. & B.R. jointly. Perhaps this was one of the mollifying schemes conceived at the time. Trans-shipment facilities are absent; perhaps these were retained at Llan Ffestiniog.

The heady wine of slate traffic figures had not only reached Paddington. The London & North Western Railway was always ready to fight the G.W.R. in the Principality. In January 1879 it too found its way into Blaenau Festiniog and opened to traffic on 22nd July (though not before the seeds of a Great Western outlet from the town had already been planted). This line was to give J.W. Greaves at least, an outlet for his slate to the north, and other quarries including Holland's under its successors, came to use it. In the Festiniog & Blaenau story however, it plays no part.

It is convenient at this stage to examine in a little more detail, the Merionethshire Railway proposals, and then the Bala & Festiniog's successful birth. Firstly, the Merionethshire.

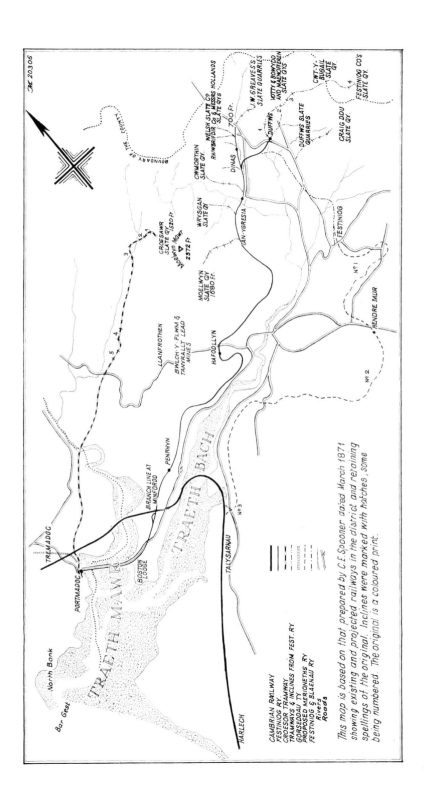

FL 20305

North Bank

Bar Gest

TRAETH MAWR

PORTMADOC

TREMADOC

BOSTON LODGE

BRANCH LINE AT MINFORDD

PENRHYN

TRAETH BACH

TALYSARNAU

HARLECH

LLANFROTHEN

BWLCH-Y-PLWM & TANYRALLT LEAD MINES

CROESAWR SLATE QY. 1520 Ft

Moelwyn Mawr 2372 Ft

HAFODLLYN

MOELWYN SLATE QY. 1680 Ft

TAN-Y-GRESIA

CWMORTHIN SLATE QY.

WRYSGAN SLATE QY.

DINAS

700 Ft.

WELSH SLATE CO.

RHIWBRIFDIR

RHIWBRIFDIR Co & MESSRS HOLLANDS SLATE QYS

DUFFWS

J.W. GREAVES'S SLATE QUARRIES

VOTTY & BOWYDD AND MAENOFFEREN SLATE QYS

DUFFWS SLATE QUARRIES

CWT-Y-BUGAIL SLATE QY.

CRAIG DDU SLATE QY.

FESTINIOG CO'S SLATE QY.

FESTINIOG

HENDRE MUR

No 1

No 1

No 2

No 3

BOUNDARY OF THE COUNTY

CAMBRIAN RAILWAY
FESTINIOG RY.
CROESOR TRAMWAY
TRAMWAYS & INCLINES FROM FEST. RY
GORSEDDAU TY
PROPOSED MERIONETHS RY
FESTINIOG & BLAENAU RY
Rivers
Roads

This map is based on that prepared by C.E. Spooner dated March 1871 showing existing and projected railways in the district and retaining spellings of the original. Inclines were marked with hatches, some being numbered. The original is a coloured print.

MERIONETHSHIRE RAILWAY
(Gauge: Mixed)

Incorporated: 34/5 Vic. Cap. 72 29th June, 1871.
Other Acts: 39/40   77 27th June, 1876 Extension of time.
           42/3   53 3rd July, 1879   "
           45/6   16 19th May, 1882   "
           50/1   108 12th July, 1887 Abandonment Order.
Registered Office: 2 Westminster Chambers, Victoria Street, London, S.W.
Capital: £80,000 in £10 Ordinary Shares.
Loans: £28,000
Time for completion: Railways Nos. 1 & 2 – Five years.

The F.&B.R. had only been working for three years when this scheme was given Parliamentary approval. The intentions of the rival factions were immediately clear. They threatened to build a 'mirror image' railway of the Festiniog which, instead of making its way westwards along the north side of the Dwryd valley to Portmadoc, would wind its way westward along the south side and make a triangular connection with the Cambrian Railways just east of their Talsarnau station. At Llan Ffestiniog there was to be an end-on junction with the F.&B.R. Completion of the Festiniog 'image' was finalised by adopting the same gauge (given in the Act as "Two Feet") and providing for exchange facilities near Talsarnau. The jargon of the Act simply described the line as intending 'to construct a junction between the Cambrian and Festiniog Railways' of length 10 miles.

There were to be three sections. Railway No. 1 was 3 m. 1 fur. 8 ch. 35 links in length from a junction in the parish of Ffestiniog with the Festiniog & Blaenau Railway, and terminating in the parish of Maentwrog in the plantation of a farm called Hendre mur – (the property of Morgan Lloyd, a director). Railway No. 2, 6 m. 7 fur. 8 ch. 5 links, was from a junction with Railway No. 1 at Hendre mur and terminating in the parish of Llandecwyn in a junction with the Cambrian Railways. It was stipulated that both Railways 1 & 2 should be built simultaneously, and that one should not be opened before the other. They were to be worked as one railway by the owning company. Railway No. 3 was simply the short curve forming the south connection at Talsarnau junction.

The Act also required the Company to run a train every morning of the week save on Sundays, from the junction with the Cambrian to the station at Llan Ffestiniog calling at all stations, and a similar daily return working. The outward journey was not to be made after 7 a.m. and the return not before 6 p.m., as might be most convenient. Quarrymen and labourers 'having daily occupation at the quarries in the parish of Ffestiniog . . . must be carried at fares not exceeding ¼d. per mile . . .' If during any period of three months less than 100 persons availed themselves of this service, the Board of Trade might allow the Company to discontinue it on application, but might reinstate it by order, under certain conditions. The Company might issue weekly tickets only for this service.

Arrangements might be concluded with the Cambrian and Festiniog & Blaenau companies.

As regards ownership of land and the interests of the promoters, it would seem that all landowners involved were earmarked to serve on the Board of seven directors save one. He was William Thearsby Poole through whose land ran Railway No. 2 for the last 5 chains before its junction with the Cambrian. Protection here was given to him by limiting the amount of deviation from the planned course.

Capital was £80,000 in £10 shares with loans up to £26,600 authorised.

Many of the names associated with the F. & B.R. reappeared – the Chairman was Samuel Holland, M.P. and though nephew Charles (then of Manchester) was not a director in this case, he was designated Engineer (resigning the position in September 1871) in collaboration with J.W. Grover, M.I.C.E. of Westminster (then acting for the Hemel Hempsted & L.N.W. Railway). John Casson, J.P. (Banker) and Morgan Lloyd, M.P. (Barrister) were on the board of both lines, and additionally the Merionethshire included William Casson, J.P., Hugh Owen, A.A. Robinson and J.H. Foulkes, J.P., a Wrexham industrialist. Foulkes and Owen were directors of the 'Duffws Casson Slate Co.' and Robinson had been a slate merchant. The offices were in Victoria Street, Westminster, initially, then moved to Oswestry and latterly to Pâle, Corwen, where the son of A.C. Sherriff (M.P. for Worcester), a director of the Bala & Dolgelley and many other lines, then lived. According to who was holding office of Secretary, so the address of the Company's headquarters was changed! One of the auditors was the redoubtable James Frazer the younger, who included in a large portfolio of similar associations the Portmadoc, Croesor & Beddgelert Tram Railway Co. Ltd.

A Bill lodged for the 1873 session of Parliament covering a railway between Bala and Festiniog (and with that title) referred to a proposal of working agreements and interchange of traffic between such a line and the Festiniog and Blaenau & Festiniog (sic) railways but when in fact the Act was obtained, reference to arrangements with the Festiniog did not appear! With the likelihood of much improved facilities open to the F. & B. and the same promoters being involved, it is not surprising that no actual construction work was begun on the new Merionethshire Railway; the Bala & Festiniog plans included a triangular junction with the Merionethshire Railway south of Llan Ffestiniog which would thus have had such a junction at each end of its line. On the Merionethshire, the section between Duffws and Llan Ffestiniog was to be of mixed standard and two foot gauge, using three lines of rail. The Enquiry of 23rd March, 1871 before the House of Lords Select Committee had emphasised the company intended to take the standard gauge up inclines right into the Festiniog quarries if necessary!

Although the Merionethshire obtained further Acts on 8th November, 1875 and 27th June, 1876 extending time for completion to 29th June, 1879, and another on 3rd July, 1879 extending to 29th June, 1882 and finally on 19th May, 1882 allowing until 29th June, 1885, these were simply a method of buying time until the position *vis-à-vis* the G.W.R. (or Bala & Festiniog Railway) and Festiniog relations had been resolved. As no work had been done by 29th June, 1885, Merionethshire powers automatically lapsed. An Act for abandonment was obtained on 12th July, 1887.

The G.W.R. thrust westwards from Ruabon had taken place through nominally independent companies which the G.W.R. worked and later absorbed; the progress westwards was marked thus–

Vale of Llangollen Railway.	Ruabon to Llangollen. Act of 1st August, 1859. Opened to passengers on 2nd June, 1862.
Llangollen & Corwen Railway.	Llangollen to Corwen. Act of 6th August, 1860. Opened on 1st May, 1865.
Corwen & Bala Railway.	Corwen to Bala. Act of 30th June, 1862. Opened on 1st April, 1868.
Bala & Dolgelley Railway.	Bala (junction station with C. & B.R.) to Dolgelley. Act of 30th June, 1862. Opened 4th August, 1868.

As from 4th August, 1868, the G.W.R. worked over the whole route as a branch line from Ruabon; on 29th May previously, the little Festiniog & Blaenau Railway had opened. The Bala & Festiniog was planned to bridge the gap between them.

By 21st December, 1872 a Bill had been lodged 'for railways from Bala to Festiniog and Blaenau' and for 'working traffic and other agreements with the Great Western, Vale of Llangollen, Llangollen & Corwen, Corwen & Bala, Merionethshire, Festiniog & Blaenau and Festiniog' railways with powers of some of those companies to subscribe. The Act was passed on 28th July, 1873 for a line between the Corwen & Bala at Llangower Junction to Festiniog, of length 22¼ miles and in mixed gauge. The companies ranging westwards from Ruabon were invited to subscribe, as was the Great Western. Working arrangements were confirmed with the G.W.R. and Merionethshire, but not the Festiniog Railway, which receives no mention in the Act. On the other hand 'BRADSHAW'S MANUAL' of 1873, recording the incorporation etc. of the B. & F.R., states that arrangements *had* been concluded with the Festiniog. The directors were an influential lot including Sir Watkin Wynn, M.P. of Wynnstay, Ruabon (industrialist etc.), Samuel Holland, M.P., John Robertson of Pâle (a director of all lines between Ruabon and Dolgelley), William. H. Darby (the ironmaster of Brymbo), Sir Daniel Gooch (of the G.W.R.), and William Wagstaff (director of all local lines, also of the Much Wenlock and certain Somerset railways). If businesses as today were valued by management potential, then the Bala & Festiniog was a strong team!

It was not long before the Bala & Festiniog Railway showed additional teeth. A scheme to extend westward from the south-west corner of Duffws station, traverse the north side of the Market Square and cross the open portion of ground opposite where the L.N.W.R. and Festiniog Exchange stations were to be sited, would have run roughly parallel to the Festiniog main line westwards out of Blaenau Festiniog. Then turning north-westwards, the line would have crossed the Festiniog immediately east of the Glan-y-Pwll level crossing and continued northwards along the site of where the Festiniog Deviation Line of 1899 was laid. A Plan dated 8th January, 1872, showing this proposal, underlines the aspirations of Holland and his associates to tap Hollands' and Greaves' quarries independently of the Festiniog and the track layout with the proposed narrow gauge Bettws & Festiniog Railway.[2]

Arrangements between the Bala & Festiniog Company and the Merionethshire were interesting. The Merionethshire's line between Llan Ffestiniog and a point where it crossed the Maentwrog–Trawsfynydd road at Hendre mur* was designated their Railway No. 1. This section of line was to enjoy reciprocal running powers for Merionethshire and B. & F.R. alike; the equipment, staff etc. to be of similar status. The B. & F.R.'s line was to connect with the Merionethshire at Hendre mur and for these last four miles of the M.R. to Llan Ffestiniog, a mixed gauge was to be laid. This would allow M.R. narrow gauge trains working east into Llan Ffestiniog and B. & F.R. trains working west to the same destination, to use the same set of mixed gauge rails.

Of course, all this was hypothetical so far as the M.R. was concerned, as no construction had begun. Section 49 of the B. & F.R. Act refers to that railway as 'running parallel to the Railway No. 1 as authorised by the Merionethshire Railway Act 1871' and not having powers to impede the M.R. from completing that length. Nor did the Act relieve the M.R. from any obligation to which they were liable to construct and open Railways Nos. 1 & 2 simultaneously; nor were they permitted to use their running powers on Railway No. 1 until Railway No. 2 had been completed.

In practice, the two concerns intended that Railway No. 1 should not only be 'parallel' but to save expense, they should use the same

*This approximates to the present end of the Blaenau-Trawsfynydd line spur as currently truncated near the nuclear power generating station.

formation and set of tracks. (Mixed narrow and standard gauge did not of course, ever come into existence on this length, but it is believed to have been used temporarily between Llan Ffestiniog and Duffws during gauge conversion.)

It is now convenient to return to affairs on the Festiniog & Blaenau Railway. The 1877 accounts show that during 1876 some heavy additional expenses had to be borne, especially by the Locomotive Department. In the same year the practice of running mixed trains ceased and goods/mineral trains ran separately. Train mileage increased by almost 30% and for the time being at least, it seemed that the promoters should be well satisfied with their success, even if the extraordinary figures for passenger traffic eventually turned out to be a once and for all phenomenon and were possibly boosted by development at Holland's and Rhiwbryfdir Quarries which had been re-entered by Oakeley after the lease expired.

Possibly influenced by increased traffic, the change-of-mind of the L.N.W.R. and the now-approaching *standard gauge* railway of that Company from the north and the promise of the standard gauge Bala & Festiniog Railway from the south-east, the directors of the F. & B. did some quick thinking. Their relations with their narrow gauge neighbour the Festiniog, were not of the best and their own existence had sprung from lack of cordiality. To be sandwiched between standard gauge schemes and out of tune with the line to which they physically attached was unhealthy.

Besides the somewhat uncomfortable position just described, there was the problem of financing considerable sums for refurbishing the line, which had taken some severe punishment since the opening. The obvious channel was through Holland himself and his position on the Bala & Festiniog; the outcome of some astute lobbying was that an Agreement was reached on 15th July, 1876 whereby (a) the F. & B.R. would be purchased by the B. & F.R. for £14,000, (b) shares in the B. & F.R. would be taken up by the F. & B.R. and (c) three years would be allowed to complete the purchase. Meanwhile the B. & F.R. would pay interest at 5% annually on £14,000 pending completion of the purchase. This followed a Directors' Meeting of the Bala & Festiniog Railway at Paddington on 11th July, 1876. The minutes state 'Arrangements with the Great Western Company were discussed and specially the necessity of a subscription contract before the time of compulsory powers expired.' The following subscriptions were arranged:

Great Western Railway Co.	£100,000
Llangollen Company	42,000
Henry Robertson	28,000
Parties on behalf of the Blaenau & Festiniog (sic) to subscribe for (on the understanding that they are to be released hereafter to the extent to which that sum should exceed the value of their property under agreement with them)	12,000
Mr. Holland & Merioneth landholders	8,000
	£190,000

On 3rd August following another meeting took place, considering especially the heavy costs recently borne by the Festiniog & Blaenau. Among those in attendance (not a director) was Henry Robertson, M.P. (who had promised to subscribe as above) who said he had been applied to with reference to the 'working of the Blaina and Ffestiniog railway and that he had instructed the Secretary and Manager to continue the present staff and mode of working under the discretion of Mr. Holland until further notice'.

[Henry Robertson (1816–1888) then of Pâle, Corwen, was a natural intermediary in these matters. Born in Banff, he came to North Wales in 1842 and among other interests, formed the Brymbo Mineral & Railway Company and the Brymbo Steel Company in 1884. He was responsible for the conception of most of the original railways in North Wales and its border counties. Benjamin Piercy was an assistant to him when surveys were made for the Shrewsbury & Chester Railway. His perception in seeing Blaenau Festiniog as a natural terminus of the nominally independent standard gauge railways driving westward from Ruabon is clear when a list of the companies for which he was then Chairman and/or Engineer, is made:

Vale of Llangollen
Llangollen & Corwen
Corwen & Bala

and though indirectly important, he had close connections with Beyer, Peacock & Co. whose locomotives were in use in the district, and the potential of the Brymbo steelworks and associated collieries and brickworks. More than any other, the influence leading to the arrival of Great Western Railway trains in Blaenau was his.]

The Chairman added that 'Mr. Kelley would be instructed to examine and report as to the future working of the railway'. 25th October next saw another meeting. Messrs. Kelley and Chapman sent in a report on the F. & B. line, of its estimated revenue and expenditure. By then its track was in a poor way and '10 Tons of rails and 600 sleepers were required for immediate repairs'. A purchase was authorised. Mr. Kelley was instructed 'to make such arrangements as may be

necessary for putting the working arrangements of the line in a satisfactory state including obtaining indemnities in case of accident from
the workmen carried over the line at low fares'.

From 28th February, 1878, when the first sets of 'F. & B. New' and
'F. & B. Ltd.' accounts appeared, they were published separately but
mounted together and got up in the same manner. F. & B. New had no
Capital Account; F. & B. Ltd. had no entries under heading 'Working
Stock' but under the same heading F. & B. New was said to possess '2
Engines, 2 Tenders, half a 1st Class Coach, half a 2nd Class Coach, 3
2nd Class Coaches, 20 Workmen's 'carriages' and 7 Goods Wagons' –
little if any of which agrees with the B.O.T. Returns for stock made by
the Company that same year! Whilst some explanation is that the
figures were pure accountancy only, it could be that the two engines
and tenders were Festiniog property – or was this a deliberate error to
allow non-existent tenders to be written-down in the end-year
accounts? If the motive power was Festiniog, perhaps on hire, had the
F. & B.'s original engines been taken out of stock or 'forgotten' conveniently? Fortunately it is not essential to have answers to these
intriguing reflections.

The principal income of the F. & B. Ltd. was the £700 'By interest
received on part of the purchase money to be received in cash'. F. & B.
New's Revenue Accounts are similar to those of a Company operating a
railway and include such items as Maintenance of Way and Works.
Griffith Griffith Davies, Manager of the F. & B. New, certified that line
and rolling stock was in good order.

Accounts of this type appeared again in 1879, 1880 and 1881 but
nowhere is the legal status of F. & B. New defined.

Payment of debts incurred by F. & B. Ltd. were recorded in a special
book and from the time of the founding of the 'twin companies', the
records have survived. A wage account for August 1876 lists the
following employees: 1 Fitter, 1 Driver, 1 Master, 1 Porter, 2
Platelayers, 1 Manager, 1 Secretary.

One may properly ask if a fireman or guard was employed or did the
fitter drive and the driver fire when there was little to do in the
workshop? Perhaps the porter doubled up as guard? The wage bill was
£43 5s. 11d. and was paid by cheque drawn on the North & South
Wales Bank by the 'Trustees of the Bala & Festiniog Railway Co.'.

Connection with the G.W.R. is also clear from 1877 items; for
example an account of 13th March from Paddington for putting a new
set of brass tubes in a locomotive (obviously at Llan Ffestiniog and not
at Swindon!) for a cost of £8 8s. 6d. This item was paid by the Bala &
Festiniog Railway Company. In the following November the G.W.R.
sent an account for supplying 2,000 card tickets, possibly due to the
heavy demand on tickets for that season. There was also a bill for 'Nov.
1 & 2; To Mr. Kelley's travelling expenses to Barmouth and Blaenau to
meet Mr. Spooner relative to signals'.

A Board Meeting of the Bala & Festiniog agreed to spend more money on the F. & B.R. when it met on 3rd April, 1878. Another 10 tons of rails were taken and the fencing was to be renewed in iron wire. The stations got a budget of £25 for repairs.

In June 1879 new junction arrangements between the F. & B.R. and the Festiniog Railway at Dolgaregddu were inspected by Colonel Rich. He did not like the arrangements and would permit only goods trains to use it – Festiniog trains were not affected . . . would it be wicked to suggest this was a purposeful layout?![3]

Mr. Kelley reported on an arrangement with the Festiniog Railway. This was on the basis of using each others wagons, four Festiniog to one F. & B. The F. & B. had not been playing the game and the Festiniog had given notice to end the arrangement: worse, they had rubbed it in by proffering an account for hire of wagons up to December 1877 of £18 11s. 5d. Kelley was authorised to make the payment and patch up the quarrel with the Festiniog as best he could, as the use of Festiniog 'trucks' was essential to the F. & B.

There had clearly been complaints about the spartan nature of F. & B. passenger stock and it was agreed that estimates be obtained 'for enclosing the existing carriages'. There was a shortage of it too, and it was agreed that two new 3rd Class carriages be sought. The existing carriage stock was to be repainted.

In the outcome the G.W.R. supplied the new fences and fixed them for £150 and in July 1878 purchase of one 1st–2nd Class composite coach for £90 and one 3rd Class for £65 was authorised, suggesting that the earlier decision had been amended.

From 1st June, 1879, maintenance of the F. & B.'s track was given to the G.W.R. at least in part, as they submitted an account for the subsequent six months' work of £95 10s. 0d.

On 26th October, 1880 Mr. Breese, Solicitor to the F. & B.R., wrote to the Secretary of the Bala & Festiniog reminding him that the time for completing their purchase of the F. & B. had now expired and asking if they were now in a position to close the deal. The B. & F.R. man-oeuvred round this question by referring it to their legal advisers, and matters dragged on, complicated by queries as to interest upon calls on certain shares. The last available B. & F. Minutes referring to the matter are dated 3rd February, 1881 and it was settled on 24th February.

During 1882 the F. & B.R. were using Festiniog wagons for their own needs and these were charged by weight. This may have been a change of situation for in 1873 C.E. Spooner had stated that F.R. vehicles were used 'at no charge'. The Festiniog also charged the cost of working the junction at Blaenau at £66 per annum, plus costs of any repairs; Spooner refused to share the cost. A Festiniog account of 14th July, 1880 reads 'To use of engine to work the traffic: £1 0s. 0d.' but no period is given.

Work on the new railway's difficult terrain between Bala and Llan Ffestiniog took its time; but under an agreement of 17th March, 1879,

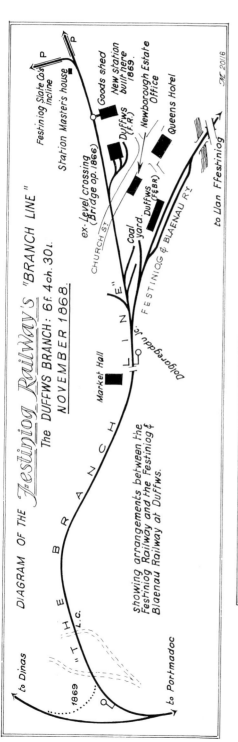

DIAGRAM OF THE *Festiniog Railway's* "BRANCH LINE"

The DUFFWS BRANCH: 6f. 4ch. 30l.

NOVEMBER 1868.

showing arrangements between the
Festiniog Railway and the Festiniog &
Blaenau Railway at Duffws.

to Dinas

"THE BRANCH LINE"

1869

to Portmadoc

Market Hall

Dolgaregddu

FESTINIOG & BLAENAU RY.

coal yard

Duffws (F&BR)

CHURCH ST.

ex-level crossing
(Bridge op. 1866)

Queens Hotel

Newborough Estate Office

Duffws (F.R.)

Goods shed

New station built here 1869.

Station Master's house

Festiniog Slate Co.'s incline

to Llan Ffestiniog

JMC 2016

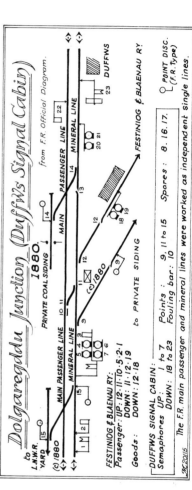

Dolgaregddu Junction (Duffws Signal Cabin)

1880.

from F.R. Official Diagram.

to L.N.W.R. YARD

(c) 1880

MAIN PASSENGER LINE

MINERAL LINE

PRIVATE COAL SIDING

MAIN

PASSENGER LINE

MINERAL LINE

(c) 1880

to PRIVATE SIDING

DUFFWS

FESTINIOG & BLAENAU RY.

FESTINIOG & BLAENAU RY.:
Passenger: UP: 12·11·10·5·2·1
DOWN: 11·12·19
Goods: DOWN: 12·18

DUFFWS SIGNAL CABIN:-
Semaphores UP: 1 to 7
DOWN: 18 to 23

Points: 9, 11 to 15
Fouling bar: 10

Spares: 8, 16, 17.

POINT DISC. (F.R. Type)

The F.R. main passenger and mineral lines were worked as independent single lines.

JMC 2015

it was to be worked by the G.W.R. The Great Western seems to have had second thoughts about this responsibility for, through the good offices of Henry Robertson, they enquired in the following May if the Festiniog Railway would work the line (presumably until gauge conversion?) The F.R. agreed to do this 'subject to the line being put into proper working order and sidings for the interchange of traffic be put up and approved of . . .'. Obviously the F.R. had its own terms: they were not acceptable. However, the aforementioned new layout at Dolgaregddu was made.[4]

[At the risk of interrupting the narrative, it would make reference to the Bala–Ffestiniog section incomplete if it was not put on record that it was a tradition on the Great Western Railway, and in the Chester Division especially, that the branch was 'originally a private line to reach Porth Dynllaen and to convey mails to Ireland' though whether by that date it was thought that Robertson was aiming for an all-Paddington line to counter the L.N.W.R. Holyhead route so long after all other Porth Dynllaen dreams – as an alternative packet station for Ireland – had been put to bed, seems hard to accept. If such campaigns had been stilled by time, they were recalled in a Divisional Report of 1924.][5]

Even before this, it was clear that the time for completion under the original Act was insufficient; another Act of 16th April, 1878 extended the time to 28th July, 1881. The official record of 1882 no longer gives 'mixed gauge' but 'narrow gauge', probably to distinguish the G.W.R. connection and to use a term so often made to distinguish it from the two gauges of the G.W.R., the standard (or 'narrow') and the broad! Under the Great Western's Act of 6th August, 1880, the B. & F.R. (with which the G.W.R. was associated) received power to absorb the Festiniog & Blaenau Railway and on 23rd May, 1882 it was resolved that the F. & B.R. Co. Ltd. be wound up voluntarily. William Davies of Ca'er-blaidd, the F. & B.R. Manager, was appointed Liquidator. He was able to report that his work was completed on 21st April, 1884. On 13th April, 1883, the little F. & B.R. became vested in the Bala & Festiniog, so finally becoming to all intents and purposes, part of the Paddington empire.

Out on the ground, so to speak, the 22-mile new railway from Bala opened to Llan Ffestiniog on 1st November, 1882, but not until further powers were granted for an extension of time. Conversion of the remaining 3½ miles of two foot gauge, for which most of the necessary civil engineering had been done when the F. & B. was built, was completed by 10th September, 1883. J.P. Edwards of Chester was the contractor, the estimated cost of conversion being £11,131. Trains on the F. & B. continued to run as, when the standard gauge rails were laid, a third was provided for them. At the site of the wooden viaduct a diversion was made to improve the curvature and bring the standard gauge away from the hillside onto a stone viaduct. Though the winter was a rough one, sidings at Blaenau were ready by April 1883, though the new station building (and that at Manod) were not ready until after s.g. trains began to run.

Col. Rich for the Board of Trade inspected on 31st July, 1883 but would not permit opening for another month until all the works were complete, giving permission on 1st September. Narrow gauge trains ceased to run on 5th September. The third rail was lifted but in some places did duty by being moved to become a check rail along the many severe curves of the line: formal opening took place on 10th September. Although the new standard gauge line almost obliterated its predecessor, it had now to provide for the carriage of slate; in one respect this presented no problem as it could be carried in open wagons. In another, and with special reference to loading arrangements at Tan-y-Manod station, 'pick-a-back' type wagons had to be built to carry the loaded narrow gauge wagons. The G.W.R. was not the first main line company to adopt this system at Blaenau Festiniog; the London & North Western had adopted it for their traffic north through the Conway Valley. Both companies built their own narrow gauge wagons for the traffic, and as with the Festiniog Railway, offered them to the quarries for use within their workings. On opening of the standard gauge over the F. & B., trans-shipment wharves and goods shed were provided between G.W. and Festiniog Railways, together with a dock for off-loading the 'pick-a-back' wagons.[6]

The Route described (Field Survey begun 1943)

(Generally speaking, the district through which the railway passed has changed little over the last one hundred years. Although Llan Ffestiniog, Manod and Blaenau Festiniog have grown, the basic nucleus of these places already existed by the mid-1860s. The route of the railway in the 1970s presented in general, a similar appearance to that of the 1860s. The re-gauging of the line, and the improvement of structures etc. by the Great Western Railway, together with the levelling of extreme gradients carried out in the years before the First War, swept away some of the civil engineering of the first railway. The course of the line between Duffws and Llan Ffestiniog is still occupied by a single line of track used for access to the Nuclear Power Station at Trawsfynydd. The section of line between Llan Ffestiniog and the present terminus at Trawsfynydd is almost exactly on the course of the proposed Merionethshire Railway, never built.)

The railway was laid through undulating country, lying between 600 and 700 ft up the upper east side of the Vale of Ffestiniog. To its west side the ground fell steeply into the Vale, and to the east there was a less steep rise towards the twin summits of Manod Mawr (2,166 ft) and Manod Bach (1,575 ft) which overlook the town of Blaenau Festiniog. The first two miles of the journey were through rugged upland country, largely treeless and often rocky.

The terminus station at Llan Ffestiniog lay just to the south-west, but some 30 feet below, the later standard gauge station. It was at the junction of the Dolgelley and Bala roads, the latter having been diverted south round the end of the station – and diverted even further when the line was linked up to form a continuous standard gauge branch. Opposite the station was a toll house and adjacent was built a chapel with inscription 1868, the year of the opening of the Festiniog & Blaenau line. When the standard gauge station was closed, a brick kiln embodied in its embankment was discovered beside the old narrow gauge station site; this is now a garage. From the terminus, the line climbed (gradient unrecorded) to the existing bridge at the north end of the standard gauge yard. The alteration in course and gradient between the two lines under this bridge is still perceptible.

The Dolgelley road forms in part the old Roman highway of Sarn Helen, which now accompanies the railway for a very short distance to the north-east. It connected Roman Forts at Kanovium (Conway) and Tomen-y-Mur (near Trawsfynydd). Near here is the site of the Graves of the Men of Ardudwy, a spot which may be picked out from the line. Legend has it that the local men of Ardudwy, tired of their own women, raided the Vale of Clwyd; after capturing a number of women, they set off for home. The men of Clwyd pursued them over the mountains and overtook them just outside Llan Ffestiniog where they were slaughtered. Apparently the women were not best pleased about this and not wishing to return with their own men, drowned themselves in a near-by lake, now a reservoir. The existence of the gravestones does not seem to have been officially vouched for during the last one hundred years!

Returning to the more material matter of the former terminal station; there was a long wooden building with slate roof along the east side; this appears to have done multiple duties as locomotive, carriage and repair shops. It is believed there was a small additional building used for station office, store and passenger shelter. Siding accommodation included a coal siding and possibly a wharf for slate loading, the latter being unconfirmed. The official G.W.R. diagram of 1923 shows a double-road building marked 'Slate Shed'. Certainly the G.W.R. received sufficient slate here to build a slate transfer shed (latterly owned by the Manod Quarry) in addition to a goods shed. In F. & B.R. days, Morgan Lloyd's Drum Quarry sent slates here by cart. There was no platform. Signalling was of simple form; a common post just inside the station limits served to admit incoming trains and as a starter. Like early Festiniog examples, there were two arms on either side of the top of the post. These were worked by hand levers on the post at the foot.

The line climbed from the terminus in a slightly north-easterly direction and passed under a small road bridge (not the existing one) to climb a short distance at 1 in 121. After a level crossing (now an underbridge), it curved more easterly and began a fall at 1 in 68 which eased to 1 in 460 and then became level for a little time. The track now ran along the south edge of the Afon Teigl valley, the prominent feature

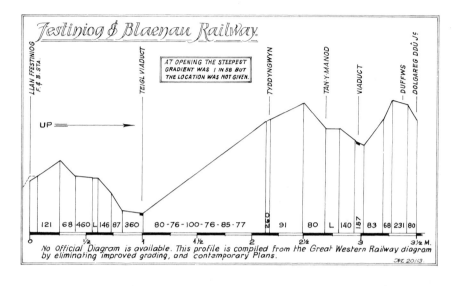

Festiniog & Blaenau Railway.

LLAN. FESTINIOG F.& B STA.

TEIGL VIADUCT

AT OPENING THE STEEPEST GRADIENT WAS 1 IN 58 BUT THE LOCATION WAS NOT GIVEN.

TYDDYNGWYN

TAN-Y-MANOD

VIADUCT

DUFFWS

DOLGAREG DDU J'S

UP ⟹

121 | 68 | 460 | L | 146 | 87 | 360 | 80 - 76 - 100 - 76 - 85 - 77 | 91 | 80 | L | 140 | 157 | 83 | 68 | 231 | 80

0   ½   1   1½   2   2½   3   3½ M.

No Official Diagram is available. This profile is compiled from the Great Western Railway diagram by eliminating improved grading, and contemporary Plans.

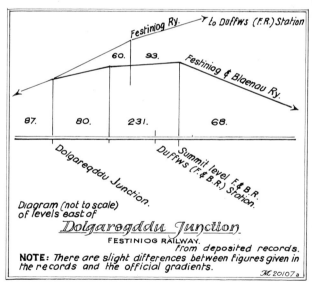

Festiniog Ry.   Y To Duffws (F.R.) Station

60.   93.   Festiniog & Blaenau Ry.

87.   80.   231.   68.

Dolgareqddu Junction.

Duffws (F.& B.R.) Station.

Summit level F.& B.R.

Diagram (not to scale) of levels east of

Dolgareqddu Junction

FESTINIOG RAILWAY.
                    from deposited records.
NOTE: There are slight differences between figures given in the records and the official gradients.

being the dome of Manod ahead and the rough upland country to the east. Beginning a semi-circular sweep anticlockwise, the fall began at 1 in 146, increasing to 1 in 87 and then 1 in 360. Here there was an embankment and the Teigl was crossed by a curved stone bridge. The railway had fallen about forty feet since Llan Ffestiniog and this was the lowest point on the line (1 mile). Rounding up from the bridge there was a cutting followed by a stiff climb along the north flank of the Teigl valley in short lengths between 1 in 76 and 100; behind, the line could be seen swinging in a great curve back towards Llan Ffestiniog and ahead, but to the west, the wooded Vale of Ffestiniog fell towards the open sea beyond, so much in contrast with the present surroundings of the line. The original starting level of the line was now reached, but climbing continued, now in a northerly direction on a high embankment and somewhat above the Llan Ffestiniog–Blaenau Festiniog road, past the hamlet of Telei-bach and with another slight curve to follow the contour of the hill, the line crossed the road on the level at Rhiwlas and left the open country behind (2 miles). From here into Duffws, housing and quarrying changed the whole picture. Groups and clusters of whitewashed small dwellings huddled wherever rock outcrop or contour permitted. The track passed over the Maentwrog road and the grade eased to 1 in 260 momentarily for Tyddyngwyn station, named after a large (for those times) residence nearby. There was no loop here, but probably a short siding, with a small building (2 m. 14 ch.).

In standard gauge times – and much more recently at that – a standard gauge branch was put in just beyond this point to serve the Pengwern Granite Quarry. Its course is still very clear. It crossed the main street to reach the granite bins and immediately beyond the site of this siding there lie the remains of its predecessor – high and low level standard gauge exchange sidings where they met a narrow gauge branch from the granite quarry. This installation does not date from F. & B. times of course, but the point where the narrow gauge branch crosses the street and dives under the Tan-y-Manod slate quarry incline, is probably an alteration in arrangements which followed the conversion of the F. & B. from narrow gauge.

These two sets of standard gauge granite sidings were on a rising gradient of 1 in 91. It brought the former F. & B. onto a steep prominence overlooking the valley of the Bowydd, which fed below into the Vale of Ffestiniog. From this excellent vantage point the whole of Blaenau Festiniog and its quarries can be embraced, and the translation of Blaenau into 'valley' becomes quite obvious. The clockwise curve of the line continued before it fell under an occupation bridge at 1 in 80 to level out on a reverse curve on which Tan-y-Manod was sited. In doing so it exchanged a cutting on the hillside for embankment construction. Tan-y-Manod was the largest intermediate stop. There was a long loop, a wooden building on the east side together with double-armed signal, and sidings accommodation. On the south side was a slate wharf and connection leading to an incline which climbed to nearby road level and

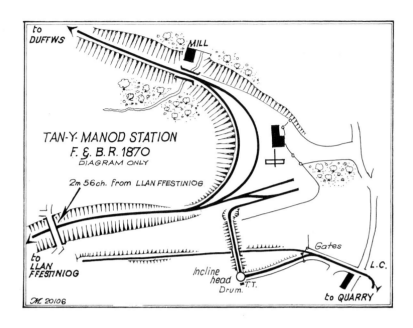

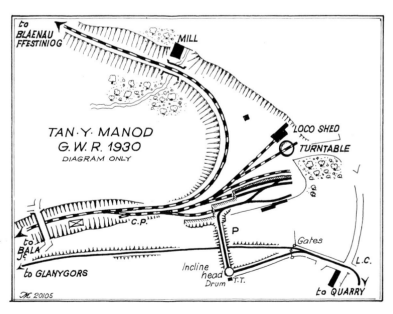

at its summit, a track therefrom led over the road by a level crossing. Here was a reversing neck and by means of two inclines 1,326 yards long, built in the mid-1860s, a tramway reached Craig Ddu Slate Quarry and, by means of a third, Manod Slate Quarry. These were the most important slate feeders to the F. & B.R., and it would seem that the station loop at Tan-y-Manod was used more as a slate wagon storage siding than for passing purposes. (The importance of this interchange point was not dimmed with the coming of the standard gauge. Wharfage and interchange facilities were provided on an even greater scale by the G.W.R. who also had a locomotive shed and turntable on the site of the F. & B. station premises. It was between here and Blaenau that the G.W.R. ran 'pick-a-back' flat wagons carrying narrow gauge slate wagons.)

On leaving Tan-y-Manod, the Afon Du-bach and a mill leat were crossed. For the remaining distance into Duffws the line was mainly on intimate terms with the backs of houses on the west side of the main street which tumbled down beside the railway in untidy fashion sometimes to sprawl below it. Their intensity grew as Duffws was neared. The railway was obliged to pick its way between housing and small side streets, very much the intruder. Various forms of construction were involved, mainly using earthen embankment and some considerable slab walling on the west side to shore it up.

Just north of the Afon Du-bach bridge, an awkward fall in the ground had to be crossed. Presumably the Engineer, working on the principle of least expense, decided that a cheap viaduct rather than filling would be better. There thus arose the wooden spanned bridge, 320 ft long with timber girders mounted on masonry piers, about which the Inspecting Officer was none too happy and which doubtless contributed to delays in opening the line. In order to reduce these and to connect either side of the bridge, a temporary railway was laid down along a shelf on the steep slope below the west side of the main street. The quality of work here was, of course, much inferior to the permanent work but oddly enough this temporary length remains as the only memorial on site of the old narrow gauge section, and may still be inspected. All other work was swept away when the route was rebuilt for standard gauge, including the feature which a Paddington-directed railway would not tolerate, the wooden bridge. In its place an eleven-arch stone viaduct arose.

North of the bridge, permanent and temporary F. & B. courses merged and a westward curve continued. Then followed a short length of line which must have proved most expensive. On the route at the present day there first comes a road crossing (gated) followed by a deep cutting taking a reverse curve through the edge of the town. On this section are three overbridges carrying streets; one is a stone arch and two are wrought-iron spans with ornamental railings, the latter supplied by Brymbo Ironworks in 1882 (the year of conversion) as their inscriptions prove. The middle bridge is the stone one and on the only site of an overbridge shown on contemporary maps of the F. & B.R.

The present arch is not the original. The streets flanking it, and for which the Brymbo bridges were used, did not exist in 1868 but may have come into being before the F. & B. was converted. Lest it might be concluded that the Brymbo bridges were exclusively used in converting the F. & B. section, this is not so, as they are to be found in other locations on the Bala line and on other railways of North Wales, notably in Flintshire. They would seem to have been a standard product of the foundry. Beyond the last of the three bridges, the deep cutting's sides are now walled, and in the cutting bottom is the summit level. As for gradients, there was a fall from Tan-y-Manod of 1 in 140 and 1 in 187, then a sharp pull up to Duffws at 1 in 83 and 68. The summit (720 ft) was just before Duffws station through which was a downgrade of 1 in 231 (3 m. 32 ch.). On entering the station the Afon Bowydd was crossed on a low span.

Duffws was a stone building, suitably semi-pretentious enough to house the Company's offices! That was about all, there being no platform, but only a run round loop and, beyond the station, a single siding for coal. A lane ran up beside the station towards the Queens Hotel to reach the main street; across and over on the other side was (for the first year or two anyway) the even more primitive station of the Festiniog Railway.

Westwards from Duffws, the F. & B.R. fell at 1 in 80 for about ten chains to Dolgaregddu Junction, where it merged with the Festiniog's 'Branch Line' (3 m. 40 ch.).

A feature of 1878 was an apparent increase in trackage reflected by the much larger Works and Way expenses for that year in the Returns. The First Schedule, made up annually for the Board of Trade, sheds a little light on this. Up to 1874 the Schedule had not been returned; in 1875–6 the railway stated it had one connection with a passenger line, one with a goods line (presumably the same one, i.e. with the Festiniog Railway) and the main line made junction with sidings at four other points. B.O.T. regulations had been complied with at five of these six and one point was fitted with locking. There were no safety points. In 1877 whilst the junction point remains, no less than thirteen points made junction with the running line, suggesting that nine other sidings had been laid in during the year to cope with traffic. These seem to have been controlled by fourteen ground levers having no locking.

The Second Schedule was first returned in 1874 and in that year the length of line was given as 4 miles. Thereafter it shrank to '3 m. 60 chains' for the remainder of its narrow gauge life. In fact, it was somewhat less than this!

Permanent Way

The Board of Trade report regarding the Inspection of May 1868 is one of two sources of reference concerning the track. Vignes' account appeared ten years later. The Inspection Report unfortunately does not specify the type of rails used in words, but uses a small drawing which if taken literally would mean they were of conventional flat-bottomed type. The date on which these rails were first used in North Wales is not known, but possibly the Talyllyn of 1865 was the pioneer of them, and even then its Engineer, James Swinton Spooner of the Portmadoc family, appeared uncertain of their behaviour and put the rail into keyed chairs. Perhaps then, if the B.O.T. Report is taken on its face value, we may conclude that the F.&B.R. was the first passenger-carrying, locomotive-hauled, narrow gauge railway to be laid in what became a conventional form, using dog spikes to hold the flat bottomed rails to wooden sleepers. The predecessor of this type of track was the T-bottom-flanged rail held in chairs used by Gorseddau and Croesor, to name two of many users [and probably in mid-Wales on the Corris, Machynlleth & River Dovey Tramroad when opened in 1859, but not copied by its neighbour the Talyllyn seven years later].

Details of the track as inspected in 1868 have already been given. The weight of rails (38 lb. per yard exactly as quoted by C.M. Holland to the Board of Trade) was another point of similarity with Talyllyn. If this rail is the curious section of flat-bottomed material still to be found as anchorages in the present standard gauge section embankment on the F.&B.R. route, then it was unique to the Railway. [There is a near-identical section in Cyfarthfa Museum, Merthyr Tydfil, rolled by Dowlais Foundry 1894 (Item No. 82). This example is slightly wider in the head but shorter in height.] By 1878 Vignes said the track was 'similar to the old Festiniog Railway track material save for certain replacements in more recent years'. He describes the rails as being 18 kilos per metre (about 39 lb.) without fishplated joints. These may have been the flat-bottomed rails just described, or something else. At this period the Festiniog was dispensing with its Phase Three track as quickly as possible. It was not standing up to the steam locomotive working over it. Introduced first in 1846, it had parallel section rails (the first forms had had fish bellies) in wrought iron, 21 ft long and weighing 30 lb. per yard. In 1868 Holland specifically stated the gauge of the F.&B. was 1 ft 11¼ in. – 'similar to that of the Festiniog Railway . . . (the rails upon the Festiniog Railway weighing 32 lb. per yard)'. In 1852 the same form of rail had been strengthened up to 42 b. per yard and both weights of this rail were in use on the Festiniog main line until 1868 when double-headed wrought-iron rails were first laid. The Phase Three rail was of T-bottom-flange type once again, but much heavier than Gorseddau or Croesor specimens. Chairs held by iron pegs to wooden sleepers were used; by 1868 the iron keys had given way to wooden ones. If these two accounts, ten years' apart, are accepted, then clearly the flat-bottomed track first installed did not stand up to usage and in 1878 in particular, the B.O.T. Returns show an exceptional rise in costs of Works and Way – possibly a most necessary injection of new (second hand) material into the track?

The original Festiniog four-wheeled engines worked regularly over

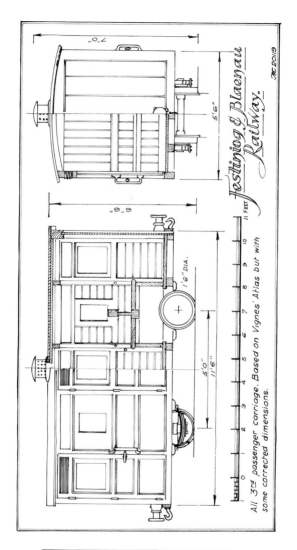

Festiniog & Blaenau Railway.

7'0"

5'6"

6'6"

5'0"

1'6"

1'6" DIA.

All 3rd passenger carriage. Based on Vignes' Atlas but with some corrected dimensions.

1 FEET   0 1 2 3 4 5 6 7 8 9 10 11 FEET

JIC 20119

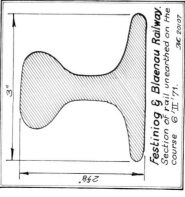

Festiniog & Blaenau Railway.
Section of rail unearthed on the course 6'III'71.

3"

2⅝"

JIC 20107

the F. & B., especially in its latter years. They would not take kindly to track of a type which by then would no longer be in use on their parent line. The F. & B.R. engines, with their extra axle and a 5 in. shorter fixed wheelbase, would not be at such disadvantage.

When the gauge was converted and the old rails lifted, some were sold by Edwards the contractor without authority, but the G.W.R. sold 153 tons to The Patent Nut & Bolt Co. Ltd.

Signalling

Where positions are known, these have been mentioned in the description of the line. Vignes states there was no signalling nor method of working the single line by staff; instead, the One Engine in Steam system was in force. Vignes was obviously wrong about both! The semaphores were of the Festiniog variety having double arms at the top of the post. The F. & B. types were more sophisticated as the red and green lenses and the attendant lamps were fixed lower down the post in the manner of the times. Hand levers which could be pinned through small quadrants at the foot of the post, worked the arms. Painting was conventional for left-hand running at the passing loops. The posts were surmounted by an iron finial and from the limited evidence available it is possible that the equipment was supplied by Messrs. Saxby & Farmer of Kilburn, London.

Train staff working was insisted upon by the Board of Trade inspector in 1868 though admittedly the 1878 Passenger Timetable could be covered by one engine alone.

Locomotives

(Official Gauge; 1 ft 11¾ in. Gauge in maker's catalogue and 'ENGINEERING'; 1 ft 11¼ in. Gauge in Vignes' survey; 1 ft 11½ in.)

No.	Name	Type	Builder	Works No./date	Sold or Scrap
1	Scorcher	0–4–2 ST	Manning Wardle	258/1868	1883
2	Nipper	0–4–2 ST	Manning Wardle	259/1868	1883

'ENGINEERING' for 15th April, 1870 contains the following article:

We publish . . . an engraving of one of a pair of tank locomotives constructed by Messrs. Manning Wardle & Co. of Leeds, for the Festiniog & Blaenau Railway . . . which forms an extension of the well-known Festiniog Railway. It is worthy of notice here that although Messrs. Manning Wardle & Co. have never supplied any engines for the Festiniog line itself, they were the first locomotive builders who got out complete designs for engines to work on that railway . . .

It would be out of place here to go into detail concerning the introduction of steam locomotives on the narrow gauge in these islands. It is sufficient to summarise by saying that C.M. Holland, nephew of

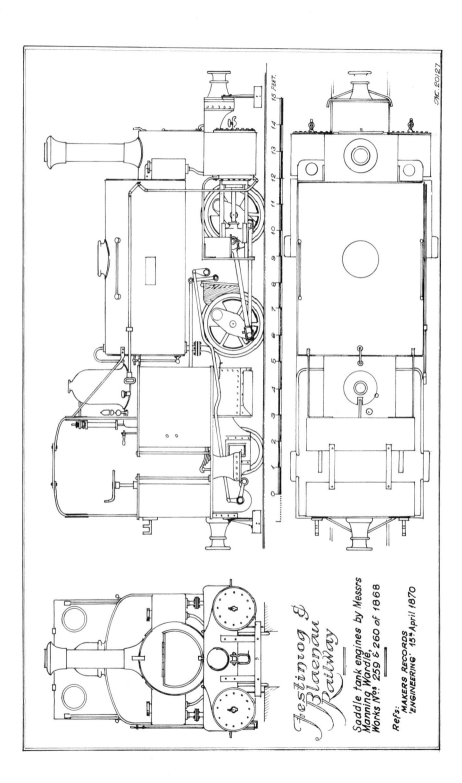

15 FEET.

_Festiniog &
Blaenau
Railway_

Saddle tank engines by Messrs
Manning Wardle,
Works Nᵒˢ 259 & 260 of 1868

Refs:
MAKERS RECORDS
'ENGINEERING' 15ᵗʰ April 1870

JC 20/27

Samuel Holland Jnr., director of the line and engineer to the Merionethshire Railway appears on the evidence to have been responsible for much of the design of the first two-foot gauge engines, which began work on the Festiniog Railway in August 1863. Clearly however, other manufacturers had submitted designs and in fact that of Manning Wardle, received on 7th November, 1862, was the *last* of twenty nine submissions.

Of Manning's previous experience, their Official List gives a 3 ft gauge engine as being the first to leave their works in 1859; nothing of lesser gauge appears until the entry for the F. & B. engines which, with charming unreliability states that they were built to the order of the 'Ffestiniog Railway Co.'. They were delivered new to 'Ffestiniog'. (Manning's were later to build a number of even narrower gauge engines, for in 1871 they supplied the first of a series of four-coupled saddle tanks for the 1 ft 6 in. gauge railway at Woolwich Arsenal.)

Whilst the first Festiniog engines were small for the gauge, the F. & B. examples were little larger. For some reason their width was restricted to a maximum of 5 ft 6 in. and may have been due to lack of certainty on the part of early designers as to how 'top heavy' a saddle-tank engine full of water might be on the narrow gauge! Free of any inherited limitations on loading gauge, it is difficult otherwise to see why F. & B. stock was so small – it would not appear that there was any intention to work it through over the Festiniog proper.

No record exists of the paint colour but it is suggested they were in Indian Red with double lining in yellow. The engine number was carried on the bunker panel in paint and oddly, maker's plates do not appear on any illustration. After delivery, the names *Scorcher* and *Nipper* countersunk on brass plates, were fixed to the flat sides of the saddle tanks.

The chimney was the slender elongated form of the maker's standard pattern; there was no footplating at all save in the cab and bunker. Frames were inside as was the Stephenson valve gear. The smokebox door was of the flat, horizontally hinged type covering the lower part of the box and flanking the smokebox sand boxes were fitted after delivery. Beneath the beams at each end was a plough-shaped device to clear obstructions from the rails. Coal was carried in pocket bunkers before the front cab sheet and braking was limited to a handbrake working wooden blocks on the driving wheels only (not the front drivers). The rear wheels were carried in outside bearings in the main frame plates but given adequate sideplay for curves. The outer firebox, as usual with the makers, was of larger diameter than the boiler and carried the dome.

The springs from the Salter safety valves, on top of a large brass dome cover, were carried through the front cab sheet in the customary way. The rear protection was a separate cab sheet, the overturns of each sheet being connected by two stiffening members over which a canvas sheet might be thrown in bad weather. *Nipper* was modified in this respect, the turnover from the back sheet being removed and the stiffening members cut back short to the extent of the front turnover. Both engines had stiffening stays fitted to the front sheets after delivery. A step alongside the motion bracket was fitted each side to enable the fireman to reach the tank filler, at the same time. Between the cylinder and the motion bracket, a cover plate was fitted to protect valves and motion. All springs were laminated, the rear pair projecting considerably up through the cab footplate across the entrance openings. Overall length was 18 ft over buffers; width 5 ft 6 in.; driving wheels 2 ft 3 in. diameter (Manning Wardle's own pattern with boss-type counterweight and having only four spokes); trailing wheels 1 ft 6 in. diameter; wheelbase 4 ft 1 in. + 4 ft 9 in.; outside cylinders 8½ in. × 14 in. at 3 ft 5 in. centres. Tractive effort 3,853 lb.; boiler pressure 120 lb.; boiler 6 ft 11 in. × 2 ft 5 in.; tubes 92 of 1½ in. diameter; grate area 4¾ sq. ft; total heating surface 284½ sq. ft; water capacity 300 gallons; weight empty 8 tons; in working order 11 tons. (Holland had estimated 8½ tons.)

Tradition has it that as traffic grew, work became too heavy for one engine and they were often used as a pair: this was Festiniog practice at the time. Twice Festiniog engines helped out when both were underpowered.

Once the Bala and Llan Ffestiniog line was complete, heavy repairs were done at Wolverhampton (to one engine once, the other twice) not by the new link however, but along Festiniog metals to Minffordd and thence by Cambrian to Dolgelley and so to the G.W.R. and Ruabon. For lighter repair, the G.W.R. sent men to Ffestiniog.

Neither engine came into G.W.R. stock and William Dean, then in charge of the Locomotive and Carriage Dept. at Swindon, had made at least some effort to dispose of them for on 7th November, 1883 he approached Arthur Wyatt of Penrhyn Slate Quarries offering all the rolling stock when the G.W.R. had finished with it:

Dear Sir,
    We have for sale 2 Locomotive Engines, 2 ft gauge, which have been working on the Festiniog & Blaenau Railway; also 2 Composite Carriages, 4 Third Class Carriages & 17 Workmen's Carriages, all in very fair condition. I enclose herewith an outline tracing of the Engines . . .
    If you are likely to require any of these for use on your N.G. Railway I shall be glad to receive an offer for them. The stock can be inspected at Llan Ffestiniog at any time.
                    Yours truely
                    Wm. Dean[7]

In August 1884 the carriage stock, still awaiting the interest of a buyer and finding none, was consigned to Swindon where it was scrapped in the following November. William Dean sent £178 19s. 8d. to the Bala & Festiniog Railway, the value thereof! The locomotives were sold to the Ruabon Coal and Coke Company, and one source suggests they did not carry names until this buyer obtained them – if this is so, what inscription did the plates on the saddle tank carry? There were links between this Company and the Great Western Railway; Sir Daniel Gooch founded it. Collieries were worked at Brandie and Hafod, both near Ruabon, but details of a narrow gauge railway system at either place remain unconfirmed.

Passenger Carriages

In 1878 there were six passenger carriages, two 3rd class being new that year as already noted (but not agreeing with the numbers shown in Statutory Returns). There was another of unknown type, possibly a special vehicle for the use of the Board and others. The public vehicles were built by Ashbury Railway Carriage & Iron Co., of Belle Vue, Manchester, and were quite similar to the four-wheelers built by them for the initial public service on the Festiniog Railway. (Details of the Festiniog specimens are scanty as they were all out of use before 1914, though some bodies went over to the Welsh Highland Railway for use as shelters at Halts. Nantmor had two.) For comparison, dimensions are shown for both varieties:

	Festiniog & Blaenau	*Festiniog*
Length over body (not couplings etc.)	11 ft 6 in.	9 ft 9 in.
Width over body (not handles etc.)	5 ft 6 in.	5 ft 0 in.
Height rail to roof (except lamp)	6 ft 6 in.	6 ft 9 in.
Wheelbase	5 ft 0 in.	5 ft 6 in.

The later vehicles for the F. & B.R. were of different sizes. Holland made a point of reporting that they were an improvement on the F.R. design whose latest carriages were raised 1 ft 3 in. above the rails in order to clear the wheels etc., whereas the F. & B. carriages 'are lowered to within 9 inches of the rails and the wheels are recessed . . . under the seats . . . thus affording more stability . . . and headroom'. They both had standard Linley oil lamps in the roof, projecting 6 in. The Festiniog had the longer wheelbase but in the F. & B.R. examples, three doors instead of two were provided and from the drawing it will be seen that though the wheelbase was shorter, the seats were almost contained within it. The seating arrangement was unusual, there being no seat against each end wall. The drawing shows one of the three all 3rd coaches; the fourth had two 2nd class flanking a central 1st. The 3rds were plain wooden interiors, but the upper classes had upholstery proportioned as to class. The mixed vehicles had double small side windows, the thirds a single small pane, due to full partitions in the mixed class and none in the thirds. Unlike the earliest F.R. vehicles, the bodies were lower slung like later F.R. types; for this reason the wheels projected through the floors, accounting for the arrangement of seats whereby these were used to encase the wheel boxes and through the floors of which lubrication was done. At each end was a large central buffer with screw coupling and hook below. Dimensions corresponded with F.R. standard, for obvious reasons. The bodies were low enough to dispense with footboards and station platforms.

The oil lamps were arranged with two for the mixed class, and one for the thirds, but the latter may have been so insufficient as to cause at least one of the all-thirds to have two lamps fitted later. There were no end steps for access to the roofs.

The carriages were painted in a single colour livery (unknown) with 'First' etc. in gilt lettering under each door drop-light.

The accommodation for passengers proved to be insufficient. From three 3rd Class, one composite 1st/2nd Class and a Guard's Van, there was added in 1878 by the G.W.R. another 3rd and an extra composite: these cost £65 and £90 respectively. Apparently there was extra brake power beside that provided by the Van, for one 3rd Class compartment of one of the Ashbury carriages could be used by the guard: it had 'the double variety' of brake (presumably shoes on each side of the wheel?)

The G.W.R. List can be summarised:

	Passenger				Workmen's
Class	1 + 2	3*	1 + 2	3	
No. of vehicles	1	2	1	2	19 (max.)
	ft in.	ft in.	ft in.	ft in.	ft in.
Body length overall	12 2	12 2	12 7¼	11 10¼	7 8
Body width overall	5 11	6 0	5 6	5 6	4 2½
Height inside	6 3	6 4	6 3	6 3	?
Wheelbase	5 9	5 9	6 6	5 9	4 5
Wheel diameter	1 6	1 6	1 8	1 8	1 5
Frame	Outside framing				Inside framing
Date of build	July 1868		July 1878		?
Built by	Ashbury		G.W.R.		J.H. Williams & Sons

*One compartment contains brake.

Bodies were made of oak, carried on laminated springs and had sprung drawgear; and buffing shocks were taken by a rubber block. As Vignes only gives dimensions for a 3rd Class carriage (and whilst his text is probably correct, there are errors in the figures of his drawing) one can only compare them with a similar carriage on the G.W.R. list, only to find considerable differences. On balance it seems the bodies were 11 ft 6 in. – 11 ft 9 in. long, 5 ft 6 in. wide (excluding door furniture) having a 6 ft 6 in. height outside (rail to roof) and a 5 ft wheelbase. The G.W.R. figures are at variance, the wheelbase of 5 ft 9 in. is especially questionable: what value may one place on the other G.W.R. dimensions?!

Besides the classified passenger vehicles, there were 12–19 Quarrymen's coaches which Vignes describes as 'very similar to those on the Festiniog Railway, but without roofs'; presumably it was these which the Board agreed should be 'enclosed' in 1878 suggesting they were at first similar to those on the Festiniog Railway which were little more than open wagons. Nos. 1–6, 8–15 carried these numbers but five more carried no number; they were not sprung but were given the same large rubber block to serve as a buffer as the other carriages possessed, and the woodwork was of deal. The builder was (according to William Dean) J. Henry Williams & Sons, of Portmadoc (later, The Britannia Foundry).

Holland's 1868 Report to the Board of Trade mentions that 'The waggons are precisely similar to those used on the Ffestiniog Railway – their length from hook to hook is 7 ft 6 in. – the width 3 ft 3 in. and height from rails 3 ft – when fully loaded they weigh 2¾ tons and empty 12¾ cwt.' (these were frame-sided). 'A few of the largest size coal waggons weigh when fully loaded 3¾ tons and when empty 15 cwt.'

As in other features, accounts of contemporary arrangements are contradictory: there was a system with the Festiniog to hire four of their wagons for every one on the F. & B., but this fell through in 1878 at a time when the F.R. only owned six wagons anyway: thereafter the F. & B.R. hired them for 4d. per ton carried.

Vignes remarks that goods traffic is carried in Festiniog Railway wagons if destined to run over that line. For F. & B. internal use only, he also describes their own wagons as 'similar to those on the Festiniog Railway'.

Directors

A list of original directors is given: there were few changes during the life of the enterprise. John Vaughan and J.W. Greaves joined the Board at an early date in place of Capt. T.H. Wynne and George Casson. The Board at the time of the September 1866 prospectus was:

			Shares held
George Casson (Chairman)		Festiniog	?
Samuel Holland	Glanwilliam,	Maentwrog	50
Capt. T.H. Wynne	Nerquis Hall,	Flintshire	?
John Casson	Blaenydelos,	Festiniog	30
Morgan Lloyd	5, Chester Terr.,	London	50
William Davies	Bryllewellyn,	Festiniog	20
Robert Roberts	Tyhwyntirbwch,	Portmadoc	10
Solicitor			
Edward Breese, Morfa Lodge, Portmadoc			10
Secretary			
Robert Griffith, Melbourne House, Festiniog			
Engineer			
Charles Menzies Holland, Liscard Vale, Wallasey			10
Bankers	*Offices*		
Messrs. Casson & Co., Festiniog	Melbourne House, Festiniog.		

(Figures following indicate number of £10 shares taken up, where known.)

The Seal of the Company was a roundel containing the name of the Company encircling a Shield on which appeared a rampant goat.

A commentary on the Company's originator and moving spirit, Samuel Holland, is to be found in the Minutes of the Select Committee, re the Festiniog Railway Bill of 1869, sitting on 6–9 July, 1869. This was shortly after the F.&B.R. had opened to traffic. The issue in discussion was the Festiniog charges for carrying goods to Blaenau; the rates were condemned by all the opponents of the Festiniog's proposed Bill. It was agreed that in comparison with other Welsh railways, they were high. Samuel Holland was cross-examined and his remarks were typical. His appearance was not entirely to his credit however. Reading between the lines, one may visualise the apparently public-spirited benefactor whom everyone locally knows is revelling in the occasion, for he is likely to benefit from the publicity and probably materially if the examination goes in favour of the opponents. His manner and speech were pompous, and he took up cudgels on behalf of the people of Blaenau Festiniog by complaining that fuel and foodstuffs which had to come from Portmadoc by train, were unreasonably charged for so doing. However, Mr. Michael, counsel for the promoters of the Bill, was a match for him.

Mr. Michael obtained information from Holland concerning the rates paid to quarrymen in general and his own men in particular. The cost of living had been rising and there had been much complaint among the men regarding the low wages. Holland had no intention of increasing wages if he could, and was brought to the point of admitting that his principal interest in the Festiniog rates was to keep them as low as possible with a view to keeping the cost of living down and avoiding labour problems in his own quarry. In short, he was made out to be more fearful of a cut at his own pocket than concerned for the welfare of the local workpeople.

Thrust and counterthrust were typical of these Enquiries, but there is nothing to suggest that Holland was any worse or better than other contemporary employers. In his defence it may be added that all the quarry owners complained of the dictatorial agreements which they had been forced to draw up with the Festiniog Railway, but which almost all expired about the period of the proceedings.

Shareholding

The promoters of the railway put great store by the way in which local people might participate in the ownership of the railway, with what degree of success may be judged by extracts from the Annual Returns:

31 Dec. 1867	976 issued to 110 holders. 44 of these were Quarrymen, most holding only 1 or 2 shares.	
27 May 1874	1148 issued to 110 holders.	
	Samuel Holland	215 shares
	Mrs. Casson	120 shares
	All others:	less than 70 shares
23 June 1879	Similar to above, but:	
	Samuel Holland	290 shares

Traffic

It was people rather than slate who were the mainstay of the line: 1879, an average year, saw passenger receipts at £1,406 against £416 for goods. Workmen were the bulk, and numbers soared to new heights when the B. & F.R. took over, holding their own above the independent times of the Company. There was a peak of 20,122 tons of goods traffic in 1881; about half of this was in slate but all coal for the district came up from ships and was distributed by rail to the Ffestiniog district: quarries and private customers alike burned many tons. Rail links to slate quarries were not a feature of the line, only Tan-y-Manod Quarry having one – there were quarries at some distance (of which Drum – opened 1840 – has had mention and had been suspended in 1883) which carted to the line. [Of these the largest was Braich-Ddu (Map Reference SH 718385) which had a road exchange at Tomen-y-Mur, Bryn Golen and was served by a ¾ mile tramway in 2 ft gauge laid in T-section chaired rails (as for Croesor) and may have taken products from the rail end to Llan Ffestiniog by sled. Its branch lines were made up in very light bridge rail and a very stubby section of flat bottom. With a long almost straight course falling in shallow gradient it was a cheaply-worked site, ideal for rail usage and having some strange features not fully explained. Working in the early years of the F. & B. its owner advertised it for sale then, a favourable issue being the passage of the B. & F.R. close by. It was acquired by The Maentwrog Slab & Slate Quarry Co. Ltd. (incorp. 1887) who were succeeded by The Braich-Ddu Slate Quarry Co. Ltd. in 1897.]

At Tan-y-Manod, Craig Ddu Quarry ultimately had an extensive branch rising by four inclines from the railway; the first, (last built) a short one, had a level crossing with the road at its summit, and the next three formed an impressive trio climbing high above the valley. At the summit of the second was the original Craig-Ddu Quarry and slate works, probably the former Old Manod Quarry. Extending eastwards from there the third incline terminates in Craig-Ddu Quarry proper; these inclines being especially fine examples of their kind. The site was opened in 1840 and in 1849 Smith & Brunton were appointed Engineers. In 1865 the New Craig-Ddu Slate Co. Ltd. was incorporated and took a lease to build the tramway that year. By 1880 'New' had been dropped and later it was the Craig-Ddu Manod Slate Co. Ltd.; names changed frequently and after World War I, Craigddu Slate Quarries Ltd.[7] The link with the roadway was made in autumn 1869 and the Festiniog Railway Select Committee Enquiry of July that year disclosed there was yet another 300 yards of track to complete it. There is an unique photograph showing men finishing this length at Tan-y-Manod. In 1882 3,140 tons were extracted, using 110 employees.

It was the inclines themselves which attracted outside attention; built under a proposal by C.M. Holland in December 1866, they were known for their unusual Car Gwyllt, 'THE CARNARVON & DENBIGH

HERALD' having an account of a journey thereon on 8th March, 1883. These small 'cars' were home-made, each carrying its owner the mile from quarry down to town along the 1 in 6 incline. Apparently the men were hauled in empty wagons to work, but these left the premises loaded during the day, so the locally made gravity 'skate' came into its own, thus, one set of wheels rode on one rail, and an outrigger (which could be detached) with a roller on its end, bore on the other rail, and there was a small handbrake worked through a slot in the floor; cunningly the brake handle was detachable and made so that it was unique to that vehicle . . . no pilfering![9]

The quarry did not close until 1945.

Finally, traffic created accidents. An alarming one was when carriages were struck by rocks falling from cuttings, and though the details are not known, a passenger claimed £110 for bodily injury. The junction at Dolgaregddu had been rebuilt, but in earlier times must have given the Festiniog Railway insufficient protection for in 1878 the F.R. sent an account for '. . . to cost of damage done to our locomotive engine LITTLE WONDER by a collision at the F. & B.R. junction, £4 13s. 9d.'

Contributing to risk, trains usually ran mixed with slate wagons among the carriages, but this was stopped in 1877.

REFERENCES

1. 'THE FESTINIOG RAILWAY', Vol. I, p.121–123. (J.I.C. Boyd) [The Oakwood Press]
2. 'THE FESTINIOG RAILWAY', Vol. I, p.114–116, 119, 121. (J.I.C. Boyd) [The Oakwood Press]
3. 'THE FESTINIOG RAILWAY', Vol. I, p.128. (J.I.C. Boyd) [The Oakwood Press]
4. 'THE FESTINIOG RAILWAY', Vol. I, p.59. (J.I.C. Boyd) [The Oakwood Press]
5. "THE CHESTER DIVISION 1924–25".
6. G.W.R. Running Powers "over Festiniog & Blaenau Railway" concerning L.N.W.R. and subject to physical junction: see G.W.R.Co. 'RUNNING POWERS' (1902) p.156.
7. Gwynedd Archives PQ100/23.
8. 'THE FESTINIOG RAILWAY', Vol. II, p.438, 478. (J.I.C. Boyd) [The Oakwood Press]
9. 'THE FESTINIOG RAILWAY', Vol. II, p.479. (J.I.C. Boyd) [The Oakwood Press]

Timetables

FESTINIOG RAILWAY and
FESTINIOG & BLAENAU RAILWAY February 1878

DOWN									
Portmadoc	6.00a	7.00b	8.40	10.45	1.00	–	3.20	5.00	–
Duffws	7.17	8.15	9.55	12.00	2.15	–	4.38	6.20	–

DOWN									
Duffws	7.40A	–	10.00	12.10C	2.20	3.45	5.00AB	6.22B	8.00B
Tan-y-Manod	7.43	–	10.03	12.13	2.23	3.48	5.03	6.25	8.03
Tyddyngwyn	7.46	–	10.06	12.16	2.26	3.51	5.06	6.28	8.06
Festiniog	8.00	–	10.20	12.30	2.40	4.05	5.20	6.42	8.20

a Mondays only.
b Except Mondays.
A Workmen's Train; times of departure variable.
B Runs on Saturdays only.
C Leaves 10 mins. later on Saturdays.

UP									
	X								
Festiniog	–	–	8.30	10.30	–	3.05	4.20C	5.30B	7.15B
Tyddyngwyn	–	–	8.40	10.40	–	3.15	4.30	5.40	7.25
Tan-y-Manod	–	–	8.43	10.43	–	3.18	4.33	5.43	7.28
Duffws	–	–	8.50	10.50	–	3.25	4.40	5.50	7.35

UP									
Duffws	6.12a	7.12b	8.55	11.00	1.15c	3.35	5.15	–	–
Portmadoc	7.15	8.15	10.00	12.05	2.25	4.40	6.22	–	–

X Blank column headed X for the purpose of A above, for working empty stock and
engine Festiniog to Duffws, or for workmen's train, as required. Times not publicly
advertised. [Author's Note.]
a Mondays only.
b Except Mondays.
c Low fare carriages attached on Saturdays.
B Runs on Saturdays only.
C Runs 10 mins. later on Saturdays.

Festiniog Railway: For the period during which the Duffws-Llan Ffestiniog line was
narrow gauge, the Festiniog Railway appears to have reversed its previous 'Up' and
'Down' directions to comply with Festiniog & Blaenau Railway directions. In the period
before and after this phase, Festiniog Railway 'Up' referred literally to up-gradient
working from Portmadoc, and vice versa.

	1873	1874	1875	1876	1877	1878	1879	1880	1881	1882
Cost of Works and Way	£137	243	218	302	363	895	376	429	384	250
Cost Loco power	326	459	519	447	814	690	469	489	558	620
Cost Carr/Wag Maint.	–	9	13	9	148	362	68	88	152	143
Profit (Loss) on wkg.	456	360	497	604	910	(334)	571	545	687	461
Merchandise Tons	3510	3462	4550	4257	7823	6022	4044	8950	17702	9177
Minerals Tons	2685	3085	3968	4625	5700	2284	1820	3012	2420	9393
1st Class passengers	886	744	745	714	1350	905	807	954	903	654
2nd Class passengers	1255	1324	1514	1490	2297	2185	1678	2396	2085	1802
3rd Class passengers	35851	42309	48409	54498	82365	59723	49614	48753	48736	45537
Mixed Train mileage	13782	13728	13728	13936	–	–	–	–	–	–
Passenger train mileage	–	–	–	–	24184	14820	14617	13524	13510	13009
Goods train mileage	–	–	–	–	415	312	376	377	390	350
Locos	4	4		4	6	6	6	6		
Carriages		Returned as Two throughout period							25	23
Other carriages		Returned as One 1873–1879								
Merchandise wagons		Returned as Nineteen 1873–1880								
Other wagons	7	7		7	5	5	5	5	3	1

Comments on above: Quarrymen's open carriages ultimately taken into stock and shown on Returns from 1881.. Peak costs and peak traffic come in 1877–8; loss on working for latter year results. The Continuous Brakes Return to the Board of Trade for 1879 states: 'Two passenger train Engines. Twenty-five carriages for use on passenger trains made up of six carriages and nineteen "other wagons"'. None fitted with continuous brakes.

The House of Commons, on the evidence of C.E. Spooner on the Bala & Festiniog Railway Bill (Session 1873), was given 'Four goods & coal trucks, about 12 open Quarrymen's Carriages, no slate trucks' as the current stock of the F.&B.Rly. Still earlier (House of Commons Enquiry on the Festiniog Railway 1869) William Davies, Manager of the F.&B.R. said they owned eight wagons, charged 6d. per ton for slate, and workmen 1/- per week.

CROESOR TRAMWAY
(Gauge 2 ft)

Incorporated by Act: None.
Opened: Goods traffic: 1st August, 1864 but possibly carrying traffic over completed sections twelve months earlier. Goods and mineral line only.[1]
Office: That of Proprietor, H.B. Roberts.
Capital: None; private undertaking constructed under wayleave.

CROESOR & PORT MADOC
RAILWAY COMPANY
(Gauge 2 ft)

Incorporated by Act: 28 & 29 Vic. Cap. 295 of 5th July, 1865 to maintain the existing Croesor Tramway between Portmadoc and Carreg-hylldrem, and to extend to Borth-y-gest.
Registered Office: Caernarvon.
Length: 4½ miles (also officially given as 1¼ miles in error).
Capital: £25,000 in Shares and £8,330 in Loans (issued £15,000 and £8,000 @ 5½% loan).

PORTMADOC, CROESOR & BEDDGELERT
TRAM RAILWAY COMPANY
(Gauge 2 ft)

Incorporated by Act: 42 & 43 Vic. Cap. 171 of 21st July, 1879. Change of name and authorised to construct branch.
Incorporated by Act: 55 & 56 Vic. Cap. 44 of 20th June, 1892: Rates and Charges.
Registered Office: 99 Gresham Street, London, E.C.
Length: 5 miles (official).
Capital: £23,000 in Shares and £7,650 in Loans.
Capital per mile: £5,700.
Promoted to absorb the Croesor & Port Madoc Railway by giving it a fresh title and taking its powers. Additional powers for new line Llanfrothen–Beddgelert (3 m. 7 fur.) over period of five years. No work done. New line to be titled 'P.C. & B.T. Railway Company's Beddgelert Extension' with capital to be kept separately.
Company into Receivership: 1882.
Powers sold to Portmadoc, Beddgelert & South Snowdon Railway:
Act: 1 Ed. VII 262 of 17th August, 1901.
Closed: Embodiment of part into Welsh Highland Railway. No official closure date for remainder of tramway though all out of use by 1936. Unofficial usage continued over these sections until about 1955. A few sections extant 1971.

Historical Summary

1864	Croesor Tramway opened to goods and mineral traffic (by 1st August). Rhosydd Quarry connected to Croesor Tramway (June).
1865	Croesor & Port Madoc Rly. Co. incorporated 28/9 Vic. Cap. 295 (5th July, 1865).
1866	Croesor United Slate Quarry Co. Ltd. formed. (Into liquidation 1874).
1873–4	Rhosydd Co. fails – New Rhosydd Slate Co. Ltd. formed.
1875	Croesor New Slate Co. Ltd. formed. (Ceased 1882) Worked by S. Pope: became part of Park & Croesor Slate Quarries Co. Ltd. 1895. (Closed 1930)
1879	Portmadoc, Croesor & Beddgelert Tram Railway Co. incorporated 42/3 Vic. Cap. 171. (21st July, 1879)
1882	P.C. & B.T.R.Co. into Receivership.
1901	Powers sold to Portmadoc, Beddgelert & South Snowdon Rly. Co.
1921	New Rhosydd Slate Co. Ltd. bought out and worked until 1930.
1948–49	Portions of tramway dismantled (see text for detail).

History

Outside the Blaenau Festiniog area, and with the exception of the big Glanrafon Quarry near South Snowdon which was later to be served by the North Wales Narrow Gauge Railways, the quarries at Croesor came to be the third largest employers of labour in the district. On a small scale, quarrying was being done on a site at Croesor (or Croesawr), the head of a valley east of Portmadoc, by 1846, and this became worked by the Croicer (sometimes Croiser) Valley & Portmadoc Freehold Slate Co. Ltd. which closed down shortly afterwards but in the manner of such concerns, was revived – or revival was attempted – by a Prospectus in 1863 which read:

> Prospectus of The Croiser Valley and Portmadoc
> Freehold Slate Company Limited.
>
> Operations on the side of Cnicht. Report by James Wright states:– ". . . a railroad is being made direct from Portmadoc nearly up to the very boundary of your property and slate will be conveyed from your quarries to the port at the rate of about 1/3d. or 1/6d. per ton instead of about 10/- which would be the present cost. This railroad is now partly made and will be completed in another six or nine months and is an important element in giving value to this property."[2]

[This site could be that known as Cnicht Quarry, opened 1875 but having no rail connection. It might also be the same (or adjacent to) the trial levels of The Slate Mountain Co. Ltd., formed in July 1861 (and liquidated in June 1866) 'to purchase slate quarries on the East side of a

farm called Croesor Bach in the parish of Llanfrothen'. The only likely
site hereabouts is a Trial Level (Map Ref. 638453) but it is of significance in that a Special Resolution of 21st November, 1862 stated:

> empowered to negotiate with Mr. Hugh Beaver Roberts or the other two proprietors
> of the Croesor Valley Railroad for the carriage of slate or slabs from the quarry
> belonging to the Company, to Portmadoc . . . and also for making a roadway and
> tramway (with convenient sidings) from the Company's quarry to the said railway . . .
> including the payment by the Company to the said Mr. Beaver Roberts the sum of
> £5,000 to be applied towards the construction of this railway by instalments . . .

and this would be among the earliest references to the building of the
Croesor line.]

By 1861 there were two other undertakings working there, the
Croesor Fawr Slate Quarrying Co. Ltd. (formerly the Croesor Slate
Quarry Co.) and the Upper Croesor Slate Quarry Co. Ltd. These two
were almost working in one another's pockets for in September 1865
the Upper Co. granted the Fawr Co. permission to dump rubbish on its
land.

The two companies amalgamated after H.B. Roberts gave a new
company, Croesor United Slate Co. Ltd., a lease to search for slate on
the land of Croesor Fawr Farm. Croesor United entered business in
mid 1866 with a capital of £160,000 and a formal lease of Upper's
property was assigned to it on 1st August, 1866. Upper's champion was
Hugh Unsworth McKie who like Roberts, appears later in connection
with other local enterprises, and not surprisingly, was also a director of
the Croesor & Port Madoc Railway. As to McKie, among relevant
documents appears the following doggerel, penned suitably on black-
edged notepaper:

Private Eye Bill!
Mr. McKie is all my Eye,
And Engineers consulting
Owens 'The Boy' will make a Toy
That Dividends result in
Then let the slate come along if it will
Shares there are, ABC still
ABCD – BCDE
Shares there are quite easy still.

Owen might possibly be Robert Owen, Manager of The Welsh Slate
Company, Blaenau Ffestiniog. Development of the quarry took place in
1868–9, a contract with Beaumont, Appleby & Ashwell of London
being placed for cutting the shafts and tunnel, James Wyatt, former
agent to Lord Penrhyn's quarry was Managing Director from 1865.
From 30th June, 1867, T.H. Wyatt was Chairman and McKie Manager
& Secretary.

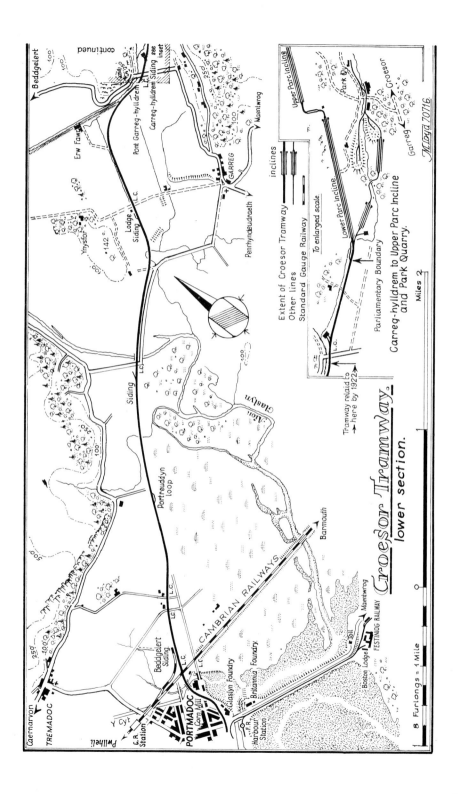

Croesor Tramway.
lower section.

Carreg-hylldrem to Upper Parc Incline and Park Quarry.

inclines
Extent of Croesor Tramway
Other lines
Standard Gauge Railway

To enlarged scale.

Upper Parc Incline
Lower Parc Incline
Park Quarry
Croesor
Garreg
Parliamentary Boundary

Tramway relaid to here by 1922 →

Miles 2
L.C.

M. Lloyd 10/76.

Beddgelert
continued

Erw Fawr
Pont Garreg-hylldrem see inset
Carreg-hylldrem Siding
L.C.
Lodge Siding L.C.
Ynystor
·142 ↑
GARREG
Penrhyndeudraeth
Maentwrog
+

Siding
Siding L.C.

Portreuddyn loop
Afon Glaslyn

CAMBRIAN RAILWAYS
Barmouth

Caernarvon
TREMADOC
Pwllheli

Beddgelert Siding
L.C.
L.C.
Glaslyn Foundry
Britannia Foundry
Cyt
C.R. Station
Corn Mill
PORTMADOC
F.R. Harbour Station
Boston Lodge
Toll
Maentwrog
FESTINIOG RAILWAY

8 Furlongs = 1 Mile

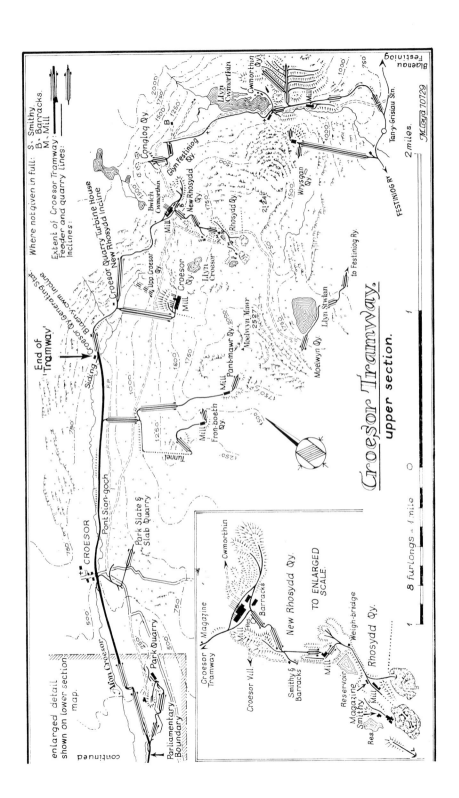

Croesor Tramway.
upper section.

Where not given in full: S = Smithy.
B = Barracks.
M = Mill.
Extent of Croesor Tramway:
Feeder and quarry Lines:
Inclines:

End of Tramway

enlarged detail
shown on lower section
map.

continued

Parliamentary
Boundary

Park Quarry

Afon Croesor

CROESOR

Pont Slon-goch

Park Slate &
Slab Quarry

Croesor Siding

Croesor by Generating Stn.

Braich y cwm Incline

Croesor Quarry Turbine House
New Rhosydd Incline

Mill

Upp Croesor Qy.

Mill Croesor Qy.

Llyn Croesor

Bwlch
Cwmorthin

Mill

New Rhosydd Qy.

Rhosydd Qy.

Llyn Cwmorthin

Conglog Qy.

Glyn Festiniog Qy.

Cwmorthin

Mill

Wrysgan Qy.

Moelwyn Mawr
2527'

Moelwyn Qy.

Llyn Stwlan

to Festiniog Ry.

Panbmawr Qy.

Mill

Fron-boeth Qy.

Tunnel

to Festiniog Ry.

FESTINIOG RY.

Tan-y-Grisiau Stn.

Blaenau
Festiniog

M.Gara 70729

2 miles.

8 furlongs = 1 mile

TO ENLARGED SCALE.

Croesor
Tramway

Magazine

Cwmorthin

Croesor Vill.

Smithy &
Barracks

Barracks

Mill

New Rhosydd Qy.

Mill

Weigh-bridge

Reservoir

Magazine
Smithy

Res.

Mill

Rhosydd Qy.

"[H.B. Roberts was the second son of Hugh Roberts at Glan-y-Menai, Anglesey. Hugh was educated at Rugby School when Dr. Arnold was the headmaster there and became a solicitor. He took over John Hughes's very successful practice in Bangor on Hughes's death in 1849 and he also succeeded him as Clerk to the Bangor Magistrates, Diocesan Registrar, Chapter Clerk and agent to the Bishop. When a District Registry of the Court of Probate was established in Bangor in 1859, he became District Registrar, a post he held until his death in 1903. For several years Hugh and Harriet lived at Bryn Menai, near the 'look out' in Upper Bangor and their five children were born there. In 1858 he purchased the Plas Madog estate near Llanrwst and the family moved to live in Plas Madog.

Roberts was a successful solicitor and businessman. Speculative slate quarrying ventures and narrow gauge railways, laid down to transport the products of quarries and mines to the ports, were his main interests. He owned the Ffridd Nant Quarry at Penmachno and the Braich Quarry in Upper Llandwrog; he was a director of the Bowydd and Maenofferen Quarries in Blaenau Ffestiniog, the Croesor Fawr Quarry in the Vale of Croesor, the Croesor and Porthmadog Railway and the North Wales Narrow Gauge Railways Co. He was associated with John Ormiston of Wigfair St. Asaph, in the development of the Flint Marsh Colliery, Flint, and the formation of the George Hotel Co. in Bangor. In addition, he played an active part in public affairs: he was appointed a Justice of the Peace for Caernarfonshire, Denbighshire and Merionethshire and Deputy Lieutenant for Merionethshire; he was a member of the Bangor Board of Health, 1850–54, and the political agent of the Hon. George Sholto Douglas Pennant during the parliamentary election campaign of 1868.][3]

Some detail of James Wyatt's interest is also desirable and a further extract from the same source is appropriate:

"James Wyatt's involvement in a slate quarrying venture dates from his retirement from the agency of the Penrhyn estate. It is appropriate to deal with the venture at this point since many of the people associated with it were members of the family who have been mentioned already; indeed, the whole saga of the slate mine at Croesor highlights yet again the closely knit character of the Wyatt family.

After 1835 the Ffestiniog area rose rapidly to prominence among the slate quarrying areas of North Wales; by 1865 slate production there had reached 100,000 tons a year and a number of speculative mining ventures were undertaken. Most of the mines were opened up on the northern flank of the Moelwynion where the slate outcropped, but a level driven into the western side of the mountains at Rhosydd in the Croesor valley had reached the slate vein, albeit some distance from the surface. James was confident that slate in marketable quantities existed under adjacent land near Croesor itself and, trusting in his intimate knowledge of the slate rock, the family supported him in founding the Croesor Slate Company in 1860. His son-in-law, Hugh Beaver Roberts, bought a tract of land at Croesor and leased it to the Company,[4] he also financed the laying down of a tramroad from the mine to Porthmadog, the natural outlet for slate in the district. Following the Companies Act of 1862 the Company was reconstituted as the Croesor Fawr Slate Quarry Co. Ltd. with a capital of £80,000. The directors of the Company were James Wyatt, Hugh Beaver Roberts, Thomas Henry Wyatt (the architect), Osmond Arthur Wyatt and Harvey Wyatt. James's son Benjamin was appointed Company secretary.

For the purpose of exploiting the slate bearing rock more effectively, the Company agreed in 1866 to amalgamate with a neighbouring slate mining company; a new company, called the Croesor United Slate Quarry Co. Ltd. was formed with a capital of £160,000. Three of the six directors were Wyatts – James, Thomas Henry and

Osmond Arthur; Thomas Henry was elected chairman and Benjamin was put in charge of the transport and marketing arrangements. A list of the shareholders in the Company in 1873 reveals that members of the Wyatt family held nearly 50 per cent of the shares and 24 per cent of the debentures. An excellent history of this Company is to be found in the 'JOURNAL OF THE MERIONETHSHIRE HISTORICAL SOCIETY,[5] suffice it to record here the fact that the venture was a complete failure due to the distance of the slate vein from the surface, the crippling expense which was incurred in reaching it, and the inferior quality of the slate once it was reached. The company went into liquidation in 1874 and no bid was forthcoming when the mine was placed on the market. The shareholders lost practically their entire investment and the whole affair must have been a traumatic experience for James Wyatt, in particular.

James Wyatt died in 1882 at the age of 87 . . ."[3]

Progress on the site was not favourable, and a private report was placed before the Board which said it might be hoped that better slate would be found below the present level of working; by then 110 men were at work. Debentures had to be issued in 1870 to meet continuous development costs, for the slate vein 'of paying quality' had still not been reached. It was a time of great anxiety and the directors reported it would be necessary 'to stop everything unless further measures are forthcoming' i.e. more capital was put up. Underground, they were hampered by a 'chert band' of hard rock. The Machine Tunnelling Co., now holding the contract for the work, made slow progress and in June 1872, the slate vein not having been reached in the Trial Shaft, the Machine Tunnelling contract was terminated and the Diamond Rock-boring Co. took over. In the November the Board appealed for more money; water could not be pumped out quickly enough, but by June 1873 the shareholders made it clear they had subscribed enough and the directors decided to wind up voluntarily and reconstitute the concern as The Croesor Slate Company: some detail of this period is revealing.

Even before the United Company was formed, McKie had reported that he could not make a good report of the existing slate chambers – there had been excessive rain. Samuel Holland inspected in November 1866 and said the present slate quality would not pay its way. They must go deeper to prove the rock. In June 1868, C.E. Spooner inspected. The machinery was always short of power and overheated the shaft. The water pouring into the workings was lifted into wagons by bucket and carried away, as £700 was needed for new pumps. McKie complained in January 1872 that the diamond borers were too weak for the rock, and then without consulting him, the Board removed all the machinery from the valley. McKie, now Consulting Engineer to the Mine, 'although deprived of the last prop he had to support his family', offered his resignation. He added, 'There has been the most reckless and wasteful destruction of plant'.

Auction of the quarry was attempted in April 1875 and the Croesor Slate Company never really began work. A second essay to sell was made in July 1875.

The undertakings all failed because of heavy costs; Penrhyn slate cost

1s. 2½d. a ton to produce, Croesor 10s. 9½d. Whereas at Penrhyn in June 1868 the output was 9,000 tons, Croesor only produced 226 tons. It need not be added that Croesor United's traffic contribution to the new tramway was miserably small.

On 9th December, 1875 the Croesor New Slate Co. Ltd. took over. Edward Breese the Portmadoc solicitor to the Festiniog & Blaenau Railway was Chairman and there was more impressive talent and wealth on the Board. Thomas Williams of Bryn Croesor was made Manager; he had been Manager of Lord Penrhyn's quarries. (Throughout there is evidence of personnel moving from one concern to another in this fashion.) John Francis of Portmadoc was Consulting Engineer.

With a capital of £45,000 they took over the workings, manager's house, eight quarrymen's cottages, workshops etc. together with a railway which linked the quarry with 'the Croesor & Port Madoc line' and it was estimated that each ton of slate would be carried from the quarry to Port Madoc wharves (sic) for less than 3s.

Croesor New went out of business in December 1882, but was purchased by S. Pope of Llanbedr, 7th July, 1883; it then became part of Park & Croesor Slate Quarries Co. Ltd., formed 21st August, 1895. It closed in 1930 and was wound up 8th February, 1931.

['THE MINING JOURNAL' carried the 1874 sale advertisement, referring to "extensive railway inclines" and "2 12 h.p. locomotive steam engines put up for temporary purposes" – clearly these were stationary and *not* locomotive type!]

The other major quarry in the neighbourhood was Rhosydd; opened in a small way about 1833 and worked more seriously from June 1853 by The Rhosydd Slate Co., it was only competitive when the cheaper transport offered by the Croesor Tramway enabled it to surge ahead under the auspices of The Rhosydd Slate Co. Ltd. formed in November 1856. True, the Company of 1853 had submitted a Bill in February 1856 to build a C.E. Spooner-surveyed railway linking the workings by an eastern route and four inclines and so down to the Festiniog Railway (with working arrangements with that Company) but the Bill was withdrawn in July the same year.[6,7] There were later Spooner-linked plans for railways in 1860 and 1862 which were equally negative.

The Rhosydd Slate Co. Ltd. had some Festiniog quarry directors on its board who included George A. Huddart with his Pennant Valley and Festiniog Railway connections. The capital was substantial for those days (£125,000), and they took over the small existing quarry which had already built a 'Branch Railway and Incline' by June 1864 to connect it to the new tramway. They were working the same vein as Lord Palmerston's Welsh Slate Co. in Blaenau Festiniog. The railway works had cost £2,500 and arrangements had been made with the Croesor Tramway to carry output for the next four years on to Portmadoc quays for 2s. 10d. per ton, reducing to 1s. 10d. per ton as traffic increased. Until the railway had opened, expansion of the quarry had been seriously hampered. A report showed that the cost of these competitive rates over the Croesor & Portmadoc Railway as £5,000, but how this came about is not stated; it certainly made a mockery of the alleged cheap terms of carriage! The local Bangor paper was quite cynical in its review of the new railway connection . . . 'The Croesor Slate Quarry – Railway to Portmadoc. Among the many signs of "progress" which may be witnessed in this district . . .'. Like newspaper errors of the present, it gave the quarry the wrong title too.

The Rhosydd Slate Co. Ltd. failed in June 1873 and its assets sold in Manchester; a New Rhosydd Slate Co. Ltd. was formed in October 1874, this time (in contrast to its predecessor which carried so many of the local 'Big Guns' on its Board) it was largely a locally-owned concern; it staggered on against the odds of the industry until July 1921 when it was purchased by the Colman's of mustard fame, only to close – albeit temporarily it was hoped – in September 1930. Fitful and small operation continued, but a roof-fall in 1900 had long buried one of the best parts of the workings and W.O. Williams of Harlech stepped in to scrap the machinery etc. in 1948. These dates are given, not so much as to underline the spasmodic nature of quarry working in these parts (which they certainly do) but also to emphasise how difficult it was for the railway historian, stumbling across the rusting rails of a mountain tramway in past years, to determine whether the line was open for traffic or not. The explanation, especially in this district, was 'that it had been, was not now doing so, but it was hoped it would do so again'.

At Rhosydd there were then five galleries, and tunnels of 550 yards and 700 yards. Output was soon 2,000 tons a year and it was recommended that some land taken be sold off to another user. Here too, C.E. Spooner sent in a full report with elaborate directions as to working the quarry in the future.[7]

The Croesor Tramway was the second railway undertaking of size in the locality to be built without Parliamentary authority and was based on a survey by C.E. Spooner in early 1863 for a railway which might have had Festiniog Railway backing in the period 1861–2.[8] [The first railway of this description had been the Gorseddau Tramway.] By the mid 1850s, trial levels for slate at the upper end of the Afon Croesor valley (about seven miles from Portmadoc and in a valley which even today is bleak and remote), were showing promise and exploitation by means of a railway from Portmadoc was considered. Throughout the district rail communications were proving their worth and to make the venture as economic and expeditious as possible, it was proposed to connect Portmadoc with the Croesor area workings in two distinct undertakings, the first given authority for its progress between the quays and Carreg-hylldrem by means of a series of wayleaves, the second being a continuation eastwards from there on land already leased to quarry owners, thus making it virtually a private tramway. The possibility of using a locomotive was envisaged. Proof of the potential of such a railway was easily to hand. The figures for slate shipments from Portmadoc from the Croesor Quarries without rail communications on the one hand, and from the Gorseddau Quarry with its new tramway on the other, spoke for themselves. They were: (in tons)

	Croesor	*Gorseddau*
1856	414	226
1857	497	478
1858	533	1006
1859	70	1338

Carreg-hylldrem is in fact, a rocky eminence just to the west of Llanfrothen village and above the roadbridge crossing the Afon Croesor, known as Pont Carreg-hylldrem. In the Portmadoc area, connections were made with the already-existing Gorseddau Tramway. The builder and owner of the portion constructed under wayleave was Hugh Beaver Roberts. The line was built between 1863–4 by Messrs. Pritchard & Gregory of Bangor to a gauge contemporarily quoted as '24 inches' and also as 'slightly greater than that of the Festiniog Railway'. The track was of primitive type similar to that at first used on the Festiniog Railway and only suited to horse, gravity or manpower – at that time even the Festiniog had done no more than contemplate self-propulsion for its trains. The rails were of wrought iron, 20 lbs. per yard laid in small chairs on wooden sleepers; extended details are given later. Writing twenty years later, Vignes says that horsepower was the mainstay but that horses were hired not owned; this was in keeping with the original Festiniog practice.

Construction was made easier at the Portmadoc end of the line by using James Creassy's reclamation embankment built in 1800 for William Madocks. Where the availability of this useful dyke ceased east of Portreuddyn a new embankment was built to Pont Croesor, where a wooden bridge was thrown over the river; in later years the bridge was well-remembered for its deplorable condition, so that later it was necessary to rebuild it completely to carry the Welsh Highland Railway of the early nineteen-twenties.

The Creassy embankment was the second of two works built in an attempt to reclaim the west side of the Glaslyn valley from the sea. It was over two miles in length and varied in height from 11 to 20 feet, and was a simple dyke of seasand covered by sods of turf to bind it, costing £2,800 excluding ancillary works. For about half of its length it ran outside of but parallel to an even earlier embankment said to have been built by William Wynn of Wern but which had only been a partial success. It was considered so fragile from the first that only sheep were allowed to graze on it. The Wynn embankment is mentioned because it is often taken to be the abandoned Beddgelert Railway earthwork.

The third, or 'Great Embankment', or Cob, is widely known and of course was a later work built for William Madocks and its seaward side is used by the Festiniog Railway to this day. Confusion between the construction of the second embankment and the Cob comes in a letter

from Madocks' agent's grandson writing in April 1900 which says
'. . .The material was carried from the surrounding high ground in
trolleys which ran upon wooden rails and sleepers . . .' without specify-
ing which of the two 'Madocks' embankments was meant. However,
there is no doubt that here The Cob is being described under construction.

Much of the western end of the route of the Croesor Tramway was
similar to a course proposed by 36-year-old James Spooner in his 1825
plan for a Moelwyn and Port Madoc Railway; this line would have
headed for the slopes of the Moelwyn massif by means of an almost
straight route to carry it up on to the col between Moelwyn Mawr and
Moelwyn Bach by means of a succession of long levels and inclines. In
the event, the east end of the Croesor Tramway and its extensions were
built on a somewhat similar theme in an adjacent valley to the north-
west, involving some splendid locations and occasional civil engineering
quite on a par with the Festiniog Railway. C.E. Spooner, though not
Engineer to the project, was engaged as surveyor and laid out the course
and civil engineering features.[9]

Because the Croesor Tramway proper went no further than Carreg-
hylldrem, it is important to note that official references to later developments do not in fact involve the tramway above this point, but the *whole
undertaking* has always been known loosely as the Croesor Tramway.
Beyond Carreg-hylldrem is the Croesor tramway, a subtle distinction
especially as even today, the 'Croesor Tramway' is shown on maps as
the part-surviving section eastwards from Carreg-hylldrem – portions
of which still exist – whilst the Croesor Tramway as such and which has
been correctly deleted from some modern maps, was demolished finally
between August 1948 and the following August. Even the official
Railway Clearing House Junction Diagram Book is guilty of the error!

A Deed of Mutual Covenant dated 1st October, 1863 between the
Rhosydd Slate Co. Ltd., and Roberts, by which Roberts granted the
quarry a wayleave to build the tramway and incline from its property to
the main tramway previously mentioned (a useful controlling factor
enjoyed by Roberts beyond the confines of the Tramway proper) was
based on a rate of 2d. per ton, reduced to 1d. per ton. This Agreement
expired on 25th March, 1906 but was then extended until 1921 and the
rate was restored to 2d. A rate for carriage was also made in an
Agreement of 1865 between the Croesor & Port Madoc Railway (a
statutory successor to the Croesor Tramway) and the Aberystwyth &
Welsh Coast Railway (later the Cambrian Railways) which concern
planned initially to build its own independent branch to Portmadoc
Harbour (The Welsh Slate Co.'s wharf), but in the event, obtained
running powers over the Croesor & Port Madoc Railway from its level
intersection with it at a rate of 1d. per ton. The sluice bridge would
have been converted into a swing bridge at the same time. The Croesor
& Port Madoc Railway was given reciprocal powers into Portmadoc
(standard gauge) station, 'if the Abersytwyth & Welsh Coast Railway

carried Croesor & Port Madoc Railway traffic from there to local wharves'. This arrangement would have involved a mixed gauge line.[10,11]

Had the Croesor & Port Madoc Railway been extended along the north side of the Aberystwyth & Welsh Coast Railway into Portmadoc station it would have had to cross also the GorseddauTramway on the level (the A.&W.C.R. obtained powers for and built a level crossing) but in any case, there seems to be no evidence that the powers were acted upon.

Croesor Quarry had formerly carted its slate to Penrhyndeudraeth on the Festiniog Railway, but began to use the new tramway in late February 1864: the final incline to the Quarry was not ready until the following August. The case would seem to have been a bid by the A.&W.C.R. (Cambrian Railways) to encourage the C.&P.M.R. to work its traffic into the Cambrian station at Portmadoc and thereafter close the C.&P.M.R./Cambrian level crossing. Under such an arrangement the Cambrian agreed to carry C.&P.M.R. traffic to the harbour, thereby placing the C.&P.M.R. traffic at the tender mercies of the Cambrian. The bait was not swallowed by the C.&P.M.R.! In early 1870 the Cambrian was toying with the idea again: this time to convert the Croesor from "a siding on the present Beddgelert Railway" to the harbour at a cost of £1,500–£1,600, or perhaps to lay a mixed gauge line.

In surviving records the first load of slate came from Rhosydd on 1st August, 1864; 4 wagons of 7 tons 8 cwts. The second load was run on 3rd August on behalf of the owner's own quarry, the Croesor Slate Company, 7 cwts. 'iron materials' at 2s. 10d. per ton. The first slates from the same quarry were on 17th August being 3 wagons containing 4 tons 1 cwt. at 2s. 3½d. per ton. The 'second Croesor' quarry must have been sending traffic by the October and a ledger entry reveals that traffic had been conveyed earlier in the year, though probably the line was not open all the way; it may be assumed that 1st August was significant only in that the whole tramway opened for business on that day. In October an entry read 'Deals & Boards conveyed for Mr. Thos. Williams about January last. 1 Ton. Rate 2s. 10d.'. These went to the Croesor Fawr Slate Quarry Co.

On 24th October, 1865 the small workings of Gerynt Slate Co. began to use the tramway. Besides the Croesor Fawr, there was the Croesor Bach Slate Co. who bought rails to build a tramway in 1864. Of the small quarries up at the top of the valley, little more was heard.

A good example of Up traffic in the first year was to Mrs. Edmunds, Park Farm, and included coal, a wheel, oats, hayseed and flour.

Rhosydd sent down 284 tons of slate in the first month of workings and almost 200 tons a month for the remainder of the year. In the same period a good business in Up coal haulage began. This was dropped at Carreg-hylldrem, Cwm and Rhosydd, some of it going to the quarry-men's barracks.

Over the Tremadoc Estate a toll of 2d. for sundries and 3d. per ton for slate was levied. The early years show good husbandry; hay conveyed at a charge of £1 14s. 0d. and 'Old wire sold £2 5s. 6d.'. Rhosydd received £23 1s. 3d. for slates broken in transit; Bryn-hyfryd Cottages, near the Siding of that name, were let out to provide income.

In the first nine days the six employees were paid by the day but after that the carriers (hauliers) received 6d. or 3d. per ton and the brakesmen (on the inclines) 3s. 4d.–4s. 6d. per day. The two platelayers got 3s. 4d. and 3s. 8d. a day and in November 1866 were provided with capes!

There was a good exchange of traffic between Croesor and Gorseddau when, from 1875, the latter made junction with the Croesor at the Gas Works. Flour traffic onto the Gorseddau was the largest item, but falling traffic hit the Gorseddau and the last wagon load was in April 1879. At the end of 1883 the Croesor wrote off £26 5s. 6d. owed by the Gorseddau as a bad debt.

Contemporary records show that the Tramway was officially opened throughout for mineral traffic on 1st August, 1864. Railway Year Book, (1911), quotes the above date – the only 'published' source to be found as yet. The year of the opening was to give problems later to its successor, the Welsh Highland Railway. This arose from the rail level crossing formed when the Aberystwyth & Welsh Coast Railway was extended to Pwllheli and was obliged to cross the Tramway on the level on the east side of its Portmadoc station. (The Coast Section was opened to traffic between Barmouth and Pwllheli on 10th October, 1867.) The successor to the Cambrian Railways, the Great Western Railway, imposed a charge on all Welsh Highland Railway movements passing over this crossing with their metals. This came to dispute in 1925, so in the same year steps were taken to find 'an oldest inhabitant' who would be prepared to make a sworn statement 'in exchange for a pound of tobacco'. Robert Morgan, then 80, made the following statement . . . 'I can remember, before the Cambrian Railway was done, crossing the Croesor Railway with the horses, drawing timber at Llyn Bach. When Mr. Jones, the Manager of the Croesor Railway, came to me and asked on whose authority I was drawing timber over his railway, I remember telling him it was the contractor's order'. Morgan also recalls that traffic on the Croesor was done under contract at this time. It was necessary to obtain more than one sworn statement, but because no other witness could be found, the idea was not pursued. As there is no doubt that the Croesor Tramway was first on the scene and the A. & W.C.R. was obliged to cross its path, there seems little enough validity in the Great Western's charge – in fact, the reverse would have been the lawful position.

Owing to the light traffic which the Croesor carried, though it was the subject of successive Acts of Parliament, no major improvements were necessary. A report by Major Spring for the Festiniog management in 1921 shows that much of the original construction survived at

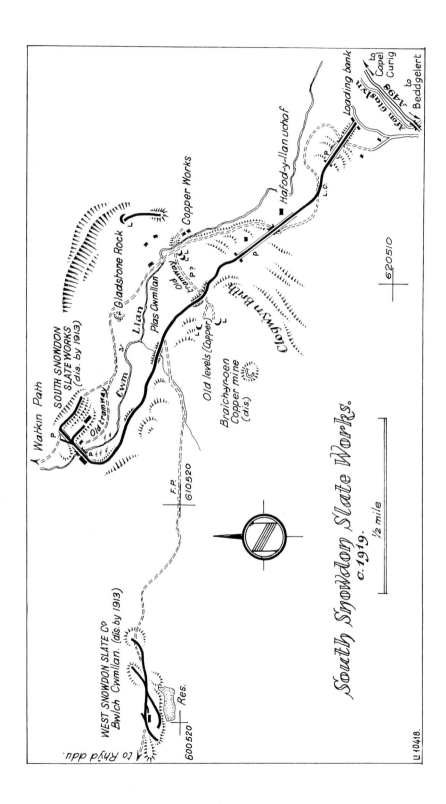

Watkin Path

SOUTH SNOWDON
SLATE WORKS
(dis. by 1913)

Gladstone Rock

Cwm
Llan

Plas Cwmllan

Copper Works

Old levels (Copper)

Braich-yr-oen
Copper mine
(dis.)

Hafod-y-llan uchaf

Clogwyn brith

Loading bank

Afon Glaslyn

to
Capel
Curig

to
Beddgelert

A.498

L.C.

P

P?
P?

P

P

Old tramway

Old tramway

F.P.
610520

620510

WEST SNOWDON SLATE Co.
Bwlch Cwmllan. (dis. by 1913)

Res.

to Rhyd ddu.

600520

South Snowdon Slate Works.
c. 1919.

½ mile

L¹ 10418.

Croesor valley looking down from the summit of Rhosydd Incline towards Portmadoc in 1934: it leads to a further incline above Blaen-y-cwm Power Station. At the foot of Rhosydd Incline another leads off left to Croesor quarries. On the lefthand slopes lie the Pant-mawr quarries' inclines.

R.W. Kidner

The farthest reach eastwards of the Croesor Tramway, New Rhosydd Quarry, seen from the rubbish tip (looking north) above the first incline there. The main adit level is immediately above the deep shadow, in the centre. October 1973. *J.I.C. Boyd*

New Rhosydd main adit level in 1934. The train is headed by a 'Megryn': the endless cable lies between the rails - it reversed around a wheel behind the photographer. *R.W. Kidner*

Rhosydd Tramway looking westwards towards the head of the Rhosydd Incline. *C.C. Green*

Pant-mawr Tramway on right, leading to the drumhouse with the incline falling to Croesor Tramway. In the valley bottom (*left*) lies Blaen-y-cwm Power Station, with the first incline of the Rhosydd Tramway rising beyond it, October 1968. *J.I.C. Boyd*

New Rhosydd Incline (foreground) c.1885, with a 'run' of that quarry's wooden-framed slate wagons at the foot. Note the slab platform in the centre foreground: Croesor Quarry Incline with river bridge at its foot, rises in the background, with rubbish tips on the skyline.   Collection J.I.C. Boyd

Blaen-y-cwm Power Station and the first of the two final inclines. A Ramblers' Association party rests beside Festiniog Railway wagons in June 1941. *W.H. Tate*

Trackwork with movable blades and diamonds at Blaen-y-cwm seen here in 1940 with a Croesor Quarry wagon. *J.F. Bolton*

Looking west from Blaen-y-cwm towards Croesor village. Note the slate fence, low embankment etc., typical valley scenery for much of the course. *J.I.C. Boyd*

Pant-mawr cable drum and incline leading to the Croesor line below. Photographed in 1934.

R.W. Kidner

A typical June day in 1941, showing the main valley towards Blaen-y-cwm. The Tramway was still in occasional use. *W.H. Tate*

Discarded wagons at Bryn-hyfryd, looking east with Cnicht rising left, August 1943.
J.I.C. Boyd

Tramway bridge at Croesor village: slab construction throughout, October 1968.

J.I.C. Boyd

Looking west at Bryn-hyfryd: Tramway in agricultural usage. *S.H.P. Higgins*

Tre-saethan embankment seen in August 1943, leading westwards from the village district to the head of Upper Parc Incline. (This was the principal engineering feature, other than inclines.) *J.I.C. Boyd*

The Drumhouse at the head of Upper Parc Incline in October 1948. *J.I.C. Boyd*

The level crossing over the road near Llanfrothen, viewed October 1947, towards the foot of the Parc Inclines. [From Croesor Junction to this point, the original track had been replaced with heavy flat-bottomed rails and was occasionally traversed by one of the Festiniog Railway's rail tractors to collect the odd loaded slate wagon.] *J.I.C. Boyd*

Croesor Quarry Mill showing overhead wiring and slab trolleys in 1938. *R.W. Kidner*

Long slabs about to enter the Mill, Croesor Quarry. *(c.1912 Sales Catalogue)*

Electric locomotive, (possibly the first electric mine locomotive) designed and built by Moses Kellow for his hydro-electric installation of 1900. *(c.1912 Sales Catalogue)*

Croesor Quarry in October 1951 when in use as an underground store for explosives. A rail tractor shelter, with three-way turnout fitted with selection lever and catch handle are visible.
J.I.C. Boyd

Another 1912 Catalogue illustration showing the trans-shipment wharf at Beddgelert Siding, Portmadoc. Apart from the leading wagon, the remainder are from Croesor Tramway-served quarries.

Baldwin rail tractor used, *inter alia*, for Croesor Tramway traffic, in the Festiniog Railway's Boston Lodge Works. It has been given F.R. number 11. *Real Photos Co. Ltd.*

Parc & Croesor Quarry wagons with remains of stencilled characters on their sides, standing on the main tramway at Bryn-hyfryd in 1946. *J.I.C. Boyd*

Obtaining details from a two-plank open wagon at Bryn-hyfryd in October 1968, after the scrap men had removed most of the ironwork. *J.I.C. Boyd*

Parc & Croesor braked wagon photographed in 1946 at Tre-saethan. *J.I.C. Boyd*

Butt-joint in the track between T rail and cast switch section, seen here at Blaen-y-cwm in October 1968.
J.I.C. Boyd

A typical butt-joint chair, seen from the inside at Pont Sion-goch; October 1968.
J.I.C. Boyd

A cast-iron 'frog' with raised wingrails, at the junction at the foot of Pant-mawr Incline in October 1968. *J.I.C. Boyd*

Varieties of chairs found in locations at Lower Parc Incline. (*Left to right*) carrying, joint and Festiniog Railway (*horse period*) all photographed in March 1957. *J.I.C. Boyd*

that time. The track was still the original material 'and most of the sleepers are rotten'. The rails and chairs were of cast-iron, some keys being of wood and others of iron strip. Wider chairs were used at joints and the chairs held to sleepers by iron pins. Pointwork was very primitive, of 'quarry type' (sic) and without switch blades. The bridge over the Glaslyn at Pont Croesor, previously mentioned, was of eight 25 ft wooden girder spans carried on slate rubble piers. By 1921 it was very faulty. All traffic was horse-drawn.

CROESOR & PORT MADOC RAILWAY

With the likelihood of the Aberystwyth & Welsh Coast Railway extending northwards from Barmouth to Pwllheli along the coast, plans were drawn up by C.E. Spooner and an estimate prepared for the conversion of the Tramway proper into a public railway with powers to extend at the western end to the seaside village of Borth-y-gest and northwards to Beddgelert.

This stated:

CROESOR & PORTMADOC RAILWAY BILL

The objects of this Bill are to incorporate "The Croesor & Portmadoc Railway Company" with a capital of £25,000 in £10 shares and £8,330 by loan, to empower them:

To maintain the Railway, length 4 miles 3 chains on a two-feet gauge, from Carrig Hylldrem, near Llanfrothen, to Portmadoc, constructed by Hugh Beaver Roberts Esquire, and intended to be vested in the Company by this Bill;

To take lands for the improvement of that Railway, and to adapt it for passenger as well as other traffic;

To make an extension Railway, length 1 mile 19 chains, also on the two-feet gauge, from the termination of the former line at Portmadoc, to Borth-y-gest;

To increase the gauge of the Railways from two feet to three feet, with the approval of the Board of Trade.

(Observations). It appears to be a question whether Parliament has hitherto sanctioned the conveyance of passengers on Railways on a gauge so narrow as those which are the subject of this Bill, viz., two feet, without imposing some restrictions as to the speed at which passengers can be conveyed.

In the case of the Corris Railway, near Machynlleth, authorised in 1858 to be constructed on a gauge of 2 feet 3 inches, the use of steam power and the conveyance of passengers were prohibited. An Act of 1864 removed the former prohibition, but restricted the rate of speed to ten miles an hour, and it continued the prohibition against the conveyance of passengers. The last mentioned restrictions, however, it is proposed to remove by the ABERYSTWYTH & WELSH COAST RAILWAY (No. 1) Bill of this Session . . .

Board of Trade   James Booth
March 1865.

The suggestion of increasing the gauge to 3 feet may have two-fold implications: (1) it might have been thought easier to find agreement in the matter of passenger traffic and (2) physical connection with the

Gorseddau Tramway might be established in Portmadoc. By Act of 5th July,1865 (28/9 Vic. Cap. 295) authority for a Statutory Company was obtained to 'maintain the existing tramway . . . and extend to Borth-y-gest with the title Croesor & Port Madoc Railway', thus regularising the existence of the Croesor Tramway as well as permitting its conversion to a public railway and of standard gauge if necessary. The cost was estimated at £14,960. Perhaps the most significant pointers were that H.B. Roberts and H.U. McKie were on the Board (the former as Chairman), C.E. Spooner was its Engineer, and locomotive haulage was authorised – in the same year when the Festiniog Railway had been operating locomotive-hauled passenger trains since 6th January – and in fact, agreements with that Company and the Cambrian Railways were arranged. (Spooner was by now virtually *the* consulting engineer for narrow gauge projects. In 1867 he was invited to advise the Belfast & Co. Down Railway on conversion to narrow gauge.) The southward extension to Borth-y-gest was to be completed within four years and of mixed gauge to be shared with the Coast Railway, (a point described as being between Trwyn-penclogwyn and Borth, by Vignes) but was never carried out in any form. As for the Croesor & Port Madoc Railway, it was destined to remain simply a new title and the existing Tramway continued its duties without alteration or extension. In the Act, the official length of the Croesor line is mistakenly given as 1¼ miles. Roberts is quoted as Chairman and his brother, Arthur, of The Towers, Mold, was also a Director, as he was also of the Mold & Denbigh Junction Railway (authorised 1861). Of the five directors, at that time only Arthur T. Roberts had other railway interests; the Company's Registered Office was in Caernarvon and its official underestimated mileage was repeatedly quoted. A capital of £63,980 was authorised and £25,000 in Ordinary Shares and £8,330 in Loans issued.

To a Festiniog Railway board meeting held in Bray in late 1869, Hugh B. Roberts had sent in a proposal that the Festiniog operate the C. & P.M.R. The board meeting was unanimous in showing disinterest in owning, operating or amalgamating with that concern 'until its track was put in order'. (Fifty years would elapse before anything of that nature would take place.)

Under a Statutory Mortgage No. 1, sealed on 23rd June, 1870 in the presence of Hugh Beaver Roberts, the Croesor & Port Madoc Railway Company mortgaged its undertaking to Mary Elizabeth Littledale to secure repayment of £8,000 at 5½%.

A sequel to this came ten years later when on 15th September, 1880 Evan Morris of The Priory, Wrexham, wrote to Edward Breese pointing out that the purchase of the above mortgage would give control of the Croesor & Port Madoc Railway to the purchaser, the borrowing powers of the Company being limited to £8,330.

It was February 1879 before any attempt was made to broaden the horizons of the Croesor & Port Madoc. In that month a circular from

Robinson Bros., Mansion House Chambers, 11 Queen Victoria Street, London, E.C. invited investment in the Company. This was headed 'A remunerative Home Investment may be accrued in the CROESOR & PORT MADOC (TRAM) RAILWAY COMPANY' and offered a premium, £25,000 in £10 shares carrying '5 per cent *guaranteed* £10 fully-paid-up Shares in the Company . . .' The offer continued:

An Act of Parliament was obtained a few years since by five gentlemen, and the necessary land having been purchased, the CROESOR AND PORT MADOC (Narrow gauge) TRAM RAILWAY was completed, and opened for Mineral Traffic only. The entire Share Capital of the Company has hitherto been held by the above-mentioned five persons only, who have not, up to the present time, parted with a single Share. Although the Act of Parliament authorised the use of Steam and the conveyance of Passengers, the Proprietors have hitherto worked the line by Horse Power, and been content with the returns of the carriage of the Mineral traffic alone.

The Tramways Corporation, Limited, having deposited plans in Parliament this Session, for powers to construct an important extension to Beddgelert, as a branch of this line, the CROESOR AND PORT MADOC COMPANY, have entered into a Three Years' Working Agreement with the Corporation to prove Passenger Cars, to develop and work the existing Line by *Steam* as part of their extended system, paying for the use of the line a rent equal to a Dividend of five per cent. on the existing Share Capital.

At the end of three years the Shareholders will have the privilege of both lines being amalgamated on an equal basis.

We are of the opinion, based upon the returns of the adjoining Festiniog Line, referred to below, that at the termination of the stipulated period, the Passenger traffic will have developed on both new and old Lines to such an extent that future Dividends will be much in excess of the present *guaranteed 5 per cent* and . . . likely to increase . . . The proposed Extension will pass along the most frequented route, and through the most attractive and romantic scenery of North Wales, including the Pass of Aberglaslyn to the celebrated village of Beddgelert, at the foot of Snowdon. When this Extension is completed, arrangements will be made with the Cambrian Railway for the joint use of their Station at Port Madoc . . . One of the principal advantages of the present line is that it possesses the monopoly of running through the Town to the Harbour and Wharves of Port Madoc, and having a junction with the Cambrian Railway* conveys at present all goods to and from the Harbour for that Railway'.

There follows a glowing account of the prospects together with references to Festiniog dividends of 12½% . . . 'must fill many a shareholder's heart with envy' etc. etc. and the brokers strongly recommend the shares compared with Bank, Gas Shares and Foreign Stocks of the times!

PORTMADOC, CROESOR & BEDDGELERT TRAM RAILWAY

No work having been undertaken under Croesor & Port Madoc Railway auspices, another Company obtained an Act which absorbed it and its powers. This was the cumbersomely-titled Portmadoc, Croesor and Beddgelert Tram Railway Company (Act of 21st July, 1879 42/3 Vic. Cap. 171) to which Lefevre & Co.† (and later Spooner & Co.) were

---

*The Beddgelert Siding.

†sometimes Lefeuvre.

the Engineers, and Hugh Beaver Roberts at first a director, was later Secretary. Once again, no new work or any outward change revealed the existence of another new Company, and the tramway continued to exist in its original form. The unbuilt line to Beddgelert was officially referred to from this time onwards as the 'Portmadoc, Croesor & Beddgelert Tram Railway Company's Beddgelert Extension', an impressive title indeed even had anything contributed toward it. The immediate goal was Beddgelert, but the ultimate target was the North Wales Narrow Gauge Railways terminus at Rhyd-Ddu.

The Portmadoc Company was given 5 years to complete its works together with the branch to Beddgelert. Under the Act, the capital of the Extension was to be kept separately; it was £23,000 in Ordinary Shares and £7,650 in Loans or Debenture Stock. Working arrangements with the Cambrian, Gorseddau and Festiniog lines were outlined. The Company was based on London with Registered Office at 99 Gresham Street, and only James Fraser (a director of the Corris Railway) had any other railway directorships.

The link between the Portmadoc Co. and the proposal of early 1879 to work the new line with its intended Beddgelert Extension by the Tramways Corporation Ltd., is not completely clear. It would seem that the five original proprietors of the Croesor & Port Madoc were able to dispose of their interests and of the five, only Hugh Beaver Roberts continued in office, not as a director, but (as just mentioned) succeeded E.F. Tremayne as Secretary. Working by the Tramways Corporation, with subsequent amalgamation, did not materialise either, though the link with tramway interest was retained through the Chairman of the new undertaking; he also held the Chair of the Preston Tramways Company. Four of his other five directors' interests seem to have been purely speculative; certainly they had no known railway influence.

The new Company issued a prospectus in October 1879, three months after formation, and invited purchasers of 1st Preference Shares at £10 each paying 6% which was of course, the Extension Capital. The accompanying propaganda ran very close to that used by the earlier Company in the previous February, and was clearly copied from it. Junctions with the Festiniog and Gorseddau Railways were mentioned additionally, and having repeated the statement about monopoly of traffic to the Harbour and *proposal* to arrange with the Cambrian for joint use of their station, reference is made to the rapid development of Llanberis since the L.N.W.R. opened a branch thereto. The extract from 'THE TIMES' giving the same figures concerning the Festiniog is quoted,and telling how it was practicable '*to make a large profit on a moderate outlay*'.

The main and additional points of interest were:

1. The Beddgelert Line was to be built by a Contractor who had consented to allow interest at a rate of 5% per annum during the period fixed for construction upon all payments made in respect of

shares (perhaps an arrangement based on the experience gained in the lamentable affairs of the neighbouring North Wales Narrow Gauge line only a few years previously).

2. W.H. Lefevre's Estimate & Report of the same month maintained that the line 'connected with the entire railway system of England' (which was partly true but involved break of gauge of course). There were 14 small slate quarries excluded from his estimate of gross income which totalled £8,325 per year and would show a profit of £4,612 10s. 0d.

3. The current rate of cartage was 8s. to 10s. per ton to Portmadoc.

4. The opening of the L.N.W.R. extension into Blaenau 'had opened up a large tourist and passenger traffic to Portmadoc wanting to be conveyed to Beddgelert'. (One envisages the queue at the non-existent booking office).*

As just mentioned, the promotion failed to attract public imagination or money in sufficient amount to justify a start on the Beddgelert Extension, and the ghastly lesson of the nearby North Wales Narrow Gauge Company was sufficient in itself to daunt the promoters – it lost £1,893 in 1879.

A further statutory mortgage of the undertaking as it now existed was given to James Cholmeley Russell on 19th June, 1882 in the amount of £330 at 5%; Russell had become Receiver to the North Wales Narrow Gauge Railways Company on 13th December, 1878.† The same year Mary Elizabeth Littledale, whose principal and overdue interest on her own £8,000 mortgage was to amount to upwards of £10,000 by 1901, put the Portmadoc Company into Receivership for the remainder of its days. In consequence of this, the proposed transformation of the Tramway was postponed for many years to come. No new work was begun under the P.C.&B.T.R. Act.

The astonishing feature of these successive failures was the drive behind them and one wonders why the apparently inconsequential Croesor Tramway should be considered to be of such strategic and bargaining importance. As has been commonly instanced throughout history, the vision of the Croesor forming part of a railway to link north and south Caernarvonshire was the dream of one man, Charles Easton Spooner, then Engineer to the Festiniog Railway. It was he who created the bullets which, with his strong local connection, he hoped others would help him to fire. In this he was only partially successful, and when in later years the vision became reality it was too late, and the reality was a failure.

---

*Did this contention lie behind the plan for a deviation at the statutory position of the P.C.&B.T. Rly. terminus at Beddgelert which would take it almost into the village centre, on the east bank of the Glaslyn (dated 12th July, 1882)?

†In view of the 1880 correspondence between Breese and Morris referred to above, and Russell's position on the N.W.N.G.R. Co., it might well be his mortgage on the Croesor & Port Madoc Railway was an attempt to purchase control of that line 'via the Back Door'. Did anyone try to buy out M.E. Littledale?(!)

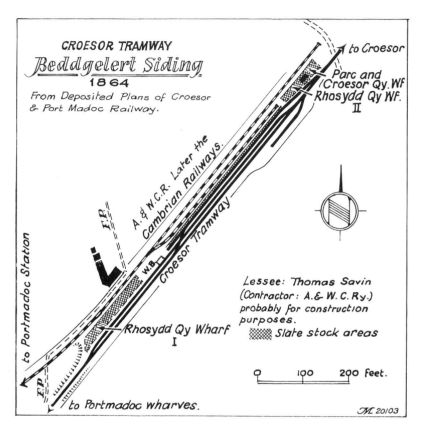

CROESOR TRAMWAY
Beddgelert Siding
1864
From Deposited Plans of Croesor
& Port Madoc Railway.

to Croesor

Parc and
Croesor Qy. Wf
Rhosydd Qy Wf.
II

A. & W.C.R. Later the
Cambrian Railways.

F.P.

Croesor Tramway

W.B.

to Portmadoc Station

F.P.

Rhosydd Qy Wharf
I

to Portmadoc wharves.

Lessee: Thomas Savin
(Contractor: A.& W.C. Ry.)
probably for construction
purposes.
▨ Slate stock areas

0   100   200 feet.

JM. 20103

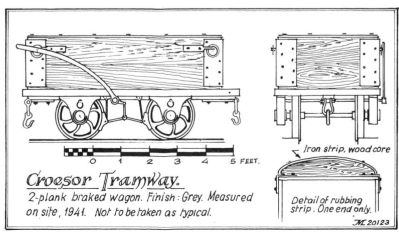

Iron strip, wood core

0   1   2   3   4   5 FEET.

Croesor Tramway.
2-plank braked wagon. Finish: Grey. Measured
on site, 1941. Not to be taken as typical.

Detail of rubbing
strip. One end only.

JM. 20123

By the early 1870s the standard gauge railway map of Caernarvon-shire was becoming complete. Spooner had recently enjoyed two triumphs on the Festiniog Railway; firstly passenger trains had been introduced with statutory backing, and secondly, steam traction had proved itself. The critics had been made to eat their words and Spooner, riding the crest of the wave, was now looking beyond the purely local horizons of the Festiniog Railway. He was concerned about the ambitions of the Cambrian, Great Western and London & North Western Railways in the neighbourhood. The Cambrian was looking north and east towards Beddgelert (their proposed route would parallel the Croesor for the first part of its way). The L.N.W.R. was already in Bettws-y-Coed and planned to extend to Blaenau Festiniog by means of a narrow gauge extension authorised by Act of 18th July, 1872 as the 'Bettws and Festiniog Railway', 12 miles long of 2 ft gauge. Under the L.N.W.R. Act of 28th July, 1873 that Company was given powers to use portions of the Festiniog Railway at Blaenau Festiniog and to enter into arrangements with the Festiniog Company. The L.N.W.R. intended in fact, to debouch from a tunnel at Blaenau, form three running lines and make an end-on junction with running powers on the Festiniog's Dinas branch. Apart from this real threat to Festiniog monopoly, powers had been obtained for a Merionethshire Railway at the instance of quarry owners who wanted an outlet from the Blaenau district independent of the Festiniog Railway; this railway would have been partly in mixed gauge and would tap the Festiniog where it hurt. The ground which had for so long been the bastion of the Festiniog was about to be infiltrated. Spooner had cause for concern.

In reply to the clouds on his horizon, his answer was firstly to baulk the Cambrian's bid to reach Beddgelert and Caernarvon by a branch line from Portmadoc and secondly, to divert the attentions of Euston by containing the L.N.W.R. in the Conway valley. Already that Company had taken over the Carnarvonshire Railway (to which Spooner had been Engineer) and being now linked with the Cambrian at Afon Wen was to obtain running powers into Portmadoc itself. To achieve a diversion, Spooner's plan was to project a new narrow gauge line northwards from Portmadoc via Beddgelert and thence to Caernarvon, so linking the important slate ports of Caernarvon and Portmadoc whilst at the same time giving interchange for all types of traffic with the standard gauge at these ports. Such a line would deter the London and Oswestry-based companies from extending their empire into territory which, while of vital interest to the Festiniog Railway, interested Spooner more person-ally in respect of his private affairs and his connections with the local slate industry. His first personal thrust came through plans for the North Wales Narrow Gauge Railways project of 1872. Not all of this ambitious scheme came to be but ultimately a narrow gauge line was built from Dinas on the L.N.W.R.'s Caernarvon–Afon Wen line (the former Carnarvonshire Railway) towards Rhyd-Ddu or South Snowdon. It opened to Quellyn Lake for all traffic by 15th August,

1877 and was a highly unsatisfactory compromise, as it reached neither Caernarvon in the north nor Beddgelert in the south, but it did have the merit of tapping most of the more important slate quarries in the neighbourhood, (such as they were).

At first, this new line had opened to Quellyn on a goods-only basis, and within three days of this event, Spooner produced a master plan in which he hoped to interest the Board of the Festiniog Railway. He entitled this:

A Project to secure Railway connections with the Festiniog Railway at Portmadoc by a connecting link with the North Wales Narrow Gauge Railways at Rhyd-Ddu on the 2 feet gauge, the latter forming a junction with the Carnarvonshire Railway near Caernarvon. Also a line to Snowdon.

In the ensuing statement he wrote:

It is daily becoming more apparent that what with the threatened Lines of the Railways between Bala and Festiniog and the Merionethshire Railway in junction with the Cambrian Railway near Minford; and also the L.N.W.R. Line in course of construction from Bettws-y-Coed to the Blaenau Quarries at Duffws, that a considerable quantity of Festiniog traffic will be absorbed, not only in respect of slates and goods, but the passenger traffic will to some extent be reduced . . .

(here he draws attention to the compensating traffic which he hoped the L.N.W.R. would produce for the Festiniog Railway)

. . . It is the passenger traffic which is the most remunerative to your Company and obvious that steps should be taken to increase the traffic . . . The mode for increasing and maintaining the traffic of your own line is in your own hands to mature. What is now required is to grasp the opportunity and give such encouragement as will allow others to construct the proposed connections. The following table is an approximate maximum estimate for the construction of the lines of railways shown in red on the sketch plan;

(a) 4 miles of Croesor Railway 2 feet gauge to be purchased (3½ miles to Junction) £13,000
     Relaying of Croesor Railway 8,000
(b) 9½ miles from Junction of Croesor Railway near Ynsfor to Rhyd-Ddu via Beddgelert 45,000
(c) 4 miles of line from Rhyd-Ddu (at Junction with the North Wales Narrow Gauge Line) to Snowdon on the Rigi system 28,000

£94,000

After setting out this idea in full, Spooner adds expenses for surveys, Parliamentary expenses, engines and stock with an estimated capitalisation of £104,000 in Ordinary Shares and £34,666 in Debentures. The estimates of traffic for systems (a) and (b) involve 120,600 passengers per annum at 1¼d. per mile. Especially revealing is that the project envisages the construction of the new link by persons unconnected with the Festiniog Board, and that the Estimate furnishes sources of traffic then obtaining (about 1875).

Croesor Slate Company	1000 tons of slate per annum
Rhosydd Slate Company	5000 tons of slate per annum
*Hafod-y-Llan Slate Company	16,000 tons of slate per annum
Pant-Mawr & Geraint Qy.	720 tons of slate per annum
Goods, Coal, Lime, Timber	4000 tons per annum

On the rack line to Snowdon summit, estimates were based on the experience of the actual Rigi line in Switzerland, opened in 1871. 55,000 passengers per annum were *anticipated*, the final net revenue for the whole system being calculated at £9,958. The House of Commons Sessional Papers of 1872 (3) p. 11, had already published a projected 'Snowdon Railway' for making a line from Llanberis to the summit of Snowdon with a capital of £30,000, loans of £7,500 and of intended length 4 miles 16 chains.

Spooner points out that working expenses would have to be lower than those on the Festiniog Railway as traffic would be mainly passenger and therefore costly to work. Only a small stock of mineral wagons would be required. His intention was that a separate company would build these railways and provide the rolling stock. The Festiniog Railway would operate the line and supply maintenance at (say) 60% of gross receipts (. . . 'or some other mode that would succeed in securing parties to raise the necessary capital to construct the lines proposed'). His estimate of actual profit to the Festiniog Railway was £1,992 per annum and that much traffic would originate from around Caernarvon and Beddgelert to pass south over the Festiniog, and then forward again by the L.N.W.R. In this respect, Spooner anticipated the circular tour which was to become such a feature of North Wales resorts' holidays with a zenith between the World Wars. Alas, when his dream became a reality, holiday makers found that the round trip from Llandudno and back via Blaenau Festiniog, Portmadoc and Dinas Junction entailed longer than they were prepared to give to a day on holiday, and the section between Portmadoc and Dinas became notorious for slow running, bad timekeeping and missed connections at Dinas for the North Wales coast.

A feature of Spooner's tourist proposals was that traffic would pass from and to the then narrow gauge Festiniog & Blaenau Railway, and he ends by adding

. . . hence making a circular tour either way through the most attractive and beautiful parts of North Wales. The public are precluded from this district for the want of it.

(i.e. the new railway link). He felt that 40,000 extra passengers per year would travel over the Festiniog and that new L.N.W.R. and G.W.R. lines now building would bring in

swarms of tourists who would want to avail themselves of the ascent by rail at so much less cost, time and fatigue.

*Not on the Croesor tramway network; slate loaded on to Croesor wagons at Pont Croesor siding.

(Here he refers to the Snowdon rack line.) He reminded his directors that half Festiniog profits came from passenger sources and urged them to consider the advantages should the lines be built.

I beg therefore to submit for your serious consideration the above scheme to improve your property. The mode I propose is to take such steps as to ensure the lines (a), (b) and (c) being constructed (not at your own cost but at the expense of a separate and independent company, such as would ensure to your company a continuously increasing revenue in perpetuity) which in the present critical and uncertain position of your company is so desirable and such as would give you a foothold of a new and good district by the same gauge line as your own.
(30th May, 1877).

The Spooner project has been referred to in some detail because it forms the basis for most of the narrow gauge development in South Caernarvonshire. Although possibly appropriate at the time, it became less so as time went by. It is now impossible to trace why the Festiniog directors did not rise to Spooner's suggestions – possibly relations between Board and Engineer were simply commercial and the Board had no wish to feather the nest of an employee who clearly had ambitious intentions further afield and had already demonstrated them. There was also the perennial question as to the future of the slate industry seen against the economic background, the growth of labour unrest among quarrymen and a lack of local enterprise. Suitable sources of capital were likely to have been deeply committed as it was, and the recent failure of the N.W.N.G. Railways' ambitious plans conceived by Spooner, could not have encouraged the Festiniog Board to further unproven enterprises where others had failed.

Throughout these negotiations, C.E. Spooner wore two hats, so to speak. He was of Spooner & Co., Engineers to the Portmadoc, Croesor & Beddgelert Tram Railway Company, and also Secretary to the Festiniog. Perhaps because of this, H.B. Roberts took over negotiations. These lapsed largely into an informal exchange of letters between Festiniog Directors (in Drogheda, Somerset and London) of which this one to Spooner is typical:

65 George Street,
Portman Square, W.

14th November, 1882

My dear Sir,

I have been endeavouring, as you are aware, for some time past, to bring about the construction of the proposed extension of the Croesor & Portmadoc Railway to Beddgelert. It has always appeared to me that the line to Beddgelert ought to belong & that it eventually must belong to your company. Possession of it would give them undivided power over the Port, and the key to all future extensions of the narrow gauge system in the only direction in which they are possible. Your company could work the line at a very small cost . . . I propose we get the extension made and the existing line put into proper order as a passenger line . . . and when completed . . . certified by Board of Trade . . . it shall be transferred to your company, they paying for it by shares in their company to the amount of £56,000 carrying a perpetual preference dividend of 4% . . . Actual cost of the line to your company . . . would be only £44,800 . . .

Kindly submit my proposition to your Directors . . .

Yours very truly,

H. Beaver Roberts

C.E. Spooner, Esqr.

The general feeling shared by the F.R. directors was that to take over the Croesor line was a highly speculative undertaking – they required further evidence from Hugh Beaver Roberts; typical was the rejoinder from J.G. Livingston 'running a great risk on our part to undertake working his Line unless we had a proviso that the receipts would amount to at least £2,750'.

The F.R. Board replied through Spooner to such attempts by Roberts to have the Beddgelert line built. The five years permitted for the work were nearing an end when Roberts proffered a 'Heads of Agreement' scheme to the F.R. Board on 15th February, 1883. In short, this proposed that the Festiniog should manage, equip and maintain the P.C. & B.T.R. Co. in perpetuity, the receipts to be divided equally between them and the F.R. The Portmadoc Co. was to build its line to Pont Aberglaslyn and bring the Croesor section up to passenger standards. As a second phase, it would extend to Beddgelert and in these two stages, the F.R. would take over responsibility. Two F.R. locomotives and three passenger trains, forty slate wagons etc. were estimated as required for this work.

This final carrot did not attract the donkey in the least. The F.R. Board was not interested; it had problems enough of its own. Firstly, they wanted to see the Portmadoc Co.'s line finished before they would discuss things. They called the scheme premature, the reward not nearly adequate enough, and no detail could be considered until construction was complete. To the P.C. & B.T.R. Co.'s suggestion that a physical junction between the two railways in Portmadoc be made at the joint expense of the two Companies, the F.R. Board replied they would not incur any further expense on their own line.

Although this outright refusal to be involved brought the matter to a close, Spooner made one more personal effort to interest his Board and show them the advantages of a tactical line to Beddgelert, not only to ward off standard gauge competitors but also to link eventually, with the N.W.N.G. line at Rhyd-Ddu. The F.R. were not drawn by this either, and clearly no support was to come from elsewhere. The almost identical Welsh Highland Railway scheme of 1922 was therefore nothing more than another re-hash of the P.C. & B.T.R. Company's plans, and perhaps on 1st June, 1923 the day of Welsh Highland opening, Spooner could be allowed a last laugh . . . from his grave in Beddgelert . . . no less!

So it was that whilst for the time being at least, the Croesor line did not materialise into the vital piece for completing the jig-saw-puzzle

map of the county, it continued to feature in fresh proposals. The first
was the Beddgelert & Rhyd-Ddu Railway of 1889 with Engineers
Charles Minns and John S. Lawrence. This would link the south end of
the N.W.N.G.R. with the Croesor line over much of the 'Tram' route
of 1879 save that it used the west side of the Glaslyn valley. Plans were
deposited but nothing further done. The next was a Portmadoc,
Beddgelert & Rhyd-Ddu Railway application of 1892: under the Light
Railways Act of 1896 another scheme dated 1898 of the same title
came – Roberts & Sons of Portmadoc were the Engineers to both.
Powers were sought to work over the Croesor Tramway between Parc
and Portmadoc and for this section of the Tramway to be embodied in
the new undertaking. A new branch was to be built from a point north
of the Croesor/Cambrian level crossing to pass along the Cambrian's
interchange siding and terminate on the site of the former Gorseddau
Junction & Portmadoc/Cambrian crosing just east of Portmadoc
station. An alternative title for this scheme was to be the Portmadoc,
Beddgelert & Snowdon Light Railway.

Proposals for building standard gauge lines, some involving the use
of the Croesor Tramway are now summarised below:

*Carnarvon, Beddgelert & Port Madoc; Carnarvon, Pen-y-groes & Pwllheli
Direct Railways.* (Session 1864–5). Engineers: H.J. and J.W.
Gridlestone. A route over much of the later Welsh Highland Railway.
Also a coastal line over the Lleyn to Pwllheli with a branch to tap the
Tal-y-sarn Quarries in the Nantlle Area. This scheme did not directly
involve the Croesor line.

Beddgelert Railway. (Acts 28 & 29 Vic. Cap. 322 of 5th July, 1865 and
29 & 30 Vic. Cap. 183 of 16th July, 1866.) This was a standard gauge
railway scheme to link the Cambrian Railways at Portmadoc and its
harbour with Beddgelert under the Act of 1865, and to extend from
Beddgelert as far as Llyn Gwynant (and deviate) under the Act of 1866
(The Beddgelert Railway – Extension & Deviation – Act. 1866). Engineers: Ordish & Le Feuvre, London. The route would be along the
west bank of the Glaslyn. It was a tactical scheme backed by Thomas
Savin, the Coast Line contractor, planned at the same period to amalgamate the Cambrian Railways with other railways. The only permanent work done appears to have been what later became The Beddgelert
Siding which the Cambrian appropriated for storing stock: all work
stopped in April 1866. The Company was the subject of an attempt to
have a Receiver appointed in order to have some of the Engineers'
unpaid bills met. 'THE WEEKLY REPORTER'of 25th February, 1871
confirms the Cambrian had been using the only portion constructed
without arrangement or payment. Ordish & Le Feuvre maintained that
The Beddgelert Railway was actually operative and based their claim on
such. There were Cambrian directors among the promoters and probably the object was to serve slate and other mineral deposits around
Hafod-y-Llan and Beddgelert, and convey them to Portmadoc Harbour
. . . all by standard gauge. Other Cambrian schemes of the time show

this to be but a part of a tactical exercise to create monopoly before narrow gauge interests pre-empted it. Length: 8¾ m. [12,13,14]
Portmadoc & Beddgelert Railway. (Session 1881–2). Engineers: Ordish & Le Feuvre. A line from a junction with the Cambrian Railways at Portmadoc using the Croesor route to Pont Croesor and then an adjacent but parallel course, eventually reaching Beddgelert, partially on the planned course of 1866 – see above. Clearly a tactical scheme to draw local narrow gauge interests – a ruse in which it succeeded.

[The Land Register accompanying the above shows the lessee of the Weighing Machine and Platform of the Beddgelert Siding, Portmadoc, to be Thomas Savin, the lessee of the Aberystwyth & Welsh Coast Railway. The land surrounding the Siding was part of the Tremadoc Estate (Francis William Alexander Roche).]

Portmadoc, Beddgelert & Snowdon Light Railway. (1897). An alternative title for the scheme described previously, but revived under the Light Railways Act of 1896. Formal application never made.

It may now be seen that this simple tramway of limited intentions formed the subject of various strategic schemes for over 35 years; some of these reached an advanced stage but none altered the physical appearance of the line. It remained a horse-worked tramway straddling the dykes of the Traeth Mawr and threading the upper valley with an isolated pair of rails which looked so improbable in such an expanse of mountainscape. Ultimately it became a part of yet another scheme to link Rhyd-Ddu, the terminal of the North Wales Narrow Gauge Railways, and Portmadoc.

On 21st July, 1883 'THE MINING JOURNAL' wrote:

> Some 18 or 19 years ago in the palmy days of slate quarrying and the opening of the Cambrian Railways powers were obtained to construct a narrow gauge line from the port [Portmadoc] to Beddgelert and about six miles of it was actually made and the metals laid but it was never carried out. At present 3½ miles of this line to the branch which goes off to the Croesor quarries is in working condition but the remainder has been dismantled and the bill lapsed . . . But the line having been strangled in its infancy it would not be wise now to resuscitate it in that form but rather to widen the embankment and lay the rails to the Ordinary gauge in connection with the Cambrian and Great Western Railway.

Which all goes to show how confused an outsider could become!!

On 17th August, 1901 the Portmadoc, Beddgelert & South Snowdon Railway was incorporated (1 Edward VII Cap. 262). Under an Agreement previously reached (18th March, 1901) the Tram Railway Co. had agreed to sell its interests to that new railway conditionally upon it receiving Parliamentary authority. So on 30th June that year, the Croesor under the mantle of the Portmadoc, Croesor & Beddgelert Tram Railway Company Limited, sold its powers to the new owners for £10,000. On the assumption of the Russell mortgage, the original investors lost all their capital.

The last entry for the Company appears in the Stock Exchange Year Book for 1901 when John Edward Jones, 16 Bank Place, Portmadoc, was Receiver. The position summarised therein was for an authorised railway of 9 miles of which five had been built. £20,000 of the authorised £48,000 in £10 Shares had been raised; Loans of £330 @ 5% and £8,000 @ 5½% had been made against the power to raise £15,980. All the capital was held by Hugh Beaver Roberts. No dividends had been paid for the past year. The two mortgagees were currently J.C. Russell and Henry William Assheton Littledale.

On the ground, so to speak, the staff employed at the end of the Tram Railway Company's life included 2 clerks, 3 horse drivers, 2 men on the track and 2 'miscellaneous'. These made a total of 9 men, 'no boys' (sic). From previous records this suggests that one horse and driver was employed between Portmadoc and the Harbour, and the other up to Parc, and beyond when necessary.

From the 1901 move, it might have seemed that the Croesor line was on the brink of bigger things and that at least some evidence of its new ownership would become tangible without delay. Not at all. With thirty-six years of life behind it, another two decades were to pass before the plans of its new masters came to maturity, and by then, even they had gone out of business under that title!

Having shown that the history of the line was more marked by paper work than track work, more by tactical moves in the office than outward signs along the railway, it is fitting to look as deeply as the meagre records will allow into the tramway as it was worked (almost without change of system) from 1864 to about 1920.

Firstly it must be said that its owners conceded it had a two-fold purpose and the accounts were divided accordingly. The line was divided into two operational units; between Portmadoc Wharves and the Beddgelert Siding, and between the Beddgelert Siding and the quarries to the north-east. The former was the 'Siding Traffic', the latter the 'Croesor Traffic'. The key to this system was the opening of the standard gauge and the connection to it via the exchange Beddgelert Siding, which continued to be of prime importance even after Festiniog Railway slate traffic began to enjoy its own private trans-shipment yard with the Cambrian at Minffordd, opened in 1872.* And it must be added, that even after this date, Beddgelert Siding continued to transship large tonnages of slate, possibly due to the fact that Minffordd was congested. Luckily for the Croesor, its route from Portmadoc wharves, over the Cambrian to the Siding, was a goldmine financially. Ex-Festiniog slate, carried by Festiniog trains, was taken forward from the Harbour station throat, and onto the quays. Here, it would be collected by horse and taken back over Croesor metals through the streets to the Siding. Consignments of Cambrian-borne goods were off-loaded at the Siding and taken down to be loaded into ships along the same route. This is a most unlooked-for feature.

Secondly there was the importance of the Flour Mill traffic, the

---

*An interesting side-issue being the objection of the Tremadoc Estate to the Minffordd yard scheme, due to loss of income from tonnage over F.R. and Croesor.

consignees being the Portmadoc Steam Flour Mill Company. The Mill was beside the tramway between wharves and Cambrian crossing and though the haul was short, tonnages were high and most of the flour was shipped out by sea. A much smaller but useful quantity was carried in the days of the Gorseddau line, from Clenenney Mills by that railway. Croesor income from this source was small, the journey being so short.

Before the opening of Minffordd yard, all Festiniog locomotive and other coal due for carriage up the Festiniog, was trans-shipped at Beddgelert Siding, taken to the wharves and left for the Festiniog Bottom Shunting Engine to marshal.

'Croesor Traffic' was off-loaded at Beddgelert Siding or continued to the quays. Coastbound traffic included slate and slab, but inland traffic was considerable in timber, foodstuffs, coal, manures, lime and occasionally track materials, ballast and machinery for quarries or repairing inclines.

The first wages were paid on 10th August, 1864 for a working week of nine days. The Croesor appears to have used the tonnage method of costing and though at the start the hauliers were paid a daily rate, later it was done by tonnage as was payment for the hire of wagons. This began in May 1870, when tonnage was about 350 a week.

Haulage was done by men who, as just mentioned, were paid by the tonnages hauled (e.g. 2s. 3½d. per ton for slate). They were obliged to find and feed their own horses, so relieving the tramway of providing motive power. In the halcyon days, two hauliers worked the top level, two the lower. When David Homfray (the Manager at £25 per year) made one of his regular inspections, a haulier with horse would call for him at 'The Sportsman Hotel, Portmadoc', and the cost of the horse etc. was paid over and above the usual slate contract. Homfray also audited the Croesor United accounts for £5 a year in his spare time! H.B. Roberts made similar inspections each February and August, and the carrier duly charged for these extra journeys. In the matter of wagons too, the tramway preferred to hire rather than own and left the quarry owners to provide their own. The Festiniog Railway appears to have been the most useful source for these, though clearly the demand fluctuated wildly and occasionally traffic was so low that no wagons were hired at all. In December 1889 only one Festiniog wagon was hired – for £1 6s. 8d. Latterly there was evidence of preference to hire from quarries on its own system, as both New Rhosydd and William Kellow are creditors for hire of slate wagons. Timber was carried on Festiniog bolsters, there being no one else who could provide them. Accountancy for these was somewhat lax as suddenly there appears an item in the books for 'Hire of Timber wagons – Three years' and then another for two years. When business was brisk wagons were hired from Rhosydd, Kellow and the Festiniog. The rates of carriage were long unchanged. On 21st March, 1893 the Secretary told the Board of Trade, 'Our railway . . . has only a small traffic consisting of slate and the old rates that were in force prior to the passing of the Railway and Canal Traffic Act of 1888 are still extant as we were bound by agreements existing between the slate quarry proprietors and our Company.'

Clearly the two men working on the line were kept busy. The horses' hooves cut the sleepers and mentions of renewals appear frequently in the accounts. The Glaslyn Bridge must have given constant trouble from the start and was consistently under repair; in September 1877 materials for this, including hire of horse, cost £19 18s. 1d. In a Return to the Board of Trade of 1896, the bridge was said to be subject to monthly inspection and be in 'Good Condition'. Floods regularly breached the line; the sea cut through the embankment near the Flour Mill at times, and flood water damage was done to stone and earthworks. Embankment walling tended to slip and an extra buttress on the Croesor wall cost £3. To repair a breach made by the high tide cost 14s. 8d. including hire of horse for the day at 7s. In 1880 Wagon No. 60 (probably wooden and Festiniog property) caught fire; repairs cost £1 17s. 6d. 'Timber keys' for one year (1877) cost £8 13s. 10d. and the Festiniog was paid £39 9s. for hire of wagons two years previously.

H.B. Roberts received irregular payments of varying sums of money, classified as 'dividends' but obviously based on what the kitty could bear; at first it was about £200 a year. There was one for £50 in February 1877 and amounts of £25 or £10 appear two or three times per year later on. In January 1882 he acted for the Company in opposing the Beddgelert Railway scheme, receiving £50 in fees. His last dividend was £10 in October 1881.

A fitful user of the Croesor system was the Hafod-y-Llan or South Snowdon Slate Quarry which was to be found at the end of a considerable tramway which included two inclines about one mile south of Snowdon summit. The Hafod-y-Llan (Snowdon) Slate Co. Ltd. issued a prospectus in June 1869 – see later – and had intended to be linked through the efforts of Mr. Lemon Hart with the erstwhile Beddgelert Railway, which had fallen victim to the national financial crisis of 1866. The tramway ended beside the road at Nant Gwynant and carts were used into Portmadoc from there. Between January and May 1875 and again between March and June 1881, the quarry off-loaded at the short siding by the Pont Croesor. This was done because the slate was to be carried by the Cambrian and trans-shipped at Beddgelert Siding. South Snowdon, though unconnected by rail with the Croesor Tramway, placed 1,600 tons of slate on the line in the early part of 1875, and was quoted in Spooner's Report of 1877.

An Agreement between Mrs. Susan Kitching and the Festiniog Railway for carrying slate over part of their line between the Croesor spur and their wharf opposite the Festiniog's Harbour station is dated 27th January, 1873. This quarry is so closely linked with the Croesor that it must be taken as if it were physically connected with it, and it would have been had there been the opportunity. The quarry agent was Allen Searell, a Devonian who had come to Wales to develop mining.

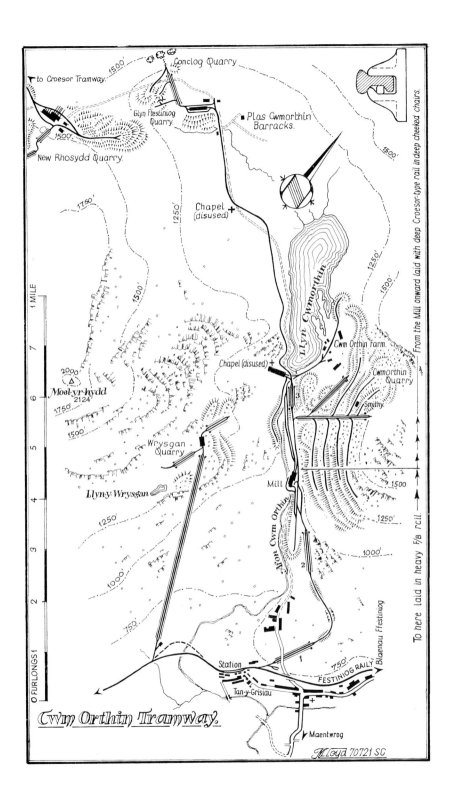

To Croesor Tramway.

1500'

Conclog Quarry

Glyn Ffestiniog Quarry

Plas Cwmorthin Barracks.

1500'

New Rhosydd Quarry.

From the Mill onward laid with deep Croesor-type rail in deep cheeked chairs.

1500'

1750'

Chapel (disused)

1250'

Llyn Cwmorthin

1250'

1 MILE

1500'

Cwm Orthin Farm.

Chapel (disused)

Cwmorthin Quarry

7

2000'

Moel-yr-hydd 2124

1750'

1500'

Smithy.

6

Wrysgan Quarry

5

Llyn-y-Wrysgan

Mill

1500'

4

1250'

Afon Cwm Orthin

To here laid in heavy F/B rail.

1000'

3

1250'

2

750'

Station

Blaenau Ffestiniog

1

750'

FESTINIOG RAILY.

Tan-y-Grisiau

0 FURLONGS 1

Maentwrog

Cwm Orthin Tramway.

J. Lloyd 70721 SC

He worked for copper at Sygun near Beddgelert* and for slate at Cwm
Orthin. He speculated at Hafod-y-Llan, successfully, and at Cefncam,
ruinously. He came to Beddgelert in 1841 and died in 1865 after which
his son failed to make headway for long. The records of Hafod-y-Llan
are partially undated, but Searell was working there in the 1840s. An
undated Specification (possibly about 1850) for a railway to Portmadoc
quay was thwarted by the same personality as faced the Gorseddau
during the 1850s, the landowner John Priestley. Searell intended to
build a complete line too, but his successors had to make do with a
truncated system which put the slate into carts at the edge of the Nant
Gwynant valley. His specification included an 8 ft wide horizontal
loading gauge, which suggests he may have considered the then gauge
of the Gorseddau, namely 3 ft. There were to be 'iron rails of a pattern
approved by the Engineer, not more than 15 ft long and to weigh not
less than eighty pounds each bar . . . to be laid in iron chairs not
exceeding three feet from centre to centre, none to weigh less than
seven pounds . . . good sound stone sleepers 14 inches square by 8
inches depth . . . and the ends of each rail to be fastened in an iron
chair etc. etc.'. Searell prepared an estimate for re-opening the quarry –
which he had ceased to work some years before – in 1856 and Wyatt of
former Penrhyn connections produced another in 1860. Searell clearly
believed that without a railway outlet there was little point in spending
money to develop the quarry, despite its potential. His papers refer
constantly to the problem of getting land for the line and the many
amendments required by the Turnpike Trustees. His death brought the
proposition to an end, and when a public company put out the aforementioned prospectus for 6% Debentures in June 1869 for the Hafod-y-
Llan (Snowdon) Slate Company Ltd., the only rail systems were to be
additional ones within the quarry.

The venture reflected the mood of the times. At Bryneglwys, Towyn
the proprietors were in the Lancashire Cotton Trade. At Prince of
Wales they were London Wine Merchants. Now it was rum; the
Chairman was Mr. Lemon Hart and co-director was brother David.
Other directors included the Rev. W. Kitching of Runnymede,
Windsor – they were all Londoners otherwise. The Resident Engineer
was none other than Hugh Unsworth McKie C.E., who of course was
still in office at Croesor United. The Company had bought the business
from Searell's son and obtained a 51-year lease. There was a barracks
for 150 men and a 50 h.p. turbine for the machinery; £5,000 was
reserved for building a tramway and inclines which were constructed
almost at once. Output was put on the Croesor Tramway whenever a
consignment had to leave the Beddgelert Siding by Cambrian
Railways.[15,16]

Another temporary user of the Croesor c.1889 was the Glistening
Valley Mining Co. of Penant (being the title on the folio in the ledger).
The whereabouts of this venture is on Moel Hebog. Why did not its
copper ore traffic pass over the Gorseddau? From the entry, one cannot

*Mining at Sygun ceased in 1903.

tell if it *did* come over that line and the charge was simply for running over Croesor metals to Portmadoc. Perhaps by then there was no traffic on the Gorseddau? At all events the phase was short-lived; but between 12th January, 1889 and 7th February, about 40 bags of copper ore were moved over the Croesor. (About 30 bags could be stowed in one wagon.) This appears to have been a healthy output and one wonders how such ponderous loads were accommodated by alternative transport afterwards . . . or was this simply a once-only consignment requiring part-Croesor transport?

A curt entry of April 1879 shows that the New Rhosydd Slate Co. repaid H.B. Roberts £20 in settlement of debt; this may have been money lent through the tramway business. There would seem to be a clerical error but it carries the implication that loans from the Roberts' to New Rhosydd were not paid off until then.

In May 1877 571 tons of new ballast were purchased and by 1883 business was brisk enough to employ two hauliers on each section again. The upper one was then termed 'Croesor Valley & Inclines'. At this period the Festiniog charged 4d. per ton mile for hire of wagons.

After the concern became mortgaged and payments to H.B. Roberts ceased, there are annual entries for the remainder of the life of the business:

Williams & Co., Bangor	Use of Incline	£19 7s. 7d.
Williams & Co., Bangor	Use of Railway	82 4 3
H. Griffith & Son, Portmadoc		57 15 9
H.J. Robinson & Sons, 2 King St., Blackburn		55 0 0

(Solicitors to the Portmadoc, Croesor & Beddgelert Tram Railway Co.)

One, if not all of these payees were lawyers, probably collecting on behalf of the mortgagees and landowners.

Wagonwork, wheels, tyres, incline rollers and the like were supplied by Isaac Williams of Portmadoc. Two new wagons were supplied by them in June 1870 and again in July 1890 for £10 11s. 6d. and presumably re-sold as none ever appeared on Croesor Returns. New wheel tyres were bought at the same time for £3. Other Portmadoc concerns to supply wire ropes, incline drums etc. were Owen Isaac & Owen, and J. Henry Williams & Sons. There was also a continual demand for yellow grease for the incline ropes.

Relationships with the Tremadoc Estate are outlined in some Instructions to Counsel prepared by solicitors Breese Jones & Casson of Portmadoc in about 1901 in connection with the preparation of a Conveyance. The Portmadoc end of the Tramway traversed Estate lands for about 2½ miles. The Estate was then the subject of a Chancery Suit. F.W.A. Roche at the time of building the line was then an infant and David Williams, Castell Deudraeth, claimed to be mortgagee in possession of the Estate. (F.W. Alexander Roche, born 1859, died 1875; grandson of W.A. Madocks and son of his daughter

Eliza Anne.) It was said that Williams had allowed Beaver Roberts to build the Tramway through the Estate without agreement being made as to terms of purchase. In 1868 the Court declared Williams to be mortgagee for about £100,000. In 1873 a Receiver was appointed pending Roche's majority, the mortgage being reduced to £82,000 by the sale of lands in 1893, the balance being re-invested in three new mortgages. When Roche's Trustees came into possession of the Estate they pressed the Tramway into terms of settlement for the acquisition of lands and about 1883 it was agreed that an annual sum of £50 should be made over. No proper Agreement was ever made, but the sum was paid annually. The Estate's land was used by every railway in the vicinity of Portmadoc.

In the matter of mileages, the Accounts have a pencilled note in the flyleaf:

Parliamentary portion of railway in	
Parish of Llanfrothen	180 chains
Private portion of railway in Parish of Llanfrothen	230 chains
	410 chains

There is a domestic note in March 1888, 'Bag of Peas, lost in transit (Value 2s. 6d.).' The Gorseddau Railway left a bad debt of £26 6s. 5d.; in July 1887 there is a note against this entry 'thought to have ceased working and have no funds'.

The most distant incline at Blaen-y-cwm was damaged by New Rhosydd in late 1874 and cost them £16 13s. 7d. in repairs; it was provided with new rollers and wire rope in November 1890 at a cost of £43 11s. 3d. Owen Isaac & Owen supplied the rollers. Perhaps this was the last renewal?

The management was clearly interested in the welfare of its employees and in this respect could have been ahead of others in the locality. In August 1891 there was an 'Excursion Trip to Chester for the Railwaymen; 7 @ 4s. plus Dinner @ 10s. £1 18s. 0d.' The following year a day out was arranged to Shrewsbury.

Officially at least, that portion of the tramway beyond the length absorbed by Statutory Undertakings, still survives and has never been closed. This is the private tramway or Croesor Tramway proper. It was auctioned on 14th October, 1936 and stated then to have been a substantial source of revenue to the Park and Croesor Estates. A Deed of 20th June, 1871 contained reference to the carriage of goods but the 1936 auction particulars stated that 'no one had exercised the rights contained in that Deed for upwards of 20 years'.

So oddly enough, it is the Croesor Tramway which may still be seen in places in a form in which it has lain undisturbed for many a year. Its link with Portmadoc has come and gone, the last rails there being lifted between August 1948 and August 1949 by W.O. Williams of Harlech using a Motor-Rail rail tractor, confusingly marked 'Shanks & McEwan Ltd. No. 14'. This was the final section of the Welsh Highland Railway dream to vanish. In the 1950s however, the 'private section' was still operational; an ancient Ford farm tractor slewed its way uncertainly along the muddy formation straddling the rails and hauling three open wagons still showing 'Parc & Croesor' lettering faintly on their sides. Their contents were not slate however, but cow dung – which is precisely the type of local traffic that Hugh Beaver Roberts intended the Tramway should convey when he started in business in 1864!

The Route described

(Field Survey made 1943–46 and ensuing account based on this.)

The most southerly tip of the Croesor Tramway was at the rear of the Oakeley Slate Company's Wharf and close by the Public Wharf on the west bank of the Glaslyn, where at the time of its building, it would be closely inter-related with the Festiniog Railway's several lines and the various connections at Greaves' and Rhiwbryfdir Wharves close by. Running northwards, it curved behind the two aforementioned wharf yards and crossed the foot of London Road (now High Street) at right angles and on the level. Coming up on its right hand would have been the Gorsedda (as it was often rendered) Tramway, which had also crossed London Road lower down and would then cross the Croesor line by a rail level crossing at an acute angle. Apart from mixed gauge trackage, there would have been no connection between the two Tram-ways for until its own Act, the Gorseddau line was of 3 ft gauge until at least 1872. These circumstances are thought to be the reason for Sections 31 of the draft of the Croesor and Port Madoc Railway Act to have been worded: 'The existing and extension railways shall be made, maintained and worked on a gauge of *two* feet; Provided that, it shall be lawful for the Company at any time hereafter, with the previous approval of the Board of Trade, to increase the gauge of the existing and extension railways from *two* feet to any gauge not exceeding *three* feet' (the italics are in the original draft). When assented to, this section of the Act had been amended on Advice to enable the gauge to be increased to 4 ft 8½ in. gauge.

The Tramway proceeded northwards (climbing at 1 in 228), passing out of the terraced housing and traversing a slow curve round the east fringe of the town and using what was to be, in 1864, the west shore of the Inner Harbour, formed by the Glaslyn above the Sluice Bridge. Turning slightly eastwards and now on level track, it entered the monotonous 'slob land' behind the town, a flat and almost treeless expanse where once the sea invaded. After a few yards of 1 in 924 a level crossing was then made with the Aberystwyth & Welsh Coast Railway (0 m. 39 ch.) on the north-west side of which an A.&W.C.R. siding came up alongside the Croesor and there was a high level interchange wharf with narrow gauge slate stockyard, weighbridge, sidings etc. From earliest times this was known as the Beddgelert Siding (loop 600 ft), taking its name from the abortive start of The Beddgelert

Railway. Here the line fell for a short distance at 1 in 833 (and six chains beyond Beddgelert Siding, facing southbound trains was a short spur of uncertain age on the east side used for loading sand).

As to the level crossing over the Coast Line, the Cambrian Railways must have considered this to be a temporary nuisance which could be overcome. But no, for on 19th August, 1875 their Engineer reported to the Board:

. . . the level crossing box at this junction has become dilapidated and a new one is necessary. I would recommend that a permanent one of brick, the cost of which would be £16 should be erected in lieu . . .

Running along the top of Creassy's 1800 embankment the Tramway rose at 1 in 3,556 along an unremarkable route with little for company save for sheep and dyke as far as Portreuddyn (1 m. 49 ch.). At this point the Creassy work turned inland and the builders were obliged to build their own embankment for the next stage to Pont Croesor. As the Croesor line was worked by horsepower and loops were provided at regular intervals, here too, was the first passing place northwards from Portmadoc. There are the remains of a slab milepost just beyond the loop (loop 180 ft).

Now at marsh level, the line climbs only six feet above the surrounding land before reaching Pont Croesor (2 m. 25 ch.), a place remarkable for nothing at all save that here the Tramway crossed the old road between Penrhyndeudraeth and Tremadoc (built as a short cut between the original Coast Road which, before land reclamation, ran inland to Pont Aberglaslyn to connect these two places) and the Afon Glaslyn – being the first road crossing of that river inland from Portmadoc's Britannia Bridge. To this point the river is tidal under certain conditions. The six foot of climb between Portreuddyn and here brought the line along the top of a low broad embankment at Pont Croesor, enabling it to cross the road there on the level and keeping it clear of Glaslyn flooding. Here and there original culverts remain, built of slab and unrebuilt in Welsh Highland Railway times. Along the south side of this embankment, within Tramway boundaries, was a substantial drainage ditch.

Seven chains before reaching Pont Croesor road crossing, a 110 ft siding, its point facing Portmadoc, ran off tangentially on the north side of the track. Its usage is problematical as, although so close to the nearby road, there was only a footpath connection to it. The Hafod-y-Llan Slate Co. was among users of it.

On the south side of the road crossing which followed, there was formerly a gate across the rails; with the road to its right, the Tramway now crossed the Glaslyn on the eight-span bridge already described. It then ran parallel to and somewhat higher than the adjacent road, one or two spans being inserted in the embankment to aid the clearance of flood waters. Slab piers and spans were used.

The line continued almost due north-east, curving very slightly eastwards, crossed a farm access road on the level and lost the adjacent road which swung away eastwards. The slow curve is now towards the north and all the way a very gentle upward inclination continues. The formation is a low embankment, just sufficient to keep the rails clear of the boggy surroundings yet at the same time, of substantial proportions. At 3 m. 30 ch. there was another access road crossing on the level where once more the Tramway was gated but not the road – this was the practice throughout. To the left was the Lodge for Ynysfor, a large house standing in the grounds of Ynys Fawr (the name being a corruption) once a considerable island in the Glaslyn estuary, and easily recognisable as such today as it stands proud above the surrounding marshland. To the north-east is a much smaller 'island', named Ynys Fach.

Occupying a similar position on the north side of the line, there was another 40 ft siding on the Portmadoc side of the occupation crossing. Unlike Pont Croesor, this was conveniently placed as a loading point and was certainly used within living memory for the carriage of farm materials, manures etc.

Now follows a straight section, flanked by drainage ditches, as far as the later Croesor Junction (3 m. 59 ch.) known locally by its original names of either Tanlan or Erw Fawr. Though the surrounding land is flat and turbary, the line lay in a positive amphitheatre of hills, a magnificent situation for a line of rails and a vantage point which was to have all too short a life for those who could visit it by passenger train. Ahead and above, lies the valley above Croesor village, Cnicht to the left with its Matterhorn peak; to the right the twin domes of Moelwyn. Each side the hills rise to buttress this central picture, certainly one of the loveliest in North Wales. In summer the semi-circle of mountains rise from the old foreshore in varying shades of green and brown, backed by blue sky; in winter a cold clear day, the greens subdued and the browns almost black, with the inevitable mantle of snow coming down to within 500 ft of sea-level, highlights the path of the old Croesor Tramway. Looking north-east from Croesor Junction, the various inclines and quarry branches stand out in a third dimension of snow and sun shadow; the great incline at the far end of the main line, and the shelf-like location of the Pant-mawr Quarry branch as it picks its way among the boulders along the flanks of Moelwyn. Imagination supplies a picture of how the slate from this remote place eventually came trundling down, past this same spot en route for shipment at the Port.

Before the coming of the Welsh Highland Railway, there was nothing to mark what later became Croesor Junction. Today, with the wheel turned full circle, there is little either. Sheep, black Welsh cattle and jackdaws have it to themselves . . . and even when the 'proper' railway came, there was little interruption to their lives from that. Forging onwards, the Tramway, still on an almost imperceptible embankment, turned clockwise through a quarter circle and made towards what at this point are correctly termed the foothills of Snowdonia, formidable as they look. Years ago, these same crags were cliffs above the shore. Today they overhang the old Coast Road which now the Tramway ran alongside and under the lee of the great bluff of rock which was considered prominent enough to feature in the Act; Carreg-hylldrem. Shortly, the Coast Road – as it was – is reached, and crossed on the level; once again gates protect the Tramway but not the road. Beside the line runs the Croesor, a tributary of the Glaslyn, and up its valley the Tramway takes its course. Once over the road, a last short rise of 1 in 302 ensues. There was a peculiar double siding in similar position, both entering a stone shed used for warehousing. The track now reached the foot of the Lower Parc Incline (length 1,725 ft) and the main line turned left for the incline foot. Ahead a branch ran level for a stretch, then rose by an incline built in the early 1870s, crossed the Afon Maegwyn and so up a second incline into the Park (or Parc) & Croesor Quarry. This working had opened as the Parc Quarries in 1866 and ultimately became part of Park & Croesor Slate Quarries Co. Ltd. which was formed 21st August, 1895. It was meanwhile owned by James Staveley in the 1880s and employed about twenty men. William Kellow bought it and after May 1893 his son Moses – then proprietor of the Croesor Quarry also, became Managing Director. Its storage sidings were dubbed by the Croesor management 'Moses Kellow Siding'. The quarry began using the Tramway about 1872. Moses Kellow, a Merioneth County Councillor, appears to have owned and managed the concern until both Park and Croesor quarries closed in December 1930, the last on the Tramway to survive.

Apart from spoil tips and the remains of dressing sheds, there is little evidence of working today; the source of slate was underground. In 1921, Spring's Report stated this quarry was sending 80–100 tons of slate a year down to the Beddgelert Siding for the Cambrian.

Returning to the foot of the incline, there was a loop line in the main tramway (4 m. 50 ch.) and storage sidings for the Park quarry. This point was the Parliamentary extent limit of the Croesor & Port Madoc Railway et seq. At the top of the Lower Parc incline was a short storage siding and an 'S' bend in the main line made necessary by the desire to make the tramway 'lift' into two shorter sections rather than one of great length involving much embankment work to keep it straight. The Upper Parc incline was 1,225 ft long and its drum house at the summit was for years a prominent feature on the crest of the hill. From 19 ft above sea level, the Lower Parc incline lifted the line to 275 ft. By the Upper Incline, the Tramway was now above the 500 ft contour. The short connection between the two inclines was less than 20 yards in length, but sufficient for operating purposes.* In 1949 all these works

---

*Incline length figures quoted are taken from those given at the Auction of Park & Croesor Estates 14th October, 1936. Sidings are quoted as being at 'Tresaethon, Brynhyfryd and at the upper terminus of the railway'. When the inclines were measured in 1884 by Thomas Roberts, C.E. of Portmadoc, he gave:

No. 1 Incline:	Blaen-y-cwm	693 ft
No. 2 Incline:	Parc	1,140 ft
No. 3 Incline:	Parc	1,716 ft

were complete though very overgrown; the track up to Croesor village began to disappear shortly afterwards. By 1965 most had gone.

The Tramway had now gone up and over the 'lip' of the upland plateau, and drove straight inland. There follows a fine drystone embankment over 100 yards long being the principal work of its type on the system. Approaching the environs of Croesor village, there was another loop and a siding was thrown off to the right to serve the former Park Slate & Slab Quarries. The branch curved sharply south-eastwards and through a narrow cutting almost 25 ft deep. Though not on the main tramway, it is the deepest cutting on the system. From the branch various sidings served the workings and one crossed the road on the level, stretched out across the valley and after climbing a short incline, served older workings long since closed. Both branch and quarry closed before World War I.

The main line now crossed the Afon Croesor by a bridge of three spans built in local material of slabs with stone piers. No wood or metal was used. Shortly it passes through the usual tramway 6 ft gate, one of several on this upper section. As elsewhere, the gates were usually kept closed across the line, emphasising the original authority for building the line and the continuance of landowners' rights. Now followed an ungated road crossing outside Croesor village, a small hamlet which during the Second War acquired something of a reputation for concealing an 'emigre' society enjoying a promiscuous life in a remote place, 'away from it all'!

Onward again, with steeply upward-sloping ground to either side, the Tramway ran beside the Croesor river along the upland valley which, even on a summer's day can be bleak. Almost treeless, it is rock strewn and sparsely populated with broken walls, deserted homesteads and farmhouses, a feature being the fencing of slates stuck end-downwards into the ground and wired along the upper ends. Mist, rain and wind are usually the companions of this place; even the lower fields are not cultivated and sheep graze there, straying up the steep slopes into boulders and gorse flanked pitches. Towering with their contrasting outlines to the left stand Cnicht (2,265 ft) and hidden to the right, the rounder Moelwyn Mawr (2,334 ft). Once a telephone system flanked the tramway between village and the quarries. At Pont Sion-goch the Croesor is crossed again by a slab bridge. Here on the left is a level with an adit, its spoil being tipped between Tramway and river; this was a loading point but there was no siding. From there the Tramway ran almost straight, earthwork being confined to an occasional cutting and most of the line a simple embankment. The only excitement brought to this length was in 1949 when one of the quarry reservoir dams high above the valley head at Blaen-y-cwm, threatened to crack and was repaired. To reach the isolated spot a helicopter was used to carry cement etc. and the Tramway embankment became a spectators' grandstand for the landing place in the adjacent field! Thus

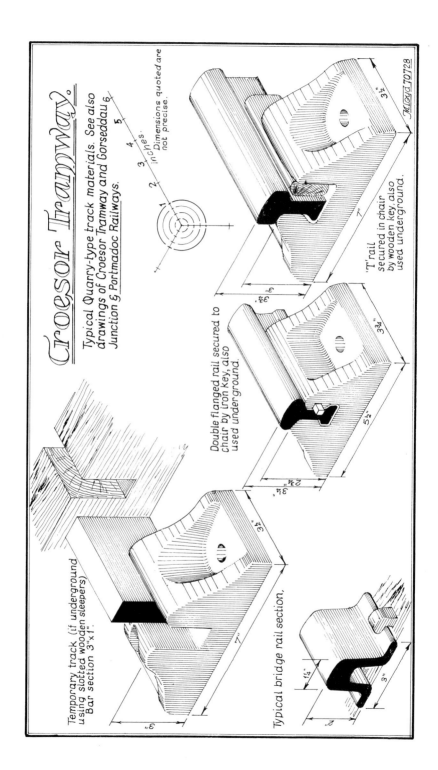

Croesor Tramway.

Typical Quarry-type track materials. See also drawings of Croesor Tramway and Gorseddau Junction & Portmadoc Railways.

Dimensions quoted are not precise.

inches.

0 1 2 3 4 5 6

Temporary track (if underground using slotted wooden sleepers) Bar section 3"x1".

3"

7"

Double flanged rail secured to chair by iron key, also used underground.

3½"

5½"

2¾"

3½"

'T' rail secured in chair by wooden key, also used underground.

3½"

7"

Typical bridge rail section.

1¼"

2"

3"

JLloyd T0728

side by side were modes of transport almost a century apart. (Ultimately the helicopter crashed.)

Earthworks now vary up to ten feet deep, embankment work being 6 ft wide, sufficient evidence that the works were built with increasing and heavy traffic in mind and quite suitable for steam locomotive traction. This straight length continues for about 1½ miles and at Bryn-hyfryd there was a short siding, entirely for agricultural traffic. The climb is steady all the way, but no dimension is on record and it is very slight; exceptionally, there is a short fall once or twice and sufficiently deterring to prevent the line being worked by gravity, however slight the general levelling may have been. Above and to the right the road to the Croesor Quarry climbs its solitary way, diagonally up the mountain face. En route it passes Bryn-hyfryd formerly the property of the Tramway, but latterly the Croesor Quarry Manager's house whose last occupant was Moses Kellow, M.I.C.E., M.I.E.E., F.R.G.S., an engineer of very inventive mind. It was he who was responsible for the electrification of the quarry, and needless to add, Bryn-hyfryd was probably the finest all-electric house in North Wales before the First War. Kellow's main private customer was Lady Owen of Croesor Hall; he built a reservoir and fitted out the Hall's electrical supply, enabling her to dispense with all but one butler. Kellow invented a hydraulic rock drill, an electrical insulator made of slate, and his car included a float in an oil bath which gave automatic control with changes of level; this was tested on the quarry roadway. Croesor Quarry was among the most efficient of its time.

Kellow's connection as Manager and Engineer with the Croesor Quarry began in 1895, the working having closed down in 1878 after the succession of unsuccessful company ventures which had encompassed it since about 1856. Under Kellow the leasehold site of 240 acres was in poor shape after this long period of disuse; worse, only ten years of a royalty-free period was left to run. This was insufficient for a return on capital which would be needed to develop the place. Kellow wrote:

> Shortly afterwards I was successful in arranging terms for the purchase of the whole Croesor Estate . . . together with the Croesor Railway on both the Croesor and Park Estates . . . the management of these estates and of the Railway were in my hands up to the time of the final sales of the properties.
>
> The Portmadoc, Beddgelert & South Snowdon Railway which linked the Croesor Railway with Portmadoc, was only under my Management during the Great War . . .

(here Kellow, writing in late retirement, is clearly confused for as this Railway had not then been completed and work was suspended, he must refer to the intention to use the Croesor line between Croesor Junction (not then made) and Portmadoc).[17]

Rodney Weaver has added much more about Kellow (1862–1943), pointing out that he amalgamated Croesor and Park, modernised Croesor with electrification and perfected the most powerful rock drill ever made. The quarry originally relied on a 39 ft diameter waterwheel in a pit beneath the floor of the slate mill but Kellow, drawing inspiration from Hungary and the firms of Ganz and Koller who were developing three-phase electrical equipment, installed machinery which was 'diametrically opposed to contemporary thinking in Britain'. The main adit level's tramway was given overhead catenary and Kellow built an electric locomotive to work it – the first so powered in Wales. He also influenced Bruce Peebles & Co. in 1906 in the supply of three-phase haulage motors to Oakeley Quarry, Blaenau Festiniog.[18] Perhaps also in acquiring electric equipment for the abortive P.B.&S.S.R.?

Shortly beyond this point was a junction to the right with a long incline which is still a predominant feature. The pointwork here was unusual; it was a special casting of bridge rails, one for each set of rails. The wing rails of the frog were raised into 'ears' which guided the outer faces of the wheels to prevent derailment; by this system, check rails were unnecessary. The Tramway which this branch incline carries was laid in similar materials to the original Tramway but was built about ten years later. The rail and chairs may have come from Festiniog surplus as a load of rails and chairs was invoiced on 11th October, 1891. The incline was divided into two sections, with an 'S' connection between them; the upper section included an exceptionally steep length at the top. South-westwards from the summit there remains, despite rock falls etc. a fine example of drystone shelf construction into the Pant-mawr Quarry. This is a remote location and the works have been disused since 1913[19]; little remains. A further short incline on to the col between Moelwyn Mawr and Moelwyn Bach ends in incomplete excavations. In these quarries all work was underground, and water-filled adits may be seen still with tramways submerged in them. Not all these are connected with the main tramway system. The more important adits have individual weighbridges at their entrances and are well preserved. They lie below the older Pant-mawr workings and above the later Fron-boeth Quarry below.

Pant-mawr Quarry opened in August 1864 but its connection to the Croesor Tramway was not completed until 1879; traffic is first recorded in September 1877 and lasts until May 1892. Work was being done until 1908 but to reach the slate strata lower down the face a new tramway was built in 1889 to serve the Fron-boeth Quarry workings. Even this undertaking was shown as 'abandoned in January 1898' in the Official List of North Wales mines.

Pant-mawr owners included Pant Mawr Slate & Slab Co. Ltd. (of London) 1873–75; a Company of similar title but of Dundee who were in liquidation by 1883, and the quarry inoperative, and the next year, though still with working suspended, the owner was William Davies, of Bridgend, Glamorganshire, trading as Fron-boeth & Pantmawr Slate & Slab Co. Ltd. – liquidated 1891. From about 1890 access to each of the above quarries could be made through each other's workings and at this time, with offices in Portmadoc, J. Lloyd Humphries owned both quarries. In 1893 the concern was run with the same title, based on

Edinburgh. Fronboeth Slate Quarry Ltd. had a brief life, September 1894 to March 1895! In 1903 New Pantmawr Slate Quarry Co. Ltd. was formed. The site closed in 1908.

The top section of the lower incline from the main Croesor Tramway was continued up through the site of the drumhouse and a line led along a ledge southwards for a distance. It then turned sharply into the mountainside and by means of a tunnel somewhat over quarter of a mile in length, reached the hillside basin below the Pant-mawr workings. Whilst underground tunnels in connection with mining etc. commonly contain tramways, this tunnel is the main 'overground' example of its type in North Wales. At the south-east tunnel mouth are extensive spoil tips, mainly of granite however, which was used in the buildings. A two-stage incline doubles back up the hillside again and then runs parallel to but below the Pant-mawr branch above it. On the way it passes the Manager's Office and Dressing Sheds. The only other item which survives is a large Lancashire boiler probably used latterly for water storage. The Fron-boeth Quarry lines were laid in more conventional flat-bottomed rails, and though they remained *in situ* for many years afterwards, work here stopped during the First War. It is a bleak place on anything but the best of days. Use of the Croesor Tramway began in 1891.

Back on the main Tramway and down below the aforementioned quarries, the Tramway continues its unrelieved course for another half mile to the former 'Kellow' Generating Station at Blaen-y-cwm, situated at the foot of a steep northern mountain barrier up against which the Tramway has now come. There was once a loop and stabling sidings here, together with Station siding. Ahead rears up the Blaen-y-cwm Incline (835 ft) which once carried both tracks and the supply pipeline to the Generating Station. This was the first of two inclines to carry the line up the face of the Bwlch-y-Rhosydd ridge and the summit is over 800 ft above the sea. There followed a spectacular section across the head of the valley by means of a mountain shelf carried on a rock wall and a bridge over the Afon Cwm-y-foel. Here there was another junction where the incline (opened August 1864) serving the Croesor Quarry rose steeply to the right, and at its foot, bridged the infant Afon Croesor. At the incline foot the Company first provided 'a hut for the horse' in December 1876.

The Croesor Quarry was the largest served by the Tramway, being 1,600 ft above sea level. Work began here about 1856 (and at the complementary Parc workings about 1866) and both were pioneers in hydro-electric power. By the building of reservoirs and the power station just noted, an output of 775 h.p. was obtained from turbines and two overshot water wheels. Alternating current was used throughout workings and mills and the half mile of main adit together with tracks outside were fitted with overhead supply wires to feed the electric locomotive, probably the first of its type. Built in the quarry workshops, it was of 30 h.p. The driver sat under the pillared-roof cab with pantograph above it and current was obtained from street-tramway type overhead cable suspension. To enable the loco to enter the workings it was both narrow and low; large headlamps were fitted at each end. The adit was near-level for some distance and then reached a vertical shaft to reach other levels. There are many natural sand-bottomed caverns and the surrounding rock is too hard even to take a scratch; a thin vein of white clay running through it cannot be removed if caught on the clothing!

Croesor Quarry was in the news as early as 1870 when a representative from 'ENGINEERING' visited the site ('ENGINEERING' 1870 (i) p. 405). The Croesor United Slate Co. had just abandoned hand labour and were using a diamond boring machine (on hire from The Diamond Rock Boring Co. Ltd., an American concern) instead. This was driven by compressed air obtained from a turbine worked by water supply to the Generating Station at Blaen-y-cwm, one of whose turbines was used for air compression. The whole rock drilling outfit was working in an inclined shaft and mounted on wagons; a tailrope was taken from thence, out through the adit mouth and a balancing wagon, suitably weighted, was fastened on its other end. The incline, apparently without beginning or end, is clearly visible on the mountainside below the Croesor workings and is commonly mistaken for an older tramway access to the quarry. The balance wagon carried a wooden tank; when the drill was down the shaft the tank lay under a mountain stream which when required, was diverted to fill the tank and draw the drilling rig clear of the face. At the balance incline foot a device automatically opened a valve and emptied the water tank. This work was begun in 1868 under contract with the Machine Tunnelling Company under the direction of John Vivian.

Work ceased in Parc (1916) and Croesor (1930); they were the last workings in the valley. After this there was spasmodic working and an occasional train on the Tramway. More often it was a single wagon drawn by a horse and even in the early thirties, Welsh Highland trains were known to stop at Croesor Junction to attach a slate wagon in the rear. Sometimes a rail tractor from Boston Lodge worked to the foot of the Lower Parc Incline (heavier units were not allowed further than the Llanfrothen road level crossing as the track beyond here had not been relaid with flat-bottomed rail). No self-propelled units worked on the section above Upper Parc Incline.

In 1942, Croesor Quarry was purchased for storage of explosives. A much-improved road now serves the quarry but not the valley bottom along which the Tramway runs. For this reason a part of this length still had track along it; in the early 1960s it was reasonably complete and a single wagon was used by farmers. A feature of the shorter inclines was that the horses transferred to different levels to pick up the wagons again; some formations were made wider to accommodate a horse-path. On most other tramways, horses were kept to their own levels.

'Train operation' within living memory has relied on horses being used without change from the foot of the Parc Incline, to the port. For this purpose horses were hired from Garreg Hylldrem, a farm near the foot of Carreg-hylldrem, as required. The largest and nearest village to this length of tramway was Llanfrothen and the inhabitants enjoyed rather a special relationship with the tramway. Llanfrothen's most convenient access to the tramway was along the rough but direct road to Ynysfor; at the level crossing there the siding was usually occupied by wagons used for bringing the necessities of the village within reach of road carts. Lime, coal and beer barrels came up from the port. Some of the more influential people of the locality would send word down to the siding that they intended to go 'to Port' the following day and for this purpose a wagon would be cleaned out; for instance, a mother would push her children in it not only the three miles to Portmadoc, but also the same distance back again. Even with the very slight descent to Portmadoc, it was said to be possible to coast along over much of the westward journey. (To these folk, Pont Croesor was a name brought in by the Welsh Highland Railway – Portreuddyn was its local name and Pont Croesor the bridge below Carreg-hylldrem.)

Returning now to the junction of the Croesor Quarry incline, there followed one of the most remarkable inclines of its type, New Rhosydd designed by Spooner. It rose like Jacob's Ladder in a seemingly un-ending parabola to carry the line above the 1,400 ft level. It was in use by June 1864, this and the adjacent tramway costing the Quarry Com-pany £2,500. It was about 1,500 ft long and at the summit was inclined at rather more than 1 in ¾, making ascent on foot almost impossible. It is a fine piece of civil engineering and its upper reaches are made from slate waste piled in an almost vertical tower. At the summit a rock wall forced the tramway to turn right along a shelf which is commonly swept by high winds as they rise up from the funnel-like valley below. Half a mile ahead is the abandoned Rhosydd Quarry, closed in 1930. Here in 1952 was a wilderness of dereliction with its broken barracks, mills and shed full of rusting machinery. Upturned wagons and dripping adits made a depressing environment; the main haulage adit was ⅔ mile long in ex.F.R. 1846-period materials latterly, and wagons were moved along it by attaching them to an endless haulage rope. This is the farthest reach of the tramway. Just over the ridge beyond, into which Rhosydd workings penetrate, are other workings which tunnel in from the south side and whose tramways are connected with the Festiniog Railway's branch system at Tan-y-Grisiau.

The early history of Rhosydd is unclear: there were numerous open-ings and closings prior to 1830 but chiefly of a trial nature. William Turner was working the site in 1833 and William Ormsby-Gore, claim-ing the land was his, took over: land ownership was ever a dispute. After working by Matthews of Aberystwyth, Thomas Jones and Edward Barker (son of Ormsby-Gore's slate agent) took over in 1851. The Rhosydd Slate Co. was formed in June 1853 and a public company of limited liability in November 1856 – it went into liquidation in June 1873 when in October 1874, The New Rhosydd Slate Co. Ltd. was incorporated under William Morris, Casson and Dr. Roberts . . . all locally-interested men.[21]

Alternative sources suggest the quarry was leased to Cwmorthin-Ucha Quarry by 1850 and had become Rhosydd Slate Quarry Co. Ltd. in 1882 with 192 employees and an annual output of 5,616 tons. This became The New Rhosydd Slate Quarry Co. Ltd. with 186 employees in 1893 and an output of 4,693 tons. These imperfections in the tale had little effect on the rail transport picture![22]

Contrasting with electrical installations in neighbouring Croesor Quarry, Rhosydd was lit by candlepower throughout its life.

In 1948 the track was in position from Carreg-hylldrem to the summit of the last incline, including the Croesor Quarry incline. At this time it was hoped that certain workings might be re-opened and the Tramway re-used. It never was. The 'SLATE TRADE GAZETTE' of February 1911 had this to say

'. . . The Croesor Tramway, 8 miles in length, serves the quarries to shipping at Portmadoc. There is 3½ miles of slate strata, and the mountains of Cnicht and Moelwyn are almost entirely slate. Croesor Quarry was opened in 1856 and Parc in 1866, the former producing roofing slate, the latter slate for manufacturing purposes. Both are underground and are complementary to one another. The Croesor Quarry is worked downwards in the usual manner, the Parc upwards to allow the spoil to fill the workings afterwards. The Croesor Quarries are 2,560 ft above sea level,' [an exaggeration of 1,000 ft] 'Electricity is generated by water power for lighting and driving machinery. This was the first case of electricity being used in a slate mine for this purpose and also later for haulage and the underground drills etc . . .'

The Croesor Tramway was the largest and longest of its kind and unique in North Wales. It was lengthy, remote and fascinating. It served quarries of interesting origin incorporating both old and up-to-date methods. Its lower length was the subject of many behind-the-scenes schemes and its upper length, no longer so cut-off from the outside world as in former days, is still out of reach of anyone without two good legs to gain it. Even today, there is still a little of the mystery and speculation which involved its progenitors over one hundred years ago. Other narrow gauge lines in North Wales were better known, but the Croesor deserves its unique place in rail transport history. It had a character unlike its contemporaries. Its quarries opened and closed in a barometric pattern of the economy: by 1914 only four remained at work – Rhosydd, Croesor, Pant-mawr and Parc.[23] The first World War closed Parc but some others remained to the slump of 1930.

Permanent Way

Writing in 1878, Vignes records that the track was exactly as laid on the Gorseddau Tramway, and the rails set to the same gauge. The rails were 20 lb. per yard in weight, though elsewhere they have been given as 15 lb. The rails were carried in iron chairs weighing 3 lb.; joints were made in wider chairs of similar pattern weighing 5 lb. Vignes describes the track as 'being like the original Festiniog Railway' which is a little misleading but accurate in general terms. The wooden sleepers were 4 ft × 5 in. × 3½ in. deep at 2 ft centres under joints and at 2 ft 9 in. elsewhere. Fishplates were never used, only butt joints. Oddly enough, though in plentiful supply, slate or slab was never used for sleepers; its disadvantages were by then well known. The rail, a T section with a rib on one side of the lower edge, was similar to the Festiniog, although the section was quite different. Unlike the flat-bottomed and bridge rail it requires the additional expense of chairs and keys. The chairs were laid with the notch cast in them to receive the lower flange of the rail inside the track; the rail was secured in the chair by a narrow iron key (later wooden) driven in along the outside of the rail. There was clearly some variation in sizes as many rails had their bottom flanges cut away to make them fit the joint chairs. Two luxuries were permitted – double chairs were cast to take check rails, and double angled chairs were cast for frog crossings. Chairs were held to sleepers by iron pins. Detail variation in chairs occurs.

The precise material used in the early pointwork is not known, but later points were built up from cast sections of left and right hand for each running rail; the switch blade was pivoted and moved over a cast plate integral with the unit. The units had 'bridge section' rails with special sockets at each end to receive the T rail without recourse to a joint chair. At frogs there was either a cast piece socketed to receive T rails at each end and having a centrally pivoted bridge rail section in the centre, or a cast piece of conventional frog and wing rail type having raised wing rails which prevented the face of the wheels from running out of alignment. The former type of frog permitted a simple and single piece of trackwork forming an X to serve the purpose of a double slip without employing check rails or blades; there was a good example at the foot of Blaen-y-cwm Incline and another at Croesor Incline.

Away from the main running line, there was later occasional use of heavier T rail in heavier chairs of identical pattern as the old Festiniog track. These were purchased from the Festiniog as its own main line was being relaid, together with a quantity of single and double slab sleepers. Croesor accounts for 1870 have 'Still owing to the Festiniog Railway Co. (Rails etc.) £234 13s. 6d.'. Obviously there must have been some crisis before this as an entry in 1866 states 'Gorseddau Quarry – loan of rails, 30 bars @ 6d. 15/-'.

Imported larch was used for sleepers and in the 1870s J. Henry Williams & Sons was the supplier – also of chair keys and other timber: sleepers were 5/6d. per dozen. In 1883 it was decided to set aside an annual sum of £500 'for reproducing New Stock and the rails and sleepers'. It is possible that the Festiniog materials were usurped in favour of those described beforehand, accounting for use of the former only in sidings etc. in latter days. At least it seems there were varying forms of track in use simultaneously!

At the end, all rails were 15 ft long: Croesor, Conclog and Pant-mawr Quarries used a similar rail in chairs, but without keys; there were considerable variations in the cross-sections of the T rails hereabouts.

Motive Power and Rolling Stock

At no period during its life did the Tramway own any motive power. Horses were used from the first, and even these were hired under contract from farms. Thus there were no stables which featured beside many a similar line. The upper section never had self-propelled units along it though farmers were known to 'borrow' wagons and use them along the main line, hauled by a farm tractor straddling the rails. This was unofficial.

The section of the line between the wharves and Croesor Junction – though not in the period under review – became in part the southern end of the Welsh Highland Railway and in this form, steam locomotives and petrol tractors were used over it. But the short section of the former Croesor Tramway between Croesor Junction and Lower Parc Incline foot still remained faithful to the horse, though exceptionally, a tractor would make its way at least as far as the Llanfrothen road crossing. Some sources refer to this traffic continuing until 1937 and certainly an odd wagon occasionally passed, but regular slate haulage had ceased by 1930. In the first flush of enthusiasm, the W.H.R. borrowed the Festiniog's Baldwin tractor (purchased secondhand in 1925) from its shunting duties at Minffordd Junction from time to time, and used it to haul longer trains of slate wagons between Llanfrothen crossing and Portmadoc Wharves. This usage was very unpopular as it left Minffordd Exchange Sidings without motive power; from 1926 a Festiniog-owned Austro-Daimler tractor began to make regular runs between Lower Parc and the wharves. It was light enough to run over Croesor rails which the Baldwin could not, and so more suited to the work. It was also tried on a passenger coach between Portmadoc and Croesor Junction (time 45 minutes for 3½ miles!), but when the slate traffic had dwindled away the tractor was pushed out of sight into the Boston Lodge Paint Shop in 1929, and never ran again.[24]

Although strictly outside Croesor Tramway days, it is amusing to note a further example of Festiniog/Welsh Highland policy of the late 1920s. This was the nominal 'posting' (to use a military term in accordance with the Col. Stephen's regime then in being) of the Baldwin tractor. In 1937 Festiniog records note it as having been transferred to the Festiniog Railway along with other Welsh Highland stock and assets, and the tractor as having been formerly the property of the 'Croesor & Portmadoc Junction Railway'. This was simply a book transfer of doubtful legality, containing proof of illicit manipulation in that there never was a Railway of the name quoted, which was a corruption of the titles Croesor & Port Madoc Railway and Gorseddau

Junction & Portmadoc Railways. Further, Festiniog accounts for 31st December, 1925 show the tractor as a Festiniog purchase for £248 13s. 4d. and the returns show an increase of one unit that year in the form of 'Petrol Tractor for Shunting'.

Though the Croesor never owned any motive power, in the quarries water, steam and electricity was used. According to a sales list of Croesor United Quarry Co. of September 1874, and another list of its successor the Croesor New Quarry Co. Ltd. of June 1883, there were probably two stationary steam engines during this time. Both quarries had closed by 1881, and again in the 1890s; sporadic working is not uncommon, nor is successive ownership. Parc & Croesor Quarries were wound up on 8th February, 1931 (having closed the previous year). Overhead wiring at Croesor was removed but the track left intact; in 1942 the premises were purchased to Cooke's Explosives Ltd. – three Ruston & Hornsby Ltd. internal combustion rail tractors have been used there.

The slate wagons used over the Tramway fell into four main types, the earliest being of the wooden-bar and cast-iron bobbin sided type so common in the district. Conversely to Festiniog practice, all wagons belonged to private owners, the Tramway having none of its own. Many of these were built at Boston Lodge to Festiniog patterns, especially in case of Rhosydd. Later, small iron-framed wagons replaced the wooden ones. Both varieties held two tons of slate and weighed empty 10–12 cwt. (wooden) or 13–16 cwt. (iron). Rhosydd preferred the frame type and an early view shows many wooden frame wagons in use.[25] Whilst Park & Croesor used frame wagons they preferred sheet-iron sided wagons of which there were several variations. All were of fixed side and end type and those fitted with brakes were peculiar in that brake shoes worked on one pair of wheels only; the wheel on one side was braked from outside, and the wheel at the other end of the axle, from the inside. Brake handles were pulled *up* to apply the shoes and these vehicles were distinguished by having horse-rings attached to the top-side strengthening rib, to which the haulage chain was attached. The fourth wagon variety was a wooden two-planked side and end wagon, again with fixed sides and ends. The owners are not positively identified.

Sheet-iron wagons were lettered with the quarry owner on the sides and the wagon number below; more recently this work was done in white stencilling but owing to extensive rusting, the iron-framed and planked wagons had lost all identification by 1940 when inspected – and worse, further investigation was made impossible at the time by the suspicions aroused in the local military by such necessary fieldwork! (The author had already been interrogated!)

All wheels were 1 ft 6 in. diameter and other average dimensions (and colours) were:

Type	Length overall ft in.	Width overall ft in.	Height overall ft in.	Wheelbase ft in.	Colour
Wooden frame	5 3	2 7	3 2	3 0	Red oxide
Small iron frame	6 0	3 4	3 2	3 0	Dark grey & black
Sheet iron side	6 10	3 6	3 0	3 0	Dark grey & black
Wooden planked*	8 6	3 6	3 2	3 0	Red oxide

*A smaller 2-plank variety existed in dark grey: it was 6 ft 10 in. long.

A sample survey undertaken by the Festiniog Railway to ascertain how many of its wagons had 'strayed' from the parent system and were being used by quarries unofficially gave, incidentally, the stock of the quarries' own wagons. In 1928, only two Croesor valley quarries were involved:

Name of Quarry	Quarry Wagons in working order	Wagons unfit	Total
Rhosydd	30	24	54
Park & Croesor	23	27	50

This high percentage of unusable wagons meant that both quarries had to hire wagons from the Festiniog. Of these many were retained illegally for internal use, the quarries not troubling to repair them at all, nor to pay the Festiniog for their hire!

A quite different form of hire (also from the Festiniog) applied only in the years 1870 and 1876 when charges were made on the Croesor: 'hire of wagons'. It is likely that this occurred when obsolete F.R. track materials were being purchased and came up onto Croesor metals for unloading – the dates agree. In April 1881 the F.R. gave notice that due to delays in returning wagons from the Tramway, it would decline to supply after 1st June.

A peculiar sidelight on this hiring was recorded in 1923; 14 ex-Welsh Slate Co. wagons had been sent to the Rhosydd Quarry. One day in April, six of these wagons came down the incline on to the Festiniog main line near Tan-y-Grisiau – the Conclog Incline. As there was never a railway between these two points or between the quarries concerned, the matter was investigated and it was found they had been let down a mountain footpath, an unrailed distance of almost two miles!

On quarry premises open ended sheet sided wagons were used for rubbish; early photos show long wheelbase flat wagons for slabs being drawn along the Tramway proper. Flat trolley types were used in the adits. Unidentifiable open wagons with outside framing (probably wooden) were used by Croesor Quarry, probably predecessors of the sheet-iron types.

To omit reference to the existence of some small and strange vehicles in the Rhosydd workings would be to overlook a curious form of

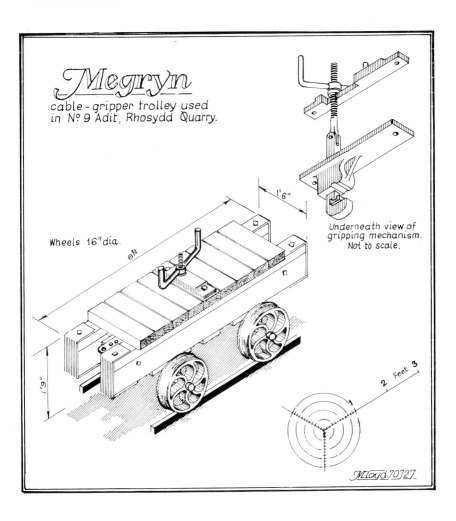

Megryn

cable - gripper trolley used
in N⁰ 9 Adit, Rhosydd Quarry.

Underneath view of
gripping mechanism.
Not to scale.

1' 6"

Wheels 16" dia.

6'½

1' 9"

2 Feet 3

M.Lloyd 70/27

haulage used in that quarry. Adit No. 9 there is said to have been the longest and deepest in the Ffestiniog district and may have taken from 1862 to 1871 to cut. It is 2,221 ft long with a gradient down from the mouth at 1 in 86 and it formed the main transport and drainage scheme of the quarry and contained a tramway system of familiar pattern having three running rails, the centre one being common to each direction of running. At a passing loop about the central point, the tracks 'ballooned out' into four rails before returning to three again (on other sites this often became but one single line, but not here). This system obviates the need for moving point blades but of necessity, each vehicle must have one flange rather than two on its wheels. Trains of wagons were moved along the adit by means of a continuous wire rope which passed round horizontal sheaves at each end, below the rails, and the sheaves were driven by water wheel. At each end of every train a cable car or 'Megryn', being a four-wheeled wooden framed trolley, was attached, having a vertical screw worked by a handle above its floor and a claw-like gripper beneath; this could be tightened to grasp the cable without stopping the cable itself. No 'driver' was needed, the car being disconnected by lineside operatives at the end of the train journey. [Similar systems but of less basic form, were commonly found on street tramway undertakings.]

Employees

The Wages Books for 1864/5 give an insight into the scope of the enteprise at the start:

9 days ending 10th August, 1864
Thomas Rees	10/-	
Robt. Anwyl	6/-	
G. Parry	5/-	rates per day
J. Edwards	3/2d.	
Thomas Parry	3/6d.	
Jno. Lloyd	3/8d.	

This gave Rees £3 10s. a week for a seven-day week or £182 per year, a considerable sum; the occupations of these men are not given. A more revealing list for 1865 gives:

Clerk		(on salary)
Carrier	paid	6d. per ton
Carrier	paid	3d. per ton
Brakesman		4/6d. per day
Brakesman		3/4d. per day
Brakesman		3/4d. per day
Platelayer		3/8d. per day
Asst. ditto		3/4d. per day

the brakesmen being those in charge of the incline drums. In 1869 three men were on haulage but there was but one brakesman with an 'Assistant', and one 'Collector' – whatever he might be! The platelayer now had two assistants.

CROESOR TRAMWAY. Relation to later Welsh Highland Railway works where applicable:

Miles	Chains	Location	Croesor Tramway	Welsh Highland Rly.
0	0	Oakeley Slate Wharf	Zero Point	—
0	8	Foot Madoc Street	—	Connecting junc. with Fest.R.
0	37	South Cambrian Rlys.	—	150 ft loop. Corrugated iron station building. Portmadoc New Station (the first).
0	39	Crossing with Aberystwyth & Welsh Coast Railway		
0	42	Beddgelert Siding	600 ft loop	Portmadoc New Station (the second).
1	49	Portreuddyn*	180 ft loop	Loop removed 1/1924; not used.
2	25	Pont Croesor	110 ft siding	Siding lengthened to 300 ft
2	27	Pont Croesor (Halt: W.H.R.)		Corrugated iron shelter.
2	28	Pont Croesor	Rail crossing of Afon Glaslyn	
3	30	Ynysfor (Halt: W.H.R.)	40 ft siding	Corrugated iron shelter.
3	59	Croesor Junction	Non existent	Loop ex Portreuddyn laid 5/1934. Corrugated iron shelter.
4	50	Foot Lower Park Incline	Parliamentary limit of Croesor & Port Madoc Rly. et seq.	

*In early 1880s also referred to as Pren-teg, probably because local slate quarry then used the name and the loop here. Connection was likely to have been by carts between quarry and tramway although a branch railway connection between the loop and the foot of the quarry incline is not impossible.

Iron bar rails with hooked ends, five feet long, and mounted on wooden sleepers, were found in Pren-teg Quarry in the mid 1960s and Croesor type track was lifted from the incline there in the late 1960s. The earliest record is 1858 when Thomas Chaffer & Co. was quarrying flagstone there.

	1871	1872	1873	1874	1875	1876	1877	1878	1879	1880	1881	1882	1883	1884	1885
Cost of Works and Way	£108	74	92	87	70	95	186	211	74	50	95	81	146	81	53
Cost Loco Power*	329	333	290	279	258	267	329	348	242	336	337	274	230	317	233
Profit/Loss on wkg.	354	55	97	17	30	5	56	79	82	115	97	137	(19)	181	34
Merchandise Tons	1575	1294	475	690	921	1694	1879	4630	4249	1471	3127	596	2361	2185	3286
Minerals Tons	25910	24904	21106	18815	16991	14952	18946	21195	15703	22263	22080	20104	12482	18615	10856
Goods train miles	6886	6326	5730	5096	5302	6014	6925	6260	5884	5302	5634	5321	5406	5634	4873

	1886	1887	1888	1889	1890	1891	1892	1893	1894	1895	1896	1897	1898	1899	1900	1901
Cost of Works & Way	£88	60	64	87	81	47	73	109	91	100	143	192	128	119	189	97
Cost Loco Power*	313	162	147	144	156	126	153	150	152	151	195	231	209	195	215	202
Profit/Loss on wkg.	95	85	72	30	59	62	65	60	107	107	93	131	154	123	43	91
Merchandise Tons	1800	1636	1949	1656	1994	1640	2652	8467	10705	13829	11051	16958	15942	11956	11155	11213
Minerals Tons	11195	6732	6332	5983	6332	5274	6250	6332	6418	5971	7690	9620	8786	8240	8811	7612
Goods train miles	3717	3087	3052	2925	3033	3030	2840	2844	2921	2736	2956	5173	4410	3950	4088	3910

Division denotes Croesor & Port Madoc Railway up to 1878; Portmadoc, Croesor & Beddgelert Tram Railway 1879 onwards.

No returns made before 1871. In 1870 Secretary states 'There are no shareholders consequently no accounts are published (private property)'.

*Note on returns: 'Cost of Horsepower, the haulage on the line being done by horses'.

*Statement by Secretary: 'The Company have no rolling stock or locomotives. The haulage is done by horses and the wagons are provided by the persons using the railway'. (1871).

Traffic Expenses of £135 are shown for 1871 and 1872, but none thereafter.

Carriage and Wagon maintenance Expenses for 1880 are £57, the only year returned.

Stock Returns: One entry made in 1880 only showing eighty wagons (type not stated). Perhaps these bought secondhand from Festiniog Railway and re-sold to quarry owners as mineral tonnages rose to over 20,000 for the next few years; such an item does not, however, feature in the Accounts but their purchase and re-sale may have been purposely omitted from the books.

Legal Expenses for years 1900 and 1901 (only) shown as £10 and £22.

In 1903 Returned as 'Purchased by Portmadoc, Beddgelert & South Snowdon Railway as from 29th October, 1903 under Act 1 Edward VII c.262 of 7th August, 1901'.

Directors of Croesor & Port Madoc Railway (successors to Croesor Tramway)

Hugh Beaver Roberts (Plas Llandoget, Llanrwst) – also initial Director N.W.N.G. Railways.

Hugh U. McKie (Hafod Tan-y-graig, Beddgelert) – also Engineer/ Contractor N.W.N.G. Railways.

Arthur T. Roberts* (Coed Du, Mold, Flints.) – also Director Mold & Denbigh Junction Railway and Buckley Railway.

Richard M. Preston.

John Ormiston.

*Brother of H.B. Roberts.

Directors of Portmadoc, Croesor & Beddgelert Tram Railway Co. (successors to Croesor & Port Madoc Railway)

James Fraser Senr.* (London, N.W.) – Director until 1883 – and also Director of Corris Railway, and Secretary of Halesowen Railway, Hereford, Hay & Brecon Railway, Wrexham, Mold & Connah's Quay Railway, Whitby, Redcar & Middlesburgh Union Railway.

Arthur Campbell-Walker (Major) – also Chairman Preston Tramways Co., and later, Chairman Brighton & District Tramways Co.

P.E. Neville (Hampstead).

J. Robertson (Finchley).

Hon. Archer Turner (Kew).†

E.R. Vyvyan (Cheltenham).

*Son of same name was auditor of the concern (and his other audits included Corris, Cambrian, Hemel Hempstead & L.N.W.R., Manchester & Milford, Navan & Kingscourt, Pembroke & Tenby, Whitland & Cardigan, Merionethshire Railways).

†Father was Sir Llewellyn Turner (Parkia, Caernarvon), Director of N.W.N.G. Railways.

The 'RAILWAY YEAR BOOK' of 1911 (and 1914) gave the same entry; the Secretary and General Manager was J.E. Jones, and Registered Office at Bank Place, Portmadoc. 'No passenger traffic. Mineral traffic worked by horses in owners' wagons'.

REFERENCES

1. A relief map accompanying the Aberystwyth & Welsh Coast Railway Bill dated April 1863 shows Croesor Tramway as existent; also a proposed A.&W.C.R. branch to Blaenau Festiniog.
2. A. Ivor Pryce Deeds and Documents No. 1317. (Nat. Lib. Wales).
3. 'The Wyatts of Lime Grove, Llandygai'. (Trans. Caerns. Hist. Soc.) – [by kind permission.]
4. Carter Vincent No. 3188. (U.C.N.W., Bangor)
5. 'The Story of the Croesor United Slate Quarry Co. Ltd.' (T.A. Morrison) [Merionethshire Historical & Record Society Journal. Vol. IV, 1872]
6. Lords & Commons Sessional Papers 1856.
7. 'RHOSYDD SLATE QUARRY' (Lewis & Denton) [Cottage Press, Shrewsbury, 1974] gives extended detail of this concern.
8. From an extract in Festiniog Railway archives per Michael Seymour.
9. Minutes of House of Commons Select Committee, 6–7th July, 1869.
10. 'THE CAMBRIAN RAILWAYS' (Christiansen & Miller) p. 78, [David & Charles]

11. County Record Office Dolgelley: item Z/CD/100 (Sheet 7) A.&W.C.R. 1865.
12. Bradshaw's Railway Manual 1866, pp. 44, 66, 70.
13. Special Meeting: Cambrian Railways, Oswestry, 26th April, 1866.
14. According to a Board of Trade Report by Lt. Col. Hutchison of 5th March, 1870, in April 1866 (when work was suspended by financial crisis),
> "about 3½ miles of low sand embankments had been constructed out of side cuttings, a rock cutting about 10 chains long . . . three culverts, a mile of permanent way laid but not ballasted . . . cost £15,429 2s. 0d. incl. a sum of £9,000 for 7½ miles . . . of permanent way material . . . about 7 miles of permanent way materials have been ? by Mr. Savin for other purposes . . . Savin's contract with the Company dated 28th April, 1865."

(who had entered into bonds with the Company). Opinion was that under the contract, Le Feuvre ("a judgment creditor") was a creditor of Mr. Savin and not of the Beddgelert Railway Company.

The Report of 1870 mentions deterioration of the work done by removal of fencing, permanent way "and the decay of the sand embankment". There is also emphasis on the disparity in accounts as to how much constructional work had in fact been done, opinion being there was little to show for Mr. Le Feuvre's statement that £31,500 had been expended; "a highly-coloured certificate of expenditure"!

15. Breese Jones & Casson: Box 142 (County Record Office, Caernarvon)
16. Searell Collection: 4–5/9 (U.C.N.W., Bangor).

Searell proposal of possibly pre-1850 for a railway to Portmadoc with 8 ft wide loading gauge, iron rails "to pattern approved by the Engineer, not more than 15 ft long and to weigh not less than eighty pounds each bar, to be laid in iron chairs not exceeding three feet from centre to centre, none to weigh less than seven pounds . . . good sound stone sleepers 14 inches square × 8 inch depth with ends of each rail to be fastened in an iron chair . . ."

The same documents refer to an estimate for re-opening Hafod-y-Llan Quarry by Searell in 1856, and by Wyatt (of Penrhyn) in 1860.

Opposition by Priestley (see Gorseddau Tramway) over acquisition of necessary land; amendments to course necessary to satisfy Turnpike Trustees.

The impression formed by these and other documents is that the Hafod Quarry's tramway as built would serve a standard gauge branch (originally conceived as The Beddgelert Railway) with trans-shipment at the foot of the tramway.

17. 'The Quarry Manager's Journal' (June 1944).
18. Festiniog Railway Society, Heritage Group Newsletter No. 7 (Summer 1986).
19. Merionethshire Historical & Record Society Journal, Vol. VI, p. 198.
20. The Quarries' Collection of 25 in. O.S. Plans was donated to the Nat. Libr. Wales.
21. 'HANES PLWYF FFESTINIOG'.
22. Cynhaiarn Papers 202–231 (U.C.N.W., Bangor).
23. Letter: Moses Kellow to J. Davies re railway potential from Croesor Quarries; 1st December, 1914. (Davies Collection) [Nat. Libr. Wales].
24. 'THE FESTINIOG RAILWAY' (J.I.C. Boyd) Vol. II, pp. 329–30.
25. 'RHOSYDD SLATE QUARRY' (Lewis & Denton) p. 80.

THE BETTWS-Y-COED & FESTINIOG
RAILWAY

In the north of Caernarvonshire the Chester & Holyhead Railway bestrode the coast, choosing for its course the narrow strip of upper foreshore for much of its journey between Chester and the Conway River. It had opened in stages, but ultimately the full route was opened on 18th March, 1850 with the bridging of the Menai Straits completed. In 1856 the working of that railway was taken over by the London & North Western Railway and became vested in it in 1858. That same year a branch 3½ miles long on the north-east bank of the Conway River was opened on 1st October by the St. George's Harbour & Railway Co., to Llandudno; an intermediate station at Deganwy (from whence at a later date it was hoped to ship considerable loads of slate from Festiniog) was opened in April 1868. Trains for Llandudno started from Conway and the present-day approach to Llandudno from the coast line was non-existent.

In 1897 the present Llandudno Junction was opened, (the original was opened in November 1858) and the Llandudno line junction re-sited to face Down trains. Into this same junction station (but in those days from the south-west and along the east shore of the Conway, and not as today) came the Conway & Llanrwst Railway whose 11¼ miles from the Junction to Llanrwst were opened on 17th June, 1863.

The Conway & Llanrwst had had a far more interesting birth than this simple recital of dates might indicate, but as the line falls more properly into the north Caernarvonshire section, it will be found in its proper context of a proposed narrow gauge railway in 'NARROW GAUGE RAILWAYS IN NORTH CAERNARVONSHIRE', Vol.3, p.214. Suffice to say that with none other than H.B. Roberts as solicitor for the promoters, a line was drafted on 28th February, 1853 to run from the Chester & Holyhead at Conway.[1] Nothing tangible transpiring, another plan for a line extending fifteen miles to Bettws-y-Coed and described as 'Secondary System; Gauge 3 ft 3 in.; Capital £45,000 in £10 Shares' appeared on a prospectus of September 1858 having such provisional directors as C.M. Holland of Liverpool and James Swinton Spooner of Beaver Grove, Llanrwst, to show it was no idle threat. The detail of these schemes, formed once more to bleed off the valuable slate traffic from Blaenau Festiniog, must await its proper place.

In 1867 the Conway & Llanrwst Railway was absorbed by the L.N.W.R. who extended it 3¾ miles to a new terminus at Bettws-y-Coed (there are various ways of spelling the name) on 6th April, 1868. The former Llanrwst terminal became the goods yard.

Only a short time after this, the North Wales Narrow Gauge Railways issued its prospectus which showed that Bettws was one of its objectives and would be reached from Capel Curig by means of the Llugwy valley. By this time the L.N.W.R. had formed plans of its own to thrust southward for twelve miles via the Lledr Valley, pierce the mountain wall north of Blaenau Festiniog, and tap the slate traffic at its heart. In order to make the line cheaply and to bring wagons of slate direct from the quarries into Bettws for trans-shipment, it intended to break the gauge there and build southward in 1 ft 11½ in. gauge and make physical junctions with slate producers in Blaenau. There was also a deeper idea of obtaining running powers over the Festiniog and Festiniog & Blaenau lines. Thus the L.N.W.R. hoped to scotch Great Western Railway plans to attack Blaenau from the southeast by means of an ostensibly independent line striking northwest from Bala. The L.N.W.R. petitioned against the N.W.N.G. Railways bill in that the lands sought for building that line were required by their own Bettws & Festiniog Railway, but resolved the problem when joint ventures for a station in Bettws were agreed upon.

To put their schemes into practice the L.N.W.R. was empowered by two Acts of Parliament. The first was the 'L.N.W.R. (Additional Powers) Act of 1872' which as 35 & 36 Vic. Cap. 87 was assented on 18th July, 1872, the relevant portion being: '. . . expedient that one of the railways by this Act authorised (hereinafter called the Bettws & Festiniog Railway) should be constructed on the same gauge as the other local railways with which it is intended to be connected. (Section 5. Para. 6) . . . The Bettws & Festiniog Railway (length 11 m. 7 fur. 1 ch.) commencing in the parish of Bettws-y-Coed . . . and terminating . . . by a junction with the Festiniog Railway . . .' In Section 15 there is reference to 9 & 10 Vic. Cap. 57 (Gauge of Railways Act) which suggests that notwithstanding the contents of said Act, the B.&F.R. should be built and maintained to a gauge of 1 ft 11¾ in., 'being the gauge of the Festiniog Railway . . . with which the B.&F.R. is intended to form a junction (or such other wider gauge etc.)' Under Section 16 it would be unlawful to run passenger trains without the consent of the Gwydyr Estate between midnight Saturday and midnight Sunday. Section 17 suggests the rates for carriage should be 2d. per ton mile for slates in private owner wagons, or 3d. per ton mile for slates in L.N.W.R. (2 ft gauge) wagons, plus an additional charge for trans-shipping at the break of gauge for traffic of all descriptions. The period for completion of the line was to be five years.

Further thought on the subject of connections at the Blaenau end of the line suggested that what was to be virtually an end-on junction with the north end of the Festiniog's Dinas branch there would only give the L.N.W.R. limited access to other quarries, and by the 'L.N.W.R. (New Works and Additional Powers) Act of 1873' which received Royal Assent on 28th July, 1873 – 36 & 37 Vic. Cap. 201 – the following is to be found among a hotch potch of bits and pieces; the preamble states:

And whereas by the L.N.W.R. (Additional Powers) Act 1872 the Company was empowered to make the Bettws-y-coed and Festiniog Railway for the purpose of connecting their system of railways with . . . the Festiniog Railway Company . . . and it is expedient that the Company should be empowered to run over and use so much of the railways of the Festiniog Railway Company as extends from the junction therewith of the . . . B.&F.R. to the terminal station at Dyffws of the Festiniog Company.

Powers were sought to purchase certain pieces of land on both west and east sides of the existing standard gauge Bettws terminus with the consent of Baroness Willoughby De Eresby (Gwydr Estate). It was intended that running powers over the east end of the Festiniog Railway should be subject to an agreement between the two Companies as to tolls etc., failure to agree being settled by an arbitrator appointed by the Board of Trade.

It has already been shown that the Festiniog & Blaenau Railway intended to link with the L.N.W.R. in the neighbourhood of Duffws, and had this taken place, there would have literally been a 'scissors movement' of the two narrow gauge companies across the tracks of the Festiniog. The matter caused great anxiety to Spooner and the Festiniog Board, and though details are outside the scope of the present account, the outcome was that the Festiniog agreed not to oppose entry of the L.N.W.R. into Blaenau so long as it did not interfere with the Festiniog's line into Duffws terminus; by this they meant the threat of L.N.W.R. narrow gauge trains running across their own tracks and down the Festiniog & Blaenau to Llan Ffestiniog would cease. Thus the matter was resolved, but it is an interesting speculation how matters would have gone had the Merionethshire Railway come into existence and the L.N.W.R. found themselves south-east of Blaenau. The interplay of Cambrian, Great Western, London & North Western, Festiniog, Merionethshire and Festiniog & Blaenau interests, not to mention mixed gauge trackage, would have been good business for the lawyers and further work for Parliament. Some of these Companies could not live together elsewhere, let alone in company!

Returning to Bettws and the building of the new narrow gauge extension south of this terminus, it was intended that the station should be of mixed gauge, and shared with the North Wales Narrow Gauge Railways. At an early date work was started on the major civil engineering obstacle, the long tunnel at Blaenau – to narrow gauge standards. By 1876 it was reported that '. . . on the Bettws & Festiniog line the tunnel works were proceeding steadily and considerable progress had been made with the remaining portions of the railway'. The bridging contractor was a local man, Gethin Jones. Between Bettws and Pont-y-pant the track crossed the River Lledr by an odd stone structure, half wall and half viaduct of six small arches plus a large one, still locally known as Gethin's Bridge or Pont Gethin. Certain other work was done by Thomas and Robert Dougall, two Scots brothers both of whom may have had previous railway building experience in Russia which may have qualified them for the peculiar problems of the Lledr Valley where they ultimately settled and took to farming near Dolwyddelen. The ruling grade was 1 in 47 to a summit 790 ft above sea-level about 400 yd. from the Festiniog end.

Whereas work on the ground went ahead steadily, piercing of the tunnel began in February 1875 and became more difficult owing to the hardness of the rock. The contractor for this work failed, and the

L.N.W.R., under William Smith, took over the work themselves. Smith was their Engineer for the Bangor District.

During this impasse there occurred the failure of the North Wales Narrow Gauge Railways General Undertaking (which would have terminated jointly with the L.N.W.R. at Bettws); there was a growing conviction that the stage was already set for the Festiniog & Blaenau Railway to be encompassed by the Great Western, and the visions of the L.N.W.R. (built to any gauge!) straddling the quarry district from north-west to south-east at Festiniog became a thing of the past, so Euston decided very wisely to revise its plans. G.P. Neele writing in 1904, ('RAILWAY REMINISCENCES' p. 230) puts it very simply:

> The line from Bettws-y-coed to Festiniog was originally intended to be constructed on the very narrow gauge adopted by Mr. Spooner for his "toy railway" from Festiniog to Penrhyndeudraeth, but in order to avoid constructing engines and vehicles of different gauge, the Directors decided on keeping to the 4 ft 8½ in. gauge throughout. The change entailed considerable outlay as many of the curves and viaducts had to be re-arranged. The cost was especially excessive in the long tunnel near the terminus at Blaenau Festiniog. So much so that the Directors called for a special report on the expenditure.

Of the tunnel he wrote,

> The contractor long back had given up the work and the Company's own Engineer, Mr. W. Smith of Bangor, had the difficulty to contend with. The line was opened in July . . . but the slate traffic itself which was a considerable factor in the calculations of the probable receipts from the line was very slow in adopting the route by rail. The quay at Deganwy was in subsequent years arranged to suit this particular traffic, but has not been phenomenally successful.

Neele ends by saying,

> . . . As the terminus of the line at Blaenau Festiniog was but a short distance from that of Mr. Spooner's line, subsequently it was extended so as to be exactly opposite his station . . . a new means of inland communication to and from the slate quarries was given by the line to Llandudno Junction . . .[2]

To complete the story of the initial invasion of Blaenau Festiniog by a standard gauge railway based on London, it should be recorded that the first L.N.W.R. "station" was at the south end of the tunnel mouth which was regarded only as a temporary terminal for mineral traffic. Traffic began here in January 1879.* Had the 2 ft gauge line come about, it would have emerged from a tunnel at this same point and made a physical junction with a branch from Greaves' Quarry. Further, nearby it was to be connected with the Welsh Slate Co. by an incline. There was to be an engine run-round and an end-on junction with the Festiniog line.

The single line tunnel under Moel Dyrnogydd was 2 miles 206 yards long, the longest on the L.N.W.R. system. Neele describes the opening inspection very fully, the inspection of the tunnel being made on foot,

---

*Elsewhere given as June 1879 and the opening to passengers on 22nd July, 1879.

followed by a carriage with its doors open on both sides propelled by an engine at walking speed '. . . the engineer's men having lanterns also showing the jagged edges of the tunnel . . .'.

The second station, about 300 yards south of the temporary one, was opened 1st April, 1881 across the road from the Exchange station which the Festiniog opened there for the exchange of passenger traffic. The narrow/standard exchange sidings north of the L.N.W.R. permanent station were opened on the same day, also the Queen's Hotel (built by the L.N.W.R.) which having lost money, was later sold.[3]

Whilst Neele was undoubtedly correct in summing up the failure of the L.N.W.R. to woo away the slate traffic (the pier at Deganwy was a White Elephant for many years, with its rows of narrow gauge tracks on to which the Earlstown-built 'slate-truck wagons' were to discharge their cargoes) the threat of traffic being enticed away by cut-price rates was very real. Cambrian representative C. Lewis met C.E. Spooner in Portmadoc and they signed a Joint Agreement on 10th May, 1881 headed 'Slate Rates and opening of the L.N.W.R. Bettws-y-coed line'. The L.N.W.R. had quoted an all-in rate of 14s. 11d. per ton for slate and 'to meet this unusual state of things' it was recommended that Cambrian and Festiniog together quote 14s. 9d. (including transshipment and loading) which broken down would mean 12s. 3d. to the Cambrian, 2s. 1d. to the Festiniog and 5d. for loading. It was further agreed that additional standard and narrow gauge trans-shipment sidings be provided at Minffordd. The rate and the work was duly carried out, and though quarry owners were continually complaining, they were conservative enough to continue, in the main, supporting the venture which they knew best.[4]

If the prospect of Crewe-built 2-ft gauge engines emerging from a 2-mile tunnel at Blaenau had finally disappeared, so had the hopes of the Directors at Euston that the order of things might change to their advantage.

REFERENCES

1. Glynllifon Collection 2241 & 2242. Caernarvon Record Office.
2. 'NARROW GAUGE RAILWAYS IN NORTH CAERNARVONSHIRE' Vol. 3, p. 215. (J.I.C. Boyd) [Oakwood Press].
3. 'THE FESTINIOG RAILWAY' Vol. I, p. 135. (J.I.C. Boyd) [Oakwood Press].
4. 'British Railway Journal' No. 15 (1987) p. 256 for details L.N.W.R. Slate Truck Wagons: some detail inaccurate.

NORTH WALES NARROW GAUGE
RAILWAYS COMPANY
(Gauge 1 ft 11½ in. – also officially returned as 1 ft 11¼ in. and Two Feet)

Incorporated by Act: 35/6 Vic. Cap. 175 of 6th August, 1872. Powers to build a 'General Undertaking'; a railway from Croesor & Port Madoc Railway (sic) to Bettws-y-Coed, and a 'Moel Tryfan Undertaking' connecting Llanwnda with Beddgelert and Bryngwyn (two railways).

Act: 36/7 Vic. Cap. 72 of 16th June, 1873. Powers to lease Moel Tryfan Undertaking to H.B. Roberts, etc.

Act: 39/40 Vic. Cap. 125 of 13th July, 1876. Powers to abandon General Undertaking, etc.

Act: 48/9 Vic. Cap. 134 of 31st July, 1885. Powers to extend to Caernarvon Harbour: separate undertaking.

Act: 53/4 Vic. Cap. 70 of 4th July, 1890. Extension of time for works of 1885 Act, and alteration in capital arrangements, etc.

Act: 55/6 Vic. Cap. 44 of 20th June, 1892. Rates and Charges.

Light Railway Order: 3rd November, 1900. Powers to extend line from Rhyd-Ddu to Beddgelert.

Agreement: 26th August, 1904 with Portmadoc, Beddgelert & South Snowdon Railway. Powers of L.R.O. of 3rd November, 1900 to pass to P.B.&S.S.R. This ratified by P.B.&S.S.R. L.R.O. of 24th October, 1906.

Light Railway Order: 6th June, 1905. Powers to work Moel Tryfan Undertaking as Light Railway.

Receiver appointed 1877.

Opened – Goods:	Dinas–Quellan (sic) (Temporary Station), 21st May 1877.*
	Dinas–Snowdon Ranger, 1st June, 1878.
	Dinas–South Snowdon (Rhyd-Ddu), 14th May, 1881.
	Tryfan Junction–Bryngwyn, 21st May 1877.*
Opened – Passengers:	Dinas–Quellan (sic) (Temporary Station), 15th August, 1877.
	Dinas–Snowdon Ranger, 1st June, 1878.
	Dinas–South Snowdon (Rhyd-Ddu), 14th May, 1881.
	Tryfan Junction–Bryngwyn, 15th August, 1877.
Closed – Passengers:	Tryfan Junction–Bryngwyn, 31st December, 1913.
	Dinas–South Snowdon, 31st October, 1916.
Closed – Goods:	Whole system run on an 'as Required' basis from 31st October, 1916.
	Purchased by Welsh Highland Railway (Light Railway) Co. as part of new system, 1st January, 1922.
Registered Office:	Parliament Street, London. (1873).
	60 Threadneedle Street, London, E.C. (1876).
	Dinas Junction. (1883).
	14 Dale Street, Liverpool. (1914).
Length:	Dinas Junction–Top of Incline, Bryngwyn, 5 m. 0 fur. 9 ch.
	Tryfan Junction–Rhydd-Ddu, 7 m. 1 fur. 8 ch.
	Officially returned as (1921):
	Length of road, 12 m. 40 ch.
	2nd track, 48 ch.
	Total, 13 m. 8 ch.
	Sidings, 1 m. 46 ch.

Maximum Gradient: 1 in 35.
Minimum Curve: 3¾ chains.
Maximum Axle Load: 4 Tons.
Speed Restrictions: 25 m.p.h. (mixed trains), (later 16 m.p.h.).
Cost per Mile: £10,434 (slight variations quoted).

Authorised Capital: Shares 1874–5 £150,000: 1876– £106,000
Loan 1874–5 £50,000: 1876–9 £35,300
1880–1900 £50,000: 1901–1921 £54,000
Further £20,437 created 1919 but not issued.

*May dates also given elsewhere as June in each case.

Issued: Ordinary: 1876–1918   £65,975

6% Pref.	1876		£2,496
	1877		£15,150
	1878		£17,140
	1880		£17,340
	1881–1918		£17,390
	1919–1921		£96,000★

Loan:	1876	@ 6% £18,500	
	1877–9	@ 5% £2,300	@ 6% £19,700
	1880	Nil	
	1881–7	@ 4% £2,800	@ 4½% £3,200
	1888–9	@ 4% £4,400	@ 4½% £1,600

Debentures:	1880	@ 4% £25,940	@ 5% £3,123
A & B = 4%	1881–4	£30,000	£3,123
C = 5%	1885–9	£30,000	£3,463–3,563
	1890	£36,200	£3,563
	1891–2	£37,807	£3,563
	1893	£38,277	£3,563
	1894	£39,177	£3,563
	1895–1921	£39,477	£3,563

★*Financial position 1921:*	A Debentures	4%	£ 9,477	
	B "	4%	£ 26,060	– part repaid?
	C "	5%	£ 3,563	
	6% Pref. Shares		£ 17,390	
	Ordinary Shares		£ 66,000	
			£122,490	

Beddgelert Extension: Authorised Capital: Shares £13,800
                                                                         Loan   £4,600
(account kept separately from Moel Tryfan Undertaking).

Historical Summary

1872 North Wales Narrow Gauge Railways Company incorporated to build two undertakings.
1873 Moel Tryfan Undertaking leased to Hugh Beaver Roberts for 21 years.
1874 Roberts repudiates lease – construction incomplete by specified date, August. Construction ceases, November.
1875 Construction resumes, April.

1876 Powers obtained to abandon General Undertaking, July.
      Agreement for hire of rolling stock, November.
      Agreement between Company and J.C. Russell to above effect,
      November.

1877 Board of Trade inspections; openings begin (see title pages).
      Receiver appointed by Grant & Co.

1878 Further Agreements re hire of rolling stock, April, October.
      Opening to Snowdon Ranger for goods traffic, June.
      Moel Tryfan Rolling Stock Co. Ltd. incorporated, December
      (registered March 1879).
      Debt now assigned to M.T.R.S.C. Ltd., December.
      High Court appoints J.C. Russell, Receiver, December.

1880 Scheme of arrangement with creditors.

1881 Railway completed and opened to Rhyd-Ddu, May.

1885 Extension to Caernarvon, and extension of Bryngwyn branch
      slate quarry feeders to improve transport to the branch: 'The
      Caernarvon & Bryngwyn Extensions', July.

1889 Moel Tryfan Rolling Stock Co. Ltd. ceases business, June.

1890 Extension of time to complete, and extended financial facilities,
      July.

1891 Regulation of Railways Act 1889 – exceptions permitted to
      N.W.N.G.R., December.

1892 2nd Class abolished. Extension of time (1890) lapses.

1894 Moel Tryfan Rolling Stock Co. Ltd. dissolved, April.

1898 Application made to Light Railway Commissioners to work as
      Light Railway under Light Railway Act of 1896, November.

1900 Beddgelert Light Railway Extension Order permits extension of
      N.W.N.G.R. south to Beddgelert, passing to rear of Goat Hotel
      and terminating there, November. Three years allowed for com-
      pletion but little work done along whole length.

1903 Powers lapse for B.L.R.E. Order, November.

1904 Agreement with Portmadoc, Beddgelert & South Snowdon Rail-
      way Co. for B.L.R.E. Order to pass to them if powers re-
      obtained, August.

1905 Powers to work Moel Tryfan Undertaking as Light Railway (first
      application had been made, November 1898) and to work by
      electricity, June.

1914 Provisional Order: P.B. & S.S.R. and N.W.N.G.R. 'Revival &
      transfer of powers'.
      A Portmadoc, Beddgelert & Caernarvon Light Railway Commit-
      tee formed to transfer P.B. & S.S.R. and N.W.N.G.R. into a
      proposed newly-formed company, and revive certain powers now
      lapsed, November.
      (This would ultimately take shape in the form of a Light Railway
      Order in 1922.)

1922 N.W.N.G.R. absorbed into Welsh Highland (Light Railway)
      Co., January.

History

By the early seventies the time was ripe for what might be termed an 'explosion' of narrow gauge schemes in North Wales. The timing could not have been better. On the premier line of the time, the Festiniog, steam locomotives had shown their mettle; Fairlie's Patent double engine had come to the forefront, and passenger traffic was not only legalised but growing.new lines to quarries at Croesor and Gorseddau had been laid down, a small extension to the Festiniog's eastern end was now open, and plans were laid to extend the line out to Croesor by making a northwards branch which might ultimately link Portmadoc with Caernarvon. Charles Spooner's involvement lay directly or indirectly with each and every scheme; he was the 'common denominator'. Spooner's advocacies had never before appeared to be more correct. The menace of other railway invaders was still contained, even though it was not long delayed. As yet, there was nothing to show that Spooner had not been right all along the line, and everything to show that nothing succeeded better than success.

So it came about that a Master Plan to link almost all the larger places in North-west Wales by narrow gauge railway – and some of much less significance also – was born. This was to be a comprehensive, worked by a Company whose administrators (as far as possible) were either experienced or would be locally beneficial and influential. The railways proposed were not all connected, but all were to be of a gauge between 2 ft and 2 ft 9 in. Chief Engineer to the scheme was Charles E. Spooner, and Assistant Engineer Hugh Unsworth McKie, now of Tanyrallt, Tremadoc, a director of the Croesor & Port Madoc Railway, and who had recently resigned (1872) from the Croesor United Slate Co. after a disagreement with the directors. The provisional promotional committee included Sir R. William M.L. Bulkeley, Sir Ll. Turner, G.A. Huddart and J.P. de Winton of the Caernarvon engineering works, and the four initial directors became Livingston Thompson (a director and past Chairman of the Festiniog), Sir Llewellyn Turner (a slate quarry owner and prominent local figure who lived at Parkia, north of Caernarvon), Hugh Beaver Roberts who has already come to notice, and J.H. Oliver.

Eight railways were proposed, but Parliament rejected application to make Railways Nos. 2, 3, 4, 5 and 8. The full proposal was:

No.1 To extend from a Junction with the Portmadoc, Croesor & Beddgelert Tram Railway Company's proposed line to Beddgelert, thence to Pen-y-Gwryd via Nant Gwynant involving reversing spirals of 2 chains radius. Thence to Capel Curig and Bettws-y-Coed.

No.2 From Bettws-y-Coed, following alongside route of Holyhead –London road to a point three miles west of Corwen.

No.3 From end Railway No.2 into Corwen, terminating behind standard gauge railway station (G.W.R.).

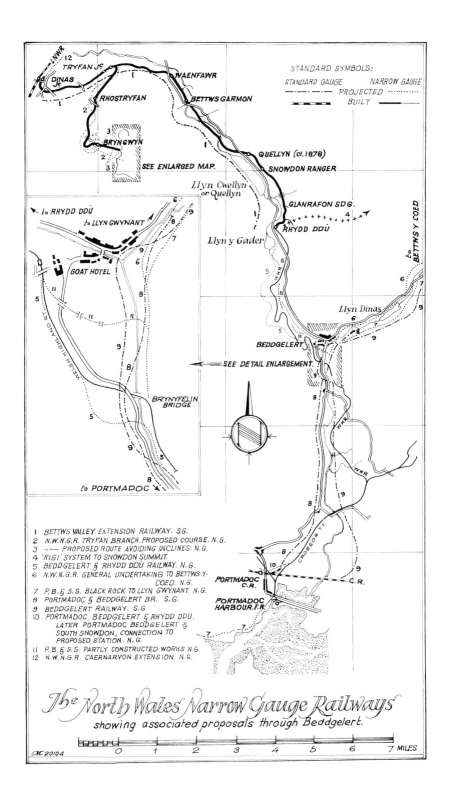

STANDARD SYMBOLS:

STANDARD GAUGE   NARROW GAUGE

PROJECTED ·········

BUILT ━━━━━

12   L.N.W.R.

TRYFAN JC.

DINAS JC.

WAENFAWR

RHOSTRYFAN

BETTWS GARMON

BRYNGWYN

SEE ENLARGED MAP.

QUELLYN (cl.1878)

SNOWDON RANGER

Llyn Cwellyn
or Quellyn

GLANRAFON SDG.

RHYDD DDU

to BETTWS Y COED

Llyn y Gader

to RHYDD DDU

to LLYN GWYNANT

GOAT HOTEL

WELSH HIGHLAND RY.

Llyn Dinas

BEDDGELERT

BRYNYFELIN
BRIDGE

SEE DETAIL ENLARGEMENT.

W.H.R.

W.H.R.

to PORTMADOC

CROESOR T.

PORTMADOC
C.R.

PORTMADOC
HARBOUR. F.R.

C.R.

1   BETTWS VALLEY EXTENSION RAILWAY. S.G.
2   N.W.N.G.R. TRYFAN BRANCH. PROPOSED COURSE. N.G.
3   -"- PROPOSED ROUTE AVOIDING INCLINES. N.G.
4   'RIGI' SYSTEM TO SNOWDON SUMMIT.
5   BEDDGELERT & RHYDD DDU RAILWAY. N.G.
6   N.W.N.G.R. GENERAL UNDERTAKING TO BETTWS-Y-
     COED. N.G.
7   P.B.& S.S. BLACK ROCK TO LLYN GWYNANT. N.G.
8   PORTMADOC & BEDDGELERT BR. S.G.
9   BEDDGELERT RAILWAY. S.G
10   PORTMADOC, BEDDGELERT & RHYDD DDU.
     LATER PORTMADOC BEDDGELERT &
     SOUTH SNOWDON, CONNECTION TO
     PROPOSED STATION. N.G.
11   P.B.& S.S. PARTLY CONSTRUCTED WORKS N.G.
12   N.W.N.G.R. CAERNARVON EXTENSION. N.G.

The North Wales Narrow Gauge Railways
showing associated proposals through Beddgelert.

JC 20104

0   1   2   3   4   5   6   7 MILES

No.4 A short branch reached by reversing from Railway No.1, to the L.N.W.R. standard gauge terminus of the line from Llandudno Junction, in Bettws-y-Coed. (The L.N.W.R.'s line south of this point was to be of narrow gauge.)

No.5 A branch from Railway No.2 in the Lledr Valley, to Penmachno.

No.6 A branch from Dinas, on the L.N.W.R. Caernarvon–Afon Wen line, to Bryngwyn, with an incline to the Moel Tryfan area slate quarries.

No.7 An extension from Railway No.6 to Rhyd-Ddu, South Snowdon.

No.8 A short line from Pwllheli (adjacent to the Cambrian Railways' terminus of that period) to Porthdynllaen, with the added possibility of joining up with the Portmadoc end of Railway No.1, by either an independent line from Pwllheli to Portmadoc or by laying a third rail along the Cambrian Railways.

The Draft Bill went before a House of Commons Select Committee in early April 1872. It listed the subscribers as including Livingston Thompson, Sir Llewellyn Turner, Hugh B. Roberts and James H. Oliver and stated that they, plus three others, would be the first directors.

Objections had been raised by:

Porthdynllaen Harbour Co.	(Opposed to Railway No.8)
Cambrian Railways Co.	('Injurious to their rights and interests')
Charles Edwards of Dolseran Hall, Dolgelley	(Opposed to Railway No.1)
G.W. Duff Assheton-Smith, (Owner of estates at Bettws Garmon etc.)	('Railway will seriously injure the amenities. No public necessity for same')
Baroness Willoughby de Eresby	(Opposition included that of the 'gauge being inconvenient')
London & North Western Railway	(In connection with their promoted Bettws & Festiniog Railway, the land would be required for their own use)
Lord Penrhyn	('Inconvenience of gauge. Injury to his Glan Conway Estate')

The petition from Lord Penrhyn was accompanied by an account from his solicitors for £50!

The promoters were 'quarry owners, landed proprietors and other gentlemen interested in the district concerned . . . the scheme had been suggested by the success of the Festiniog Railway'.

Of the eight railway developments proposed, applications were made only for Railways Nos. 1, 6 and 7, the first to incorporate the scheme for Railway No.4. Powers were granted by an Act 35/6 Vic. Cap. 175 of

6th August, 1872 and this divided the venture into two Undertakings:

1. General Undertaking. Railway No.1 (22 m. 6 fur. 4 ch.) from a junction with the Croesor & Port Madoc Railway and ending in a field called Cae Isa at Graig-glan-conway, Bettws-y-Coed.

2. Moel Tryfan Undertaking. Railway No.6 (5 m. 9 ch.) from Dinas to a farm called Vron Heulog (Top of Incline, Bryngwyn). Railway No.7 (7 m. 1 fur. 8 ch.) from Tryfan Junction with Railway No.6, ending in a field called Cae Mawr on Fridd Isa farm, parish of Beddgelert.

On the assumption that the Bettws & Festiniog Railway became law under the L.N.W.R. Additional Powers Bill in the 1872 Session (this was to be the narrow gauge extension of the Conway Valley line) and authority was given to proceed, then there was to be a junction with the Bettws & Festiniog Railway south of Bettws which would enable The General Undertaking's line to enter Bettws over Bettws & Festiniog metals. The station would be a joint one, with part of it given over to the use of the North Wales Narrow Gauge and Bettws & Festiniog Railways, the L.N.W.R. providing a third rail in their standard gauge where this was necessary. It appears that staffing would be carried out by the L.N.W.R., with N.W.N.G. running powers from the junction to the station.

The influence of local landowners was over-riding, not only in matters of the flesh, either. Under the threat of a £5 fine for every contravention, the Gwydr Estate was empowered to fine the N.W.N.G. should it pick up or set down passengers within five miles of the Waterloo Bridge, Bettws-y-Coed, between the hours of 5 a.m. and 10 p.m. on Sundays!

Under the Act the Portmadoc, Croesor & Beddgelert Tram Railway Co.'s line (still in practice the Croesor Tramway as completed in 1864) was to be relaid suitably for locomotive traffic by and at the expense of the Railways Co., between Portmadoc wharves and the junction with the south end of Railway No.1. This work was not to be carried out until half Railway No.1 was complete and land for the remainder obtained; the Portmadoc Co. would be given twelve month's notice of intention to commence. (Later, when powers to abandon The General Undertaking were sought and secured, the old tram line was left undisturbed for many years to come.)

The way was now clear for work to begin. A Prospectus was issued on 23rd January, 1873 outlining the Company's proposals, and on 23rd December, 1872 a contract had been given to H.U. McKie, co-Engineer of the Company, assisted by George Lea, for the construction of the line for a sum of £56,150. It was the Directors' intention to tackle The Moel Tryfan Undertaking first, regarding which an Agreement had been entered into also on 23rd December, 1872 between them and one of their number, the ubiquitous H.B. Roberts, who was prepared to lease the railway for 21 years from completion, according to the

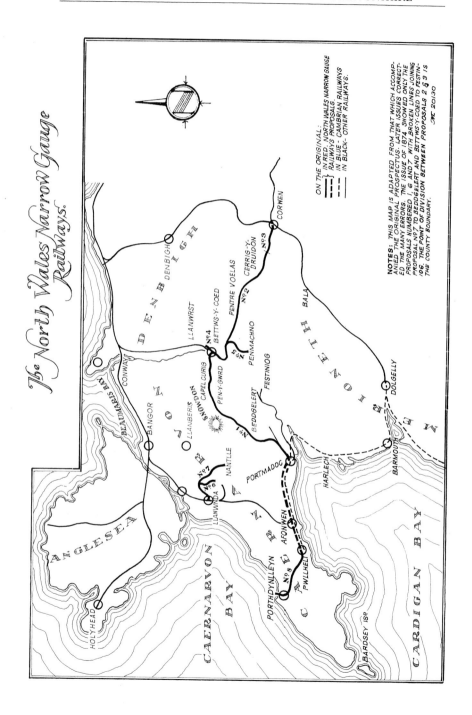

contracted finishing date. This Agreement was modified at a meeting on 23rd April, 1873 and Parliamentary authority for it was given by Act 36/7 Vic. Cap. 72 of 16th June, 1873.

The terms were that the period of leasing should now commence from the date of the Board of Trade Certificate authorising the opening. The rent to be paid was a complex sum involving Debenture Rent, Administration Rent, Fixed Rent etc. and was set down in detail in the Schedule to the Act. It was calculated on the yearly interest @ 6% of the Debenture Stock of the Company – the amount of administration costs, a rent on the borrowed capital *for the time being* – allowances being made for occasions when the net profits did not exceed the combined Debenture and Administration Rents. It is remarkable that, under the financial clauses alone of this Agreement, Roberts should have so allowed himself to be tied down; his confidence in the amount of business the railway would bring is surprising.

The lessee also agreed to spend £10,000 (covenanted to be paid to him by the Company) on locomotives and rolling stock for working the line and 'turning to the utmost profit, the demised premises'. He was to consult the Company's Engineer before providing same, and was to keep them in full repair 'so that they shall always be of the full value of £10,000 or upwards, and sufficient for the development of traffic'(!)

This last section is quite extraordinary. Whilst we currently live in an age of inflation and rising values, machinery to be used in such circumstances as this was hardly likely to hold its value. Again, the frame of mind in which Roberts agreed to this is beyond understanding.

The next portion of the Agreement shows how adroitly, while keeping himself in the background, Robert Fairlie had imposed himself on C.E. Spooner; and how strongly the influence of Festiniog Railway experience lay on the promoters. Fairlie's financial benefit was in the publicity the opportunity afforded him rather than the Royalties: how much it cost him to influence can only be hinted at. The lessee '. . . shall at all times (unless otherwise agreed) have all the locomotives (except the Shunting Engines) in use upon the demised premises constructed and maintained according to the principle known as "Fairlie's Patents" and shall pay the royalty of £300 per engine payable in respect of the same principle' (Section 12).[1]

At the expiration of the lease, locomotives and stock 'to the full value of £10,000 to be given up and if exceeding the value "The Company to have option to acquire".' Roberts was not to assign his powers without the consent of the Company who would give him £10,000 within four weeks for the purchase of the stock.

McKie started work in the spring of 1873 and the first half-yearly meeting (reported in 'THE TIMES' on 10th March) said it was hoped he would complete both lines within the twelvemonth. As time went by, it was apparent that McKie's progress was not that of a man who would finish his assignment within the hoped-for period. Payments to him began to falter and relations with Spooner were far from easy. This situation arose when McKie took up the contract and, ceasing to be co-Engineer from that time, found himself with Charles E. Spooner as Engineer remaining. Spooner's inspection of the work became irregular and as McKie was paid on results, his remuneration fell behind. As payments fell behind, McKie's interest flagged and his work became slower. The contracted completion date was 24th November, 1874 and it soon became clear to the Board that this date would not be met. Worse still, Roberts, whose co-Director McKie was on the Croesor Tramway venture, began to have doubts too, and mindful of the problems of McKie, called a special meeting in August 1874 and duly repudiated the lease. The Company, not surprisingly alarmed by this, took legal advice but were recommended not to enforce the matter; the Company was in no position to stand firmly as it was short of cash and as McKie was unlikely to finish the contract to time, Roberts might enjoy a great deal of sympathy if the matter was taken into the Courts. By 12th November, 1874 all work had practically ceased. McKie had overshot his time. The Company was behind in payment.

McKie claimed that his work had not been properly assessed by the Engineer and he was consistently underpaid; the matter went to arbitration between Mr. James Brunlees and a long battle ensued, no work being done again until April 1875. The arbitrator visited the site and discovered that the contractor should have received '£43,050 for work done to the value of £41,303, including £1,500 for rails not delivered'. Having found for McKie, he awarded him £440 costs to be paid out of the Company's retention reserves, the Company to pay the cost of Chancery proceedings and an award of £3,253 and £300. When the Board met in Caernarvon on 24th May, 1875 it reported, 'The Directors had been led to expect a different result from the reference, but they could only come to the conclusion that the Company's Engineer had not given the contractor credit for as much as had been executed, and they learned to their great surprise that the requirements of the contract for periodical measurements being regularly taken by the Engineer in the presence of the contractor, had not been complied with . . .' [In the case of the Railways Co. v. McKie (papers filed 9th June, 1874) Charles E. Spooner maintained that certain materials had been paid for by the Railway Company, such as rails. This was to be the form of 'advance' to McKie but McKie refused to accept this form of payment and pressed for £570 in cash for work already done. McKie had already received £40,000 in cash. McKie had depot sites at Llanwnda and Bettws Garmon, together with an advance store at Nant Mill. As the Company would not pay him, he refused to take rails off the Company, inferring that this would suggest he was prepared to accept them instead of money. In consequence though rails were on hand, McKie would not bring them to the laying site and all work stopped. On 1st June, 1874 McKie began to remove materials lying at the three sites, including the rails. The Railway Company sent in a squad of men to prevent him but only succeeded for a day or so. The following materials were removed:

On 4th June 5 tons of dog spikes. These left Llanwnda and were shipped to the Isle of Man for use on the railway then building. The previous day 241 rails had left the lineside at this spot, and on the same day 174 rails were loaded away. The following day another 175 left similarly (this would have laid 2,360 yards of railway line).

On 6th June materials were moved from Nant Mill and placed in a field near McKie's residence, where they were under his surveillance. McKie informed the Company he intended to continue removal of the materials.]

The Directors then announced that work would be hastened and could be completed in three or four months if 'vigorously prosecuted'; the contractor had been paid the award and there was no reason for further delay. They would use their endeavours to have the line opened as quickly as possible. Extra costs would certainly be involved. The Engineer reported that he thought £19,000 would be needed to open the line and it was added that local quarry owners wanted the railway extended so that they might use it (who 'they' were is not stated).

The McKie affair did not improve: on 23rd September, 1874 the Board reported that McKie was 'making far less progress than he should have done but that recently he had increased the number of men on the job'. They thought it unwise to make any change but gave the contractor notice to proceed 'with greater vigour generally and to direct his efforts to Railway No.6 so that traffic may be brought upon the line from quarries on that branch'.

If there were evident problems out on the line, there were equal but no-so-obvious problems within the Board Room. Half yearly meetings were poorly attended; the consistently adverse reports probably demoralised shareholders. Throughout the early period Sir Llewellyn Turner (he had been knighted for services to Caernarvon and district, had seen the Harbour improved and been a Mayor of the Town) held the Chair. Livingston Thompson was an early casualty along with H.B. Roberts, but thereafter there was some continuity through the troublesome period, the Chairman frequently having to ask for volunteers to the Board from the floor of the scantily attended meetings. (A list of Directors quoted for specimen years, is given at the end of this section.) J.H. Oliver of Brondanw, Caernarvon, served, Sir Richard William Mostyn Lewis Bulkeley (Bart) – an original promoter – came on in later 1873 and was succeeded by his son in October 1875 after the father died. There were Messrs. C. Pearson, T. Bolland, A. Fitzgibbon and C. Celyn, some of them serving as being local shareholders of varying influence but all of whom were losing money on the venture! None had other railway interests or board experience. At the end of this troublesome start, Henry Watts was still Secretary but Spooner ultimately resigned in favour of his son, young Edwin Spooner.

The method of financing of the Company's rolling stock at this time is not completely clear. From the first set of Receiver's accounts it would appear that when Roberts faded from the scene as threatened, the matter of financing the stock purchased during his time was carried out in two ways. The first way may have been the continuance of an arrangement between Roberts and the builders which was suitably transferred to become an arrangement between the Railways Co. and the builders; suffice to say that the coaches supplied by Ashbury Rly. Carr. & Iron Co. Ltd. and by Gloucester Wagon Co. Ltd. together with wagons were being paid for in instalments to the builders. The other way was of more consequence to the Company, for it tied itself to a financier who ultimately took office as Receiver and Chairman and who stood in the way of development until his death in 1912. This man was James C. Russell (a barrister), of whom more anon.

From the brief surviving accounts it appears that Russell was the owner of the Fairlie locomotives *Snowdon Ranger* and *Moel Tryfan*, and the engine *Beddgelert* from Hunslet. Nor was this all. He also financed certain coaches and wagons.

On 3rd December, 1878 The Moel Tryfan Rolling Stock Co. Ltd. was incorporated to 'purchase or otherwise acquire the locomotives, engines, carriages, waggons, trucks and rolling stock now in use by the N.W.N.G. Railways Co.' The Capital was £10,000 and the subscribers were:

Chaloner W. Chute,	Lincolns Inn,	Barrister
A.C. Humphreys Owen,	Garthmyl, Montgomery	
J.C. Russell,	86 Queens Gate, S.W.	
Alex Mortimer,	Paper Buildings, Temple	
Ernest E. Lake,	Hampstead,	Solicitor
W.L. Wiggett Chute,	Basingstoke	
Robert E. Tidswell,	Lincolns Inn,	Barrister

All were itemised when, as it will shortly be mentioned, Russell made an Agreement between The Moel Tryfan Rolling Stock Co. Ltd. and himself, dated 7th December, 1878. In this it was detailed that the aforementioned rolling stock was each fitted with a plate stating that Russell was the owner, save for *Beddgelert* which presumably had not yet been so treated. The dates of Russell's Agreements with the Railways Co. as to hire of the stock from him, were 18th November, 1876, and 27th April and 18th October, 1878.

The Agreements already made between Russell and the Railways Co. were to be continued and the first Directors were Chaloner W. Chute, Ernest E. Lake, and J.C. Russell; and of these Chute was already a Director of the Railway, Russell was shortly to be appointed Receiver and Lake was to become a Director, nearly thirty years later! (His firm were solicitors to The Moel Tryfan Rolling Stock Co. Ltd.) On 7th December Russell made an Agreement with the Rolling Stock Company to sell such stock as he hired to the Railway (and listed above), for a sum of £3,630, partly in ordinary and partly in preference shares of the Stock Company, a balance of £630 in cash to be paid within 14 days. The vendor might take shares instead of cash if he wished.

Russell also agreed to assign a debt of £882 10s. 7d. which had been obtained by him against the Railways Co. This case had been heard in the Exchequer Division on 18th November, 1878 when Russell took the Company to Court for non-payment of hire charges on the rolling stock. He obtained the above sum and costs. The judgement was recovered on the contract entered into by the Railway Co. on 18th November, 1876 – (the date of the first Agreement between Russell and the Railway to hire rolling stock.)

By indenture of 7th December, 1878 Russell assigned the debt to the Stock Company and advised the Railway accordingly. The Railway however, was still in no position to pay, and accordingly the Rolling Stock Co. lodged a petition in the Chancery Division against the Railway (the Stock Company having the advantage of considerable legal weight on its Board!) on 9th December, 1878. The outcome was obvious and it was recommended that the Railway Company's Secretary should be appointed Receiver but, in the event, Russell was decreed to be a fit and proper person to fill this role. It should be stressed that he was not the first Receiver to be appointed; a firm of financiers, Grant & Co., had previously advanced money to the Railway, and took them to Court for non-repayment; they had a Receiver appointed in the person of Samuel Lowell Price. The matter was an involved one and concerned action by the Trustees for the Debenture Holders against the Railway for not placing part of the Moel Tryfan capital. The Railway fought the decision and was successful in the Court of Appeal on 7th May, 1878. Price's 'reign' from 5th December, 1877 to 7th May, 1878 was terminated.

A little more may be said about these two Receivers, (albeit the second has been mentioned before the first!). Russell was rather more than a figure in N.W.N.G. Rlys. affairs alone, for in August 1880 he would take a further role by becoming Manager of the Manchester & Milford Railway which concern at that time had its management in the hands of the directors. This brought Russell into contact with James Szlumper (later Sir James) and together they were later to be found as fellow-promoters of a Vale of Rheidol light railway, an ambition of the Manchester & Milford which failed to materialise but to which The Light Railway Act of 1896 gave hope for fulfilment – hope which was to blossom into fact. Though Russell resigned from the Rheidol scheme in early 1899, it is significant that under Russell as its Chairman and Managing Director, the N.W.N.G. Board in 1906 included Sir James.[3]

The appointment of a Receiver by Grants must have warned the Company that in their perilous financial state there were other parties who might have a Receiver appointed; as Russell's appointment was carried out with some haste, was this a case of preferring the Devil they knew?!

As to Russell's involvement with The Moel Tryfan Rolling Stock

Company, this must have been a calculated financial operation involving willing investors who would have had an assured return and the possibility of redemption out of any surplus – such redemption taking place between 1886 and 1889.

The Stock Company was paid £1,947 in 1878 and £922 in 1879, but the Railways Co., showing deficits for the years 1878, 1879, 1880 and 1881 of £101, £1,893, £592 and £74 was finding it even more difficult to carry on. Ultimately the Stock Company was to be owed about £7,000 and the problem of repaying this was not resolved until 1880.

A return must now be made to the Board Room, for it was here that most development was taking place. The half yearly meeting of 2nd March, 1876 reported that McKie had continued to delay and had placed matters before Mr. James Brunlees for further arbitration. The Board had ultimately decided there was nothing for it but that McKie should have the works taken from him and he had been instructed to surrender all works, materials and plant by 7th February last. The Board was then negotiating with another contractor.

In the matter of shortage of funds, The General Undertaking (on which no work had been done), was the subject of an Act 39/40 Vic. Cap. 125 of 13th July, 1876. This empowered the Company to abandon the whole venture and nothing more was heard of it until resurrected by the North Wales Power & Traction Co. Ltd., who obtained a Light Railway Order in November 1903 for a line between Beddgelert and Bettws-y-Coed ('The Bettws Application' as it was known) but for which powers lapsed on 3rd August, 1907 without any work being done. The powers for the work were then transferred to the Portmadoc, Beddgelert & South Snowdon Railway who could afford to do little about it either!

The next meeting on 17th August, 1876 announced that a Mr. J. Boys had been appointed contractor to complete The Moel Tryfan Undertaking; he had already made considerable progress. Heavy losses had been incurred due to the line's incomplete state and the disputes between the contractor and the engineer. Mr. Brunlees had made a further award to McKie of £7,417 'and they had got rid of him' (McKie). There was still the matter of the lease to Roberts, who had made it clear in August 1874 he would be free of obligation if the line was incomplete by the contracted date. The Company had been unable to further the matter and never did.

The meeting empowered the Board to issue as much of the newly authorised £40,000 Share capital, as they thought fit. It was agreed that 3,000 6% Preference Shares of £10 be issued to rank next after the £22,000 mortgages and before the Ordinary Shares amounting to £66,000. £16,000 was needed immediately to meet debts and to complete the railway authorised by Parliament and the balance would be used for rolling stock and extra expenses when the line was complete. The Board was trying to arrange for some debts to be paid in shares, but if existing shareholders did not come forward and subscribe to the new issue, the Company would collapse. Several quarry-owners on the line had promised to subscribe and use the line when ready for traffic. The Directors again repeated their confidence in the future of the railway.

A circular to shareholders dated 4th September, 1876 read:

> Mr. Beaver Roberts, the lessee of the Line under the Act of 1873, attended the recent meeting and stated that he considered the lease no longer binding; the Directors are advised to the contrary, but it is open to doubt whether the Company's interests would not be best served by making some arrangement with Mr. Roberts for the cancellation of the lease. That gentleman stated that if the lease were given up he would, until the line yielded a gross revenue of £10,000 a year, pay double rates on all slates carried from his quarry.

(The Receiver's accounts for the period December 1877 to May 1878 show Roberts had been by far the biggest user of the railway. The traffic from his quarry was worth, for instance, three times the value of either the 'Moel Tryfan Crown' or Alexandra Quarries.)

The Board were to consider this and report back to shareholders; it was two years since Roberts had made his feelings known, both sides had taken legal advice. It concluded with:

> If this appeal is not promptly responded to, the Board will have no alternative but to resign the management, and the Mortgagees and other Creditors be left to take what is available to meet their claims.

Administrative matters have now taken affairs up to the autumn of 1876 and it is now desirable to return to the railway to see how Boys the new contractor was getting on. He was making good progress and by May 1877 had reached Quellyn road bridge with the main line, enabling goods traffic to begin working publicly to that point within the third week of the month. The branch from Tryfan Junction to the top of the incline at Bryngwyn was also ready and open for goods and minerals services.

On 26th June, 1877 the Secretary Joseph Oldham advised the Board of Trade that the line would be 'ready in about a fortnight'; plans were sent on 19th July and on the following day the Secretary says 'will be sufficiently completed for the safe conveyance of passengers by 23rd July'. Second thoughts now prevailed and on 31st July he writes to the Board, 'it is found we are not in a position for working the passenger traffic on some parts of our line with perfect safety in all respects. Postpone inspection.'

There had been an informal Board of Trade inspection on 23rd July, 1877. Major Marindin had then reported that the new line commenced half a mile north of the L.N.W.R.'s existing station at Llanwnda on the Carnarvonshire Railway. At the new junction the L.N.W.R. had built an exchange platform and sidings and up until then, the N.W.N.G. Railways named their station Llanwnda too; as the L.N.W.R. of that station was to remain open, the N.W.N.G. agreed to change their name to Dinas. Additional land for doubling the narrow gauge had not been purchased.

Major F.A. Marindin made his first formal inspection on 31st July, 1877 and found certain bridges and cuttings too narrow; he looked in again on 20th August but the widening had not been finished. It was not done until the year-end but on 28th January, 1878 he passed the line for passenger traffic as far as the temporary station at Quellyn, and the Bryngwyn branch. Some off-the-record arrangement must have been made on 20th August previously, as both these lines had advertised a passenger service since the 15th of that month!

It has been emphasised that in many respects the railway was a modernised version of the Festiniog line but without the physical limitations of that railway. This influence was felt in another way; certainly at the beginning, all slate trains were worked Down by gravity (though over what extent of the line is not known), and the Inspector was careful to point out that they must carry the staff 'and be considered in the same light as an engine in steam'. Presumably the decline in slate traffic obliged the Company to change to Mixed Train working.

The next section to be ready took the railway to Snowdon Ranger and the Major inspected this on 22nd May, 1878. This was 7 furlongs further than the temporary terminus which had by then 'been removed'. On the new section was a six chain curve and upward gradient of 1 in 79. The gauge was given as 1 ft 11¼ in. The terminus had a run-round 'beyond it' and only Home and Distant signals were erected; as yet there was no nameboard and a waiting room with convenience for ladies had to be built. Approval to run a passenger service on the "One Engine in Steam" principle was given.

There were a number of features about the railway which the Inspector did not like, though on the whole he thought 'the works had been well carried out'. In some places the carriages cleared the cutting wall by only 2 ft instead of 2 ft 4 in. allowed; in most overbridges and some rock cuttings the carriage doors would not fully open and it was necessary to slew the rails and cut away projecting rock or masonry.

Some of the ironwork on bridges had been in place so long that it already required re-painting; likewise some masonry required repointing. On bridges the rails had been fastened to longitudinal sleepers by spikes; these had to be altered to fang bolts. There were no nameboards or clocks on display as yet at stations; some signal boxes had clocks, but they were not all fitted up.

The new carriage stock was intended to carry four persons per side. The Major thought they were too narrow for that number and decreed that three per side was sufficient! The Distant Signal at Llanwnda was not visible from the cabin and some trees should be lopped to clear the view; similarly at Moel Tryfan Junction the top of a high hedge had to be taken off and some additional locking put into the frame. The Major disliked the layout at Bryngwyn, where he insisted that the points at the foot of the incline should be weighted to keep them open for the sidings

The end of the line (or perhaps, the beginning?). The farthest point of the slate trans-shipment wharf, Dinas Junction *c*.1920. *L.&G.R.P. Courtesy David and Charles*

Dinas Junction, looking north in 1909, showing the N.W.N.G. side of the establishment. The interchange passenger platform is to the left; the Goods Shed contains a line of each gauge.

Collection: W.A. Camwell

Dinas Junction *c*.1892 with all three of the Company's engines and most of the carriage stock present. Note 'the three small four-wheelers' carriages in the front of the train, *Beddgelert* running chimney first; the three Gloucester-built carriages appear - less the fittings on the roof shown in the maker's photographs. Westinghouse brakes have been fitted but the point and signal work required under the 1889 Act is outside the bounds of the picture.

Collection: C.C. Green

A general view of Dinas Junction looking north in 1911 with signalman about to hand the staff to the driver of the 'Cauliflower' mixed traffic engine on the Afon Wen-bound train. To the right is the substantial stone building of the N.W.N.G. and also the wooden one of the L.N.W.R.

British Rail

Although dated after the opening of the Welsh Highland Railway, this view of Waenfawr in April 1926 looking towards Dinas Junction, has the advantage of showing the station 'cleaned up' and open after the years of disuse. *Moel Tryfan* with the Festiniog coach, the dual-fitted ex-Quarrymen's coach (F.R. No. 4) and N.W.N.G. coal wagons in rear. A Festiniog Railway van is in the siding to the right. *K.A.C.R. Nunn*

The line from Bettws Garmon station, looking south, with a 'standard' N.W.N.G. bridge. At this time in 1936 an occasional train passed by. *D. Mackereth*

Bound for South Snowdon, a mixed train with wagons of coal makes for the mini-summit between Salem and Plas-y-nant. This was the kind of illegal train make-up which made the Board of Trade furious with the N.W.N.G.R. *Caernarvonshire Record Office*

A nice piece of civil engineering; the retaining wall near Plas-y-nant, April 1971.

J.I.C. Boyd

The railway passes through the gap at Plas-y-nant and makes for the shores of Quellyn Lake in the distance. This was the most severe curve on the main line. *Collection: J.I.C. Boyd*

As the line leaves Nant Mill, the Nant-y-betws opens out before it. Crossing the Afon Gwyrfai there is a short straight length: Castell Cidwm looms ahead. *Hudson's Series*

This more recent view shows the same section of railway, little changed after 35 years of abandonment. *J.I.C. Boyd*

Many Bell Tents reveal a lakeshore camp at Snowdon Ranger, but the station is in decline and the arm has been removed from the signal. *Caernarvonshire Record Office*

The ridge of the Snowdon escarpment peers over the shoulder of the nearby slopes and down onto Snowdon Ranger station. On a clear day, the exhaust of trains on the Mountain Tramroad could be seen near the ridge. *Collection: J.I.C. Boyd*

Glan-yr-afon Viaduct remains, now completely obscured by trees in the summer. For this view in April 1966 it was necessary to wade out into the river! *J.I.C. Boyd*

Seen from a point not far from Rhyd-Ddu terminus, the line falls rapidly to twist its way down to lake level at Snowdon Ranger. There is a single telegraph wire and the walling is reminiscent of Festiniog Railway practice. *F. Frith & Co.*

Seen in 1939, South Snowdon station was then coming to the end of its second phase of closure. Soon the wartime scrap men would move in. Little or nothing denotes its owners were now the Welsh Highland Railway; all the N.W.N.G. features survive in this northward view.

Photomatic Ltd.

and form an additional protection for the passenger line. Anticipating the day when more than one train would be worked and block working be introduced, the line would have to be fitted up with telegraph, block instruments, passenger loops and run-away points, with second platforms 'and proper shelter at Moel Tryfan, Rhostryfan and Bryngwyn which are on steep inclines'. The logic of the last statement is a little vague! Can one assume that at first these three stations had no buildings?

The matter of adequate clearances in cuttings had clearly been anticipated, for Oldham had written to Marindin in August 1877 with a truly Festiniog-like proposal! 'As alterations to bridges will take some time, may we run trains with bars fitted to the carriage windows and lock the doors on leaving stations?' To which Marindin replies 'altho' bars on carriage windows are objectionable, they are better than bashed heads'. The bars were to be removed when bridges were safe. Oldham contended on 3rd January, 1878 that this had been done.

Opening dates may be summarised thus:

Main line from Dinas Junction:

Goods	to Quellyn (temp.)	21st May, 1877
	to Snowdon Ranger	1st June, 1878
	to S. Snowdon (Rhyd-Ddu)	14th May, 1881
Passengers:	to Quellyn (temp.)	15th August, 1877
	to Snowdon Ranger	1st June, 1878
	to S. Snowdon (Rhyd-Ddu)	14th May, 1881

Branch line from Tryfan Junction:

Goods:	to Drumhead	21st May, 1877
Passengers:	to Bryngwyn	15th August, 1877

Though taking the narrative beyond the date so far described, it is convenient to bring matters out on the line to a conclusion; the last section was opened following inspection on 5th May, 1881, a length of 2 m. 11 ch. with a formation width of 10 ft. Sidings at the terminus were centred at 6 ft and station limits were: Snowdon Ranger (5 m. 18 ch.) 31 chains; Rhyd-Ddu (7 m. 16 ch.) 24 chains; distances in brackets from Tryfan Junction.

There was a junction with a quarry system at Glanrafon and the upgrade varied between 1 in 74 and 1 in 332; the sharpest curve was 3½ chains radius. The major work in the section, and throughout the line in fact, was the Glanrafon Viaduct. Marindin found this to be 'exceedingly strong . . . under test'. He did not pass the line, as there was no buffer stop at Rhyd-Ddu, the buildings there were incomplete, and there was no staff-key for the points there nor at Glanrafon, nor any interlocking with the signals. There was no Rhyd-Ddu nameboard and the fencing was not finished; the yard was also incomplete. 'An undertaking must be given to work the line by One Engine in Steam and a Train Staff be provided with a key for Glanrafon Sidings, which have no signals.'

In this Report there is just one reference to the progress of work under McKie before he was dismissed – the only one available; culverting and some preparatory earthwork had been done on this section as early as 1874 and the Inspector found it 'quite adequate'. It would seem therefore that McKie had not at first concentrated his efforts at the Dinas end of the line but must have prepared drainage at least throughout the length of the main line.

It appears that at first only temporary fences were installed between Glanrafon and Rhyd-Ddu; the existing stone walls were completed after the line opened. The station at Rhyd-Ddu was only temporary too; both walls and station proper were finished for mid-May 1881. On 13th May the Inspector had written to the Secretary of the Railway Department '. . . It is of great importance to this line to open tomorrow and I would recommend that upon the receipt of the undertaking as to the working which the Engineer will bring this afternoon, sanction for the opening should be given . . .' In this case the Inspector was asking for endorsement of his approval without making a further inspection at that juncture. A speed of 10 m.p.h. was to be the limit for Glanrafon Viaduct until the next visit. Temporary sanction to open was then given.

On 14th September, 1881 Marindin was back again, his main concern being guard rails on the Glanrafon Viaduct which he found had not yet been installed; in no uncertain terms he recommended that 'final sanction for opening should be with-held'. The engineer had fixed inside instead of outside guard rails to the viaduct: he was told to alter them.

So at last the whole main line was open: Quellyn (road), convenient for the contractor but little else, had gone. Snowdon Ranger to South Snowdon, a sinuous stretch, was complete. The spelling of Quellyn seems to have presented its problems in various ways; there was an extreme Welsh version of Cwellyn and English Guides of the period used Quellyn. Ward Lock's Guide of 1903 called the station 'Quellyn Lake Station Hotel' and the same Guide showed the terminus plainly as Snowdon. Caught between the local Welsh names and common usage by visitors who were deterred by pronunciation, the Company made several efforts to please all parties by altering the names from time to time; they could not satisfy the Welsh by using English titles and the passengers on whom the Company relied were not attracted by the Welsh ones; one hundred years later in a more overall sense, the matter is not yet resolved!

It is now necessary to return to 1879 to examine the problems lying behind the ultimate completion of the railway.

A finish to The Moel Tryfan Undertaking there may have been, but it did not bring much hope to the Board Room. In reporting a loss for the half year ending 30th June, 1879 the Directors complained there was 'presently a depression in the slate trade and the line is not working at a profit. The deficiency is mainly due to the line possessing no rolling stock of its own as the whole of it is hired' (this is the first mention of the matter in such a Report. 'A Receiver has now been appointed on behalf of the owners of the rolling stock whose rentals are largely in arrears.'

The background of this greater problem was not of the Company's doing, as a slate slump was being felt throughout North Wales; it was going to be another three years before losses were eliminated. The continual drain on financial reserves had made its mark; just when the line might have come into profitable operation, the slate slump hit it. To judge from the Returns, it was not so much the mineral tonnage which dropped but in the previous year over 47,000 Third Class passengers had been carried, the bulk being quarrymen and workmen; in 1879 this fell by almost half and it was 1893 before such a figure was recorded again. Second Class passengers dropped to almost a quarter and never reached the same figure again. So the Company went into Receivership, in which it stayed for the remainder of its days.

As regards the Receiver appointed by the High Court on 13th December, 1878 the information was not made public until the next June meeting. Not surprisingly, Russell was made Chairman but Sir Llewellyn Turner remained on the Board. He and Fitzgibbon were the sole survivors of the Old Guard. Chaloner W. Chute and Richard Seymour Guinness both of London, filled the vacancies. Guinness was a Director of the Banbury & Cheltenham Direct Railway.

No actual date is available but Edwin Spooner had resigned his post before the end of 1877 following the opening to the temporary station at Quellyn. He later became the first General Manager of the Federated Malay States Railway. James Cleminson M.I.C.E. (an associate of R.F. Fairlie) of 7 Westminster Chambers, London, S.W. was appointed Engineer in 1878. More usefully for the Company, R.H. Livesey, who had been made Traffic Superintendent in April 1877 at the age of 24, was appointed Manager and Secretary in November 1879 when, at the same time, the Company's offices were moved from London to Dinas Junction.

James Cleminson's reign lasted six years and as from 1st January, 1884, Livesey took up the additional duties of Engineer and Locomotive Superintendent, taking on responsibility at the same time for permanent way and all rolling stock matters. Livesey, from 1879 to August 1890, *was* the N.W.N.G. and the Company's position, though not of the status of a financial goldmine, was at least stabilized and traffic increased. He left North Wales for Donegal's Finn Valley Railway, later becoming Manager of the 3 ft gauge Co. Donegal system, on which he left a profound mark.

Robert Livesey was one of the more notable managers of the small company scene in those times: he was actually a Civil Engineer and as Secretary, General Manager and Engineer to the N.W.N.G. before he left, he was well suited to the environment of the Donegal concern. Born in Chester in 1853 he was the third son of James Livesey, a

Locomotive Superintendent of the G.W.R. (Chester Division) where Robert had his initial training, moving to the Birkenhead Joint line and then the Goods Department of the L.N.W.R. Only 24, he joined the N.W.N.G. at its opening as Traffic Superintendent; in November 1879 he was made Secretary and General Manager, his additional duties coming on 1st January, 1884. Whilst on the N.W.N.G. he was credited with devising an iron tie for keeping the rails in gauge on the sharp curves, and also for a barbed dogspike. He joined the 5 ft 3 in. gauge Finn Valley Railway in August 1890.[4] [He died in Donegal Town in 1923, having retired from management of the County Donegal Railways in 1922. His son took over from him but left shortly for an appointment in India.[5]

Considering the Donegal system to have been the best equipped narrow gauge railway in Ireland at Livesey's retirement, we may hazard that the history of the N.W.N.G. might have taken a much graver turn had not a man of Livesey's capacity been at the helm.]

When Livesey moved to Ireland, S. Tanner became Engineer, to be followed shortly by James W. Szlumper. During the Company's evolvement period of the early 1900s, G.C. Aitchison took up from March 1898, the fourfold role which Livesey had latterly held. Aitchison will also be seen as an executive of the North Wales Power & Traction Company, and the Portmadoc, Beddgelert & South Snowdon Railway, but this is to anticipate! He became Receiver on 15th January, 1912.

The shareholders met in Manchester on 15th April, 1880 and agreed to raise £50,000* by Debentures 'to rid the railway of debt and to continue the line to its original terminus'. This special meeting was to obtain the assent of the shareholders to a Scheme of Arrangement filed in Chancery between the Company and its creditors. The Scheme was approved by the Court without opposition in early July.

In March 1881 the Board was able to report that 'the profit of £263 made in 1880 has been applied towards payment of hire of rolling stock, and the claims of the Rolling Stock Company, which would amount in the whole to about £7,000, have been settled, and the rolling stock acquired for the Company by the issue of £2,650 in 'A' Debentures @ 4% and £3,350 @ 4½%, involving an annual charge of £257'.

The Rolling Stock Co. had had seventeen shareholders registered on 31st March, 1879. Russell held five times as many shares as any one of the others. By 9th August, 1884 Russell was one of seven shareholders and still the largest by eleven times of any one other shareholder. By then three of them only held one qualifying share; in March 1883 the shares were redeemed. On 31st July, 1889 the Company filed a return showing final redemption of shares and stated 'The Company ceased to

---

*Viz: £6,000 'A' Debentures in payment for Rolling Stock.
 £30,000 'B' Debentures in payment of existing Debentures and completion of line.
 £14,000 'C' Debentures for satisfying outstanding liabilities and the general purposes of the Company.

carry on business in June 1889, the cause was that the objects namely, the supply of rolling stock to a small railway company paid for by instalments over a series of years, was fulfilled.' The Company was dissolved on 27th April, 1894.

From a commercial-tactics viewpoint, it should be noted that Russell, (Chairman and Receiver), became a mortgagee of the Croesor & Port Madoc Railway in 1882 and this gave him effective control of that Railway.

At last on 3rd July, 1882, the Company was able to tell the Board of Trade that the outside guard rails had been fixed to the Dingle Viaduct (i.e. Glanrafon). Presumably the speed limit was then eased to conform with the rest of the line.

Of some of the problems explained to shareholders, 'THE RAILWAY NEWS' 23rd September, 1882, gives an insight:

NORTH WALES NARROW GAUGE
(MOEL TRYFAN UNDERTAKING.)

The twentieth half-yearly meeting was held on Monday, at the Inns of Court Hotel, Holborn; Mr. J.C. Russell, the Chairman, presiding.

Mr. R.H. Livesey (Secretary) read the notice.

The following is the report of the directors for the half-year ended June 30, 1882:– "The expenditure on capital account for the half-year has amounted to £120 15s. Of this sum £88 15s. is in respect of guards to the sides of the largest bridge on the line, which were required by the Board of Trade.

The question of Dinas Station expenses is still unsettled. The directors have made every effort to come to a settlement with the London and North Western Railway Company about the division and payment of these, but hitherto without success."

The Chairman, in moving the adoption of the report and accounts, said: The report this half-year presents rather an unfavourable aspect. The explanation of this heavy expenditure is really that, during the third and fourth years of the existence of the line, when traffic was so bad that our receipts for the half-year fell to little over £800 (whereas now they are over £1,200), everything had to be practically starved, though the line was kept in safe condition for travelling on, and repairs, no doubt, were deferred which in the ordinary course of things, had we been able, we would have done. The locomotive power shows an increase of £37 in the half-year. That is due again to really serious repairs to our Fairlie engines, and represents £90, as against £23 before. That is an excess of nearly £70; but that has been counterbalanced to some extent by a saving in oil and tallow, which we find represents a sum of only £30, as against £40. In the carriage and wagon department the expenses have not been so heavy as in the corresponding period of 1881. The repairs are low. In traffic expenses and general charges there is a very slight decrease; but these are not departments in which reductions can be expected for the future, as they are practically as low as they can ever be. On the receipts side of the account there is some satisfaction in this, that though there is a slight falling-off in the passengers, chiefly in the third class, both first and second class have increased, which is somewhat curious. In our merchandise, coal and lime, and slate, we have a considerable increase. The increase is represented by about 40 per cent in the merchandise; only about 100 tons more of coal; and an increase of about 25 per cent in slate. That increase only brings us an increased revenue of £150; and the cause of that is, when analysed, that our average receipt per ton, for slate and minerals, is only a little over 2s. per ton; and, of course, it takes a great deal of traffic at such a small return as 2s. to bring us a large receipt. There is a paragraph in the report alluding to the Dinas station expenses. We always keep in view the necessity of acting cordially with the London and North Western Company, and the settlement of money matters with them is always a question of time and negotiation; but I hope that perhaps in this coming half-year we may succeed in coming to a definite settlement about those matters. We have always kept that in view in certain arrangements we have made, which, hitherto have proved very satisfactory, though perhaps at a slight cost to this company. As to the train mileage, that of course, has increased. It has increased from 13,000 to 17,300 miles, and that is partly due to the extension to Bedgeleart,* which had been opened only two months in the corresponding half-year. It is important to keep down the train mileage as much as possible, because the greater the traffic that is carried with the smallest mileage, so much the greater profit there will be to the company. Our traffic receipts are steadily, though slowly, going up. The connecting line with the Vron Quarry is now actually completed, or will be in a week; and we may expect a considerable slate traffic, commencing at about 1,000 tons in the year and rising probably up to 4,000 or 5,000 tons a year.

In June 1883 George Imlach of 4 India Buildings, Water Street, Liverpool, asked Charles Spooner concerning the value of N.W.N.G. Stock; the reply included:

. . . I am not able to answer otherwise I should have been happy to do so. I have always felt in regard to that Line (which no doubt you must be aware is in anything but a favourable financial position) should have been continued on via Beddgelert in junction with existing Lines to make it a useful and paying concern, and was a point that steps should have been early sought to effect, but unfortunately was not done.

After this shockingly shaky start, the Company was fortunate to enter a period when the slate trade – if not as intense as it had been earlier in the century – was to enjoy a reasonable period of busy-ness. However, the geographical shortcomings of The Moel Tryfan Undertaking were obvious to all; the collection of slate from quarries which the line served was reasonably well catered for, but the drawbacks of having a terminus within three miles of a port and yet, where slate was due for shipment, having to trans-ship it into the L.N.W.R. at Dinas Junction, only for it to be put aboard a boat at Caernarvon within hours, were patently evident. By some means, the narrow gauge must be extended northwards to give it independent access to Caernarvon harbour. Powers were sought to carry out this extension, and obtained by Act 48/9 Vic. Cap. 134 of 31st July, 1885. At the same time it was intended to abandon the incline at the head of the Bryngwyn branch and substitute it by another more evenly graded route which would be suitable for passenger traffic. None of this work could be carried out under the aegis of The Moel Tryfan Undertaking, as a Receiver was in being for that Undertaking and no further capital might be raised for it. Separate capital would therefore be necessary.

In the event, authority was obtained for the following:

Railway No.1 (3 m. 1 ch.) from a junction with the existing railway near Dinas Junction, terminating on the south shore of

---

*Should be Beddgelert, and in fact was Rhyd-Ddu.

Caernarvon Harbour near the Rowing Club's Boathouse.
Railway No.2 (1 m. 5 fur. 4 ch.) from a junction with the branch near
Bryngwyn station and ending alongside the Bwlch-y-llyn–Carmel
road 95 yds. west of its junction with the Rhostryfan–Cilgwyn
Common road. An end-on junction with this Railway was the
commencement of:
Railway No.3 (3 fur. 3 ch.) which ended in the existing Drumhead at
the summit of the Bryngwyn Incline.

The whole concept was to be a separate Undertaking and distinct
from The Moel Tryfan Undertaking, and to be known as the
'Caernarvon & Bryngwyn Extensions'. Separate capital was £28,000 in
Ordinary shares or stocks in amounts of not less than £10. Borrowing
powers were £9,300 and this was conditional in part upon Railway No.1
being open to traffic. None was ever issued. Such stocks or etc. were to
be offered to those who had already invested in The Moel Tryfan
Undertaking, at par. Complicating the financing even further, Section
22 of the Act permitted the Company, following agreement at an
Extraordinary General Meeting, to allow The Moel Tryfan Undertaking to absorb Railways No.2 and 3, for which purpose the accounts
of these two lines were to be kept separate from the separate accounts of
the remainder of the separate undertaking! Three years were permitted
for the compulsory purchase of land and five for the completion of the
work. Section 28 is of formidable length, protecting the L.N.W.R.
(successors to the Carnarvonshire Railway and Nantlle Railway),
especially at the point where Railway No.1 would have passed under it.
At Caernarvon Harbour, authority was given to build a bridge over the
River Seiont and to purchase the Caernarvon ferry.

The Act was more complicated because at the summit of the
Bryngwyn Incline, Crown Lands were involved, and it was intended to
annex about 4 acres while building the new railway in order to abandon
the existing Incline. Certain quarries which sent goods and minerals
down the Incline were Her Majesty's property also, leased to sundry
operators. It was intended that the Company should lease the required
land from the Crown for 998 years from 10th October, 1885 at a yearly
rental of £5 on the basis of a draft lease signed by J.C. Russell on the
Company's behalf. Over such lines as were laid over Crown Land, the
rate of carriage was not to exceed that charged by the N.W.N.G. over
the existing Incline.

No immediate attempt was made by the Company to raise the further
capital which the act authorised. Owing to serious illness the Chairman
was unable to prosecute matters. Some evidence suggests that opinions
were mixed regarding the advantages of the scheme and, it seems
certain that it was prepared in anticipation of improvements in the slate
trade – an industry which worked on a 'Jam Tomorrow' basis for over a
century. Now and again, jam appeared, but not in the late 1880's. So it
was that the time for completion was approaching and nothing had been

done about the powers on hand. The fall in passenger traffic 'was fully accounted for by the fact that the terminus of the railway was not in the town of Caernarvon but 2½ miles from it and owing to the great delay in having to wait for trains on the main line they were not able to compete fully with the cars' (2nd October, 1886). By Act 53/4 Vic. Cap. 70 4th July, 1890 an extension of time was obtained to 30th July, 1892. Also the 'A' Debentures were redeemable, and substitution was sought for them. Lastly, as a result of the Railway Returns (Continuous Brakes) Act: 41/2 Vic. Cap. 20 of 1878 it was now illegal to operate passenger trains on any railway not exempt without continuous brakes and further capital was required to fit such brakes to existing stock and also purchase additional vehicles for working The Moel Tryfan Undertaking.

The Company was ultimately compelled to comply with both this and the Regulation of Railways Act 52/3 Vic. Cap. 57 of 1889 when the Board of Trade made an Order on the Company dated 30th December, 1890. This instructed them to: (1) fit interlocking on points and signals and introduce the Block System within eighteen months and (2) fit continuous brakes on stock used by passenger trains within three years of the Order. One unbraked vehicle might be attached to the rear of braked trains. Proportions of braked/unbraked vehicles in mixed trains were laid down, the train not to exceed 25 vehicles and 25 m.p.h. and to stop at all stations. Two slate wagons were to count as one, and two goods wagons as one if not exceeding 2 tons when loaded.

The 1890 Act repealed certain 1885 sections regarding the separated accounts concerning Railways Nos. 2 and 3, and authorised the issue of £10,000 in new 'A' Debenture Stock, enabling the Company to redeem the current issue which, it may be recalled, was issued to repay the lessee of the original rolling stock. Thus £10,000 new 'A' Stocks would redeem £6,000 old 'A' redeemable Stocks and the balance of the capital was to be used to pay for the costs of the Act, fitting continuous brakes, providing new rolling stock, installing telephone or telegraphic communication. Other improvements specifically mentioned were '. . . turntables, additional buildings, shed, sidings, signals etc.'.

In 1892 after a season 'of unfavourable weather', a decision was taken to cease catering for 2nd Class passengers at the year end and with the funds now available new stock was bought. The buying spree for rolling stock ended in 1894. Commencing in Spring 1892 and completed early in 1894 Westinghouse brake was fitted to all existing bogie carriage stock, and the locomotives. The layout at Dinas Junction was enlarged, some signalling and communications improvements carried out and in general, the railway was much uplifted from its then primitive state.

Of Railways Nos. 1, 2 and 3 nothing more was to be heard until after the First War. Nor did the turntables materialise; the practice of slewing the engines round from time to time, upon greased steel plates aided by jacks and ropes, persisted until Welsh Highland days when the Boston Lodge turntable became accessible.

Under the Railways Rates & Charges No.6 (Festiniog Railway & Etc.) Order of 1892, special provisions were laid down for the Company.

1. Slate traffic carried in the railway's own wagons on its main line to be charged at ½d. per ton mile.
2. Slate traffic carried in the railway's own wagons on the Bryngwyn branch (5¼ m.) was to be charged as for 6¼ miles which would cover the use of railway wagons by the quarry owners on the lines radiating from the 'Drumhead', all use of inclines and where N.W.N.G. services were provided over quarry owners' inclines and sidings.
3. Where slate traffic was carried in quarry owners' wagons (there were about thirty private owner quarry wagons before 1900) between Glanrafon and Dinas (8¼ m.) the Company would charge as for 9¼ miles but this would cover charges for using any of the Company's sidings at Dinas and the working of those sidings.
4. Where traffic (other than slate and other minerals) was carried in owner's wagons the rate was to be:

Bryngwyn–Drumhead–Dinas Junction   3d. per ton mile
Glanrafon Siding–Dinas Junction   4d. per ton mile

(The latter suggests that private owners' wagons originated in the Moel Tryfan quarries complex, and at Glanrafon Quarry only.)

As to returning empty wagons into quarry sidings and the shunting of the sidings, the Railways Co. was not entitled to charge over and above the rates of sections 2 and 3. An interesting addendum was to the effect that if quarry owners could load goods to or from Caernarvon without the necessity for loading or reloading at Dinas, then suitable equipment for this purpose must be provided at cost by the Company for the use by quarry owners. Perhaps some sort of 'container' which would transfer rail–road–rail was under consideration?

It was probably too much to expect that other parties would not enter the field at a period when interest in 'light railways' (the actual Light Railway Act had not then been passed) was at its height. In 1889 a proposed Beddgelert & Rhyd-Ddu Railway (Engineers Charles Minns and John S. Lawrence) was intended to link South Snowdon on the N.W.N.G. and the Croesor line on much the same course as other lines of earlier date had intended, save that south of the end-on connection with the N.W.N.G., the road would have been crossed and the new railway remained on the west side of the valley all the way south as far as and beyond the Aberglaslyn Pass where tunnels would have been avoided by circumventing the bluffs on the Pass instead of cutting through them. Plans were deposited but no development took place.

More threatening to N.W.N.G. plans was the Portmadoc,

Beddgelert & Rhyd-Ddu Railway which intended to apply for Parliamentary powers in the 1892 Session for:

Railway No.1 (4 m. 2 fur. 5 ch.) from a junction with the Portmadoc, Croesor & Beddgelert Tram Railway Co. (the Croesor Tramway) 4 fur. 8 ch. from the west side of its Llanfrothen road level crossing, to Beddgelert close to and south-west of the Goat Hotel.

Railway No.2 (4 m. 3 fur. 8 ch.) A link between this line at Beddgelert and the N.W.N.G. at Rhyd-Ddu.

Notices of intent appeared in 'THE CAMBRIAN NEWS' during November 1891, from which it was hoped to establish links with the Festiniog, N.W.N.G. and P.C.&B.T.R. Companies and to enjoy running powers over a rebuilt Croesor Tramway between the point of junction and Portmadoc. The promoters were William Hunt Scott and Joseph Wellington Burrows, neither of whom had any other local railway interests. The gauge was to be 1 ft 11½ in. with powers to increase to standard gauge.

Though nothing developed once again, the basic scheme was revived after the passing of the Light Railways Act of 1896, when a draft Light Railway Order to go before the Light Railway Commissioners in November 1897 was prepared for a Portmadoc, Beddgelert & Rhyd-Ddu Light Railway. Promoters were James W. Wyatt of Gwynant, Robert Isaac, Richard Davies and William Jones (local landowners etc.), and two Railways were proposed:

Railway No.1 (6 m. 6 fur. 3 ch.) from the Gorseddau Railways' then disused site immediately east of the Cambrian Railways' road crossing at Portmadoc station, thence along the side of the Beddgelert Siding Cambrian interchange siding and running roughly parallel to the Croesor Tramway, worked northwards along the Glaslyn's east bank and south of Beddgelert, crossed to the west side of the river and tunnelled part way through the Pass of Aberglaslyn. North of here and into Beddgelert was almost the same route as previously intended by other promoters.

Railway No.2 (4 m. 5 fur. 52 ch.) was largely on the site of the Beddgelert & Rhyd-Ddu Railway of 1889. All lines were to be 1 ft 11½ in. gauge.

These plans were brought to an advanced stage and though the Draft Order makes no reference to, or use of, the Croesor Tramway course there must have been second thoughts for an Estimate of Costs omitting the Croesor and dated 8th November, 1897 has been amended under date May 1898 and gives 'Length of Croesor Tramway 3 miles 1 furlong' and later provides for new railway and refurbishing of the Croesor line as respectively, £864 per mile and £688 per mile – indicating the major renewal of the Tramway which would be necessary to bring it up to passenger standards. There were to be stations at Beddgelert and Portmadoc only. The tunnel would have been 280 yards long. Thomas Roberts & Son of Portmadoc were the Engineers and the maximum grade would have been 1 in 41.

[In the context of narrow gauge railway work then being carried out in North Wales, it is fitting to add the estimated costs of building a new line in 1898 – including bridges, stations etc. New work was originally to cost £23,870 for 11 m. 3 fur. of railway and included all works. By May 1898, allowing for reduction in expenses but including rebuilding of Croesor, the figure was £24,720.]

Having reached this advanced stage of promotion, why was nothing further heard of this last scheme? The answer lies in an inability to carry out the necessary preliminaries before the Railways Company, alarmed by the course of events, took matters into its own hands. The projected Portmadoc, Beddgelert & Rhyd-Ddu Railway was still a paper-bound intention in May 1898 but the Railways Co., for all its earlier failings, was very much an existing railway and in the same year it gave notice of applying for a Light Railway Order to extend its line to Beddgelert; the application went before the Light Railway Commissioners in November 1898 and provisional agreement was given, subject to a local enquiry. This astute move on the part of the N.W.N.G., subdued competitive promotions for the moment.

A more subtle obstacle to various schemes for railways between Portmadoc and Beddgelert at this time was undoubtedly Russell himself. The Light Railway Commissioners themselves admitted, in a Report to the Board of Trade in 1900 regarding efforts of 1897 and 1898 . . . 'these schemes were rejected by the Commissioners owing to the legal difficulties of acquiring the Croesor Railway, a disused mineral line'(!) Clearly, the Commissioners were misinformed, as the Croesor was very much a going concern and, whether they felt the situation was too complex to tackle, or they were astute enough to appreciate how matters stood, they evaded the issue. There were in fact no real legal difficulties; at this time control of both N.W.N.G. Railways and the Croesor could be said to be in the hands of the same man though why he was disinterested is not clear. Did he feel that once he linked with other railways, control would pass from him?

The N.W.N.G. 'Beddgelert Light Railway Extension Order' was obtained on 3rd November, 1900 with James W. and William W. Szlumper as Engineers (they were currently engaged on the Vale of Rheidol Railway promotion) for a line 4 m. 6 fur. 3 ch. long to the rear of the Goat Hotel, Beddgelert, a maximum grade of 1 in 41. It was intended to work the line by steam and for the scheme to be separate from The Moel Tryfan Undertaking. Suitable and separate financing arrangements were proposed. The total cost would be £11,996. [In the event, work done under this Order was carried out by the Portmadoc, Beddgelert & South Snowdon Railway and no longer concerned the N.W.N.G. An Agreement to this effect between the two concerns was dated 26th August, 1904.]

Under the Beddgelert Extension Order a time of three years was

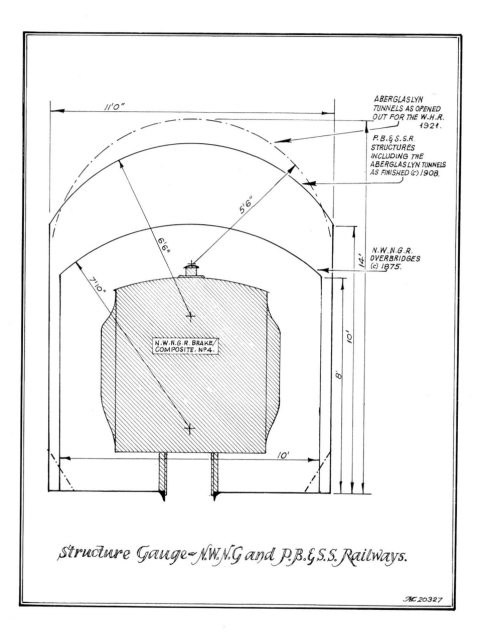

Structure Gauge~N.W.N.G and P.B.&S.S.Railways.

permitted for completion, a period which was exceeded before the work was completed – indeed, very little was done at this time. A maximum speed of 18 m.p.h. on the level or of 15 m.p.h. on grades exceeding 1 in 50 and an axle loading of 8 tons was allowed. The separate capital would be £13,800 called 'The Extension Capital', with borrowing powers dependent on the amount of subscribed capital at any time. Rails were to weigh no less than 41½ lb. per yard and curves of less than 3 chains were to be checkrailed and tied. Coachscrews and bearing plates were to be used in the track in addition to dog spikes.

In view of the Light Railway nature of the work, it is curious that provision for semaphore signalling was made. It was not carried out, but the relevant Order reads: 'At places where trains pass one another there shall be a home signal in each direction . . . near the entrance points. If (it) cannot be seen from a distance of quarter of a mile, a distant signal must be erected . . .' Signals were to be interlocked with points and each other. Shelters and conveniences were not obligatory at stations. So much for 'Castles in Spain' and to revert to N.W.N.G. matters.

A nice footnote to the Returns for 1902 states under 'Season and Period Tickets': 'Includes a receipt of £158 from a Quarry Company for settlement of a previous year's quarrymen's tickets.'

From this entry might be inferred that the quarrymen travelled 'free' at the cost of their employer, or more likely, the quarry deducted the cost of a block booking from their wages. It is also possible the booking was made by a 'Quarrymen's Club' for whom the quarry acted in this matter.

The Company now found itself in an untidy 'status'. It was a fully fledged railway with a proposed appendage as a Light Railway and with aspirations – scarcely disguised – of becoming an electric railway drawing power from its own generating stations and working its trains by overhead conductors. So no surprise was occasioned when on 6th June, 1905 an Order was obtained to work the existing line as a Light Railway and operate with electric traction. The P.B. & S.S.R. was given powers to lease the N.W.N.G. at any suitable time and work the two systems as a joint concern.

Confusing though all this interplay between companies and the exchange of powers to do this and that undoubtedly is, and accepting that this account is written with a background knowledge of the geography of the district and a clear vision of what the ultimate would be, it must be appreciated that none of this could take place without authority, usually of the Board of Trade. The various railway parties, anxious to outsmart each other, were bombarding the Department with paper and applications; basically it was the same group of promoters acting under varying titles and the Board of Trade officials might be excused for believing they were dealing with Welshmen who, with map in front of them, were endeavouring to join up every town of any size in North Wales with a narrow gauge railway. Their dismay is evident from the interdepartmental notes which were exchanged and can be found among a mass of documentation in the Public Record Office. Perusal of this is not for the faint-hearted or the dilletante: more than ten companies intended to reach Beddgelert alone, and we may wonder why? If the conception of a through narrow gauge route between Portmadoc and Caernarvon harbour was considered vital, it can only be in terms of tourist business. Would the financial return have justified the capital cost? It may have been calculated that a direct link between the Bryngwyn branch slate quarries and Caernarvon harbour would produce income enough to see such a railway through the winter months?

It was the incoming North Wales Power & Traction Co. Ltd. which changed the whole picture; its object was profit through the sale of electricity generated by local hydro-electric stations. Every possible user of such power was canvassed, some success being found in certain slate quarries which until then had relied on water power. Additional users were essential, and the conception of working the local narrow gauge railways electrically was introduced by personal links with eastern Europe. At this juncture (1903–6) certain items from the Board of Trade files derive from their view of things:

The N.W.N.G.R. Co. capital of £10,000 per mile 'is enormous for a line of this gauge.'

The Company currently earns about £6 per week and costs about £5 per week – net earnings are about £600 per year.

As to The Beddgelert Extension: 'the line has a grade of 1 in 20 for ¼ mile whereas the Order permits only 1 in 40.'

The cost of Glaslyn bridges would be 'c.£945 for a 60 ft span plus c.£1,100 for two spans of 40 ft'. A 100 yard tunnel is estimated at £650.

Capital per mile is estimated at £6,600: there was a 'mistake in the Light Railway Order – the gauge should be 1 ft 11½ in., not 2 ft'.

The Board of Trade files include newspaper cuttings of promotional activities. 'THE CARNARVON & DENBIGH HERALD' reports a meeting of the Light Railway Commissioners concerning the Portmadoc, Beddgelert & South Snowdon Railway at Beddgelert in February 1904 where the cost of electrifying the N.W.N.G. was said to be c.£12,000. This was a contract figure: alterations would be made at Dinas Junction in view of electrification, and The National Trust had objected to a tunnel. Whilst the Light Railway Order for 1900 proposes steam power (no provision for electrification), the P.B. & S.S.R. 'was really a railway company and an electric supply company at the same time.'[6]

The spectacle of an overhead-wired narrow gauge electric railway, with trains passing effortlessly over the steep gradients and sharp curves and driven by power obtained in the district from an abundant water supply is perhaps best known in Switzerland, where today there are many miles of mountain railway exactly as conceived for Caernarvonshire at the turn of the century. Even in 1988, a part of such a project in the county remains viable; but neither the Railways Co. nor

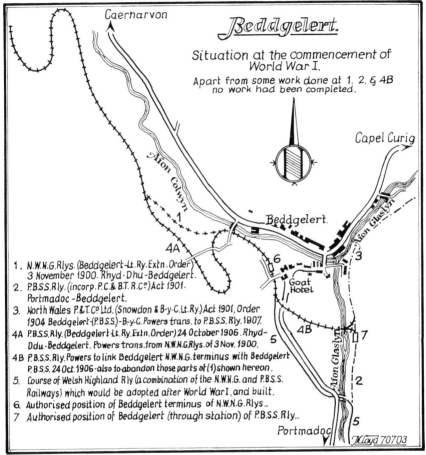

Beddgelert.

Situation at the commencement of World War I.

Apart from some work done at 1, 2, & 4B no work had been completed.

Caernarvon

Capel Curig

Afon Colwyn

Beddgelert.

Afon Glaslyn

Goat Hotel

Portmadoc

1. N.W.N.G.Rlys. (Beddgelert-Lt.Ry.Extn.Order) 3 November 1900. Rhyd-Dhu-Beddgelert.
2. P.B.S.S.Rly. (incorp. P.C.& B.T. R.Cº) Act 1901. Portmadoc-Beddgelert.
3. North Wales P.&T.Cº Ltd. (Snowdon & B-y-C.Lt.Ry.) Act 1901, Order 1904 Beddgelert-(P.B.S.S.)-B-y-C. Powers trans. to P.B.S.S. Rly. 1907.
4A P.B.S.S.Rly. (Beddgelert-Lt.Ry.Extn.Order) 24 October 1906. Rhyd-Ddu-Beddgelert. Powers trans. from N.W.N.G.Rlys. of 3 Nov. 1900.
4B P.B.S.S.Rly. Powers to link Beddgelert N.W.N.G. terminus with Beddgelert P.B.S.S. 24 Oct. 1906-also to abandon those parts of (1) shown hereon.
5. Course of Welsh Highland Rly (a combination of the N.W.N.G. and P.B.S.S. Railways) which would be adopted after World War I, and built.
6. Authorised position of Beddgelert terminus of N.W.N.G.Rlys..
7. Authorised position of Beddgelert (through station) of P.B.S.S.Rly..

JLloyd 70703

NORTH WALES NARROW GAUGE RAILWAY.

DINAS, Nᴿ CARNARVON.

DEC 29 Ans'd

Secretary & Manager's Office.

Llanberis, R.S.O.

Carnarvonshire.

PLEASE QUOTE

THIS REFERENCE.

REFERENCE TO

YOUR LETTER.

the Snowdon Co. was destined to provide it in 1905. In fact, the Railways Co. was already at its prime, and though a final locomotive and carriage was added to the stock, no further improvements to the line took place, nor did further behind-the-scenes empire-building affect the Company. The slate trade continued to decline in importance, whilst passenger traffic was suspended on the branch on 31st December, 1913 and *all* regular traffic on the main line on 31st October, 1916.

Evidence of a run-down in conditions may lie behind a rumour which was circulating of which a notice in 'THE TIMES' for 20th April, 1910 might have been significant. This suggested that the L.N.W.R. was to take over the Railways Co. 'between Dinas and Beddgelert'. (A similar story that the L.N.W.R. would take over the Cambrian was rife about 1900.)

With the coming of the First War passenger returns dwindled and the railway fell on particularly hard times, as most of the quarries closed completely (never to re-open in many cases) and only a few worked with reduced output. The main line to Rhyd-Ddu was especially hit and proved quite uneconomic with its long arm and dwindling return. It was a sorry decline, and the whole railway gradually fell into that state which the Festiniog line experienced during the Second War. The passenger stock was pushed into a siding and the best of it went under such cover as Dinas Junction could provide; most of it deteriorated rapidly through lack of paint. Damaged slate wagons filled the yards as there was no work for them and no men to repair them even if required. The locomotive stock contrived to keep going, with *Russell* doing the brunt of the work. The newest engine *Gowrie* was sold, and the signalling equipment, with a railway worked 'One Engine in Steam', decayed and fell out of use. The sleepers rotted and the rails hogged; nature began to reclaim the track bed.

An 'epilogue' to a railway which began with high hopes and extensive aspirations, which for many years had been not only a doubtful investment but a constant source of problems to its operators, came in the form of an ex-Royal Engineer's Report compiled by Major G.C. Spring in 1921. By then, all traffic was confined to the Bryngwyn branch and slate quarries, save for a small amount of coal working. The two engines were in good order, *Moel Tryfan* had been rebuilt in 1903 and retubed in 1912. It would haul four composite coaches up the steepest gradient; *Russell*, the other engine, would haul nine coaches, each holding 50 passengers. The coaches, however, were not in use and having received a minimum of paint, were extensively deteriorated. There were eleven composites, two brake-composites and a four-wheeled brake van. All were fitted with Westinghouse brake.

The various pattern of slate wagon numbered ninety. Additionally there were twelve open wagons of 2 tons capacity, thirteen coal wagons, fourteen bolsters and twenty bolster runners (flats).

The two-wire telegraph used on posts throughout the system, was

The train is drawn up at South Snowdon, awaiting departure for Dinas Junction. In this broad landscape it resembles a child's toy. The outermost flanks of Snowdon fall towards the track; beyond is Llyn-y-gader, with Y Gader and Moel Hebog rising behind. *Hudson's Series*

Moel Tryfan with a mixed train at Rhyd-Ddu (now named Snowdon), in August 1922 after the restoration of passenger services. *C.R. Clinker*

Another Snowdon scene, used on a highly-coloured postcard and showing a most unlikely driver and small boy on the engine, with the remainder of the family posed on the platform. The recipient of the card added "smoke to taste".   *National Library of Wales*

Rhyd-Ddu before the First War. *Moel Tryfan* (with corrugated iron Refreshment Room behind) and a typical train of "no-two-alike" stock.   *Locomotive Publishing Co.*

The east end of Bryngwyn in N.W.N.G.R. times shows a rake of coal-loaded slate wagons ready to ascend the Incline, the locomotive water tank at the run-round neck, and two high-capacity coal wagons in the Coal Yard on the right. *Collection: W.H.R.*

Although this view dates in 1934, illustrations of the passenger station area at Bryngwyn have not survived from an earlier date. The passenger accommodation had been disused here for almost two decades by then, but there was still slate coming down the Incline beyond. In the right foreground are the remains of the signal box - the locomotive water tank has also disappeared. Optimistically, the building still carries its nameboard! *R.W. Kidner*

Snowdon Ranger outside the sheds at Dinas in the early part of the century. Continuous brakes and sandboxes have been fitted but there is the customary tub of sand on the footplate before the smokebox.

Locomotive Publishing Co.

Moel Tryfan, attached to a passenger train, at Dinas platform. Sandboxes, brake reservoir, square lamp sockets and the generous size of coal carried are evident.

Locomotive Publishing Co.

After the fatuous demolition of *Moel Tryfan* in 1954 at the Festiniog Railway's Harbour station (the engine survived in Boston Lodge shed throughout the Second War), only the rear bogie remained, a pitiful reminder of the early N.W.N.G.R. locomotive stud, January 1958.

J.I.C. Boyd

Beddgelert, now turned so as to be able to run up to Bryngwyn bunker-first and with a shorter chimney, is ready for duty beside Dinas Signal Box. Sandboxes on the tank-side are prominent in this 1905 view. *Locomotive Publishing Co.*

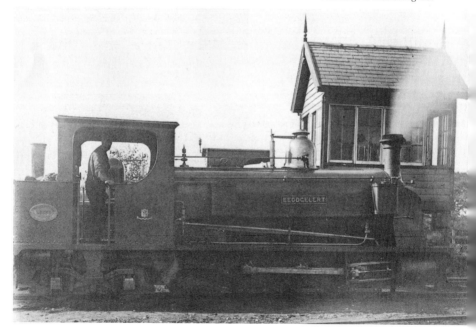

1909, and a very new *Gowrie* (nameplates not yet fitted) is probably undergoing tests; *Russell* may in fact be 'dead' and dragged from the shed for photographic purposes. Polished domes are 'de rig.æur'.

Locomotive Publishing Co.

Right. Russell was possibly about three years old when this portrait was taken in 1909. The Westinghouse brake pump is just visible in front of the smokebox, and the footplate there has acquired an old box to carry extra sand.

Locomotive Publishing Co.

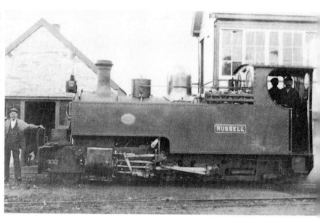

Right. The daily freight working pauses at Waenfawr in 1920. While the depth of undergrowth denotes the economic state of things, the engine however, is comendably clean and polished!

C.R. Clinker

Right. Taken at the same period as the previous scene, *Russell* shunts at Snowdon on the daily working. (There are going to be some noisy collisions between wagons and engine *en route*, if they cannot be coupled more closely!)   *G.H.W. Clifford*

Gowrie at the goods yard throat, Dinas Junction: the engine weighed less than *Russell* in working order, carried less water and its theoretical tractive effort was well short of that engine. The purchase suggests it was a replacement for one of the earlier Vulcan engines.

Collection: W.A. Camwell

Still a youngster, *Gowrie* heads a Dinas train at Rhyd-Ddu c.1909: it is hoped that the fireman moves the headlamp to the bunker before his driver accuses him of giving all his attention to the photographer.

K.A.C.R. Nunn

Probably in about 1910, *Gowrie* with a full head of steam seems about to set off for Bryngwyn with the slate empties.

Collection: *W.A. Camwell*

Gloucester Wagon Co.'s Second/Guard/Third Cleminson six-wheel carriage before delivery to North Wales. The roof ventilators and the legend above the windows had their lives cut short!

Gloucester Carriage & Wagon Co. Ltd.

Similar to the foregoing, this vehicle was an all-Third carriage. The makers were also suppliers of garden sheds etc., and the fact is scarcely disguised!

Gloucester Carriage & Wagon Co. Ltd.

Above. The Gloucester carriages survived for a surprising time, but were ultimately put to the saw and shorn of their running gear, finding other roles in their old age. Dinas Junction in 1934.
R.W. Kidner

Right. Ashbury Railway Carriage & Iron Co.'s carriage of 1874 stands on an L.N.W.R. wagon for despatch from the makers.
Collection: M. Seymour

Above. Another Ashbury coach (as yet unlettered or numbered) mounted on a twin six-wheeled flat wagon at the builder's Manchester premises.   *Collection: M. Seymour*

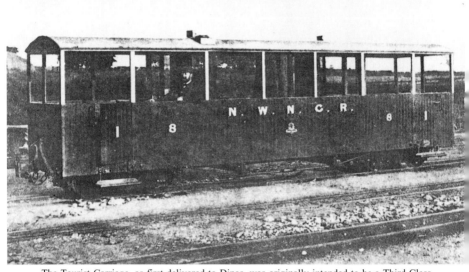

The Tourist Carriage, as first delivered to Dinas, was originally intended to be a Third Class vehicle; the potential of this lovely coach compared to the workaday air of its sister carriages must have prompted the Board to 'up-market' their business! *Collection: J.I.C. Boyd*

One of the batch of 'Summer Coaches'. *Collection: J.I.C. Boyd*

Pickering of Wishaw built two composite Guard's Vans to replace the two original Ashbury vehicles of similar type which had been supplied for the opening of the N.W.N.G.R.

R.Y. Pickering & Co. Ltd.

As detailed in the text, the origins of the Company's slate vehicles are not on record, so how many of these Gloucester Co.'s wagons were supplied is not known. The date reads 'December 1877'.

Gloucester Carriage & Wagon Co. Ltd.

A more sophisticated slate wagon is credited to the Company, and was one of a lesser number supplied by an unknown builder. These wagons were quite unlike most others in the Welsh slate industry.

Collection: J.I.C. Boyd

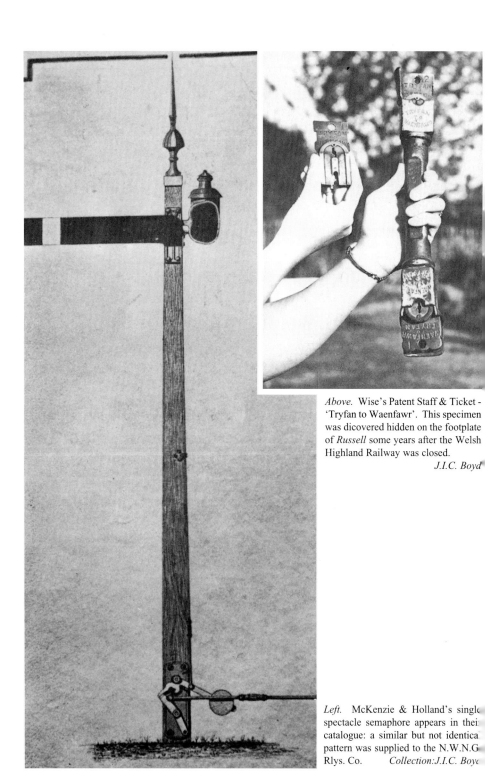

Above. Wise's Patent Staff & Ticket - 'Tryfan to Waenfawr'. This specimen was dicovered hidden on the footplate of *Russell* some years after the Welsh Highland Railway was closed.

J.I.C. Boyd

Left. McKenzie & Holland's single spectacle semaphore appears in their catalogue: a similar but not identical pattern was supplied to the N.W.N.G. Rlys. Co.   *Collection:J.I.C. Boyd* out of order. The telephone, Dinas to Snowdon with a tapping at Waenfawr, was working. The block instruments provided throughout, were already taken out save those at Tryfan Junction and Waenfawr which were passing places and where they were *in situ*.

Trains ran on the Bryngwyn branch four days a week and when required, ran up to Snowdon also with coal 'and smalls'. Only two men were employed to maintain the whole track which was in a poor state; new sleepers and tie bars had recently been put in on the branch; more were needed and Bryngwyn station 'needs immediate attention'. The main line was unsafe for passengers, requiring 300 new sleepers per mile; all curves needed packing, but from 8½ miles to Snowdon, the track was in good order. Timber on bridges and signal cabins had rotted away.

Distant, Home and Starter signals existed but were dilapidated and useless. All the machinery had gone from the Running Shed and repairs put out to contract. 'There was no place of any importance for passengers on the line.'

The track was 41 lb. U.F.F. steel rail in 30 ft lengths, carried on 11 sleepers. Owing to spikes being loose, the rails had worked down-grade and together with the sharp curves, some station yards gave constant trouble; Bryngwyn for instance, was now unfit to take locomotives.

The Bryngwyn Incline to the Amalgamated Quarries was ¾ m. long and 1 in 10 grade; it was worked by the Railway employees and connected with Alexandra, Moel Tryfan, Braich and Cilgwyn Quarries at the top; Vron was about to re-open. The Incline rope was weak and only 3 slate wagons could descend at a time. In consequence, it took four hours to handle a 20-wagon train. (Spring preferred abandonment of the Incline and as the country was suitable, a new line incorporating reversing necks. He also recommended an approach to the Pen-yr-orsedd Quarries to suggest they might divert their traffic to Drumhead instead of consigning it via the horse-worked Nantlle Railway.)

The existing signalling was extremely lavish; Tryfan Signal Box had 10 signals and a 20 lever frame. The Report confirms that the last Aberglaslyn tunnel on the railway then building, had yet to be pierced; no viaducts were built, but 41 lb. rails were laid for a mile south of South Snowdon and had recently been used for 'timber logging', but this mile was now out of use.

As a result of an intensive period of rehabilitation to bring the main line up to passenger standards, passenger services were resumed from 31st July, 1922 using the Festiniog's *Palmerston* which had been on hire to the contractors and was conveniently available. Passenger services on the branch, though intended, did not materialise.

Henry Joseph Jack – of whom much will follow – became Receiver on 9th April, 1921.

In 1922, Evan R. Davies, a new N.W.N.G. director, wrote to S.E. Tyrwhitt the newly-appointed Manager of the Festiniog and the new Welsh Highland Railway – into which the North Wales Narrow Gauge

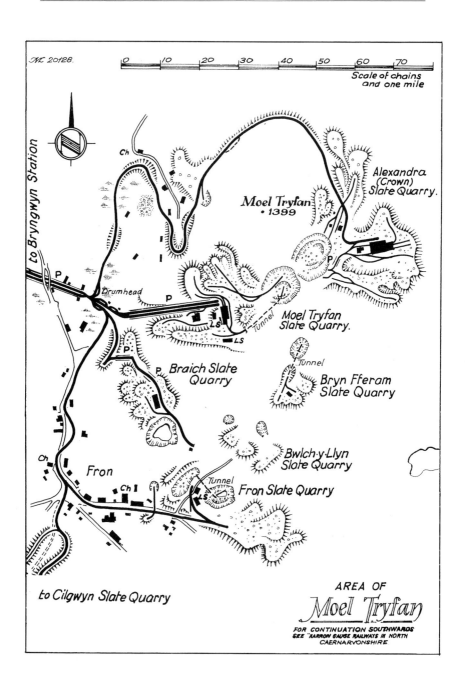

N.C. 20128.

0   10   20   30   40   50   60   70

Scale of chains
and one mile

to Bryngwyn Station

Ch

Moel Tryfan
•1399

Alexandra
(Crown)
Slate Quarry.

P

Drumhead

P

Tunnel   Moel Tryfan
          Slate Quarry.

LS
LS

P

P   Braich Slate
     Quarry

Tunnel

Bryn Fferam
Slate Quarry

Ch

Fron

Ch

Bwlch·y·Llyn
Slate Quarry

Tunnel

LS

Fron Slate Quarry

to Cilgwyn Slate Quarry

AREA OF

Moel Tryfan

FOR CONTINUATION SOUTHWARDS
SEE "NARROW GAUGE RAILWAYS IN NORTH
CAERNARVONSHIRE

Railways was absorbed as from 1st January, 1922. Advice was given that all matters of finance would now pass to Dolgarrog, the Welsh Highland headquarters. It was anticipated that the L.N.W.R. would begin its summer service on 10th July, 1922 and Tyrwhitt was instructed to see that the Rhyd-Ddu line would be ready for opening on that day. D.O. Jones had tendered a draft for a restored passenger service on the N.W.N.G. which could be worked with little addition to the then skeleton staff. (D.O. Jones was the factotum at Dinas Junction.) So almost unnoticed, the N.W.N.G. ceased its independent life.

The Route described

(from fieldwork 1940–54)

The Main Line

The railway began at a junction at Llanwnda with the Carnarvonshire Railway* (as it was locally still known) a standard gauge line which had commenced at a temporary station south of Caernarvon at Pant, had absorbed the old Nantlle Railway (opened in 1828, gauge 3 ft 6 in.) and extended for 18¾ miles southward across the neck of the Lleyn Peninsula to a junction with the Cambrian Railways (Coast Section) at Afon Wen. The Carnarvonshire Railway was in practice part of the London & North Western Railway which had opened to Caernarvon (a separate station at the north end of the town) in July 1852 and had had aspirations of reaching Portmadoc as one point where the slate industry might be tapped.

At Llanwnda the Nantlle Tramway (or Railway) ran roughly parallel but to the west of the main Caernarvon–Pwllheli road, and the absorption of this horse-worked narrow gauge line permitted the Carnarvonshire Railway to use limited portions of its course between Caernarvon and Pen-y-groes for its new standard gauge line. The evidence of old photographs suggests that the new owners built their standard gauge track leaving not only most of the Nantlle Railway in use but re-siting some (including the section at Llanwnda) alongside its own new line, probably for contracting purposes. An early scene at Dinas Junction – the name for the station where interchange with the North Wales Narrow Gauge was made – shows narrow gauge track apparently of 3 ft 6 in. gauge running alongside and west of the standard gauge through the station (where later the L.N.W.R. was to provide a passing loop and Up platform). L.N.W.R. passenger trains began to call at Dinas from September 1877.

The N.W.N.G. occupied a narrow site between the L.N.W.R. and the main road on the east side of the standard gauge. There was an interchange platform between standard and narrow gauges, the former being of traditional height and the N.W.N.G. at rail level, but having

*The statutory title and spelling.

in common with all N.W.N.G. stations, slab curbs to define the passenger area. The northern end of this platform was occupied by a similar two-level wharf for interchange of slate and later of timber. The central portion contained a stone station building for N.W.N.G. purposes, the L.N.W.R. not having a building of its own at the time. East of this was a large stone goods shed containing tracks in both gauges divided by an exchange platform; at its north end was a goods platform with a crane at its extremity and later, a weighbridge for narrow gauge was added.

A feature of the site was a road crossing of the station premises at the south end. The N.W.N.G. bridge was in its standard brick and stone design, and the L.N.W.R. had its own overbridge alongside, the two being connected by an earthen embankment carrying the road. An early drawing (undated) headed 'Proposed Station and Transhipment for the North Wales Narrow Gauge Junction with the Carnarvonshire Railway at Llanwnda' undoubtedly comes from Spooner's office at Portmadoc though it is not marked in any way. Additional sidings in both gauges are provided on the drawing, but these do not appear to have been built at the outset, clearly due to shortage of funds. Lime and coal sidings on the east side (with high level L.N.W.R. tracks discharging into low level N.W.N.G. wagons) together with a tippler, did not materialise until further capital was available for such improvements under the N.W.N.G. Act of 1890.

A second early drawing with estimate of costs is dated 22nd February, 1874 which appears to arise from the Engineer's Office, Bangor, and is signed by C.E. Spooner and has various possible omissions with consequent reduced costs pencilled in. Basically the arrangements would have been similar but probably by the example of Nantlle quarries' wagons which were now being carried pick-a-back by the standard gauge, two end loading docks at the Caernarvon end would allow slate wagons to run on and off standard gauge opens . . . not a very desirable arrangement unless the narrow gauge wagons could be run through the standard gauge train in the manner of a modern car ferry train. The tippler's purpose is now clear – it was for 'ore traffic', this presumably being iron ore from the Bettws Garmon district, and the tracks through and below it were gauntletted.[7]

South of the road overbridges, where in later years carriage and wagon shops, loco shed and workshops etc. were to be found, no detail is given and the tracks simply converge.

The Company was obliged to 'make do' with this limited arrangement until additional funds came to hand and extended facilities were provided:

1. Additional sidings were laid east of the goods shed for coal and lime traffic. The L.N.W.R. provided a single high level siding with tippler there, held up on a retaining wall. The double line and end

tipper for the standard gauge, envisaged by Spooner, did not materialise.

2. The latterday facilities south of the road overbridge were erected. There was a three road carriage and wagon store shed and repair shop in corrugated iron with a long siding giving access. A feature of this in latter days was the string of broken wagons on it which, because of diminishing traffic, never had need to enter the works for repair.

Across on the west side of the curve was a double road engine shed built in timber with store and sand oven in stone alongside. (An original and smaller loco shed on this site is likely to have been a stone-built affair.) Here too, stood an iron water tank on a stone plinth, a feature which must have existed from the beginning. There was a small stone smithy beside the shed which, though not specifically provided, doubled up as a workshop. A wooden signal box on stone base completed the buildings; the box was at first to be placed north of the goods platform on the other side of the bridge so presumably at this period no intention of works and sheds on the south side was anticipated. Detail alterations and periods of disuse and refurbishing of certain pointwork throughout the life of the N.W.N.G. according to the times when no passenger trains were running at all, are evident in the trackage which it was necessary to retain or revive on the wharves.

It will be noted too that on the standard gauge side, an Up loop and platform were laid in the early 1880s and the signal box (which had been some way north of the station near the sidings' throat), was placed on the Up platform before 1885 where it was also more convenient for handling the single line staff etc.

On the Down platform, the principal building remained the stone station of the N.W.N.G., but after the First War the Snowdon Mountain Tramroad and Hotel Co. operated a Refreshment Room at the north end – a large wooden affair on stone foundations – and a small wooden Booking Office was added south of the stone station.

Standard gauge facilities remained throughout the period of the narrow gauge's existence.

On leaving Dinas Junction the railway curved left through a right angle turn, entering a cutting to pass under the Caernarvon–Pwllheli road by means of the customary pattern of N.W.N.G. overbridge built in stone with brick lining to the arch – usually of four courses in either red or yellow. On the outer side of the curve, in front of the bridge, was the Advance Starting signal to cover movements made from the loco and carriage yard when using the main line as a headshunt.*

Once under the roadbridge past the Home signal, after ¼ m. the track emerged from the cutting and after threading a narrow wooded belt ran along the left bank of the Gorfai stream for about ⅛ m. before crossing it by a 12 ft span girder bridge and passing under a secondary road (200 ft above sea level). The surrounding land is low lying and tends to be marshy; the climb began from Dinas at 1 in 136 but the real

---

*On the Spooner-projected station plan of 1874, this post is shown carrying a Distant signal – the only signal on the whole plan.

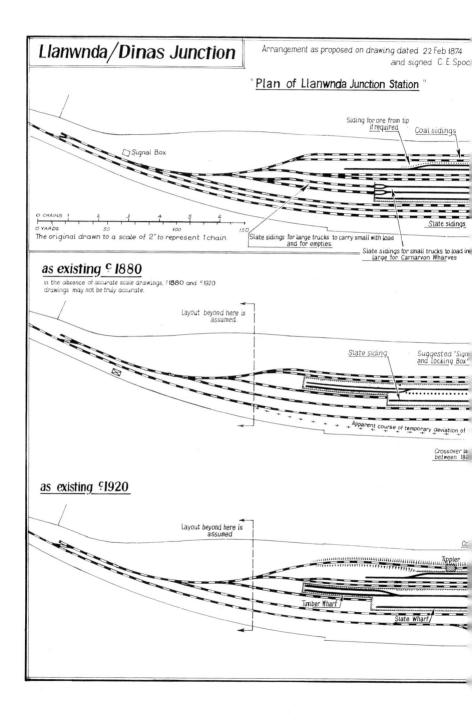

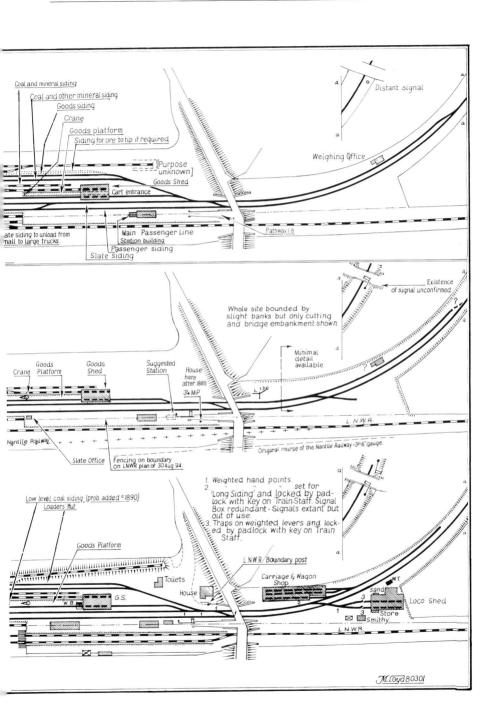

Distant signal

Coal and mineral siding
Coal and other mineral siding
Goods siding
Crane
Goods platform
Siding for one to tip if required
[Purpose unknown]
Goods Shed
Cart entrance
Weighing Office
ate siding to unload from mall to large trucks
Main Passenger Line
Station building
Passenger siding
Slate siding
Pathway 1:8

Whole site bounded by slight banks but only cutting and bridge embankment shown
Existence of signal unconfirmed
Minimal detail available

Crane
Goods Platform
Goods Shed
Suggested Station
House here after 1885
3/4 MP
L 136
L.N.W.R.

Nantlle Railway
Slate Office
Fencing on boundary on LNWR plan of 30 Aug '94
Original course of the Nantlle Railway - 3ft 6 gauge.

1. Weighted hand points.
2. " " set for 'Long Siding' and locked by padlock with key on Train Staff. Signal Box redundant - Signals extant but out of use.
3. Traps on weighted levers and locked by padlock with key on Train Staff.

Low level coal siding (prob. added c1890)
Loaders Hut
Goods Platform
Toilets
House
L.N.W.R. Boundary post
Carriage & Wagon Shop
W.T.
Sand
Loco Shed
Store
Smithy
G.S.
W.B.
L.N.W.R.

JMLloyd 80301

collar-work had yet to begin.* A straight run of about ¼ m. brought the line to Bodaden where another secondary road was crossed and the first milepost passed. In the next ⅜ m. the stream was crossed twice more and the main road to Rhostryfan came in alongside on the left. The ground each side remains flat and somewhat uninteresting, besides being boggy and wet. The road on the left mounted over the railway by a bridge rebuilt in concrete in 1933 during road widening. The railway turned north-west here and followed a virtually straight course until the second milepost. The height is now 300 ft as Wernlas-Ddu is passed and climbing from here begins in earnest. There was a long pull up of 1 in 47 mainly on low embankment and through an ever-increasingly pleasant countryside. The course used the tip of the foothills of the mountain bloc, keeping it out of the wet lands below but still avoiding heavy earthworks and confining the gradient to a steady climb. The line was bounded by substantial stone walls, 12 yd. between each, and gated in wood where necessary. Much use of slab and worn flat-bottomed rails was made for gate posts; of the latter, perhaps most were taken from the N.W.N.G. when substantial relaying was done by the W.H.R. in the early 1920s. Some are marked 'Leeds Forge 1904' and 'Darlington Steel Co. Ltd.'; they are about 40 lb. weight and if in fact were taken from the N.W.N.G., were in very poor condition when renewed. This length of line must have been delightful in railway days; the land slopes upwards to the south in pasture and woodland, whilst to the north are water-meadows with grazing Welsh Blacks dotted over them. Farms tend to be large, by local standards.

Now came a slow right-hand curve and from a nominal 1 in 47 the gradient stiffened as the foothills' slopes steepened. The long low embankment ceased, there was a short length of open ground and after a short length of 1 in 37, a cutting and road overbridge. Immediately beyond extended a brief embankment and by means of a stone over-bridge, the adjacent stream was crossed for the last time (2 m.). Almost at once there is another road overbridge – all within a length of about 75 yd. Beyond the second one and a slight reverse curve, the railway entered Tryfan Junction station (originally named Moel Tryfan Junction).

Tryfan Junction (2 m. 15 ch.) (372 ft) must have been something of a disappointment to the stranger, but on the other hand, totally in keeping with that type of isolated meeting place of railways perhaps more commonly met with in Ireland than in Wales. Apart from the small stone and brick station building, with its generous nameboard below the eaves, giving the title in full, it was one of the remotest of places. Even today, a small road passes along the rear but it only serves two farms. In yesteryear, it would have been quieter still. It must be presumed that occasionally some folk changed from a Dinas-bound train for a Bryngwyn-bound one, but that would be about the whole of

---

*Gradients are quoted where known but the figures are insufficient to produce an accurate Gradient Profile.

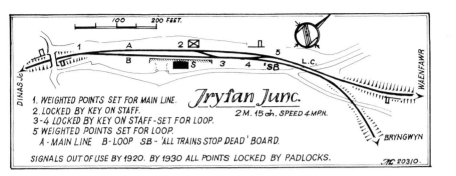

Tryfan Junc.

2 M. 15 ch. SPEED 4 M.P.H.

1. WEIGHTED POINTS SET FOR MAIN LINE.
2. LOCKED BY KEY ON STAFF.
3-4 LOCKED BY KEY ON STAFF - SET FOR LOOP.
5 WEIGHTED POINTS SET FOR LOOP.
 A - MAIN LINE   B - LOOP   SB - 'ALL TRAINS STOP DEAD' BOARD.

SIGNALS OUT OF USE BY 1920. BY 1930 ALL POINTS LOCKED BY PADLOCKS.

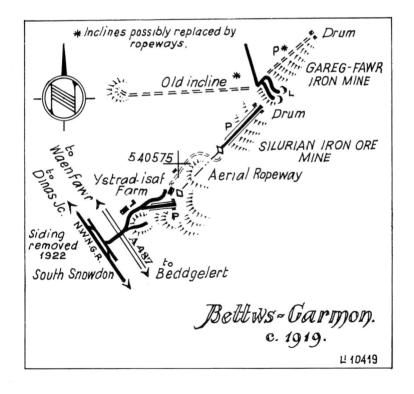

Bettws-Garmon.
c. 1919.

it. Originally the signalling was luxurious, with a Down Home signal before the first overbridge previously mentioned, and six other signals to keep it company. At the east end the Bryngwyn branch came in at a fearsome 3¾ chain curve which lay at the foot of a long 1 in 39 fall, so occasionally there may have been some exciting moments. Whether this had anything to do with the branch not having a Home signal but only a stop board is not known (!) but branch trains were required to make a dead stand at the incline foot in any case. However, the Junction was one of those places where one is bound to conclude that operating methods were evolved which suited the place and whereon management seldom gazed. There was one long passing loop which contained a facing crossover and from the south side of which the junction was made to Bryngwyn. This simple layout allowed great flexibility of movements – if ever they were required. There was no siding and no goods facilities. Opposite the station was a wooden signal box on stone base and the passenger platform, as at other stations, was simply a neat 6 in. edging of slab to retain a gravel stand. From a full passenger station, Tryfan Junction was reduced to Halt status in 1934, before the Welsh Highland lost its passenger services.

Resuming its course north-eastwards from the Junction, the line continued to rise at 1 in 690 and began to curve slowly in a more easterly direction. First there was a low embankment and a farm road came alongside on the left. This road then passed over the line which fell into a cutting below it. Now east of the bridge, there followed a considerable embankment pierced by a fine example of the Company's stone underbridges which carried the line over the road to Gwredog-isaf, a large farm now derelict. This place is of special interest as early 25-inch Plans show it to have had a railway system in the barnyard. Today there is no sign of railway connections save for inventive use of ex-Nantlle Railway fish-bellied rails to support the roofs of some out-buildings . . . indeed, such is the extensive use of these rails (presumably available when the Caernarvon–Pen-y-groes section was superseded by the standard gauge) that they may be found in remote localities all over the area serving as fencing posts or etc.

Eastwards of here the countryside becomes more wooded and the gradient steepened then eased as the line reached the south side of the Afon Gwyrfai, now meandering some way below to the left. After a short cutting the railway was carried on a shelf on the valleyside, with the river steeply down below (3 m.). This steep slope takes on a partially escarpment-like quality for a short distance below Tanyrallt, and the railway was forced to wind its way along to keep contact with the valley side. Now enveloped in woodland, it was a charming section of the train journey as the river gradually comes up alongside.

The climb which was such a feature up to, and for quarter of a mile beyond Tryfan Junction, had reached a plateau thereafter; after a short fall at 1 in 200 the line into Waenfawr was level.

Another detail noticeable during the threading of the 'shelf section' was that four foot boundary walling topped by two wires had ceased and when fencing was resumed a mile or so west of Waenfawr, it was of the seven-wire and four foot wood-post variety which was retained almost for the whole of the remainder of the main line. Presumably stone walls were built where loose boulders from river deposits were available on the lower stretches of the line. They resume again between Snowdon Ranger and Rhyd-Ddu in Festiniog pattern with wire fence on top.

Before Waenfawr is reached the 400 ft contour was crossed and there came a most intimate length where the river, now alongside and occasionally broken by rapids and islands, is enhanced by hillocks and large trees. Waenfawr itself, on the hillside to the north which is now a noticeable feature from the line, tumbles down in scattered fashion to meet river and railway. On this length of line some curious track spikes were found – they were of standard N.W.N.G. domehead pattern but no less than 8 in. long, perhaps a Livesey type? On this section the railway was heading almost due east but as Waenfawr Down Home signal was passed, it curved right and south-easterly, entered a short cutting and emerged from under a stone overbridge carrying the Caernarvon–Beddgelert road to enter Waenfawr station (3 m. 70 ch.). After the delightful mile or so preceding Waenfawr, this was something of an anticlimax. The countryside has changed and for some distance the railway was to run along the flood plain of the Gwyrfai, the foothills tending to hang back for a time as the valley widened out ready for an even more dramatic narrowing higher up.

After 1895 this had become the largest station between Dinas and South Snowdon. Up to that time it was neither a staff nor block station but then a loop siding – similar to that at Bettws Garmon was put in. Whilst it had catch points at each end it was not signalled. The points each end were locked by Annett's Key from the signal box. One ground lever at the south end was actually in a corner of the box, and the Dinas end alongside the turnout. Only one set of points could be worked at a time as there was only one key, which interlocked with the signals.

Col. R.A. Yorke reported on 28th November, 1895 that if facing point locks were added the loop might be used for goods traffic but as the intention was to use it for all traffic the following must be done now it is both a block and staff station:

1. Signal the station as a proper passing place.
2. All trains to use left-hand side of loop.
3. Home signals capable of being lowered only for proper line.
4. Removal of catch points.
5. Starting signals at each loop to be installed.
6. Facing point locks fitted.

Until this had been done, subject to fitting facing point locks, the loop could be passed for goods traffic only.

Mr. Russell met Major Marindin and Col. Yorke and it was agreed

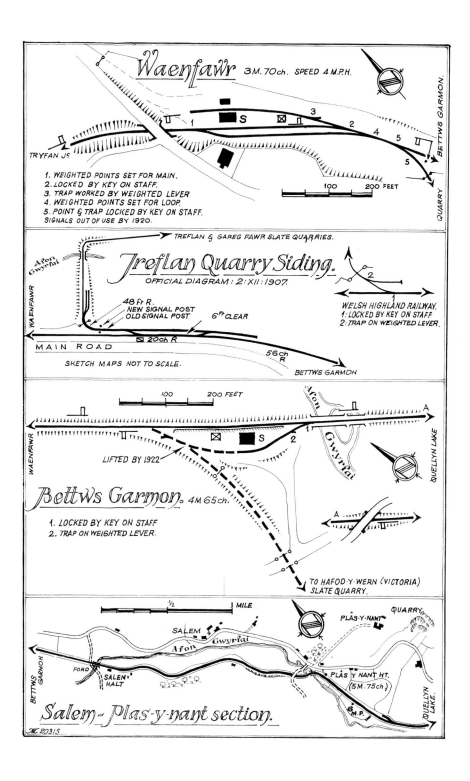

Waenfawr 3M. 70ch. SPEED 4 M.P.H.

S

1

3

2

4

5

5

5

TRYFAN Jⁿ

100   200 FEET

BETTWS GARMON.

QUARRY

1. WEIGHTED POINTS SET FOR MAIN.
2. LOCKED BY KEY ON STAFF.
3. TRAP WORKED BY WEIGHTED LEVER
4. WEIGHTED POINTS SET FOR LOOP.
5. POINT & TRAP LOCKED BY KEY ON STAFF.
SIGNALS OUT OF USE BY 1920.

TREFLAN & GAREG FAWR SLATE QUARRIES.

Treflan Quarry Siding.

OFFICIAL DIAGRAM: 2·XII·1907.

Afon Gwyrfai

WAENFAWR

48 ft R.
NEW SIGNAL POST
OLD SIGNAL POST

6ᶠᵗ CLEAR

2

WELSH HIGHLAND RAILWAY.
1: LOCKED BY KEY ON STAFF
2: TRAP ON WEIGHTED LEVER.

1

MAIN ROAD

20 ch R

56 ch R

SKETCH MAPS NOT TO SCALE.

BETTWS GARMON

---

100   200 FEET

Afon Gwyrfai

A

WAENFAWR

QUELLYN LAKE

S

2

1

A

LIFTED BY 1922

Bettws Garmon. 4M 65 ch.

1. LOCKED BY KEY ON STAFF
2. TRAP ON WEIGHTED LEVER.

TO HAFOD·Y·WERN (VICTORIA)
SLATE QUARRY.

½   MILE

QUARRY

PLÂS·Y·NANT

SALEM

Afon Gwyrfai

BETTWS GARMON

FORD

SALEM
HALT

PLÂS Y NANT HT.
(5M·75ch.)

6 M.P.

QUELLYN LAKE.

Salem - Plas-y-nant section.

Ⅎ 20315

that Starting signals would not be required. The other work was carried out using Saxby & Farmer materials and the layout came into use on 21st July, 1896. Trains could use it as a passing place (though most timetables did not require it) which could not be said of all stations, even though others boasted loops. There was the usual stone building, a signal box and one siding (with small goods shed) facing South Snowdon. After the demise of the box's locking frame, the point hand levers were weighted for left-hand running through the loop which was 250 ft clear at 8 ft centres. The traps in the siding were locked by the staff key. A quarry branch, south of the station, was opened to a nearby granite quarry in later Welsh Highland days.

The climb from Waenfawr was a slighter one of 1 in 150, with the main road alongside on the right hand. The fencing which survives along the rail route in this section is worth a second glance – few railway museums have such a fine collection of various rail sections!

The fourth mile post was passed just south of Waenfawr; the line was now sandwiched between river and roadway, a rather boggy place. The next feature is to the left where a junction (facing South Snowdon) with a tramway to the Treflan and Gareg-fawr Slate Quarries was made. These quarries were open when the railway was built.

Though there may have been an earlier non-railway connection, it seems that the junction here was not made until 1901–2. It was the ironstone mine and not the slate quarry which wanted the link, but it could not obtain any more suitable land from Rev. Parry (the land-owner) and the junction was the best that could be made in the circumstances. In the event a connection in the form of a stabling loop was made, the points being worked by Annett's Key attached to the staff. There were two signals (one at each end of the layout) and a small ground frame for each end. The work was inspected on 7th May, 1902 and the Inspector's final recommendations carried out in the July. The two slate quarries, in practice, made far more use of the siding than did the ironstone mine adjacent to them.

Treflan ceased regular working in 1883 and Gareg-fawr closed in April 1885. The former was working again in the early 1920s as the Treflan Slate & Granite Co. Ltd. and in 1928 as the Welsh Standard Slate & Granite Quarries Ltd. of Liverpool. By then, work had ceased. The tramway itself passed through a gate, made for the far bank of the river by means of a very sharp curve from the N.W.N.G., a low embankment, a stone-piered span river bridge, yet another sharp curve, and a long low embankment made of quarry spoil to divide into two branches at the foot of the inclines. The tramway was probably laid in bridge rail, and was about half a mile long.

Returning to the main line, a feature of the course here was the width of the land purchased for the railway. It must have been cheap, for a double-tracked standard gauge railway could be made along it with room to spare. (Height 414 ft).

Bettws Garmon (4 m. 65 ch.) is now reached. Several variations in spelling have been used and the N.W.N.G. did not always spell in accordance with local custom! To keep the track clear of low-lying floodland, the route was now raised on a five foot embankment. The adjacent road swings away from the line which, quite straight for a distance, entered the station which, like others, was really outside the hamlet of its namesake. The usual stone building and signal box were on the right, and a siding in the form of a loop passed round the rear of both. It had been installed in the Spring of 1902 and the points at each end were controlled by local ground frames each with locking lever released by a key on the Waenfawr–Rhyd-Ddu staff. Major Druitt would not pass the installation until facing point locks were fitted. Off this siding a branch line, just over half a mile long, took a tramway to the Hafod-y-wern Slate Quarries, a working which provided the railway, in its time, with considerable traffic. This quarry, latterly one in the Moel Tryfan Crown group, was disused when the railway opened, but started work again as Wilson & Co. in the mid-1880s and on a moderate scale of output. The road was crossed on the level and here the rails were of grooved street-tram variety. Before the line closed, north-end loop points and quarry branch had been taken out.

Still rising, the railway crossed the Gwyrfai on leaving Bettws by one of its 'standard' bridges. This was a bowplate steel (originally wrought iron) structure of 48 ft on stone piers. Immediately following it was a stone and slab spillway beneath the line, to carry flood water away. A field's length away, the line passed under the main road, which was carried above it by a curious bridge having cast-iron joists and some unusual brackets to hold up its span walls. The line was now in the centre of the narrowing valley, following a shallow cutting beneath farmlands until it was obliged to cross the river again by means of a second 'standard' bridge with adjacent spillway. Shortly before this and on the left, there was originally a branch with loop and sidings to the Gareg-fawr Ironstone & Copper Mines, a series of remarkable 'rabbit holes' which climb ladder-like up the mountainside to the east, and which have enjoyed a chequered career since before 1850 and have used both rail and wire ropeway haulage.

The branch crossed the main road – road users in this age must have been quite familiar with quarry tramway crossings along this route! – to reach a loading platform at the hill foot. What appear to be tramway inclines are not necessarily so. The branch was lifted during 1922 reconstruction and loop etc. removed.

Gareg-fawr iron mines were worked by Sir Alfred Hickman Ltd. and in 1911 employed over thirty men below ground. Work was abandoned in October 1913. Ystrad Mine hard at hand was worked by Bettws Garmon Iron Ore & Smelting Co. Ltd. up to 1916, and in 1919 by Silurian Iron Ore Co. Ltd. It shut down on 21st February, 1920.[8,9]

At the incline foot a crusher could produce 100 tons a day; the incline was 460 yards long with 25 lbs./yard flat-bottomed rails on 6 ins. × 3 ins. wooden sleepers; but 128 yards of track in the quarry had rails but of 14 lbs./yard; the aerial ropeway was no less than 2,466 yards long. In 1917 the Geological Survey reported that the railway was moving 300 tons of ore per week from Ystrad Mine.

This branch line junction faced Dinas and was at the fifth milepost.

The main line now reached a lovely section of the valley. The steep mountainsides close in upon the river and force water, road and railway closer together. The railway wound its way around the slopes on the west side, the road passing through the hamlet of Salem on the east. Opposite a wooden footbridge over the river, a Halt was provided (not opened until 21st July, 1922!). There was a rough 'platform' and wooden hut (5 m. 40 ch.). Climbing now at 1 in 122 this steepened to 1 in 84 at 5 m. 53 ch. and then came some more picturesque curves, the rugged hillsides now closing in more closely and forcing the railway on to a shelf which, to carry it above the river below, was now supported by a lengthy and fine piece of stone walling. On the right-hand side, a short siding trailed in which served the railway's ballast pit known as Salem Quarry. This was controlled like Treflan Siding, by a small 2-lever ground frame. Rock and boulder rise up steeply above the railway's course. At the head of this defile the railway passed under a road bridge and made a reverse 3.12 ch. radius curve beside the river and Falls at Nant Mill (or Plas-y-nant). This was the sharpest bend on the main line. The old mill is but a memory but the water supplies now form part of a reservoir; railway travellers were the most fortunate for the train was carried in a continuous curve above the water, supported by stone walling five feet above it. Next, the course reversed its curve, passed round a rocky eminence and immediately this intimate setting became lost. The defile ended with the line crossing the river for the last time (using the standard 48 ft bridge plus a stone spillway) and entered the flood-plain again. Here the mountains recede and ahead extends a magnificent view of mountain and lake with Snowdon to the left and the crags of Craig Cwm Bychan overhanging Llyn Quellyn to the right. Over this section the climb eased from 1 in 400 to 1 in 551.

Just south of the river bridge was Plas-y-nant Halt, a semi-official stop before 1924 when in July it appeared in the Time-table, (5 m. 75 ch.; 486 ft) served by a gate in the road wall and a pathway on the river bank. There was no other facility other than the 17 yards 'platform' and just beyond was the sixth milepost.

There followed a short straight length down towards the lake, on embankment. There must have been subsidence here for the embankment suddenly becomes very narrow and sunken, and has been built up in milled quarry waste, to judge by the saw-cuts in the spoil. At the south end of this earthwork traces of a 40 yds. siding are visible on the left. This served the nearby Plas-y-nant and Brynmanllyn Slate Quarries, the latter very small. Both had closed before the turn of the century and though an actual tramway connection to the former is possible physically (including the inevitable level crossing of the road) there is no tangible evidence of it today. No records survive for

Brynmanllyn, but Plas-y-nant was hard at work with 28 men in 1883. The slump hit suddenly: one man survived in 1885 and work stopped the next year.

Shortly after this siding, the railway quit the river bank, swung east with a short cutting in rising ground, and then passed under the main road again by means of the usual stone overbridge, this time arranged on the skew. There is a wide and considerable – though shallow – cutting on the south side where the temporary terminus was sited. On the north edge is a slab built wall, the remains of a top level roadway for offshooting materials from carts, and a good deal of milled slate and slab of cruder shapes and sizes. If this could tell its story we should be much wiser. Some of this material was obviously loaded here and the best of what there was has long been 'acquired' for local building purposes! Probably much of the residue has provided the railway and other users of filling with the necessary material over a great number of years. There is space for a run-round loop and at least two sidings (6 m. 45 ch.)

Despite the obviously ample space for a temporary station here, by the time of the Board of Trade inspection the layout was specifically described as having 'only 2 signals and no points'. If sidings or loop were put in here temporarily either before then, or later, they were not there at the time of inspection. This leaves the unanswered question; how did Marindin pass the layout if there was no means of running the engine round the train?

Perhaps with the satisfaction of having completed the last stone bridge on the main line, the stone mason had permitted himself to carve 'W.E.W.' on a corner stone of the Quellyn road bridge.

Ahead there comes this new and mountainous scene. The somewhat melancholy lake is below to the right, a fine sweep of Mynydd Mawr behind it. For part of the day in summer and most of the day in winter, its western shore never receives any sunlight. To the left of the track, slopes pile on one another until the summit of Snowdon itself is reached and from suitable viewpoints, the mountain train may be seen climbing the final stages to the summit station. On the N.W.N.G., the grade steepened to 1 in 67, then 1 in 96, 79 and 94 along a superb run above the lakeside. There was not much civil engineering work here, the contours being kindly and allowing the course to meander slightly along the lower flank of Foel Gron. Numerous mountain streamlets are crossed by stone arches; these are dry for some seasons. Milepost 7 was passed and then came what was to become Snowdon Ranger station. At first it was named Quellyn Lake, but soon it was changed to that of the Hotel hard by which carried the name 'Snowdon Ranger'.

From the road in the Quellyn Lake area a sledgeway was built about 1810 to carry copper ore to Caernarvon on sledges for shipping to South Wales. These sledges carried 6 cwt. apiece and were drawn by two horses. In the main the workings were on the west side of the Snowdon bloc and the sledgeway extended from the Beddgelert road to the Upper

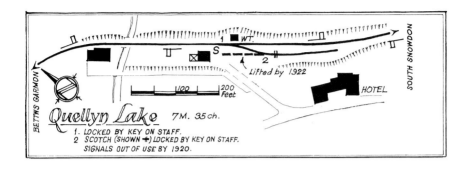

Quellyn Lake   7M. 35ch.

1. LOCKED BY KEY ON STAFF.
2 SCOTCH (SHOWN +) LOCKED BY KEY ON STAFF.
   SIGNALS OUT OF USE BY 1920.

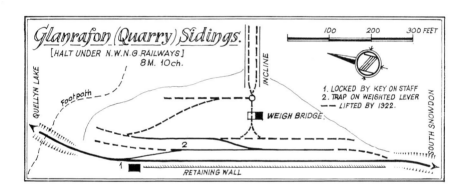

Glanrafon (Quarry) Sidings.

[HALT UNDER N.W.N.G. RAILWAYS]
8M. 10ch.

1. LOCKED BY KEY ON STAFF
2. TRAP ON WEIGHTED LEVER
--- LIFTED BY 1922.

WEIGH BRIDGE

RETAINING WALL

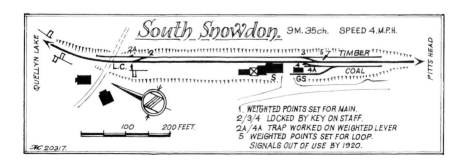

South Snowdon   9M. 35ch.   SPEED 4. M.P.H.

1. WEIGHTED POINTS SET FOR MAIN.
2/3/4 LOCKED BY KEY ON STAFF.
2A/4A TRAP WORKED ON WEIGHTED LEVER
5 WEIGHTED POINTS SET FOR LOOP.
   SIGNALS OUT OF USE BY 1920.

Mine at Bwlch Glas, thence there was a footpath to the mine in Cwm Glaslyn. The proprietors also built a horse path (for pack animals) from Gorpwsfa – beyond Llanberis – to Bwlch Glas. The name Cwellyn (Quellyn) is assumed to be from Cae-uwch-y-Llyn (The Field above the Lake) and a large residence nearby was owned by the Quellyn family who took their name from the place. It had been demolished by 1813.

The station (7 m. 35 ch.) had a siding with backshunt, a stone building (the only survivor and now a bungalow) with signal box alongside, and across the track, a water tank on a stone plinth. It was close by the road. The next feature was a natural interception in the path of the railway, the Afon Treweunydd gorge over which a wrought iron bridge of 93 ft 6 in. and 8 ft width on stone piers had to be thrown at a height of 50 ft above the ravine. The building of this was a subject of some delay in the already protracted construction of the line. The eighth milepost was at its south side.

The comfortable contour site now became more difficult to follow. But firstly after a cutting came a shelf-situation supported on a high stone wall. Here was the triangular junction to the Glanrafon Slate Quarries (8 m. 10 ch.; the northern side of the triangle was later lifted) the largest quarry on the main line. During its lifetime it had owned four locomotives but was closed down during the First War; this was almost the final nail in the coffin, for shortly afterwards, regular working over the South Snowdon section ceased, save for timber trains as required. The quarry had opened as the Glanrafon Slate Quarry Co. before the railway came. Together with Alexandra, it was the largest working quarry served by the railway. It survived the slump of the 1880s, employing about 190 in 1887. The quarry stands above the line, connected to it by incline and having a considerable trackage within its workings, including a quarter mile tunnel. The loop on the main was a stopping place for quarrymen's traffic.

For the last part of the journey the line, climbing at 1 in 47, was obliged to twist and turn its way through rugged terrain which was quite unhelpful to the surveyor. For the passenger however, there was a feast of views either side of the train including an 'end-on' scene of Quellyn Lake as the carriage wound its way round a final curve. Hereabouts the superelevation on curves was highly distinctive. On this length at 8 m. 52 ch. there was a 50 yd. interchange siding for the Rhosclogwyn Slate Quarry. This connected to an incline which was closed before 1890; the connecting point was taken out but the siding survived and was reconnected again for the Snowdon Slate Co. in September 1903. The points were worked from a ground frame unlocked by a key on the staff. Major Druitt (16th September, 1903) insisted that the engine be at the lower end of the train for all shunting here, in view of the gradient. There was a second period of activity in the 1920s and 1930s and output was taken down to the line by wire ropeway for which a new 20 yd. siding was put in at 8 m. 66 ch. Inside the curve which follows was the ninth milepost and after a reverse, the terminus was reached at 9 m. 35 ch., over the last ¾ m. the grade rose at 1 in 191, 100, 146, 430, (Level), 224, 1100 and 200 before levelling at the station!

Rhyd-Ddu (Black Ford) can be a bleak spot even in summer. The village is very small and at 600 ft it is the summit of the pass between Caernarvon and Beddgelert. However, it was the first point south of Llyn Quellyn where the line could strike the main road and thus secure a measure of passenger traffic. ('The Caernarvon–Pont Aberglaslyn road was reconstructed by public subscription in 1802 and levelled 'so that a horse could trot or gallop all the way'.) Local traffic would be very small, and would perhaps have included a few quarrymen. It was also hoped to link up with the Llyn-y-gader Slate Quarry to the southwest across Llyn-y-gader which had its own tramway to the roadside at a point near the old woollen factory but which started to build a causeway and low viaduct across the marshland and river in the direction of Rhyd-Ddu station. This connection was never completed, and a few drunken slab pillars stand as mute memorials to the unfinished bridge work.

The year 1885 saw the start of a quarry here, owned by the North Wales Quarrymen's Union. It changed hands almost at once and closed down. In 1922 it was owned by Gader Lake Green & Rustic Slate Quarries Ltd. and was worked occasionally for a time.

Rhyd-Ddu was more in fact a bridgehead, perhaps in the eyes of the promoters a springboard from which Beddgelert and other goals beyond might yet be reached. As it was, road services by horse bus were provided in the summer and the timetable helpfully stated connections. Mail and goods vehicles also ran.

As time went by, Snowdon station – as it came to be known – assumed more importance for its timber traffic than anything else. Parry's timber yard grew enormously on the east side of the station during the First War, when the unfinished section of the P.B. & S.S.R. beyond stretched into the Forestry Commission's woodlands around, using an ex-Glanrafon Quarry locomotive.

The layout was simple, with a 300 ft long run round loop at 8 ft 6 in. centres, station buildings in stone, a wooden refreshment room: part of the station building served as a signal box. One siding served a corrugated iron goods shed but did not enter it. There were Home and Distant signals and a Starter. A Bench Mark at the station rear read 627 ft.

In terms of the usual terminal station, Snowdon, like Tryfan Junction, was an anti-climax to the traveller and a delight to the connoisseur of the remote rail ending. Bog, bracken and rock surrounded it on all sides. Mist and rain enveloped it in winter, snow lay for long periods, blizzards funnelled up either side to blanket it. At least the road ran alongside and the place might be left reasonably easily, even if the train service was not running! Until 1896 it enjoyed the distinction of being the nearest railhead to the summit of Snowdon.

Looking back over the route of the main line, it was remarkable for its many changes of character. The first section of two miles was through farmland of increasing interest, then followed a wooded valley of peculiar beauty and not typically Welsh character, to Waenfawr. Here came complete contrast where the run up the flat valley floor ended with the defile at Plas-y-nant and yet another widening took place. From here to Glanrafon the course followed the side of a clean glacial slope, with fine views of lake and mountain. Lastly there ensued a rough mountainous section so commonly found in the Highlands of Scotland or the wilds of north-west Ireland. Tourists got full value for their money!

The station nameboards followed L.N.W.R. pattern using cast-iron lettering on a wooden board: these were fitted under the eaves of the buildings instead of the more conventional method of mounting on posts on the platform. In a reply to a Board of Trade circular the Secretary stated on 2nd February, 1895 that three years ago station names 'were fixed up with 10 in. deep cast-iron letters . . . which catch the eye very well there being no advertisements near either of these nameboards'. (It is assumed that for 'either' he meant 'any'.)

The four 'standard' 48 ft river bridges were built in wrought iron but rebuilt in steel plate after 1895.

The Bryngwyn Branch

If the main line had many faces, the branch added an extra one. From it one of the most typical aspects of Caernarvonshire might be seen, perhaps not that of the country best remembered by the visitor, but the more natural ones of stone cottages, stone walls, sheep farms and low uplands stretching down towards the Menai Straits. The branch gave something which the main line failed to do – a view to the north-west of coast, sea and Anglesey, with Caernarvon Castle for good measure. The Guide Books of 1900 recommended a journey on the branch for its scenery '. . . you leave the main line at Tryfan Junction and should sit on the right-hand side, from which you will have an extensive view of Anglesey . . . Yr Eifl (The Rivals) and neighbouring chain form a prominent . . . object. Moel Tryfan is interesting to the geologist on account of its cap of marine deposit containing shells, which shows it must have once been submerged.' It must have been a dour slog for the train. Starting from rest at the Junction, the track rounded a 180 degree curve of 3¾ chains and the train would have to start a long pound at 1 in 39 (the official figure, but certainly there were some steeper pitches). First came a cutting on the curve which when straightened, set the railway going in exactly a parallel and opposite direction to the main line, just one field's width away. The cutting ended with a stone road overbridge (408 ft) followed by an embankment over that same stream which follows the main line down to Dinas. A long uphill but straight climb, easing to 1 in 48 took the line into

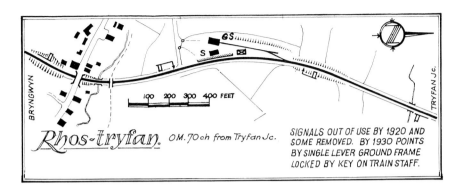

Rhos-tryfan. 0 M. 70 ch from Tryfan Jc.

SIGNALS OUT OF USE BY 1920 AND
SOME REMOVED. BY 1930 POINTS
BY SINGLE LEVER GROUND FRAME
LOCKED BY KEY ON TRAIN STAFF.

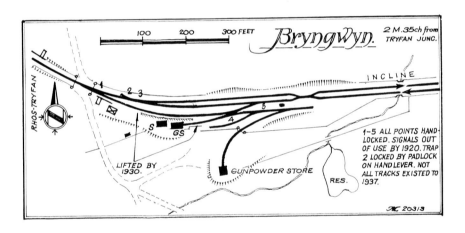

Bryngwyn. 2 M. 35 ch from
TRYFAN JUNG.

1-5 ALL POINTS HAND-
LOCKED. SIGNALS OUT
OF USE BY 1920. TRAP
2 LOCKED BY PADLOCK
ON HAND LEVER. NOT
ALL TRACKS EXISTED TO
1937.

North Wales Narrow Gauge Railway.

(MOELTRYFAN UNDERTAKING).

TRAFFIC RETURN.

*Week ending_____189_*

	Miles.	Pas-sengers.	Goods and Minerals.	Total.	Per Mile.	Passengers for weeks.	Goods, &c., for weeks.	Grand Total for weeks.	Per Mile.
		£	£	£	£ s. d.	£	£	£	£ s. d.

Rhostryfan station, a scattered community of cottages littering the hillside, and apparently without a centre. By now the railway, still with sufficient local stone to fence its boundary with stone walls, was able to struggle up the face of the hillside without much earthwork. Up the slope to the left may be seen the ancient site of a prehistoric village and the nearby Gaerwen Camp. This part of the county is well blessed with ancient monuments such as these.

The station (0 m. 70 ch. from the Junction: 482 ft) was a simple affair, built out on filling from the hillside and consisting of the stone station building, and signal box. There was one siding with a goods shed at the end, which faced the Junction. Latterly the only signal was the Home arm for descending trains; perhaps speed was always slow enough to prevent accidents to trains coming up the bank – certainly the other three signals had disappeared.

From the station, a cutting was entered, a stream crossed on a stone arch and the main road through the village passed over the line which then set off across moorland terrain of open uplands, giving pleasant views over sheep country. Earthworks were slight but curves frequent to allow the track to use the contours.

Shortly after the second milepost the Bryngwyn "road" was crossed on the level, an awkward site for both rail and road users.* Here the builders of the line were obviously faced with Hobson's Choice; they could either have crossed the road on the level (as they did) or spent a good deal of money (of which they were short) in building a bridge. The former course resulted in a horrifying gradient immediately beyond the road crossing which, ignoring the official figure, is clearly nearer 1 in 30 than the 1 in 39 usually quoted. Coming at the end of a long pull it must have tried the fireman's art if they were hauling a long train of slate empties. The track went straight up the side of a large hillock and curved round to the left through a cutting on a 3¾ chain curve, all without any easing of the grade. On leaving the cutting, the railway flattened out and yet another of those changes of scene took place as the line passed round another 180 degree curve, now out and above the surrounding hillside and riding round on an embankment. Ahead stretched a wide open expanse of upper moorland; more walls, bracken, gorse and on the sky line, the outlines of grey tips of slate rubbish – the objective slate quarries almost in sight!

The curve now swung the other way and over an easy grade of about 1 in 200, passed round Bryngwyn Farm, came up alongside the road and crossed it for a second time. The gates were set on the skew. Immediately over the road was Bryngwyn station (2 m. 35 ch. from the Junction: 650 ft) and if visitors had by now become used to the N.W.N.G.R., they would not be surprised in feeling they had not really arrived anywhere. Like Snowdon station, it happened to be the place where passenger trains stopped, but for real business the railway always looked beyond to the point known as the Drumhead, at the top of an ensuing incline.

*If considered a "road", this was the only level crossing, anywhere on the line.

The station with its runround loop lay entirely to the south of the line. It was a curious layout with the signal box beside the crossing gates, a storage loop for slate wagons and a passenger loop south of it. This cunningly allowed passenger trains an element of safety if runaway wagons came down the incline, and allowed freight working clear of the passenger platform. There was a goods shed alongside the station and set apart to the south, a gunpowder shed.

Rising reasonably easily for a slate line, the incline in double track rose from 650 ft to 895 ft over half a mile. The land it crossed is still rough and untended, intersected by stream and by-road; the course simply went straight up the face of the hill, passed under the Fron road near the summit and after a cutting beyond, reached the drumhouse at the top. Unlike other similar situations, the Railway Company owned this mineral extension right up to the winding drum, and private tramways did not begin beforehand. A curious mystery in the working of the incline was the existence of one road which crossed it on the level in the middle of the slope; perhaps a flagman was on duty here and if traffic wished to cross, they allowed the wire haulage rope to slacken on to the road surface.

Beyond Drumhead lay a network of private tramways; an odd fact of the railway at this point is that whilst Dinas is only about two miles distant, the railway has covered over four miles to reach here.

Quarry Tramway Feeders (Quoted gradients are estimated).

According to an account of the 1840s,[10] most of the quarries in the Moel Tryfan area had opened in the 1840–50 period. These were among those about to be considered. An older group of quarries, connected to the Nantlle Railway, was to be found to the south.

At the Drumhead the line forked into three branches, the most southerly also dividing into what was known as the 'New Line' built in the early 1920s to connect with the Fron and Cilgwyn systems near Fron village. Of the three lines fanning out from the summit, each had a storage loop at its end which might also be used by locomotives running round the wagons.

The most northerly line took a sinuous course to the Alexandra Quarry and was 1½ miles long. Between Drumhead and the Quarry it climbed over 350 ft. Setting off in a northerly direction through a cutting it began climbing at approximately 1 in 50, steepening to 1 in 30 through a further cutting. Sleepers were spaced at yard intervals, but on the sharp right-hand curve below the Hermon Congregational Chapel, this was reduced to 2 ft. Rails were of 25 lb./yd. flat-bottom type. Below the chapel, shelf and cutting were to swing the line through a semicircle south-west; there followed an extremely steep section, almost straight, rising at about 1 in 20 and at its end, a formidable 1¾ chain curve, steeply superelevated and carried on a 30 ft embankment, swung the track anti-clockwise through another semicircle below the rubbish tips from the Quarry far above. The course now took a long slow climbing semicircle round the summit of Moel Tryfan, climbing in the early stages at approximately 1 in 40 but easing at the most northerly section of the bend where the track could follow the contours. On the way up the west face of the mountain, a more recently opened section of the quarry (isolated from its parent) is found. The track ran between slab walls; there was an overbridge and sidings. An amount of Nantlle fishbelly rail was utilised in the workings, and some tracks were laid in chaired T-bulb rail (as Croesor).

Beyond the junction for this quarry was a passing loop. Now up on the flanks of Tryfan superb views are available where the line ran round the hilltop; this is undoubtedly one of the finest vantage points in all North Wales, with the mountains of Lleyn stretching away to the south-west, Anglesey and Holyhead Mountain to the west, and ahead a sweep which embraces the valley along which, out of sight and below the hill flank, drove the main line of the N.W.N.G. on its way to Waenfawr. Rounding east and disappearing from view behind the hill on which the tramway ran, was the whole Snowdonia bloc – a viewpoint from which few visitors must have seen it.

Ultimately the line reached the quarry, the largest and most profitable of any served by the N.W.N.G. and employing almost 200 in the 1880s. Until 22nd April, 1918 it was known as the Alexandra Slate Co. Ltd., or locally Cors-y-briniau Quarry and changed its name on reopening after the 1914–18 war. It closed again in June 1929 and on 1st April, 1934 was included in quarries owned by the Amalgamated Slate Association Ltd. (which had gone into liquidation on 9th January, 1931) in the name of Caernarvonshire Crown Slate Quarries Co. Ltd., formed 1st April, 1932. Work began again in July 1934 but by 1939 it had closed and much equipment had been taken away. By September 1963 the rubbish was being taken away by lorry as filling. There is a tunnel connection with the Moel Tryfan Quarry adjacent, where the tramway was working up to 1966. (All these quarries have a tendency to sporadic working under varying titles, making them exceedingly difficult to discuss.) The first owners of this quarry were Spooner & Sons.

The Alexandra Tramway was a microcosm of Welsh narrow gauge practice; a practical demonstration of Spooner doctrine and an engaging little example of what could be done in an inhospitable terrain. The site is still worth seeing on this score, if only to appreciate how overseas systems like the Darjeeling–Himalayan line developed along this basis.

Returning to the Drumhead: there was a tramway which went off along an E.S.E. direction and being on the level for only 10 chains, included two storage loops on this short stretch. It then curved almost eastwards and went up the west slope of Moel Tryfan on a double line incline. This lifted the track to 1,250 ft and achieved almost the same level as the Alexandra line but in a much shorter distance and by different means. [Quarry owners were mixed in their opinions as to whether Inclined Planes or more conventional tramways were most suitable. The Plane was expensive to construct, needed more men to operate, and when requiring repair was more delaying than a tramway.] Here within a mile of each other, two tramway-accesses of varying type worked to the same end.

The quarry had been worked by C. Pearson until 1875, by a further operator up to 1st November, 1879, and was known as the Moel Tryfan Slate & Slab Quarry Co. Ltd. until 22nd April, 1918. In the 1880s, nearly 100 men were employed; it was then the third largest quarry in the neighbourhood. Like Alexandra, it was closed during 1914–18. It was part of the Amalgamated and later, the Crown companies (see previously) and pre-Second War, opened and closed much as Alexandra. It was closed for about two years from 17th September, 1958 and in September 1966 lorries took over. A rail tractor was observed working the line through the tunnel earlier that year; this tunnel had always connected the quarry with the slate mill, and latterly the quarry workings of Moel Tryfan and Alexandra had broken into each other. Material from this combined site was taken to the Moel Tryfan mills by rail.

The third and most southerly line from Drumhead built about 1884, ran south for 20 chains to a reversing neck, and included one storage loop at the Drum.[11] The neck held only two or three wagons and there were two short inclines upwards from here, divided by a brief length of level tramway. The tramway for this quarry has, owing to the time since its abandonment and the marshy nature of the ground between Drumhead and incline foot, almost disappeared. Its principal interest lies in the fact that whilst Alexandra was owned from the first by the Spooner family, the Braich Quarry, the destination of this tramway, was owned by Hugh Beaver Roberts, the builder of the Croesor Tramway. He sold it in 1881 at the time when his connection with the Croesor had terminated in October that year. It became the Braich Slate Quarry until 1887, Braich & Coedmadoc Slate Co. to 1891, John Robinson to c.1897, Thomas Robinson to 15th May, 1904 and Talysarn Slate Quarry Co. Ltd. to 2nd November, 1908. Thereafter it was the New Braich Slate Quarries Ltd., who went into liquidation on 10th October, 1915. Work at the quarry had ceased in 1911. In size it was the second largest in the district, employing 125 men about the time the N.W.N.G. was opened. It was working again in 1915.

The fourth and final branch from Drumhead was not built in its entirety until 1923. It diverged from the Braich line 7 chains from the Drumhead and fell away downhill slightly, curving south and westerly to run between either slate walls or fences – the only tramway so protected in these parts. It ran on to the east side of the Fron road and proceeded southwards along the roadside. To keep the gradient as reasonable as possible, the track crossed over to the west of the road and almost immediately came back again, beginning a climb of approximately 1 to 25 and leaving the roadside for its own cutting a little distance east of the road. This diversion maintained the gradient and this short length was bounded by slab walling. Passing along the side of the main street in the village of Fron it now regained the roadside, crossed over, swung back again, used the east side down past the Post Office and then turned round the corner. Almost immediately opposite the Post Office there was a junction and a new connection crossed the junction of roads at this point and running due south, traversed open ground to effect a junction with the Cilgwyn 'Horseshoe' – an unusual loop of tramway entirely carried on embankment and a prominent local feature. [This line was laid in and the connection to the Fron tramway made after 22nd April, 1918 when the Amalgamated Slate Association Ltd. began working Alexandra, Moel Tryfan and Cilgwyn Quarries.]

Meanwhile, back at the Post Office, the original Fron branch crossed over to the south side of the road (now little but an unfenced rough track) and quarter of a mile further on, made a backshunt connection with the slate mill of the Fron Quarry. This working consisted of two open quarries connected by a small-bore tunnel. Connection with ground level and the mill was by an incline up and out of the workings. Fron Quarry opened at an unknown date but had closed by 1881. Connection was laid in to the Drumhead in 1884. It was first named Vron & Old Braich Slate Quarries Co. Ltd. to 24th July, 1902 (ex Vron Slate Co. – John Robinson) becoming Vron Welsh Slate Quarries Ltd. (Thomas and John Robinson were also associated with Talysarn quarrying, Nantlle.)

A similar working situation was to be found a little distance to the north of Fron Quarry, at the Bryn-fferam (or Brynefferam) Quarry, where two pits connected by a tunnel are to be seen. This quarry had cart but no rail connection with the Drumhead: it is of interest in that it was owned by the Chairman of the Railways Co., Sir Ll. Turner. In 1887 it only employed two!

Although these tramways were not strictly N.W.N.G. owned or worked, they were provided and owned by persons of influence on that Railway. The Bryngwyn branch may be seen as the trunk of a tree, with roots spreading out to tap the rich slate deposits of Moel Tryfan. There was nothing quite like this arrangement elsewhere on the Welsh narrow gauge, and the spectacle of locomotives bringing trains to the Drumhead would be fascinating indeed . . . especially as some were designed by Spooner & Co. for this particular purpose.

Locomotives

Name	Type	Builder	No.	Date	Withdrawn
MOEL TRYFAN	0–6–4T	Vulcan Foundry Ltd.	738	1875	1937
					1954 Scrap
SNOWDON RANGER	0–6–4T	Vulcan Foundry Ltd.	739	1875	1917
BEDDGELERT	0–6–4T	Hunslet Engine Co. Ltd.	206	1878	1906
GOWRIE	0–6–4T	Hunslet Engine Co. Ltd.	979	1908	Sold 1915
					period

[The Company did not number its locomotives. All were driven from the right-hand side of the footplate.

Moel Tryfan was taken into Festiniog Railway stock in June 1923 and numbered 11. The locomotive *Russell* which ran on the N.W.N.G. Railways line was not built for that Company and will be found under Portmadoc, Beddgelert & South Snowdon Railway.]

Moel Tryfan and *Snowdon Ranger*

Under Section 12 of the Agreement regarding a lease of the Railway, the lessee was committed to supplying engines of the Fairlie type. This resulted in two identical engines coming from the Vulcan Foundry in 1875. Coming as they did just a year before a similar but four-coupled engine from the same makers for the Festiniog Railway, the same parentage is obvious. The designer was nominally George Percival Spooner, a son of Charles Easton;* they had a six-coupled bogie under the boiler and a four-wheeled one under cab and bunker. Though not the first engines to be built on the Single Fairlie principle (as opposed to the Double Fairlie which in practice was two engine units mounted on bogies swivelling beneath a double-ended boiler having a divided firebox in the middle) the Single was more conventional though it retained the motorised bogie unit swivelling under the single boiler barrel. In both types, a full-length carrying frame was discarded and the boiler served as frame in the manner of a road engine.

The N.W.N.G. engines were the first 0–6–4 tank engines in the British Isles, being followed a few months later by a well-tank of this arrangement for the Great Southern & Western Railway of Ireland (5 ft 3 in. gauge) and it would be hard to find two more differing conceptions of the same arrangement! The original drawings are signed 'C.E. Spooner per G.P. Spooner 12th January, 1874' and stamped 'North Wales Narrow Gauge Railway. Engineer's Office, Portmadoc', and the maker's drawings are dated 10th October, 1874 – these are preserved in the City of Liverpool Museum. The leading frames carried outside cylinders, a six-coupled wheel arrangement with disc wheels and having inside bearings and valve gear. Steam entered the valve chest via a pendulum swung pipe pivoted immediately below the smoke box and, in order to reduce the movement of the flexible union as much as possible, the steam pipe was continued into a reception chamber behind and below the valve chest by means of a second flexible union. The exhaust pipe was similarly treated but owing to the smoke box being to the rear of the chimney centre-line, it was arranged to slope back into the smoke box. As usual on Fairlie designs, the front coupler was attached to the bogie frame. Stephenson valve gear was fitted.

*Other published drawings stated C.E. Spooner was the designer (e.g. in 'ENGINEERING', 23 November, 1877).

The main dimensions were:

Cylinders	8½ in. × 14 in.	Driving Wheels	2 ft 6 in. dia.
Weight in		Tractive Effort	3538 @ 75%
working order	14 tons		boiler pressure
Heating Surface	366 sq. ft	Grate Area	5.9 sq. ft
Pressure	140 lb.	Tank Capacity	303 galls. (also
			given as 350)
Wheelbase:	Bogie: 6 ft	Total:	14 ft 11½ in.

The driving bogie pivoted under a cast-iron saddle on the underside of the boiler barrel and centrally above the middle axle. The main frame was carried along below footplate level from the hind end up to nearly the front of the firebox where it rose sufficiently to clear the driving bogie frame. About the centre of the length of the boiler barrel the frame plates were connected by transverse stays to carry the centre of the driving bogie. At the rear end, the footplating was carried on the main frame but at the front end, on brackets from the smokebox. In front of the firebox a strong transverse stay between the frames carried a spring which controlled the movement of the rear end of the driving bogie. The water tanks were of 'winged' type; brakes were applied on all wheels save the leading pair of the driving bogie: both bogies had Adams' Patent centre with india-rubber cushions and Vicker's cast steel wheels. Ten and a half tons rested on the driving bogie and the engine would pull (according to 'ENGINEERING', and at variance with intended figures which follow), one bogie passenger carriage, two four-wheeled passenger carriages weighing all together 10 tons 5 cwt. full; the full load was 30 tons, the remainder being made up of coal and goods trucks, and empty slate wagons.[12]

The cylinders drove on to the trailing driving wheels. Height to top of chimney was 8 ft 9 in. and over the footplate was 6 ft 7 in.; as on Festiniog designs the boiler was pitched low resulting in a neat design with tall boiler mountings and cab (backless and open to the elements), rounded tops to side tanks and to the corners of the footplating. The rear wheels were disc pattern of 1 ft 7 in. diameter; the bogie frame was inside and wheelbase 3 ft 6 in. The boiler was 12 ft long (8 ft between tubeplates) and 2 ft 0½ in. diameter without clothing . . . not large. There were 104 tubes of 1½ in. outside diameter. The Klotz safety valve was mounted on the dome; the stovepipe chimney was typical of G.P. Spooner and used on his Spooner & Co. designs also.

Rear weatherboards (detachable) were fitted by the Company soon after delivery, a feature which the footplate staff clearly preferred for it persisted on the surviving engine until the end. When fitted, the

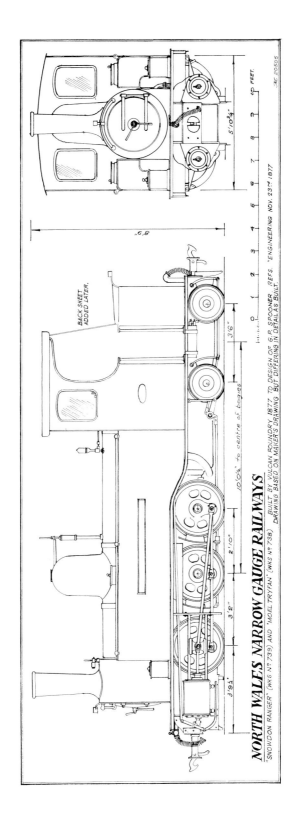

NORTH WALES NARROW GAUGE RAILWAYS

"SNOWDON RANGER" (WKS NO 739) AND "MOEL TRYFAN" (WKS NO 738)

BUILT BY VULCAN FOUNDRY 1877 TO DESIGN OF G. P. SPOONER. REFS. "ENGINEERING" NOV. 23RD 1877. DRAWING BASED ON MAKER'S DRAWING BUT DIFFERING IN DETAILS AS BUILT.

BACK SHEET ADDED LATER.

10'0½" to centre of bogies

3'6"

2'10"

3'2"

3'9½"

8'9"

5'10¾"

FEET

7C 20505

Westinghouse brake reservoir was slung under the right-hand footplate under the cab and the compressor was carried inside the cab. When new, the domes were of polished brass but had been painted over by 1890. Westinghouse brakes were fitted between 1890 and 1894.

The design was intended to handle 280 tons on the level, 140 tons on 1 in 100 and 75 tons on 1 in 50, figures which seem extremely optimistic! (The Festiniog Railway's first Double Fairlie of 1869 hauled 206 tons on 1 in 100.) Wiener in 'ARTICULATED LOCOMOTIVES' maintains that the Vulcan Single Fairlies – and the later Hunslet *Gowrie* – all with only a 4½ Ton axle loading, did in fact achieve these loadings over curves of 60 ft radius (metres and not feet are more probable!).

In 1902 *Snowdon Ranger* went to Davies & Metcalfe Ltd., near Stockport, for a new boiler and heavy overhaul. Brass oval plates were fitted reading 'Davies & Metcalfe Ltd: Rebuilt 1903: Manchester'. It was previously considered that continuous brakes were fitted then, but if the Returns are to be believed, all stock had been fitted by 1894. In 1908 it was 'repaired by Hunslet' in Leeds.

In 1903 *Moel Tryfan* was treated similarly – it received new tubes in 1913.

In 1917 the frames of *Snowdon Ranger* were placed under *Moel Tryfan* and the latter was put into the best working order possible under wartime conditions by cannibalising the sister engine.

It is convenient to add that under Welsh Highland Railway auspices, *Moel Tryfan* went into the Festiniog Railway's Boston Lodge Works in 1923, when the cab and boiler mountings were cut down in height to enable it to work over the Festiniog line. Vacuum brake was substituted for the Westinghouse so as to make fittings standard on both Railways. Between 1924 and 1936 the engine worked regularly between Dinas Junction and Blaenau Festiniog. Occasionally it was turned so as to run bunker first Up to Blaenau. *Moel Tryfan* was like the Festiniog's own Single Fairlie, a free steamer, a good and fast runner and well-liked by the enginemen. In 1937 the engine went into Boston Lodge for boiler and firebox repairs. The dismantled parts lay in various parts of the yard throughout the Second War, the boiler and driving bogie in the Engine Shed. In 1954, under the auspices of the Festiniog Railway's 'New Order', the boiler etc. was towed across to the Harbour station and cut up for scrap. The trailing bogie survived.

Beddgelert

Though of the same wheel arrangement as the two previous engines (and curiously, an arrangement which the Company chose for every one of its own engines) *Beddgelert* was not of Fairlie type nor of Spooner design. A saddle tank with outside frames and cylinders and having outside bearings to the rear bogie together with a typical Hunslet full cab, the result was entirely different from her predecessors. And if these had been greyhound-like in their sleekness, then *Beddgelert* was a bulldog built for rough going, but none-the-less a good looking piece of machinery – as one would have expected from her makers. Said to have been built for the Bryngwyn branch traffic (there is but pictorial evidence of her working on the main line) she was 80% more powerful than the Fairlies.

It could be that the engine was delivered facing up-grade so that the firebox would be better covered on the hill and perhaps this resulted in overheating of the upper tubes; it may be calculated that a horizontal boiler might be up to 4 in. sloped from end to end on the steepest part of the journey and this might uncover the front end of the tubes if the water level was slightly low. So it might be that a visit to Hunslet in 1894 was to overcome these problems by replacing the smokebox with a taller one and reducing the chimney height consequently. The boiler would then be inclined by a few inches: by returning the engine so that it ran bunker first up the branch, the boiler would be near-horizontal. Some opinions have been expressed about the sloping smokebox front shown in the maker's drawings and suggesting the engine was not built in that way, but whatever the truth of all the foregoing, there are no N.W.N.G. records to substantiate it!

The effect of running the engine bunker first up-grade would be to improve adhesion: with the heavy rainfall of this district, train operation on wet rails would be a permanent hazard. Notwithstanding any of the aforementioned, controlling a rake of loaded slate wagons (none fitted with but handbrakes which would be put on before leaving the top) on a greasy rail, would have called for much care.

The main dimensions were:

Cylinders	10 in. × 16 in.	Driving Wheels	2 ft 6 in. dia.
Weight in		Tractive Effort	6400 lbs.
working order	17 tons	Grate Area	7½ sq. ft
Heating Surface	416 sq. ft	Tank Capacity	450 galls.
Pressure	160 lb.	Driving Bogie	
Wheelbase total:	17 ft 8 in.	Wheelbase:	6 ft 2 in.

The rail gauge on the drawings is shown as 1 ft 11¾ in.

The rear bogie had a 3 ft 6 in. wheelbase with 1 ft 10 in. wheels.

The smokebox was skirted out at the waist to meet the contour of the outside cylinders: with its built-up chimney the front end was quite in a "Beyer Peacock" tradition. The saddle tank did not extend over the smokebox but covered the firebox; the latter made full use of the ample width between the frames and the length between driving and bogie wheel flanges. The boiler was 9 ft long in the barrel and 2 ft 10½ in. diameter, pitched low into the frames. Chimney and cab were 8 ft 11 in. from rail level. One sandbox was placed for either direction of travel, two on each side of the tank.

The total length was 22 ft 1⅝ in. and width over footplate was 6 ft 3¾ in. Stephenson's Valve Gear was fitted behind the driving wheels. The engine is reputed to have been worn out in 1906 and scrapped that

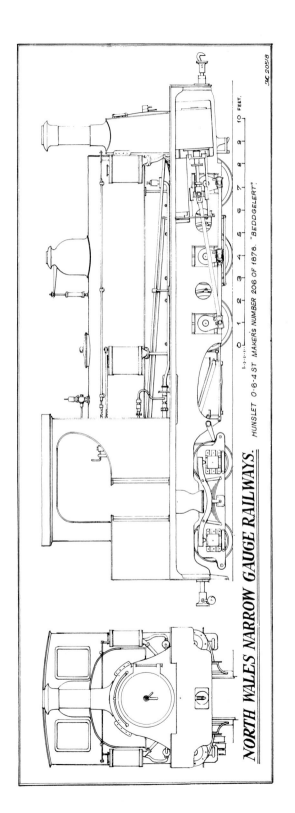

NORTH WALES NARROW GAUGE RAILWAYS.

HUNSLET 0·6·4 ST MAKER'S NUMBER 206 OF 1878. "BEDDGELERT".

FEET.

JC 20518

year. Another engine from Hunslet of quite different type replaced it; some doubts exist about its condition and suitability by 1906; it probably had its original boiler and perhaps a replacement firebox. These are likely to have been worn out. Tonnage of slate had declined in the new century and did in fact continue to do so; the peak of mineral traffic was reached and passed in 1897.

Gowrie

The last engine was purchased in 1908 in anticipation of the completion of the link between Rhyd-Ddu and Portmadoc where a modern powerful engine would be needed to surmount the steep gradients north of Beddgelert and the several reverse curves on the same section. The basic design was that of the makers but Aitchison influenced it to the extent that the Single Fairlie arrangement was reverted to, perhaps some indication of its success in the Vulcan engines and its suitability to the Company's conditions. So far as is known, it was the last Single Fairlie to be built, and certainly so as regards these Islands. The maker's influence was complete in the standard components used for side tanks, cab, bunker, firebox etc.; the rear part of the engine was mounted on footplating in the usual way, but forward of the side tanks the boiler and smokebox extended without adornment or footplating. The engine was really an up-to-date version of the Spooner 1875 engines; there was an inside framed six-coupled bogie with outside cylinders though now the valve gear was Walshaert's outside. Many features such as cab, boiler mountings and firebox outlines were similar to *Russell*.*

Despatch from the makers was on 2nd September, 1908 and for a time the engine ran without nameplates; ultimately it received the name *Gowrie* (Aitchison's Christian name) and together with *Russell*, (the Hunslet-built engine which the P.B. & S.S.R. bought and which was Aitchison-influenced) eventually meant that the Company operated two engines each named after a Receiver . . . though admittedly the same gentlemen also filled other positions with the Company!

The rear bogie had outside frames and the rear bunker sheet was flanged out to increase the capacity for coal. The saddle beneath the boiler which supported it on the driving bogie was pivoted slightly to the rear of the centre axle. The asbestos-covered main steam pipe was taken externally from the dome and led between boiler and side tank vertically down to a ball and socket coupling between the frames; from here it was carried forward horizontally to the valve chest. The movable exhaust pipe showed nakedly beneath the smokebox. Sandboxes for forward running were on the bogie frames; for backward running in the top rear end of the side tanks. To allow for swivelling, they had rubber feed pipes. The brake equipment had the compressor on the right-hand side of the boiler barrel and the main air reservoir under the footplate;

---

*A General Arrangement drawing was delayed until May 1921 – some components were of Sierra Leone and minor Indian railways' design. ('THE NARROW GAUGE', No.118, p.12) on the left-hand side under the footplate there was an auxiliary reservoir. Main dimensions were:

Cylinders	9½ in. × 14 in.	Driving Wheels	2 ft 4 in. dia.
Weight in working order	18½ tons	Tractive Effort	5415 lb. at 75 per cent b.p.
Heating Surface	282 sq. ft	Grate Area	5 sq. ft
Pressure	160 lb.	Tank Capacity	400 galls.
Driving wheelbase	5 ft 6 in.	Rear Bogie wheelbase	3 ft 3 in.

The boiler barrel was 8 ft 10 in. long between tubeplates and 2 ft 5 in. diameter; it was pitched 4 ft 7½ in. above the rails. The engine was 22 ft 2 in. long over the beams, and 6 ft 7 in. wide over footplating; from rail to chimney top was 8 ft 6 in.

Tradition has it that the engine was not a success and this may be due to having a smaller boiler but larger cylinders than the Vulcan Fairlies. After the 'wedding' of the two Vulcan engines in 1917, *Moel Tryfan* and *Russell* were adequate for the reduced service of the War period. By then there were no passenger trains and an opportunity was taken to sell the engine while prices were high.

The engine's movements when sold by 1918 (one source gives 1915) for Government use, are unknown. In 1919 she was in Wake's Geneva Yard, Darlington, bearing the number 1516 and still in possession of Westinghouse brake. In 1922 she was on contract work at an aerodrome site at Marske-by-Sea, Yorkshire, and was advertised for sale, along with other engines on this contract, by Messrs. Hughes, Bolckow & Co. Ltd. in 1928. This is the last trace.

Proposed Rack Locomotive

To appreciate the mood of optimism following the First War, and the expansive ideas of the promoters of the new Welsh Highland Railway (as it was shortly to become) one can but only give examples. Certainly the talk of increasing business in terms of a complete narrow gauge link between Dinas Junction and Portmadoc (now so near an accomplished fact) and the possibility of through running between Dinas and Blaenau Festiniog via Portmadoc, seems to have gone to the heads of the new 1922 Board.

Someone must have turned up a copy of Spooner's Grand Plan of 1875 among the papers which passed to Dolgarrog in the fusions of that time. Why had they not thought of it themselves? 'Let's have a Rack Railway to the summit of Snowdon!'

No English firm had ever built a rack engine for use in these Islands, but a letter dated 12th April, 1922 on N.W.N.G. notepaper was received by Beyer Peacock & Co. Ltd. of Gorton, Manchester followed on 27th April by another on Aluminium Corporation notepaper. (It may have been that second thoughts prevailed at Dolgarrog; the Corporation was certainly more credit-worthy than the N.W.N.G.)

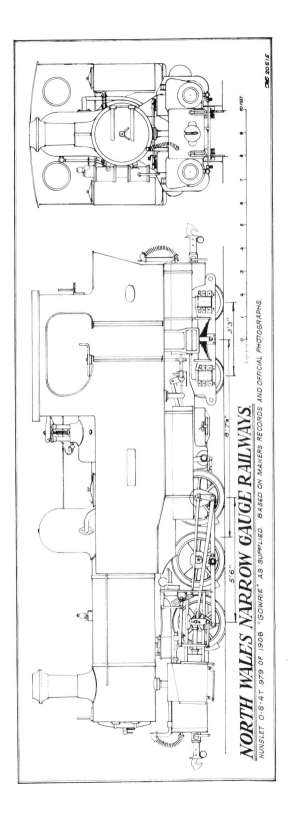

NORTH WALES NARROW GAUGE RAILWAYS.

HUNSLET 0-6-4T 979 OF 1908 "GOWRIE" AS SUPPLIED. BASED ON MAKERS RECORDS AND OFFICIAL PHOTOGRAPHS.

Beyer's noted the following from the letters: 'Can we let them know where they could buy a loco suitable for a 2 ft gauge rack railway. To run part on rack and part on ordinary track. Either new or secondhand, want approx. price or could we give them a rough idea of the cost of making such an engine for hauling light passenger coaches'. Other details noted were: '2 ft Gauge; Grade 1 in 6; Maximum load to be hauled 12 tons.'

Beyer duly sent sketch design No. 93574 for an outside cylinder 0–4–2 side tank with rack equipment; the drawing was dated 9th May, 1922. The design was a modification of sketch No. 81294 for a similar engine prepared on 31st July, 1912 for agents Sumner & Co. which never materialised into an order.

(Beyer Peacock archives record nothing further following submission of design and quotation.)

Contractors' Locomotives

It seems highly likely that both McKie and Boys would have used locomotives during the building of the railway. It is assumed that a spare England-built four-coupled tank-tender engine from the Festiniog Railway was hired for the purpose, for the Festiniog was certainly passing through a period when a small engine might have been available for the task. A Minute of that Railway dated 16th February, 1876 reads 'To let Mr. Bray, the Contractor, of N.W.N.G. lines, hire one of the small locomotives for six months at £130'. It could be 'Bray' was a mistake for 'Boys'.

Passenger Stock – General Note

No official list exists and several hypotheses have been attempted to unravel certain mysteries, some of which arise from the vernacular used by the staff or from the maker's drawings – or the absence of same! However, since the First Edition new facts and photographs, together with further research into the known records, has enabled a fresh account to be prepared. The Annual Returns (first made in 1877 and therefore unable to confirm the pioneer position) have been linked to the summaries of stock shown in the Spring's Report and Robert Williams' (sent from the Festiniog Railway for the purpose) list of stock stored at Dinas Junction, both in the early 1920s and in anticipation of the forthcoming Welsh Highland Railway opening. Before launching into a description of what existed and what had been, it is informative to recall the 1921 scene at the Junction; no passenger carriage had been in use since 1916. Only the 'Summer' coaches were stored under cover, the rest languished outside and some must have been there, out of service, for many years. Of the last year of passenger trains over the main line it had been written:

The line is in a precarious financial position, as a journey over it makes it apparent. The signals, station buildings . . . and signal box have long ago been abandoned:

grass almost buries the track; whilst holes in the outer panelling of the coaches were noticed by the writer: and the Branch to Bryngwyn has been closed to passenger traffic. The rest of the line has two trains each way . . . a motor bus service which follows the course of the line bids fair to prove the proverbial "last straw".[15]

Between the opening and the time of these pre-W.H.R. investigations, the Railway had seen the following types of passenger carriages over its metals:

Four-wheel (2-compartment) carriages	3
Six-wheel on Cleminson's Patent Flexible Wheelbase carriages	3
Bogie Guard's brake/Composite carriages	4
Bogie 'Workman' carriage	1
Bogie 'Corridor' carriages	2
Bogie 'Tourist' carriage	1
Bogie 'Summer' carriages	4

a total of 18 in all. As only two Guard's brake/Composite vehicles existed at the same time, the total of 16 is the maximum stock at any period. So to the Annual Returns, and the stock as shown therein; total vehicles can be summarised:

In 1877	5
1878–1890	8
1891–1892	10
1893	12
1894–1908	16
1909–1921	13

Thus it may be seen that the basis of a Stock List is available. From Board of Trade records two facts emerge to upset the foregoing; firstly the four-wheelers are said to be withdrawn in March 1897 and secondly the six-wheelers in 1908, yet the Annual Returns continue to show the former until 1908 and the latter are still listed in 1921! This could be explained by 'putting out to grass' (literally perhaps) the former until they were scrapped (their running gear etc. may have gone into goods stock) and that the latter had not been dismantled (or) when the 1920s arrived. [It is commonplace for Returns to continue with similar figures year after year, for the job of counting vehicles is a chore and is only done 'out in the field' when Management calls for it . . . certainly not when all that is required is an entry to complete the Return. However, in a small place like Dinas, the Secretary could correctly give all surviving stock which lay around his premises, and probably the Company Returns are an honest reply.]

Hereon a list of carriage numbers can be suggested for the dates around the major changes in totals:

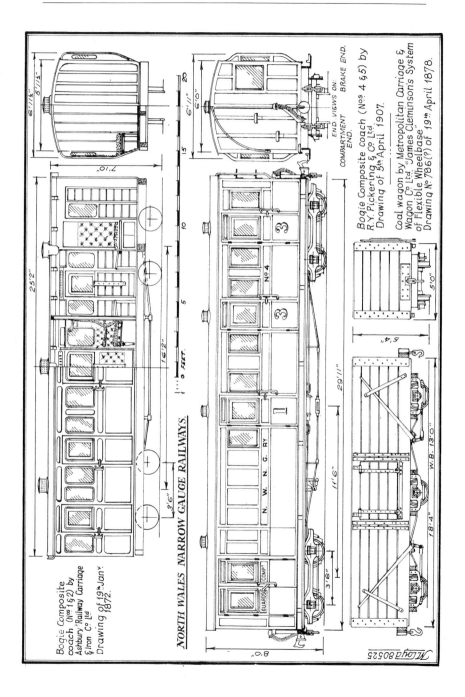

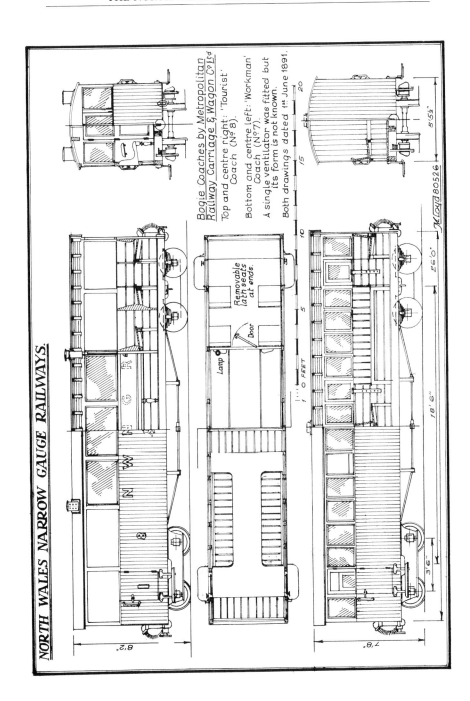

NORTH WALES NARROW GAUGE RAILWAYS.

Bogie Coaches by Metropolitan Railway Carriage & Wagon Co Ltd

Top and centre right: 'Tourist' Coach (Nº 8).

Bottom and centre left: 'Workman' Coach (Nº 7).

A single ventilator was fitted but its form is not known.

Both drawings dated 1st June 1891.

M.Lloyd 80526

Removable lath seats at ends.

Door

Lamp

5'5½"

2'6 0"

18' 6"

3' 6"

FEET

8'2"

7' 8"

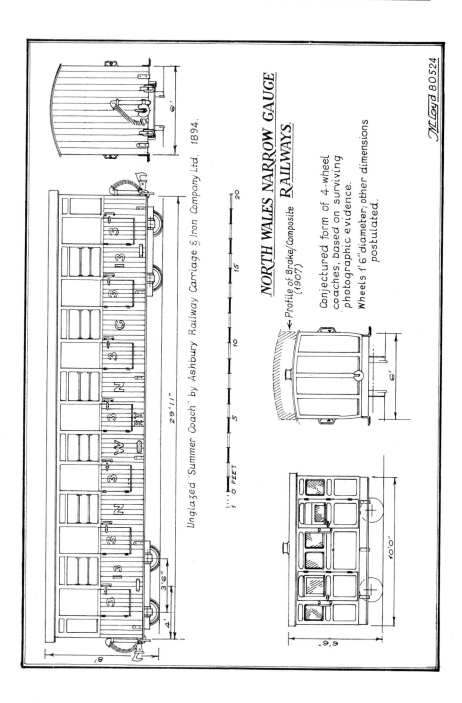

NORTH WALES NARROW GAUGE RAILWAYS.

Profile of Brake/Composite (1907)

Conjectural form of 4-wheel coaches, based on surviving photographic evidence.

Wheels 1'6" diameter; other dimensions postulated.

Unglazed "Summer Coach" by Ashbury Railway Carriage & Iron Company Ltd. 1894.

M Lloyd 80524

1878 (8 vehicles)

Nos. 1-2	Guard's brake/Composite	Ashbury	pre 1877
Nos. 3-5	Four-wheel	Ashbury?	pre 1877
Nos. 6-8	Six-wheel	Gloucester	1878

In 1891 one 'Workman' carriage and one 'Tourist' carriage (both bogie) were added to stock, making:

1891 (10 vehicles)

Nos. 1-2	(extant)		
Nos. 3-5	(extant)		
Nos. 6-8	(extant)		
No. 7	'Workman' bogie carriage	Metropolitan	1891
No. 8	'Tourist' bogie carriage	Metropolitan	1891

By 1893 the two 'Corridor' bogie carriages (each of different type) had come from Ashbury so that Nos. 9–10 were added, making twelve vehicles in all.

The final tranch was to come in 1894 when Ashbury delivered four 'Summer' bogie coaches, two of each type and carrying numbers 11–14, bringing the total stock to sixteen at which it remained until 1908 when the three four-wheelers, officially withdrawn since 1897, were deleted from the total.

It may be seen that the Company received its vehicles in two eras; pre-1878 and post-1891, the former including four-, six-wheeled and bogie stock, and the latter bogie only and fitted with continuous brake on delivery. These eras seem to have been marked by two numbering systems; the first may have been:

Nos. 1-2	Bogie Guard's brake/Composite	Ashbury	pre 1877
Nos. 3-5	4 wh. 2 compt. (Workmen's?)	Ashbury?	pre 1877
Nos. 6-8	6 wh. 3rd & Guard's brake/Comp.	Gloucester	1878

With delivery of 'Tourist' carriage in 1891, carrying '8' there was a change in the system; together with Williams' description a possible list with numbers carried in 1922 can be assembled:

1	6 wheel	Gloucester	2/G/3	1878	
2	6 wheel	Gloucester	2/G/3	1878	
3	6 wheel	Gloucester	3rd	1878	
4	Bogie	Pickering	G/1/3/3	1907 (replacing orig. No. 1)	
5	Bogie	Pickering	G/1/3/3	1907 (replacing orig. No. 2)	
6					
7	Bogie	'Workman'	Metropolitan	3rd	1891
8	Bogie	'Tourist'	Metropolitan	1st	1891

9	Bogie	'Corridor'	Ashbury	3rd		1893
10	Bogie	'Corridor'	Ashbury	1st/3rd		1893
11	Bogie	'Summer'	Ashbury	3rd	semi-glazed	1894
12	Bogie	'Summer'	Ashbury	3rd	semi-glazed	1894
13	Bogie	'Summer'	Ashbury	3rd	non-glazed	1894
14	Bogie	'Summer'	Ashbury	3rd	non-glazed	1894

Williams did not list anything against Nos. 1, 2 and 6. Nos. 3 and 7 he called '3rd class closed carriages' and if he was prepared to make no distinction between the fact that one was a 6-wheel and the other a bogie of quite different appearance (each now probably relegated to carry workmen), but was only concerned with the passenger content (which is likely), only the identity of No. 6 is in doubt. Nothing is known of the circumstances whereby *both* the Ashbury Brake/ Composite bogies were replaced (evidence available is only for one) by the new Pickering vehicles of 1907.

The omission of Nos. 1 and 2 could be accounted for by their having been taken off the track – one had certainly become a shed at Dinas Junction. Reverting to No. 3, to accept Williams' list in terms of 'passenger content' must be to allow that he was in error in stating 'they have 11 bogie carriages . . .' for he has listed ten and one 6-wheeled: if the Returns are correct, never at any time did the Company own eleven bogie vehicles!

Major Spring listed a Road or Brake Van (4-wheeled) in his 1922 Report: though there were in fact two Vans, one not having been 'fitted' as was the other, and the identity of No. 6 was possibly the fitted Road Van.

Although further consideration will be given under the Welsh Highland Railway, an allocation of Festiniog/Welsh Highland Railway numbers was given to the stock at Dinas in 1922; this took up a series beginning with No. 23, No. 22 being the last Festiniog vehicle. The Guard's brake/Composite carriages were numbered after their fellows in the Festiniog's series. The new numbering classified the vehicles by type rather than in numerical order, thus giving:

F.R./W.H.R. No.	*N.W.N.G.R. No.*	*Type of Vehicle*	
23	11	'Summer'	semi-glazed
24	12	'Summer'	semi-glazed
25			
26			
27	13	'Summer'	non-glazed
28	14	'Summer'	non-glazed
29	8	'Tourist'	
30			
31			
32	3	6-wheeled	
33			

F.R./W.H.R. No.	*N.W.N.G.R. No.*	*Type of Vehicle*
34	7	'Workman'
35	9	'Corridor'
36	10	'Corridor' (became 'Buffet Car')
8	4	Guard's brake/Composite
9	5	Guard's brake/Composite

and the above conveniently account for the ten bogie vehicles. What of the six other numbers allocated – had the Festiniog been misled by the reduction from 16 vehicles to 13 in 1909? Probably not, but if No. 32 was the surviving Gloucester coach and the other two had been allocated Nos. 30 and 31, then Nos. 25, 26 and 33 must remain unallocated until evidence appears.

Confusion has arisen in that at some stage after the formation of the Welsh Highland, No. 24 'disappeared' and No. 26 (one of the unallocated numbers) appeared: this may be due to an oversight when repainting the numbers, the figures '26' being painted on what was actually '24'; certainly No. '26' was returned to Portmadoc in the 1950's having served as a bungalow since the sale of all stock and has since been returned to running order; it is more accurately the former No. 24 (ex-12).

Stock in existence before 1878 had no continuous brake; Westinghouse brake was fitted to carriages supplied thereafter, to the six-wheelers in 1892–4, but the small four-wheelers were only 'piped'. The Company Chairman had complained to the Board of Trade (who were responsible for seeing that the Regulation of Railways Act 1889 concerning the fitting of Continuous Brakes was followed up) that the low bodies of the six-wheelers made it impossible to fit brake cylinders, but this was done despite by putting the cylinders (quite small on the Westinghouse principle) on the carriage floors.

Guard's brake/Composite bogie carriages Nos. 1 & 2

These were supplied by The Ashbury Railway Carriage & Iron Co. Ltd. in 1874 at a time when construction was in its infancy and following the lease of the undertaking to H.B. Roberts in the previous year, and ordered by Charles Edwin Spooner before he resigned.[13] They were a Guard's brake/Composite carriage with one 1st and two 3rd Class compartments with look-out duckets for the guard and surmounted by three oil lamps, the central one serving the 1st Class compartment. The drawing was stamped 'North Wales Narrow Gauge Railway. Engineer's Office, Portmadoc' and the job was Ashbury's Works No. 2040. The drawing date is 17th January, 1872, and is signed 'C.E. Spooner' but it does not show running gear – this was usually the subject of a separate drawing – but possibly in this case (as with the

Festiniog bodies) the bogies may have been supplied from Boston Lodge. The body was 25 ft 2 in. long by 5 ft 11½ in. wide (6 ft 11½ in. over duckets) and rooftop to rail measured 7 ft 10 in. not including the height of the lamps. [They were probably higher than 7 ft 10 in., perhaps 8 ft 3 in. if mounted on larger wheels at later date.] It was carried on 1 ft 7⅛ in. diameter wheels mounted in 3 ft 6 in. wheelbase bogies (Festiniog standards). The 3rd Class compartments were in bare wood with moulded seats, but the 1st compartment was upholstered in blue broadcloth, with padded doors and sides, coat-hooks, mirrors, and floral decorations on the interior panelling.

Coupling gear is not shown but the Festiniog/G.P. Spooner type of central buffer-coupler was fitted for most of the coach's life. Both these vehicles were replaced by new similar ones in 1907.

Doubtless the Company would have benefitted from further elegant coaches of this type, but with Spooner's departure from the N.W.N.G. scene in 1876 or early 1877, James Cleminson was appointed Engineer, and so far as carriage design was concerned, the clock was turned back to the Dark Ages when three carriages to his 'Patent' were ordered in 1877.

Four-wheeled carriages Nos. 3–5

Virtually nothing is known about these three carriages. From their small size and primitive accommodation, they were of vintage appearance by the time the first N.W.N.G. track was laid: though the Company did not Return them they ran them among their own stock. They appear to have been 3rd Class and each had only two compartments; from their appearance they resemble the early Festiniog coaches from Ashbury or the similar vehicles on the Festiniog & Blaenau Railway. There is no reason to suppose they had been built for either and not taken up; the design suggests Ashbury or Brown, Marshalls was the builder and the style that they were built in the 1860s. The wheels are known to have been 1 ft 6 in. diameter; the bodies are estimated at 10 ft long, about 6 ft 6 in. from rail to roof excluding lamp, and slightly less than 6 ft wide. One large lamp did duty for both compartments and there was unlikely to have been a full division between them. The Board of Trade made the Company withdraw them in March 1897 because they had only been piped for brakes and the Company said it would be too expensive to fit them fully.

The drawing by J.M. Lloyd (p.222) is intended to compare the N.W.N.G. vehicles with the drawing in Vignes (Plate 11), the latter including a four-wheeled carriage in a Festiniog train: did Vignes purport this to be a N.W.N.G. specimen?!

Six-wheeled carriages Nos. 6–8

These three remarkable coaches are something of a mystery. It could be that they appealed to the Company in its financially embarrassed situation because of their cheap and simple construction, which was in the manner of vertical planking with outside framing, the spartan interiors having a modicum of seat upholstery for 2nd Class and bare boarding for the 3rds. The classes and Guard's central compartment were separated by light partitioning without communicating doors and the seats arranged round the perimeter. Two were 2nd and 3rd Class divided by the Guard's compartment with its lookout ducket, the third was an all 3rd Class: the finish was simple varnished boarding and for the official photograph the makers suspended a board reading 'North Wales Narrow Gauge Ry.' from the cant-rail. The class was printed in full above each door and on the solebar was the maker's plate and an oval plate reading 'James Cleminson's Patent Flexible Wheel Base'. The initials of the Company were in yellow above the right-hand windows and the number above the left-hand. On top of each coach were some grotesque lamp cases which doubled up as ventilators; there were three on those with the Guard's compartment and two on the other. Coupling was by simple 'chopper' buffer-coupler, held down by counterweight. Being low-slung, there were no footboards and such was this deficiency that a step under each door was soon added. The extraordinary ventilators were also removed, for their clearance under bridges must have been minimal. [An ingenious suggestion that the ventilators were not removed but that at some stage the very small wheels shown in the official photographs were replaced by larger, and the lamp tops were removed in consequence of that, cannot be substantiated.]

There was a droplight in each door and the furthest window from each door (on either side of the partition) opened too.

The builders were the Gloucester Wagon Co. Ltd. to Orders 249/50. The advantageous weight/seating ratio may have been attractive to the purchasers; the vehicles carried 40 in a 4¼ ton vehicle whilst Nos. 1 and 2 carried 30 in a 5½ ton one. [Gloucester was then a builder of station buildings, signal boxes and the like, and the style of these vehicles suggests a garden-shed origin!]

The flexible wheelbase consisted of mounting each pair of wheels on its own small sub-frame. The middle pair was allowed generous lateral movement and, connected to the sliding frame so formed, radius arms stretched to either side and were fastened to the subframes on which the end pairs of wheels were mounted. When the middle pair slid laterally, the end pairs (which were pivoted to the coach frame) were angled in such a way as to take up something of the radius of the curve and offset the conventional stiffness of a rigid six-wheeled vehicle passing over a curve. In point of fact, such a system was unnecessary on the N.W.N.G. main line which had no severe curves, but Cleminson's Patent was later used elsewhere in the British Isles, among the owners being the Southwold Railway (1878), Manx Northern (1878), and several Irish railways (1879–1887), all 3 ft gauge.

Although Cleminson appears to have been the first to use this idea on rail vehicles, a similar scheme is described and illustrated in 'MECHANICS MAGAZINE' 10th September, 1825 for a six-wheeled road vehicle in which the central pair of wheels were rigid but the outer pairs swivelled and were connected together at their extremities by a pair of crossed chains 'upon a principle of leverage, from its counterpoise motion upon the centre wheels . . .' The inventor was Sir Sydney Smith.

These carriages were 30 ft long over body, 5 ft 11 in. wide, 7 ft 10 in. from rail to roof-top and the wheelbase was equally divided over 23 ft. The non-Guard's vehicles carried 42 passengers and weighed 4¼ Tons tare.

'Workman Car' No. 7

The curious title of this carriage comes from the heading given to Metropolitan's drawing of 1st June, 1891, 'Workman's Car'. In outward appearance it resembled Nos. 9 and 10, except there was only one central ventilator and the body dimensions were reduced to length 26 ft, width 5 ft 5½ in., height 7 ft 8 in. rail to roof centre line, bogie wheelbase 3 ft 6 in., bogie pin centres 18 ft 6 in., wheel diameter 1 ft 10 in. The only illustration which shows the type reasonably well is of a train at South Snowdon whereon – reading from the engine – is shown No. 5, No. 10, a Gloucester 6-wheeler and a vehicle which conforms to the 'Workman's Car' drawing. Westinghouse brakes were fitted as supplied and all windows were glazed, and the seating was of plain wooden perimeter type. It survived to 1923.

'Tourist Carriage' No. 8

This coach was one of the first attempts to encourage tourist travel on any narrow gauge railway in Britain; it went further than any previous design in recognising the attractions of open balconies and yet having somewhere to retire when the weather turned unfavourable. This lesson seems to have been very slow in making its mark upon railway carriage designers though shipbuilders had been practising it for many years!

The Company's staff looked upon it with special favour and it received more maintenance than the rest of the stock! By 1922 it had been given a coat of vermilion paint and with 'N.W.N.G.R.' flanked by '8' each end and the crest on a plaque below, it looked very smart indeed. The body had open end balconies with a central all-glazed saloon, curtained, upholstered and carpeted. It was an all-1st Class vehicle and, along with No. 7, the first to be supplied new with continuous brake. Each door had an individual step and the sides were of matchboarding. Automatic central couplers with safety chains were fitted, lighting and those various small appointments which place a vehicle in a class of its own. Mr. Gladstone, then well over eighty, travelled in it on the way to a holiday at Nant Gwynant, so we read in 'DOCTOR IN THE WHIPS' ROOM', the autobiography of Sir Henry Morris-Jones. Thereafter it was nicknamed the 'Gladstone Car'. When new, it was painted with cream upper works and white roof, with the customary red waist; the lettering etc. was in gold-shaded vermilion. The builders were The Metropolitan Railway Carriage & Wagon Co. Ltd. of Birmingham and the drawing is dated 1st June, 1891; the original intention was clearly for a spartan 3rd Class coach with four individual lath seats plus a full-width seat in each balcony, and the interior had side seats in street-tram style having contoured and perforated seat and backs in wood. The balcony seats were to be removable and four Colza lamps were to be fitted, one in each corner of the compartment, up against the partition which had a perforated zinc panel inserted in it behind the lamp. The body was 26 ft long over headstocks by 5 ft 5½ in. over sides; it was carried on platesided bogies having 3 ft 6 in. wheelbase and 1 ft 10 in. wheels. The drawing shows a customary plain and sprung buffer at each end, strengthened by a supporting framework to take lateral shocks; these and other features did not appear in the finished vehicle which had its official photograph taken at Dinas shortly after delivery, complete with upholstered seats, carpets and curtaining.

'Corridor Coaches' Nos. 9 & 10

The next two were bogie vehicles of 'saloon' type having end doors and glazing all along each side: they were supplied by Ashbury.

The pair was known as 'Corridor Coaches' by the staff; there was a door in the partition between the two compartments into which the Composite saloon was divided: the all-3rd had none. In their latter-day form they had been refurbished at Dinas. (The term 'Corridor' did not imply there was any passenger connection with the adjacent vehicle in the train, nor that they were side-corridor.)

General dimensions of the carriages (there is no drawing) are estimated to be: length 29 ft over body, width 5 ft 11 in. over body, height 7 ft 9 in. from rail to roof centre-line, bogie wheelbase 3 ft 6 in. at 23 ft bogie centres, and mounted on 1 ft 10 in. diameter wheels. There was no visible solebar as the vertically planked sides masked it. The roof had two (three in the all-3rd) large lamp cases and louvred ventilators ran below the cant-rail. By 1914 No. 10 was fitted up with a small 1st Class saloon at one end, the relevant door having '1' on it on a white ground: the lettering 'N.W.N.G.R.', flanked slightly lower on each end with '10', appeared on the upper waist and, in the centre, the Company's arms were mounted on a panel. The coaches were very smart and nicely proportioned. Westinghouse brakes had been fitted as supplied; there were steps under each door individually.

These two vehicles survived to become Nos. 35 and 36 in W.H.R./ F.R. books, the latter being rebuilt into a Buffet Car in its latter days.

'Summer Coaches' Nos. 11–14

The Company went to The Ashbury Railway Carriage & Iron Co. Ltd. of Belle Vue, Manchester, for four tourist carriages in 1894. Each carried the plate 'Ashbury Co. Ltd. 1894': Nos. 11 and 12 were semi-glazed whilst Nos. 13 and 14 had no glazing; otherwise the bodies were quite similar, having seven 3rd Class compartments and being open throughout inside: all of them survived until 1923.

The carriages came new with Westinghouse brake, class numbering on doors and 'N.W.N.G.' flanked by the vehicle number on the side in the same colours as No. 8. The number of characters on the waist was seventeen, there being at the foot of the fourth door 'Ry.'. The non-glazed bodies had stable doors like the semi-glazed variety, but where the other bodies had glass Nos. 13 and 14 were given window bars. 'Norwegian' couplers and side chains, lighting and ventilators were fitted.

The principal dimensions of these vehicles were: length over body 29 ft 11 in., width over body 6 ft, bogie wheelbase 3 ft 6 in., wheels 1 ft 8 in. diameter, height of body centreline from rail 7 ft 5 in.

STOCK LIST – 1907

N.W.N.G. Rlys.	Builder		Vernacular Title	Arrangement
1	6 wh.	Gloucester Wagon Co. Ltd.	–	3/G/2
2	6 wh.	Gloucester Wagon Co. Ltd.	–	3/G/2
3	6 wh.	Gloucester Wagon Co. Ltd.	–	3/3
4	Bogie	R.Y. Pickering & Co. Ltd.	Guard's/Composite	G/1/3/3
5	Bogie	R.Y. Pickering & Co. Ltd.	Guard's/Composite	G/1/3/3
7	Bogie	Metropolitan Railway Carriage & Wagon Co. Ltd.	'Workman'	3/3
8	Bogie	Metropolitan Railway Carriage & Wagon Co. Ltd.	'Tourist'	1/1
9	Bogie	Ashbury Railway Carriage & Iron Co. Ltd.	'Corridor'	3/3
10	Bogie	Ashbury Railway Carriage & Iron Co. Ltd.	'Corridor'	3/3 [later 1/3]
11	Bogie	Ashbury Railway Carriage & Iron Co. Ltd.	'Summer'	3/3/3/3/3/3
12	Bogie	Ashbury Railway Carriage & Iron Co. Ltd.	'Summer'	3/3/3/3/3/3
13	Bogie	Ashbury Railway Carriage & Iron Co. Ltd.	'Summer'	3/3/3/3/3/3
14	Bogie	Ashbury Railway Carriage & Iron Co. Ltd.	'Summer'	3/3/3/3/3/3

Guard's brake/Composite bogie carriages Nos. 4 & 5

Vehicles of this type would be likely to run in every train formation and it can only be assumed the original Ashbury carriages of this type were beyond repair after three decades of use. Certainly it is known that No. 4 took the place of one of the Ashburys in 1907, but there is no manufacturer's photographic evidence nor documents to support the supply of a second. Not until photographs taken on the same day in 1935 were examined for detail, was doubt shed on the demise of the second Ashbury, for on the same day in August of that year two carriages of Pickering likeness with different details were pictured – by then successive coats of paint given at Dinas Junction had obliterated their numbers . . . nor has, as yet, any illustration of a Railways Co. period vehicle carrying No. 5, come to light. On the other hand, supporting the suggestion that both Ashburys had gone before World War 1 is an absence of photographs showing them latterly . . . though dating old pictures is treacherous!

They were the last to be supplied and, giving more space for luggage, they were arranged as a Guard/1st/3rd/3rd coach finished in red with gilt lining etc. a truly attractive vehicle. The makers, R.Y. Pickering & Co. Ltd. of Wishaw, built the body to their standard design for 60 cm. gauge and it was offered in their catalogue, including the French-language version. The drawing is dated 5th April, 1907. The 1st Class was fully upholstered, the 3rds having lath seats. The guard's end had duckets and end windows, the other having steps and handrail for access to the roof oil lamps. 1st Class seating was 2 ft 4½ in. wide, the 3rds 'making do' on 1 ft 11 in.; leg space between seats was 2 ft in both cases and the floor of the 1st was covered in 'linoleum and rugs' the 3rds being plain Red Deal. The body was 29 ft 11 in. over headstocks, 6 ft wide (and 6 ft 11 in. over duckets) 8 ft in centreline from rail, and the 3 ft 6 in. wheelbase bogies with their 1 ft 8 in. wheels were at 23 ft centres. The bogie side frames were of Great Northern Railway type outline with boxes and springs behind the frames.

The Company's initials appeared on the waist band, together with the number. Each door bore the Class figure: the carriages survived into the combined series stock.

General Note

So much for the Railways' carriage stock, all of which had Colza oil lighting by 1909 but which was said by the Festiniog staff to be 'very poor'. The last nine vehicles built i.e. those introduced from 1891, which had Westinghouse brake from the start, were not only a most useful selection of stock primarily intended for holiday traffic, but were handsome as well. Of the North Wales narrow gauge lines, the Company had no competitor at the turn of the century in the recent acquisitions of carriages it had made. The Festiniog (by comparison) made a poor showing and it was not until the last year or two of the century that other lines like the Lynton & Barnstaple, the Welshpool & Llanfair and the Rheidol followed a trend which the N.W.N.G. had begun a decade earlier.

Goods Stock

One fact may be stated about N.W.N.G. goods stock with positive certainty – very little is known about it! Nothing is available for the original purchases and building of stock, only the Annual Returns showing totals of wagons survive. A summary of this reads: 1877, 114; 1878–90, 120. A House of Commons Sessional Paper for 1890 discloses 105 wagons fitted with hook and link couplers and 15 wagons fitted with 'Norwegian' type hooks and fitted with the usual eccentric with weighted ball so as to draw the chopper-hooks close together and prevent buffer 'chatter', thus making the 120 total of open wagons. The standard coupling height was 1 ft 8 in. The Paper also states the Railway employed two shunters but no shunters' poles were used – '. . . They were able to do this' (couple wagons) 'without going between or under them'. The distance between adjoining wagons was 1 ft 3 in.

As no information exists for the type of traffic carried for quarry or local district use, but assuming this took in general the form of other local lines, the Company, somewhat akin to the Festiniog's equipment, provided small wagons – apart from slate wagons – for quarry traffic, and a large type for the main line; the latter would not travel over the inclines nor enter quarries as their loading gauge would be excessive. For quarries and mines a fleet of small open wagons (which could be tipped on their sides to empty them if need be) did duty: in addition 15 large open wagons for main line purposes including local coal traffic, had the 'Norwegian' coupler suited to the passenger stock and locomotives. We can assume that almost all mineral exploitation (slate included) would rely on steam power and coal traffic was considerable. These 15 vehicles may have been a separate number series 1–15.

Reverting to the Annual Returns; these were 1891–2, 147; 1893–6, around 135; 1897–1907, around 145. About 1910 there was severe reduction – perhaps many broken wagons were now written off as having no purpose whilst traffic was falling away. No Returns were made during the First War and in that decade were shown: 1910, 118; 1911, 117; 1913, 92. A useful Stock Return for 1897 has survived; this gives; covered vans 3, open goods vehicles 6, slate wagons 120, coal wagons 14 (presumably the large main line type), timber bolsters 4. It is tempting to link the 3 vans as being the fourwheeled coaches stripped of their interiors, but the dates do not fit! Six open wagons would be for coal etc. into quarries and mines.

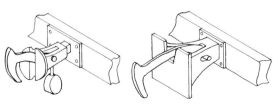

N.W.N.G.R. COACHES   N.W.N.G.R. OBS'N CAR

N.W.N.G.R. SLATE WAGONS

After the First War, more informative Returns were made:

	Open Merchandise & Mineral Wagons	Rail/Timber Wagons	Misc.	Service
1913	98	–	29*	4
1919	107	34	1	–
1920	107	39	–	–
1921	82 open + 13 other = 95†	18	–	–

*Presumably some of this total were converted into rail or timber bolsters which swelled the total for 1919; forestry traffic was at its height during the First War.
†It is likely that 82 were wooden or iron-frame slate wagons, and 13 coal wagons.

Slate Wagons (Wooden frame and slatted type)

Supplied by The Gloucester Wagon Co. Ltd. in December 1877 to Order 248 (the next order number being that for the six-wheeled 'carriages) was a number of conventionally-built all-wooden wagons; and the official photograph shows one fitted with handbrake which could be applied to wheels on the handle side of the wagon only. Link and hook couplings were recessed into the curved buffing plate ends and the capacity would be about 1 ton. There are similarities in the design with the rough drawing of an early slate wagon in Festiniog Railway records, especially in the running gear.[16]

Slate Wagons (Steel slatted, with wooden or steel frames)

Three versions of this wagon have been traced. Basically they were of the design in use far and wide over the county, but in detail they were entirely different from those used by other companies. The framing was of bar and angle, the top member being angle. The 2 ton wagons (specimen Nos. 120 and 127) were most common, and had a rectangular plate buffing pad at each end with hook and chain coupling. Some had brakes with shoes and handle on one side only; handles were fitted in various positions and were shaped in S, J or straight varieties. Wheel bearings were unlike other Welsh lines. Some were lanky plain pedestals, others had a somewhat sophisticated axlebox cover on a bevelled face with grease-box lid occasionally fitted at the top of the pedestal, and another version was sprung with small W irons to hold a box whose body and spring were behind the W iron. Bearings were swopped about. Probably dimensions were 5 ft 6 in. long × 3 ft 6 in. wide. The 3 ton wagons were similar to the two ton, but wider. They were distinguished by having curved buffing plates at each end and most had spring boxes in W irons. Probably dimensions were 6 ft long × 4 ft 6 in. wide. (Specimen Nos. 46 and 52.)

The above types had wooden floors and their top rails varied in height with each other depending on bearings in use and wear and tear. A suggested rail-top side dimension is 3 ft.

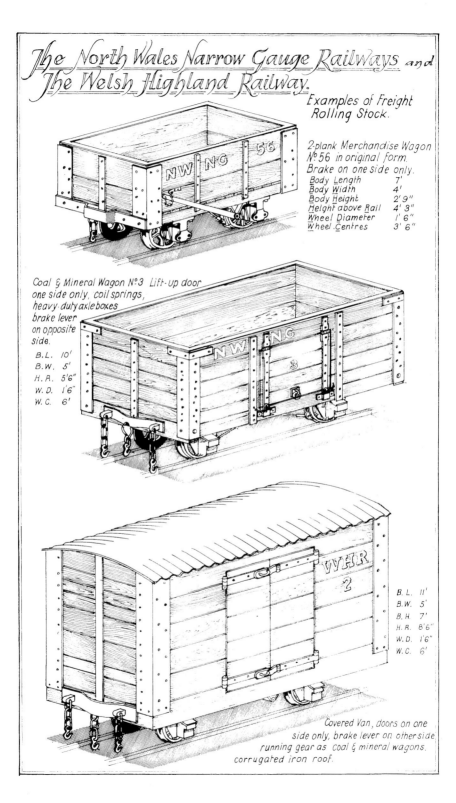

The North Wales Narrow Gauge Railways and The Welsh Highland Railway.

Examples of Freight Rolling Stock.

2-plank Merchandise Wagon Nº 56 in original form. Brake on one side only.

Body Length	7'
Body Width	4'
Body Height	2' 9"
Height above Rail	4' 3"
Wheel Diameter	1' 6"
Wheel Centres	3' 6"

Coal & Mineral Wagon Nº 3 Lift-up door one side only, coil springs, heavy-duty axle boxes brake lever on opposite side.

B.L.	10'
B.W.	5'
H.R.	5' 6"
W.D.	1' 6"
W.C.	6'

B.L.	11'
B.W.	5'
B.H.	7'
H.R.	8' 6"
W.D.	1' 6"
W.C.	6'

Covered Van, doors on one side only, brake lever on other side, running gear as coal & mineral wagons. corrugated iron roof.

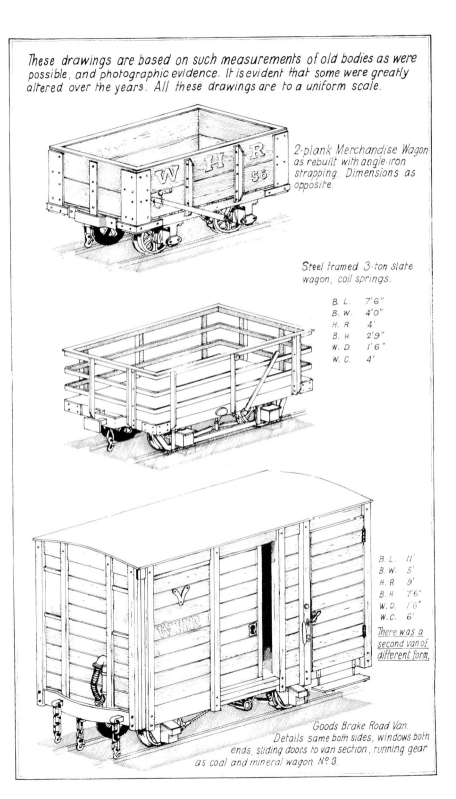

These drawings are based on such measurements of old bodies as were possible, and photographic evidence. It is evident that some were greatly altered over the years. All these drawings are to a uniform scale.

2-plank Merchandise Wagon as rebuilt with angle-iron strapping. Dimensions as opposite.

Steel framed 3-ton slate wagon, coil springs.

B. L.	7'6"
B. W.	4'0"
H. R.	4'
B. H.	2'9"
W. D.	1'6"
W. C.	4'

B. L.	11'
B. W.	5'
H. R.	9'
B. H.	7'6"
W. D.	1'6"
W. C.	6'

There was a second van of different form.

Goods Brake Road Van. Details same both sides, windows both ends, sliding doors to van section, running gear as coal and mineral wagon N°.8.

The final variety of steel frame wagon was quite the most sophisticated design to be seen in Wales. Of 3 tons capacity, a chassis with axleboxes supporting coil springs and with central sprung buffers, a handbrake working on all wheels and having the axlebox horns suitably 'tied' with a frame connecting solebar and boxes, these wagons were much in advance of anything else to be seen on such humble duty. One source suggests the builders were Kerr Stuart & Co. Ltd., of Stoke-on-Trent, but this cannot be confirmed and the number purchased is not known. There cannot have been many of them but their chassis appear (stripped of their bodies) in the demolition train where they were used as rail bolsters. They may have dated from the capital available with the Act of 1890.[17]

Slate Wagons (Two plank wooden type) (also used as general purpose wagons, coal, manure, etc.)

These may be part of the initial stock, possibly built at the Festiniog Railway's Boston Lodge Works as they were very similar to their own construction.

The smallest type held 2 tons of slate (or), and was of fixed two-plank type with rectangular buffing plates each end. Some had brakes, and levers (also wheel bearings) enjoyed the same wide variety as did the framed wagons. Two vertical members of square section timber were bolted from frame to top on each side. Dimensions appear to be similar to the frame wagons of this capacity, but their height was lower.

The next size held about 2½ tons and though similar to the above, had higher sides and levelled up with the 2 and 3 ton frame wagons. Probably due to damage in the quarries, many of the vertical side frame timbers were replaced with T section steel strip.

The largest wooden slate wagons were of dimension similar to the 3 ton frame wagons i.e. were wider in the body but otherwise built in the same way as the smaller wooden wagons. Specimen Nos. 50, 56 and 70.

Side Tip Wagons

There were about half a dozen three-plank wooden-bodied side-tippers, and their bodies overhung the underframes from which they tipped on one side only. They were larger than any of the slate wagons and probably held 4 tons of stone, and were likely to be conversions from redundant slate wagons. Specimen Nos. 123 and 124.

Coal Wagons

It is possible these too were the fruits of the finance available under the 1890 Act and certainly they were kept in good condition to judge by illustrations of the First War period. Perhaps they were not so abused. There were fifteen of them and in general style they resembled the large wooden mineral wagons on the Festiniog, and they were usually used for coal, but in the First War, for pit props also. There was a lift-up door of 4 planks in the five-plank side on the one side; the other side was masked by the brake lever, and the doors were arranged on the west side. Large curved metal buffing plates were fitted, some wagons having additional side chains as well as the central link and hooks which, unlike any other concern's link and hook varieties, had two links plus hook – replacing the original 'Norwegian' choppers. This arrangement had its dangers as a disengaged hook would trail along between the rails and tend to hook up point blades 'en passant'. Specimen Nos. 3, 9, 10 and 12. All these wagons had heavy duty axleboxes in W irons and coil springs and these fittings were similar to those on Festiniog Railway Quarrymen's Coaches. Suggested dimensions: 10 ft × 5 ft wide × 5 ft 6 in. from rail. Average capacity was 4.31 tons.

Covered Vans

There were three covered vans, two carrying Nos. 2, and 4; and they were based on the 5 ton Coal Wagons and may have been conversions. There were double opening doors on one side only, the brake handle being on the east side. No. 4 had wider doors arranged with the opening in the form of an arched curve; quite unusual. Buffing and couplers, and running gear was the same as the Coal Wagons.

Cleminson six-wheeled Patent Wheelbase Open Wagon

No illustrations survive showing this wagon(s) but a drawing was prepared and presumably at least one wagon went into service. It may be compared with the Cleminson six-wheeled Open which the Festiniog used for coal traffic from 1878.

Four-Wheeled Goods Brake or Road Vans

One was Westinghouse fitted and survived to receive a W.H.R. number. It had outside framing, two windows in each end and was of 'Road Van' type, completely enclosed. The van portion had a single sliding door each side and at one end there were full-height solid outward-opening doors (one per side) for personal access. It was mounted on sprung axleboxes and approximately 11 ft long by 5 ft wide. It carried 'No. 2'. There was certainly a second van distinguished by having no roof ventilator or Westinghouse brake.

Private Owner Wagons

The slate quarries ran about 30 open wagons over N.W.N.G. metals. They are believed to be of wooden frame and wood plank varieties and appear in pictures before the turn of the century.

Goods Stock – General Note

Wheelbases were generally (except for the large coal wagons and covered vans) as for Festiniog stock, with 3 ft on the 2 Ton slate wagons and 6 ft on the coal wagons and closed vans. All wheels were 1 ft 6 in. diameter.

Timber Bolster Wagons

Prior to the First War the Company began timber traffic over the uncompleted portion of the P.B.&S.S.R. There were two varieties of bolster wagons, one in iron and the other of wood. The latter had curved buffing plates like the coal wagons and pedestal bearings of considerable height, unlike any others. The solebars were cut away to allow the grease-box lids to be lifted. Dimensions were approximately as for the 2 Ton slate wagons where relevant. Most had a brake fitted and average capacity was 2 Tons. There were thirty-nine of them in 1920 reduced to eighteen in 1921, some being adapted from slate wagons.

Flat Wagons

These were used as runners between bolsters for long timber, and were braked, having tall plain pedestal bearings of singular design.

Finally it must be recalled that one wagon chassis was fitted with a water tank and served at Pont Croesor on the Welsh Highland line of 1923. The most striking feature was the Thompson Patent buffers fitted to it – no other N.W.N.G. vehicle has been noted with them . . . dare it be suggested that it came from another place?

Goods Stock in 1922

Spring's Report summarises the survivors as:

     1   4-wh. Brake Van (fitted continuous brake)*
    90   Slate Wagons (various)
    12   2-Ton Open Wagons
    13   4½-Ton Coal Wagons
    14   Bolster Wagons
    20   Bolster Runner Wagons

These figures differ slightly from the Official Returns.

Permanent Way

An accident report of 1883 verifies the construction of the main line track of the period. The gauge was 1 ft 11¼ in. (on a later accident

*There were certainly two.

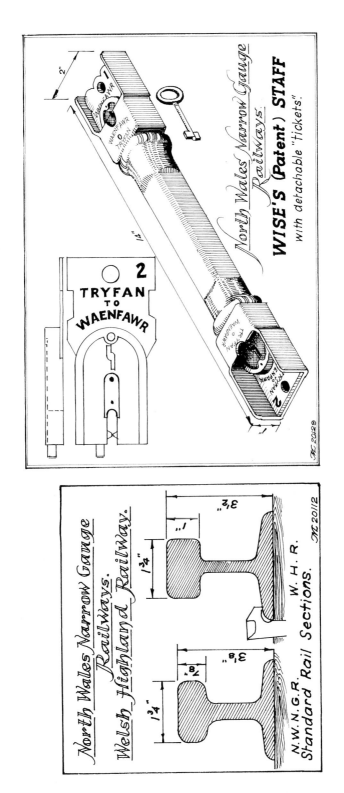

report this becomes 1 ft 11½ in.) with flat-bottomed rails in 24 ft lengths weighing 35 lbs. per yard. Fang-bolts and dog-spikes were used alternately on the sleepers which were of half round section, in larch, measuring 4 ft 6 in. long, 9 in. × 4½ in. section laid at 2 ft 5¼ in. centres except at joints where they were 2 ft. Fishplates had four bolts. Ballast was of gravel mixed with shale or cinders to a depth of 7 in.

Another report of the same period refers to 'iron rails' and says that 35, 38½ and 40 lb. sections in 24 ft lengths were in use. At joints there were two fang-bolts to hold the rail, and intermediately single spiking. This account also refers to half round *and* rectangular section sleepers in use at the same time. Clearly, there was some variation in the materials used along the line. Starting in January 1884, 41¼ lb. Indian Metre Gauge standard rail of steel in 30 ft lengths, spiked with four dogs per fastening took the place of iron rails. At first, three miles were so treated and this was ultimately extended to the whole line. The balance of steel rails was purchased in the latter half of 1886 when it was reported that 2,000 replacement sleepers had been laid too. At this time the increase in working expenses was almost entirely due to relaying. In the 1922 reconditioning of the line, the 'Indian' rail was replaced by 40 lb. B.S.S. rails, 33 ft long. Smaller sleepers only 4 ft long and a shallower depth of ballast were among the economies practised in the 1922 relaying.

The formation level width was 10 ft.

An account in 'RAILWAY PRESS' of 21st June, 1889 refers to the numerous sharp curves of 3½ to 4 chains radius on gradients of 1 in 36 to 1 in 48 (obviously on the Branch Line) and the continual problem caused thereby of the tendency of rails to spread on the 'excessively sharp curves' and cause derailments. (The Company enjoyed plenty of these.) In 1886 Livesey designed iron ties which were fitted, three to each rail length, to hold the gauge on the sharpest curves. These proved very successful and were later extended to almost every curve on the line. So poorly had the track stood up to traffic on curves that in the early days platelayers were constantly respiking the rails until the sleepers quickly became useless. Livesey introduced barbed dog spikes which, together with ties, reduced maintenance and derailments considerably.

By 1921 only two men were employed on the whole railway to tend the track. Some new sleepers had been put in on the branch and tie bars inserted. Bryngwyn station was unsafe for a locomotive. All curves needed packing, joints had broken and sagged. From a point north of Glanrafon and into Rhyd-Ddu the main line was good. Otherwise it was 'unsafe for passengers'.

Signalling

The main line and branch was of single line and no land was obtained for doubling it. The Official Returns of Single Line read:

1877 9 m. 0 ch.—Dinas-Bryngwyn 4 m. 50 ch.: Tryfan Junc.-Quellyn
                                                           4 m. 30 ch.
1878 9 m. 70 ch.—Dinas-Bryngwyn 4 m. 50 ch.: Tryfan Junc.-Snowdon Ranger
                                                           5 m. 20 ch.
1880 on. 11 m. 70 ch.—Dinas-Bryngwyn 4 m. 50 ch.: Tryfan Junc.-Rhyd-Ddu
                                                           7 m. 20 ch.

Goods/Mineral Traffic only:

1892   1 m. 8 ch. Incline & Above
1893 on 0 m. 44 ch. Incline only

It will be seen that on the latter Returns, a change of emphasis prevailed, the tramways above the Bryngwyn Drumhead not being shown as N.W.N.G. property!

Frames and semaphore signals were supplied by McKenzie & Holland of Worcester; block instruments (not an original installation) came from the Railway Signal Company of Liverpool.[18]

There were signal boxes at the following stations, and at those marked * it was ultimately possible for the engine to run round a train (from which it must not be assumed that the Board of Trade viewed the loop as a suitable passing place for passenger working): Dinas Junction*, Tryfan Junction*, Waenfawr*, Bettws Garmon*, Snowdon Ranger, Rhyd-Ddu*, Rhostryfan, Bryngwyn*. [At first there were no instruments of any kind, the railway being worked on the One Engine in Steam method.] At opening the equipment was:

Llanwnda	12 levers	3 spare included
Moel Tryfan	20	1
Rhostryfan	8	2
Bryngwyn	8	3
Waenfawr	8	2
Bettws-y-Garmon	12	4
Quellyn	2	–

These are the original spellings; probably Quellyn was just a ground frame for the temporary layout. After 1895 track alterations, Waenfawr had 7 levers and 1 spare. By 1921 the timber work on the signal boxes had 'quite rotted'.

Distant, Home and Starting signals were installed: there were no Starters at Waenfawr, but only those at Dinas, Tryfan, Bettws Garmon, Snowdon Ranger and Rhyd-Ddu remained intact (though out of use and derelict) by 1922. Previously all stations were signalled. The signals were of the single spectacle type showing a white light for clear and having a blue spectacle back light.

There was a telephone link between Dinas, Tryfan and Rhyd-Ddu, with tappings at Waenfawr and all intermediate quarry sidings. The block instruments were connected by 2-wire circuits on overhead poles, some of which were cast-iron tubes: they were at Dinas, Tryfan Junction, Waenfawr and Rhyd-Ddu, also at Bryngwyn on the branch. All these had been taken out before 1920 save Tryfan Junction and Waenfawr, and both these were out of order.

From the time of opening until at least 1888 both main line and branch were worked on the One Engine in Steam principle or when required, by using the only available staff for a section and sending a train(s) ahead on a ticket. Only the engine carrying the staff would be able to enter any sidings as the key was attached to the staff. The Company returned this method of working over the 2 m. 35 ch. Tryfan Junction–Bryngwyn branch for the whole period of its history. The Returns show that on the main line, Wise's Patent Train Staff & Ticket system and Absolute Block working was introduced over the 9 m. 35 ch. mainline in 1892; presumably in the period 1888–1892 there was a mixture of working while Wise's system was being installed.

The Interlocking Returns of 1888 gave nine sidings and one crossover, and five sidings in main and branch respectively where interlocking was fitted. There were ten main line and five branch locations where point and signal locking was concentrated, i.e. signal boxes or ground frames.

[Wise's Staff is not commonly found; there are samples of it in the Armagh Museum (ex-Clogher Valley Railway), the Science Museum (that used by McKenzie & Holland who were agents for it) as a sample from India, and the Narrow Gauge Railway Museum, Towyn, has an original N.W.N.G. example. The staff is metal and has pockets attached at each end into which metal tabs are slipped. Berkeley D. Wise was Engineer to the Belfast & Co. Down Railway having been previously on the Belfast & Northern Counties line. His aim in designing the staff was to eliminate the use of card or paper tickets in connection with ordinary staff working; these were vulnerable and had to be collected and returned to higher authority. Wise's system used metal tabs as tickets; engraved on each was the section for which the ticket was intended and the direction of travel, i.e. A–B or B–A. A ticket from one end would not fit the pocket at the other. At the issuing station the Station Master had a key to unlock the staff; he did so in front of the train driver who saw the staff and was given a ticket from it. At the end of the appropriate section the ticket would be given up; the Station Master there, on receipt of the staff itself which followed on the last working, would be able to slip the one or more tickets into the appropriate end of the staff; he would not of course, have a key for the end into which he replaced the tickets, but only for the other end which released tickets for the return journey. The staff was customarily used with its full complement of tickets for the contrary journey, locked in the one end of it; this was an added safeguard as not only would a ticket from the other end not fit, but the end having its full complement of tickets, there would be no vacancy to enable anyone to try and force in a ticket.

Users of the System, which lasted well into the time of the Electric Token, included the Clogher Valley as mentioned, Great Eastern and parts of the (English) Great Northern Railways, The Belfast & County Down, and the Seacombe, Hoylake & Deeside Railway. Most of these installed it in the 1880s and McKenzie & Holland illustrated it in their catalogue.]

LIVERY

Locomotives

The main colour was difficult to define because in weathering it changed its tone. It began as a red-brown which some sources say was like that of the North British Railway, and others as Midland Railway red. The latter is the likely starting shade, and being unstable, it would become more brown with weathering and rubbing down. The lining was black, edged each side with a thin yellow line. Hall cranks on outside framed engines, and buffer beams were vermilion, as was the ground of all brass name etc. plates. Frames, smokebox and cab roofs were black. The Company's initials were not carried. *Beddgelert* carried the Coat of Arms on the cab panel. *Gowrie* was in Midland red as delivered.

Coaches

The six-wheelers were teak with black ironwork and white roofs. Lettering etc. was in gilt with black shading, under the eaves.

Bogie coaches were Midland Railway red lettered and lined in gold but by the early 1900s the lining had begun to disappear. Roofs were grey latterly, white originally.

When delivered, the bogie coaches from Ashbury had light brown upper panels and were chocolate below the waist in a style similar to that used by the Lancashire & Yorkshire Railway. Roofs were originally white; lettering etc. was gilt and each door had the Class number on it together with 'N.W.N.G. Ry.' and the vehicle number . . . all of which somewhat cluttered up the waist panels!

The Observation Carriage No. 8 was similarly treated and for good measure had the Company's Arms on a plaque mounted on the side.

By the end of the First War some carriages were grey without marking of any kind save for the number in small figures in a bottom corner of the side.

Goods Stock

Slate wagons were Midland red but became grey with black running gear. Vans may have been Midland Railway red originally but were grey latterly. On some open planked wagons, the top plank would read (for example) 'N.W.N.G. 58' in white, but this gave way to stencil characters on soles or elsewhere. No additional marking was given; tare weight or loaded weight was not shown. The large open coal wagons were always smartly turned out, the number being in a large white stencil on the top right-hand plank or in the centre of the side.

Extremely little is known about wagon colours and clearly no basic method of painting, numbering etc. was used. Paint was simply a medium to preserve the vehicle and identify it by a number.

Crest and Garter

The Company used two 'devices'. There was a proper Coat of Arms 8 in. × 8¾ in. having a Red Dragon against a white decorated background. Beneath, on an elaborated scroll, read 'North Wales Narrow Gauge Railways Company'.

There was also a Garter Device. This was the same as that used by the Festiniog Railway and may have been introduced by Spooner, for instance, before a Coat of Arms proper was sanctioned. The Garter was 6 in. diameter and read 'North Wales Narrow Gauge Railways' and was surmounted by a Red Dragon. The garter could encircle a vehicle number, but an illustration of it in use on any vehicle has not come to notice. The Crest on the other hand, was used on engines and carriages but probably not all received it. The Ashbury delivery of the 1894 period did not have it, but it is thought that the 6-wheelers apart, coaches up to that time were given it when new. On the carriages, it was customarily mounted on its own panel.

Notes on Timetables

The Company never ran trains on Sundays.

The nature of the surviving documents makes it impossible to be precise in comment on timetables, and these notes are observations only. No copies of Working Timetables, Rule Book or Minutes are available.

February 1878

1. The Railway had only just opened; the branch was complete and probably provided the bulk of all traffic – certainly the bulk of slate traffic.
2. The Timetable would require two engines in steam. The Company only possessed two at this time, *Beddgelert* not being delivered until the end of 1878. There was thus no margin for engine failures.
3. The service was probably based on through trains between Dinas and Bryngwyn with a branch service (so to speak) on the unfinished main line from Tryfan Junction to Quellyn. Presumably the engine on the latter service would fill in its duties on materials' etc. trains for the contractor. It is likely that during the course of the day the engines on the two duties were swopped over, for instance, the 5.00 p.m. arrival at Dinas Mondays–Fridays with the 5.03 p.m.

February 1878 — Week-days only — 1st & 3rd Class — General Manager & Secretary: J. Oldham

UP

Station	Gov.		A	B	Gov.	A
Quellyn	8.20	11.40	1.30	4.20	6.15	8.20
Bettws Garmon	8.33	11.53	1.43	4.33	6.28	8.33
Waenfawr	8.40	12.00	1.50	4.40	6.35	8.40
Bryngwyn	8.30	11.50	1.40	4.30	6.25	8.30
Rhostryfan	8.40	12.00	1.50	4.40	6.35	8.40
Tryfan Junction	8.50	12.10	2.00	4.50	6.45	8.50
Dinas	8.58	12.18	2.08	5.00	6.55	9.00

DOWN

Station	Gov.	SO	A	B		A
Dinas	7.20	9.58	12.30	3.03	5.03	7.43
Tryfan Junction	7.30	10.08	12.40	3.13	5.13	7.53
Rhostryfan	7.40	10.13	12.45	3.18	5.18	7.58
Bryngwyn	7.55	10.22	12.55	3.27	5.27	8.05
Waenfawr	7.45	10.17	12.50	3.23	5.23	8.03
Bettws Garmon	7.55	10.22	12.55	3.28	5.28	8.08
Quellyn*	8.05	10.32	1.10	3.40	5.40	8.20

A Saturdays only   B Saturdays excepted   Gov = Parliamentary   (*Temporary station)

August 1892 — Secretary: S. Tanner

UP

Station	SE	SO	Gov.				SO
Beddgelert (coach)	—	9.40	12.50	3.10		6.10	—
Rhyd-Ddu (train)	7.20	8.20	10.35	1.45	4.05	7.05	—
Snowdon Ranger	7.34	8.33	10.48	1.49	4.17	7.18	—
Bettws Garmon	7.47	8.46	11.01	2.12	4.29	7.31	8.55
Waenfawr	7.53	8.51	11.06	2.17	4.34	7.36	9.00
Bryngwyn		8.35	10.50	2.00x	4.17	5.35	8.55
Rhostryfan		8.43	11.00	2.10x	4.27	5.45	9.04
Tryfan Junction	8.03	9.00	11.15	2.27	4.42	5.52	7.45	9.11
Dinas	8.13	9.10	11.24	2.37	4.51	6.00	7.55	9.20

DOWN

Station	Gov.	SO					SO	SO
Dinas	6.00	7.45	9.40	12.47	2.12	5.00	7.00	8.25
Tryfan Junction	6.09	7.55	9.50	12.56	2.21	5.10	7.09	8.35
Rhostryfan	—	8.04	9.58	1.05x	3.30	5.18	7.15	8.43
Bryngwyn	—	8.14	10.06	1.15x	3.40	5.28	7.24	8.53
Waenfawr	6.18		10.00	1.05	3.30	5.20		8.45
Bettws Garmon	6.23		10.05	1.10	3.35	5.25		8.50
Snowdon Ranger	6.36		10.18	1.23	3.47	5.38		—
Rhyd-Ddu*	6.50		10.31	1.36	4.00	5.55		—
Beddgelert (coach)	—		11.15	2.15	4.30	6.30		—

Gov = Parliamentary   SO Saturdays only   SE Saturdays excepted   x = Saturdays only   *2½ miles from the summit of Snowdon' departure on all weekdays would not allow the same engine time to run round, coal and take water.

4. Working over the steep gradient between Tryfan Junction and Bryngwyn the following times were allowed between the three stations involved for Down (uphill) trains:

Tryfan Junction to Rhostryfan   10   5   5   5   5   5   mins.
Rhostryfan to Bryngwyn   15   9 10   9   9   7   mins.

The first train was the morning Government or workmen's train which would have the heaviest loading. The third train was Saturdays only and would carry a greater passenger load that day. The last train, at a not-very-late hour of evening, presumably carried little traffic between Rhostryfan and Bryngwyn – as might be expected!

On the Up (downhill) run ten minutes were allowed for each of the two sections of the branch journey between the three stations. All trains were timed the same. This would allow opportunity for braking of slate wagons when required.

5. The timetable shows passenger workings only. It is believed that other-than-passenger workings were run as required and not provided for in the working timetable. Most advertised trains ran with wagons at the rear of the passenger portion. The accounts show that Saturday passenger takings were five to six times those of Monday to Friday inclusive.

August 1892

1. This table could be worked by using one engine on the main line and one on the branch. On Saturday evenings the last working Bryngwyn–Dinas which made connection with the last train Tryfan Junction to Dinas, would either have to combine and form one train with two engines at Tryfan, or run the branch set back to Dinas as empty stock.

2. The Saturday evening train to Bettws Garmon only and back is a feature of this period. Presumably lack of population beyond did not warrant extending this service. There must have been a suitable layout for running round the engine at Bettws but there is no record of it before spring 1902 when the latterday loop was put in. Perhaps the coaches were pushed into a siding and hand-shunted behind the engine again?

3. Some of the turnround times at Rhyd-Ddu were quite short but probably time could be made up on the downhill return run if late starts from there were involved.

June 1909

1. This table could be worked with one engine on the main line and another for the branch. The main line engine could work the same

June 1909 'Snowdon & Beddgelert District' – N.W.N.G. – Secretary & Manager G.C. Aitchison

DOWN	A	SO	SO	SO	SO	SO
Dinas	6.51	9.55	12.48	3.10	5.25	7.00
Tryfan Junction	7.00	10.03	12.56	3.18	5.34	7.09
Tryfan Junction		10.08	12.58	3.20	5.36	7.10
Rhostryfan		10.15	1.04	3.25	5.42	7.15
Bryngwyn		10.25	1.14	3.35	5.52	7.25
Tryfan Junction	7.00	10.04	12.57	3.19		7.11
Waenfawr	7.09	10.17	1.05	3.29		7.19
Bettws Garmon	7.13	10.25	1.10	3.25		7.24
Quellyn Lake	7.26	10.38	1.23	3.48		7.37
Snowdon*	7.38	10.50	1.35	4.00		7.50
Beddgelert (coach)		11.15	2.10	5.40		

UP	A	SO	SO	SO	SE	SO	SO	SO	SO
Beddgelert (coach)	–	10.00	12.30	–	–	4.00			
Snowdon (train)	7.45	11.05	1.40			5.30			7.55
Quellyn Lake	7.58	11.17	1.50			5.43			Sig.
Bettws Garmon	8.10	11.31	2.00			5.54			Sig.
Waenfawr	8.15	11.40	2.04			5.58			8.25
Tryfan Junction	8.25	11.47	2.14			6.05			8.32
Bryngwyn	–	11.30	2.00	4.28	5.34		6.00	7.27	–
Rhostryfan	–	11.40	2.10	4.38	5.44		6.10	7.35	–
Tryfan Junction	–	11.45	2.15	4.44	5.49		6.15	7.40	–
Tryfan Junction	8.26	11.48	2.16	4.45	5.50	6.05	6.16	7.40	8.32
Dinas	8.35	11.58	2.25	4.54	6.00	6.13	6.26	7.50	8.40

A 1st Class & Gov. SO Saturdays only SE Saturdays excepted *About 3 miles to the summit of Snowdon'
Sig. Stops to set down on notice being given to Guard.

set of carriages to and fro throughout the day except that on Saturdays, after arrival at Dinas at 6.13 p.m. of the 5.30 p.m. from Snowdon, the engine and train would have to work back empty stock as far as Tryfan Junction to make connection with the 7.00 p.m. Dinas–Bryngwyn train (also Saturdays only) to extend this Saturday service to Snowdon.

By the above arrangement, the Bryngwyn branch engine would make all its journeys on a revenue-earning basis.

2. The ample Up Dinas–Bryngwyn service on Saturdays is notable though it ceases at an early hour; the last trip of the day on the branch is notable for the two minutes allowed to hook on and off the train and run round at Bryngwyn. This train was then allowed only eight minutes to Rhostryfan, the fastest of the day. Doubtless it seldom failed to keep time, as last workings-of-the-day and a homeward run enjoy a beneficial effect!

3. Branch times vary from 5 to 7 minutes for the climb from Tryfan Junction to Rhostryfan, and 10 minutes were allowed thereafter. With the exception of the working just mentioned, Up trains were also given 10 minutes for the return journey and 5 or 6 minutes from Rhostryfan to Tryfan Junction.

4. The fastest main line run was the Up working at 5.30 p.m. from Snowdon which was allowed 43 minutes for the 9½ miles.

March 1916

Weekdays only					G.C. Aitchison	
DOWN			UP			
Dinas	9.35	3.20	Beddgelert (coach)		10.00	3.20
Tryfan Junction	Sig.	–				
			Snowdon (train)		10.45	4.15
Tryfan Junction	–	–	Quellyn Lake		Sig.	Sig.
Rhostryfan	–	–	Bettws Garmon		Sig.	Sig.
Bryngwyn	–	–	Waenfawr		11.25	4.40
			Tryfan Junction		Sig.	–
Tryfan Junction	Sig.	–				
Waenfawr	9.55	3.40	Bryngwyn		–	–
Bettws Garmon	Sig.	Sig.	Rhostryfan		–	–
Quellyn Lake	Sig.	Sig.	Tryfan Junction		–	–
Snowdon	10.35	4.10				
			Tryfan Junction		Sig.	–
Beddgelert (coach)	11.20	4.50	Dinas		12.05	5.10

(Footnotes as for June 1909.)

March 1916

1. This was the nadir of the passenger service. The branch line had gone and nothing was provided for passengers (at least as an advertised service) in place of the ample schedules of seven years previously. It now took an hour to work from Dinas to Snowdon and an hour and twenty minutes to return – presumably to allow time to pick up slate wagons bound for Dinas.
2. The table could be worked entirely with one engine; between 12.05 p.m. and 3.20 p.m. there was opportunity to make a freight working up to Bryngwyn and back when required.
3. On the main line, Tryfan Junction, Bettws Garmon and Quellyn Lake had been reduced to 'Halt' category.

The passenger service finished entirely at the end of this year.

A Report of 1921–2 implies that there was fair traffic on the Bryngwyn branch (freight only) and the track was in good order. Tryfan Junction–Snowdon was used only about once a week and very unprofitably, mainly for timber off the incomplete P.B. & S.S.R. This somewhat contradicts Spring's Report of 1921 which quotes Bryngwyn workings on four days a week (etc.) and implies that little of the track was in good order. Latterly both surviving engines were said to be in 'good order' and *Moel Tryfan* would haul four coaches and *Russell* nine on the Bryngwyn branch . . . (One may ask, "why?"!)

Under the Board of Trade's Prevention of Accidents Rules 1902, 'the movement of vehicles by means of a prop or pole, being the operation commonly known as "propping", shall not take place, except in cases where no other reasonable practicable means can be provided for dealing with the traffic, . . .' after the next twelve months. Further, 'tow-roping . . . effecting the movement of vehicles on a railway by means of towing with a rope or chain attached to a locomotive, or a vehicle moving on an adjacent line, shall not be allowed except in cases where no other . . .'.

'The North Wales Narrow Gauge Railway Company is exempted from the operation of this rule as relates to tow-roping'.

(Further along these same Rules, the Festiniog Railway was exempted from attaching brake vans to trains, but *not* the N.W.N.G.R. Co., the distinction being in the basic gravity train working scheme used by the former.)

Incidents and Accidents

From the number of reported accidents, the Company had one of the worst records with a predilection to derailments. Whether this was due to an honest streak which would not hide the slightest reportable incident, or whether only the worst was notified, cannot be said. What is clear is that whether during the time of the hire of rolling stock, the early Company stock or the later bogie stock, trains were prone to leave the rails and there having been plenty of opportunity to put the running gear of stock into good order, we can only assume there was insufficient manpower, available finance or materials to keep the track in fair order. A sample of reported items will illustrate this.

1878		One collision between passenger trains
		One passenger train derailment
		One passenger injured
		One Railway Servant killed by falling from engine on moving train
24th February, 1883		(See separate account of collision)
1892		One non-classified accident – carriage blown off rails at Bettws Garmon
1894	January–March	One passenger train derailment
1896	January–March	One goods train derailment
1899	June–December	One goods train derailment
1901	June–September	Two passenger train derailments
	September–December	One Railway Servant killed (Cause classed as 'Miscellaneous')
1902	June–September	Three passenger train derailments
1903	March–June	One passenger train derailment
		One Railway Servant injured
	September–December	One passenger train derailment
1906	January–March	One goods train derailment
		One passenger train derailment
31st July, 1906		(See separate account of collision)
	September–December	Collision between passenger and goods trains; one passenger injured
1907	January–March	One goods train derailment
	March–June	One Railway Servant injured whilst shunting
	June–September	One passenger train derailment
		One goods train derailment
	September–December	One coupling failure

Over a span of twenty years on what had been a newly-built railway, this list makes impressive reading. The two most interesting occasions deserve separate mention.

On Saturday 24th February, 1883 the 8.25 p.m. left Rhyd-Ddu for Dinas in darkness and in good order. The Single Fairlie engine ran, bunker leading, followed by Gloucester brake composite six-wheeler coach and two small third class four-wheelers. They duly stopped at Snowdon Ranger and shortly after re-starting, the two four-wheelers at the rear left the rails, coming to a stand 960 yards west of the station. Parted from the derailed coaches, the engine and coach sped on for another 580 yards and it was Quellyn Bridge before the guard sensed they were alone. He managed to signal the driver to stop and ordered him to set back along the line to find the missing carriages. The driver lost no time in doing so and contact between the Gloucester and the four-wheelers was so violent that the former was considerably damaged and the latter thrown off down the lineside on their sides. The only passenger was in the Gloucester and no one was injured.

At 11.30 p.m. Guard Morris knocked up R.H. Livesey at his Caernarvon home and told him that some of the 8.25 from Rhyd-Ddu lay battered at the foot of the bank near Snowdon Ranger. Livesey went at once to Dinas Junction where he found Driver Jones asleep on the engine. He was drunk but the fireman was sober. The guard too had been drinking, but was not so drunk as the driver. The engine being in steam, Livesey drove out to Ranger. He found the derailed coaches lying on one side of the line. The fireman had admitted they (the three trainmen) had been drinking at the Snowdon Ranger Hotel and were running fast to make up time. The guard had not made up the train correctly; the brake vehicle should have been at the rear. The derailed vehicles had run for 420 yards along the ballast.

William Roberts the ganger arrived on the scene at 2 p.m., Sunday. He found the track there true to gauge and the materials quite sound. Thomas Morris the guard had been a fireman on the L.N.W.R. at Crewe but came to the N.W.N.G. when it opened. They had arrived at Snowdon Ranger at 8.37 p.m., a minute early, and left at 8.50 p.m. he thought. He maintained he was with the stationmaster from Rhyd-Ddu all the time, 'who had come down with the train' . . . 'doing the accounts and changing the date in the press ready for Monday' . . . 'I did not go to the Hotel. I did not have anything to drink . . . I noticed the carriages were missing at Quellyn Bridge and we set back at not more than 4 miles an hour . . . I went into Caernarvon for Mr. Livesey and had two glasses of beer before going to him. I did not know that the driver and fireman had been to the hotel at Snowdon Ranger. I spoke to the driver at Quellyn Bridge; I was too frightened to notice what state he was in . . . I know I should have gone back with my handlamp to look for the missing coaches instead of setting back . . .'

John Williams, fireman, had been cleaner and fireman almost since the line opened. He said they all went into the hotel for a glass of beer and were there about five minutes. 'I don't think any of us had more than two glasses' . . . 'the stationmaster from Rhyd-Ddu never does come down on that train on Saturday night' . . . 'put my brake on a little harder than usual that night as I must admit we were running a little faster than usual'.

The Inspector concluded that the two light carriages must have been jerked off the track by a sudden application of the break (sic) when the train was running at a high rate of speed to make up time lost at Snowdon Ranger, the guard having disobeyed the rule about having the heavy brake carriage at the rear of the train. The second collision was caused "by the carelessness of the driver and disregard of the rules shown by the guard; had the coupling merely broken and the coaches following the train downgrade at a high rate of speed, the collison would have been greatly magnified. The disregard for the truth on the part of the guard and the gross mismanagement of the train by all three servants was something about which it was hard to imagine anything more unsatisfactory" . . . so Major Marindin summed up. He recommended that a better class of employee be engaged and though there was insufficient work for a stationmaster at Snowdon Ranger, had a man been there in that capacity, the accident would probably not have happened. He thought the conduct of the landlord at the hotel deserved the attention of the county's licensing authorities '. . . to have allowed the driver to get so drunk upon his premises that he was a serious risk to the public'. The driver was discharged from employment.

A less colourful accident occured on 31st July 1906 when the 10.00 a.m. excursion train from Dinas to Rhyd-Ddu hit a vagrant coal truck which had become detached from the 9.47 a.m. mixed train from Tryfan Junction which was running ahead. The coal truck ran back and impaled itself on the engine of the excursion near Nant Mill overbridge. This train was headed by a Single Fairlie engine. Due to the train running over a section where a speed restriction was always in force and the coal wagon having slowed on a more level grade, the impact was not too great. Engine buffer and coupling were broken and the cylinder covers cracked; headstock plate was bent, steamchest covers cracked and rear beam and trailing buffer coupling bent. The rear engine bogie left the rails. The coal wagon survived with a broken end and coach No. 9, behind the engine had its end smashed in and some glass broken.

Driver Beaumont came on duty at 7.45 a.m. to work until 5.30 p.m. He took the excursion, giving the staff to Hughes, Waenfawr Stationmaster who gave him the Waenfawr to Snowdon staff without making any remark. After two minutes they set off and as he was slackening speed for the restriction, he only had a 15 yards view of the oncoming wagon due to the curve and the bridge. He closed regulator and applied brakes before the impact.

Hughes had been at Waenfawr since the line opened. He was offered the mixed train from Tryfan at 9.57. He accepted it and received 'Train entering section' for it at once. Snowdon accepted it at 10.3 and it left Waenfawr at that time. Snowdon did not give him 'Train out of section' for it. He accepted the excursion at 10.19 a.m. and got 'Train entering section' at the same time. He offered it to Snowdon who accepted it at 10.25, at which time it left Waenfawr. He said that on that day, and the day previously, he did not receive 'Out of section' for the mixed train from Snowdon but worked to the timetable. On the latter day, at 10.37 a.m. he got a message from Idwal Owen, Snowdon Stationmaster, saying, 'Not one of the trains arrived here yet', but could do nothing.

Owen had spent all his 17 years at Snowdon. He accepted the mixed at 10.03 a.m. and got section for it at the same time. He was offered the excursion at 10.25 a.m. and accepted it, although the mixed train had not arrived. 'We never give "Train arrived" signal, as under our regulations this need not be sent unless special instructions are given for so doing.' The mixed train arrived a little after 11.00 a.m.

The Inspector maintained that the collision was due to failure to carry out the ordinary rules for signalling by block telegraph. Owen should not have accepted the excursion when the mixed had not arrived. Worse, the mixed, on finding the wagon was missing short of Snowdon, had set back down-grade to find it! He had at least instructed the passengers to alight first. Apparently the centre buffer-coupler of the wagon had jerked undone and it was recommended that additional chains be fitted.

Some of Lt. Col. E. Druitt's comments are apt:

> The Company's Regulations which say that 'The signal "Train out of Section" is only to be given at stations where special instructions are used to that effect' should immediately be altered and the signal invariably be used.
>
> The centre buffer hook couplings on coal wagons are evidently not to be relied upon and, to prevent breakaways, chain couplings should be fitted as a precaution.
>
> It is to be hoped that in future, the block regulations will be strictly enforced.

As to the movements of the mixed train, the loss of the coal wagon had been noted by the guard and he stopped the train. After making the passengers alight, he had the train backed down the line to pick up the wagon. The Inspector was very concerned 'at this improper proceeding', emphasising that the train should have continued to Snowdon and the Waenfawr stationmaster informed from there that the train had divided.

Personnel

(Extracted from Official Returns as available.)

31st March 1884
General Manager, Secretary.
Superintendent's Dept.: 8 Station Masters (also act as Signalmen), 2 Guards, 1 Porter/Messenger.
Goods Dept.: 1 Inspector, 5 Porter/Messengers.
Loco Dept.: 2 Mechanics, 2 Drivers, 2 Firemen, 2 Labourers.
Engineer's Dept.: 1 Ganger, 4 Platelayers.

1st December 1898
General Manager, Secretary, 1 Clerk.
4 Station Masters, 2 Guards, 1 Porter (boy), 2 Labourers, 8 Sheeter/Loaders, 4 Mechanics + 1 boy, 2 Drivers, 2 Firemen, 1 Cleaner, 6 Permanent Way.

1911
Secretary, Manager, 2 Clerks.
7 Station Masters &/or Clerks, 5 Porter/Ticket Collectors, 1 Traffic Supt., 1 Fitter, 3 Locomotive Dept. men, 5 footplate men, (Permanent Way not stated).

July 1886	Drivers and firemen working 12 hour day, occasionally 14 hour; 2 Station Masters occasionally working 14 hours day; 'Examiner' did not work 12 hour day.
1905	3 Passenger Guards & Brakesmen (same the following July) 5 Drivers & firemen (6 the following July) 1 Guard/1 Driver/1 Fireman work 6.20 a.m. to 8.30 p.m. with two hour rest at mid-day.
Spring 1922	20 men employed; they were all paid by daily rate.

Wages

			Weekly Gross £ s. d.
D.O. Jones	Traffic Superintendent		4 5 0
M.O. Jones	Booking Clerk		1 10 9
M. Williams	at Snowdon station		1 2 6
T. Morris	General duties		not quoted
T.R. Thomas	Foreman		3 16 0
Caradoc Jones, Thomas Ore, W. Ll. Jones, R.J. Roberts, J. Williams, W.G. Jones	Slate Loaders	each	2 7 3
D. Lloyd Hughes	at Bryngwyn		2 9 4
W.H. Williams, John Williams	Drivers	each	2 10 1
A.E. Bailey	Fitter		3 3 9
Jeff Limerick	Ganger		2 11 8
S. Williams	Platelayer		2 5 9
D. Daniels	Carpenter		2 12 6
R. Williams	Blacksmith		2 12 6
W. Ll. Thomas	Striker		19 6

The gross fortnightly wage bill was £89 12s. 2d. and it was currently proposed to reduce wages by 15 per cent to enforce economies.

Relations with the Board of Trade

Having set down most of the available information concerning the Company, its financial problems, its physical difficulties regarding the finding of traffic, the working of trains and its instructions from higher authority to do certain work, it is possible to see more clearly the day-to-day worries of the Company.

The Board of Trade must have found the Company a grievous trial! This stemmed in part from lack of experience on the part of the railway staff and stubbornness on the part of the Company Board; each stemmed from shortage of money. For instance, the constant succession of accidents, large and small, was religiously reported to the Board of Trade and from their records it is clear that in true Civil Service manner, each case was examined from the roots upwards, the ground being covered again and again to ascertain whether the Railway Company was working according to the previous instructions of the Board of Trade. The fact that these enquiries had probably been invest-igated a mere week or two previously by the Board made no difference – each case was opened without reference to earlier decisions and the facts quantified on the Report Forms . . . a policy of full employment at the Board of Trade?

The Railway was ever quoting that the Board had given it authority to run all trains as mixed trains save for one train in each direction per day. In 1890 it maintained that this authority was still in force and all trains were mixed. The Chairman of the Railway complained that they could not adhere to the Board's instruction of 30th December, 1890 (re fitting of continuous brakes, block signalling etc.) having insufficient time and money for the work. He asserted that working One Engine in Steam should be sufficient to meet the Board's requirements, and that in any case, in his view, the instructions of 30th December, 1890 did not apply to the Bryngwyn branch! There was no telephone or telegraph along the line. The Chairman made his point and won the day; the Board allowed him another three years to carry out the work. General Hutchinson of the Board complained to the Railway, regarding One Engine in Steam working, that 'there was a somewhat lax observance of the regulations'.

The correspondence at first stated the Company's coaches weighed 4½ tons, later corrected to 6½ tons and added that at the time, there were no separate brake vans – an important point when later accidents were investigated.

By early 1891 the Company said that four large passenger vehicles contained a Guard's compartment and had brakes. (By 'large' they meant either bogie or six-wheel stock, and not the four-wheelers.) A train usually consisted of one passenger vehicle and wagons, the passenger vehicle contained the brake and was used as a brake van and marshalled at the rear of the train. The Board of Trade 'saw red' at this and reminded the Company that if the coach was fitted with continuous brake it must be marshalled next to the engine or else the brake would be ineffective. In reply the Company said that if this was done, the vehicle would not be available as a brake van for a mixed train. This was typical of correspondence passing between the two parties and emphasises the gulf between them – deliberately dug by the Chairman no doubt, who was no fool. From time to time the Chairman wrote to emphasise the Company's poverty, that it could not afford brake vans, and of the 'unnecesary restrictions'.

The correspondence also shows that before the large coal wagons were built in 1890s, the small mineral wagons were used for it and ran into the various slate quarries to serve the boilers of stationary winding engines etc.

The Board of Trade wanted more facts and were told (November 1890):

1. The grade was 1 in 47 between Dinas Junction and Tryfan Junction. After that 'there were comparatively easy grades' to the original terminus at Quellyn. The line then rose at 1 in 76 to Snowdon

Ranger and to Glanrafon Siding at 1 in 79–290 there being 3½ chain curves between there and Rhyd-Ddu. On the branch the grade was 1 in 41 to Rhostryfan, then 1 in 41 and 1 in 35 to Bryngwyn. (These figures do not exactly accord with the limited selection available from other sources.)

2. The six-wheeled stock was piped for brakes but could not be fitted with brake gear (presumably because the floors were too low). Two of these coaches had Guard's brake compartments; the third had not. The Chairman wanted 'to run these piped coaches in trains of fitted coaches, if permitted . . . without great expense the six-wheelers could not be fitted with continuous brake and could not be altered to bogie (the Board had made this suggestion) as the cost would be half that of building new stock.'

This last observation is dated 1st July, 1892.

By 5th November, 1894 the Company, through their Secretary, S. Tanner, reported that *all* stock now had continuous brakes 'except the three small four-wheeled coaches fitted with blow-through pipes'. It was hoped to fit brakes on them this year, if it could be afforded.

That same year the main line was fitted out with Wise's Staff and Tyer's One Wire Block Telegraphing System. A Sealed Undertaking was given to the Board of Trade to the effect that the branch would be worked by One Engine in Steam or Two Engines Coupled Together which would carry the staff (29th November, 1894).

Further details of composition of trains were available in 1896; one coach was used on the branch and two on the main line. This was sufficient except on Saturdays. Between Dinas and Tryfan Junction, passenger and goods trains now usually ran separately. The Company appeared to be unable to keep from under the Board of Trade's feet; the goods train derailment (listed earlier but without details) which occurred on 14th February, 1896 was typical. The 4.50 p.m. Down from Bryngwyn had proceeded only 800 yards from that station when a wagon came off the track and brought five others off the line with it. The cause was a loose wheel on an axle – a common enough happening. This derailment happened at probably the nastiest section of the whole railway, being on the very steepest part of the branch involving a sharp curve and a road crossing on the level. The Board of Trade got its teeth into the case. After evasive replies by the Company, the Secretary at last admitted that the coach with the brake was at the rear of the train, and the whole weary investigation began again! The Chairman said that it was not necessary for the Company to marshall the passenger portion next to the engine 'the usual load on the branch was three or four passengers anyway, not more'. The train had consisted (in order), of *Beddgelert* leading chimney first, seven loaded slate wagons, a bogie brake composite carriage and four empty coal wagons at the rear, an assemblage which might be calculated to make the coolest Inspector at the Board hot under the collar. The Board advised the Company of its obligations in the most direct language. They also took up the matter of continuous brakes again and in April of the same year the Company reported that thirteen bogie or six-wheeled coaches had the brake but that the three small four-wheelers had not. From this may be deduced that the Cleminson carriages had had to be fitted (perhaps by mounting the brake cylinders Festiniog-fashion inside the coaches, on the floor). Under further pressure, Russell told the Board of Trade that he would rebuild or withdraw the four-wheelers by the end of 1897 and the Board wrote back that this was not good enough. The outcome was that it was agreed they be withdrawn from service on 31st March, 1897 and there was instead 'a new large coach (fitted) in place thereof'.

The Company's passenger tickets did not adhere to regulations by showing the fare on the face.

Reference has been made to tip wagons and that the Company owned side tippers. There must also have been a number of privately-owned side tip wagons for iron-ore traffic because on 9th August, 1902 such a wagon left the track and overturned, pulling two other wagons off the line with it. This was between Tryfan Junction and Waenfawr. Once again the Company was in dire trouble with the Board of Trade. The train's composition was now the first question the Board asked; once more it was a mixed train with the brake coach in the rear! This time it was Aitchison who was in trouble; he pleaded that he had only been appointed in 1898 and had been given nothing to guide him, 'matters being in a very mixed condition' and no instructions about train working. Instructions from the Official Receiver were verbal and vague, he hinted.

In December 1904 the B.O.T. wanted to know more about explosive carried on the line. It was carried in metallic cylinders in quarry owners' wagons and passed off the N.W.N.G. onto their branches. The Board wanted vans to be used instead of open wagons, but were told these were unsuited to the Bryngwyn Incline, where the winding drum at the summit would have fouled their roofs. Though the Company was adamant that this traffic was small, the Board imposed a limit of five wagons to be dealt with at a time if containing explosives – which was probably more than generous or likely to be the case. There were no Gunpowder Vans; all powder was loaded at Dinas Junction.

At this same period – the turn of the century – there was correspondence with the Board of Trade regarding the Company's proposals to extend to Beddgelert. The Board wanted an explanation of the choice of route and the cause of delays to the scheme. It was revealed that the route had been surveyed for electric traction (a feature which has been mentioned earlier in respect of the sharp curves and steep gradients at first proposed) and that one reason why the Company would have to seek an Extension of Time was that the main landowner involved was still away at the Boer War and had been unable to finalise matters with them.

[Among documents at the Public Record Office is a batch of material dealing with the proposed electrification of the N.W.N.G. and Portmadoc Beddgelert & South Snowdon Railway; this is dated 20th March, 1905 from Messrs. W.A. and H.W. Harper, Consulting Engineers and for a 600 volts 3-phase system, two phases from overhead wires 27½ inches apart and 16 ft 10 in. above the rails. The third phase was to come from the running rails. Steel sleepers were to be installed in tunnels and there were to be ten substations between Portmadoc and Caernarvon. The electric locomotives would have had an output of 90 B.H.P.]

The Company – a concluding note

The Company was the most complex undertaking of any of the narrow gauge railways in the Kingdom. Whilst possibly the Festiniog Railway (because of its great age) holds a pioneering place in Welsh lines, the Narrow Gauge Railways Company has no equals when it comes to sheer qualities of survival against all odds. Where else could be found a Company whose start was marred by the failure of a Director to lease the line as he was bound? Whose contractor began to ship the Company's materials overseas instead of laying them himself? Which was saddled by an extraordinary agreement to work with Fairlie engines? Which threw one Receiver off its back only to be saddled by another within weeks? Whose constant embarrassment was shortage of capital? Whose constant burden was a Chairman/Receiver who held all the aces but refused to play them? Whose rolling stock was hired from one who assigned his recognised credit from the Company, to a new company in which he himself was the largest shareholder and through which he became Receiver of the Railway? Whose traffic began to fall away almost from the time of opening, due to the end of the slate boom? Which held on to what it had, operating in similarly neglected conditions as did the Talyllyn, until absorbed by an even more starry-eyed undertaking which far from bringing success, brought the end – which was sooner or later inevitable.

Needless to say, the loss carried forward from year to year, the fact that no dividends were ever paid on the ordinary shares and that vast monies were poured out and lost, is not peculiar to the North Wales Narrow Gauge. But against all the other odds, the Company stood out; it was certainly one of the few outstanding railways of any gauge.

Right from the start it was a compromise . . . only two parts of an eight-part dream achieved. On the purely physical side it may be commented that there were no tunnels, heavy earthworks or embankments despite a mountain location; there were no level crossings over public roads nor turntables. Even the sharpest curves had no check rails. But the worst feature was not so clearly perceived; the Railway had no money, and never made any. Or not enough!

Directors (Quorum = Two)

Director	ORIGINAL	1873	5/1875	3/1876	6/1879	1880	1891	1893	1900	1906	1911	1914	1919	1920	1922
Sir Ll. Turner	X	X	X	X	X	X		X	X						
Livingston Thompson	X														
H. B. Roberts[10]	X														
Ja. H. Oliver	X	X	X	X	X										
T. Bolland		X	X	X	X										
C. Pearson[9]		X	X	X	X										
Sir R. W. M. L. Bulkeley (Senr)[1]		X	X												
Sir R. W. M. L. Bulkeley (Junr)				X											
C. Celyn		X													
Abr. Fitzgibbon		X	X	X	X	X									
C. Davidson			X	X											
— Hill				X											
Chaloner W. Chute[2]						X	X	X	X						
J. C. Russell[3]						X	X	X	X	X	X				
R. S. Guiness							X								
John Menzies						X									
Hugh Pugh						X									
Chas. Davison[4]										X	X	X			
Ernest E. Lake[5]										X	X	X			
Sir Jas. W. Slzumper[6]										X		X			
G. C. Aitchison[7]													X	X	
G. W. Fosbery													X	X	
Sir J. H. Stewart[8][11]															X
Henry J. Jack[8][11]															X
Evan R. Davies[11]															X
J. W. Cassells[8]															X
Total	4	7	7	8	5	6	3	3	3	4	3	3	2	2	4

1. Replaced by his son at death in June 1875. Prominent Anglesey etc. landowner.
2. Barrister and quarry owner.
3. Receiver N.W.N.G.R. Co.; Director, Barking Gas Co.; ex Moel Tryfan Rolling Stock Co. Ltd.
4. Firebrick manufr.; ship owner Connah's Quay; Director, Hawarden & Dist. W.W., Halkyn District Mines Drainage Co. etc.
5. Solicitor; later Chairman N.W.N.G.R. Co. (following Russell).
6. ex Director Vale of Rheidol Rly.; Civil Engineer to N.W.N.G. and V. of R.R.
7. Receiver N.W.N.G. also Secretary & Engineer; also connected P.B. & S.S.R., N.W.P. & T. Co. Ltd. and Snowdon Mountain Tramroad.
8. Director, Aluminium Corporation Ltd., Dolgarrog.
9. Owner of Moel Tryfan Slate Quarry until 1875.*
10. Owner of Braich Slate Quarry until 1881.
11. Became the new Board of Festiniog Railway, June 1921.

In the period 1919–1920, two Directors only (Aitchison and Fosbery). Both of South Collingham, Newark-on-Trent; the former of Smith Woolley & Co., Land Agents, Civil Engineers etc. of South Collingham.

*Same family also owned: Coed Madoc Slate Co. Ltd., Nantlle (John Pearson until 1887; C.E. Pearson to 9th October, 1896).

m. ch.	Original Name	Open Goods	Open Passenger	Closed Goods*	Closed Passenger†	Changes in Title
0 0	Dinas	21/5/1877	15/8/1877	19/6/1937	29/9/1936	6/1891–9/1938 Dinas Junction
2 15	Tryfan Junction	21/5/1877	15/8/1877	29/9/1936	29/9/1936	
3 70	Waenfawr	21/5/1877	15/8/1877	19/6/1937	29/9/1936	
4 65	Bettws Garmon	21/5/1877	15/8/1877	19/6/1937	29/9/1936	
5 40	Salem Halt	–	31/7/1922²	–	29/9/1936	
5 75⁷	Plas-y-Nant Halt	–	⁴	–	29/9/1936	
7 35	Snowdon Ranger	1/6/1878	1/6/1878	19/6/1937	29/9/1936	By 7/1922 Quellyn Lake
8 10	Glanrafon Halt	prob from c.1878	³	19/6/1937	31/10/1916¹	
9 35	Rhyd-Ddu⁵	14/5/1881	14/5/1881	19/6/1937	29/9/1936	By 4/1895 Snowdon; 7/1922 South Snowdon: 10/1922 Snowdon; 10/1923 South Snowdon.
Mileage from Tryfan Junc.						
0 70	Rhostryfan	21/5/1877	15/8/1877	19/6/1937	31/12/1913⁶	
2 35	Bryngwyn	21/5/1877	15/8/1877	19/6/1937	31/12/1913⁶	

* Date of last Goods Train.
† Tryfan Junction–Rhyd-Ddu closed to passengers also between 31/10/1916 and 31/7/1922.
1 Not re-opened by Welsh Highland Railway.
2 Not strictly a N.W.N.G. Rlys. Halt, but may have been unofficially used before 31/7/1922. Regularised at this date.
3 Unofficial Halt for quarrymen and etc. probably from time of line opening.
4 No precise date available; thought to have been an unofficial stop before 7/1924 when regularised. Did not always appear in timetable.
5 Usual footnote '2½ miles from the summit of Snowdon' but mileage given as 3 miles (or) at various times; later '1½ hours for ascent and 1 hour for descent of Snowdon'.
6 Bryngwyn branch. It was intended to restore the passenger service in 1924 but this was never done.
7 Between 21/5/1877 and 1/6/1878 there was a temporary terminus at 'Quellan (Station for Beddgelert)', open for goods and passenger services at dates of preceding section of railway (6 m. 45 ch. from Dinas).

ANNUAL RETURNS

	1877	1878	1879	1880	1881	1882	1883	1884	1885	1886	1887	1888	1889	1890	1891
Cost hire r/stock	26	211	1947	922	–	–	–	–	–	–	–	–	–	–	–
Maintenance Works and Way	27	231	131	178	374	512	629	634	475	768	1150	932	978	1010	836
Loco Power	417	728	605	720	713	802	753	694	758	806	822	705	797	757	743
C and W maint. and repair	45	186	193	357	650	355	446	482	582	312	370	318	250	163	136
Traffic Expenses	543	880	618	664	719	715	769	783	903	858	851	866	794	729	759
Legal Expenses				29	50	20	20	25	18	–	23	–	15	45	232
Profit/Loss on Wkg.	4	(101)	(1893)	(592)	(74)	168	211	355	367	450	466	470	450	427	279
Merchandise Tons	304	839	509	611	698	1054	647	720	594	670	1118	1053	973	739	726
Minerals Tons	5418	9736	8707	10,809	13,306	13,847	15,599	16,573	17,544	18,803	21,752	17,957	17,763	17,179	15,677
Class 1st	359	598	540	531	462	496	433	409	431	362	282	325	385	400	331
Class 2nd	–	1712	435	848	953	1204	1073	1076	1012	1139	719	810	877	911	554
Class 3rd	18,518	47,294	26,905	31,859	30,042	29,074	29,210	32,266	33,114	33,944	34,501	37,752	36,362	27,606	
*Season tickets												193	190	214	198
Pass. train miles	9388														
Goods train miles	953														
Mixed train miles	10,341	27,118	23,479	27,953	28,341	31,405	31,456	31,703	31,102	30,912	30,685	30,697	30,466	30,573	
Locos (own, not hire)	2	3	3	3	3	3	3	3	3	3	3	3	3	3	3
Carriages Total	5	8	8	8	8	8	8	8	8	8	8	8	8	8	10
Wagons Merchandise	114	120	120	120	120	120	120	120	120	120	120	120	120	120	147
Other Wagons															
Other Vehicles															

(Pass. and Goods train miles: Mixed from 1878)

*Mainly Quarrymen's Seasons paid for by the quarry in certain cases.

	1892	1893	1894	1895	1896	1897	1898	1899	1900	1901	1902	1903	1904	1905	1906
Cost hire r/stock	—	—	—	—	—	—	—	—	—	—	—	—	—	—	—
Maintenance Works and Way	952	1024	841	1011	1370	1275	668	602	481	447	380	388	390	555	409
Loco Power	829	1050	1367	1435	843	949	1096	969	1006	1023	1079	763	814	840	875
C & W maint. and repair	263	369	337	444	636	479	359	390	428	342	596	353	268	428	307
Traffic expenses	710	827	944	895	926	955	952	913	891	891	853	911	862	883	862
Legal Expenses	20	26	26	32	30	14	—	10	12	14	26	15	29	14	17
Profit/Loss on Wkg.	348	502	455	502	704	615	971	899	586	563	570	419	700	483	532
Merchandise Tons	842	756	1087	1352	1241	1363	1448	1328	1169	1168	1160	1060	1873	1754	885
Minerals Tons	16,112	17,055	17,093	18,210	21,626	23,057	23,020	21,791	20,519	20,436	25,234	20,238	17,950	18,030	18,126
Class 1st	473	643	642	699	726	716	659	494	572	585	660	491	582	805	489
2nd	515	415	—	—	—	—	—	—	—	—	—	—	—	—	—
3rd	38,550	54,162	51,305	55,072	52,069	49,709	45,626	53,688	35,878	37,917	37,891	37,233	42,853	51,451	48,713
*Season tickets	220	328	351	331	362	312	309	13,575	4949	806	7	15	9	8	8
Pass. train miles															
Goods train miles															
Mixed train miles	30,747	31,645	33,206	32,637	32,631	30,228	30,636	32,714	31,363	29,314	28,631	27,569	28,011	31,632	28,798
Locos (own, not hire)	3	3	3	3	3	3	3	3	3	3	3	3	3	3	3
Carriages Total	10	12	16†	16	16	16	16	16	16	16	16	16	16	16	16
Wagons Merchandise	147	134	137	137	145	147	148	148	148	147	147	147	147	147	147
Other Wagons											1	1	1	1	1
Other Vehicles															1

	1907	1908	1909	1910	1911	1912	1913	1919	1920	1921	
Cost hire r/stock	–	–	–	–	–	–	–	–	–	–	No Returns
Maint. Works and Way	432	350	391	413	353	299	333	–	–	–	
Loco Power	972	1022	884	842	925	687	735	–	–	–	
C & W maint. and repair	353	339	372	293	286	87	225	–	–	–	
Traffic Expenses	912	894	853	782	800	678	675	–	–	–	
Legal Expenses	14	15	67	27	24	43	27	–	–	–	
Profit/Loss on Wkg.	535	466	177	(10)	(165)	220	(205)	(62)	(246)	(1208)‡	
Merchandise Tons	799	532	553	535	797	827	1784	4203	2550	185	Tons General Merchandise
							4353	–	–	–	Coal
Minerals Tons	18,235	17,724	18,523	16,915	14,364	14,422	7017	7297	7588	7320	Other Minerals
Class 1st	497	347	343	245	285	174	226				
Class 2nd	–	–	–	–	–	–	–				Closed to Passengers
Class 3rd	44,141	41,394	43,632	40,549	40,351	23,419	23,399				
*Season tickets	24	25	3	1	1	1	2				
Pass. train miles											
Goods train miles								7987	7054	5330	Goods Goods Goods
Mixed train miles	30,072	31,565	31,907	27,423	27,471	18,516	18,800				
Locos (own, not hire)	3	1	4	4	4	4	3	2	2	2	
Carriages			8	8	8	8	8	8	8	8	Carriages of uniform class
			5	5	5	5	5	5	5	5	Carriages of composite class
Total	16	15	13	13	13	13	13	13	13	13	
Wagons Merchandise	143	143	118	117	117	92	98	197	107	95	= 82 Opens + 13 Mineral Merchandise and Mineral wagons (slate, etc.)
Other Wagons	4	4	4	4	4	12	29	34	39	18	Rail and Timber trucks / Miscellaneous wagons
Other Vehicles	1	1	1	1	1	1	4	1	–	–	Service Vehicles

*Mainly Quarrymen's Seasons paid for by the quarry in certain cases.
†13 fitted continuous brake and 'three exceptionally small coaches'.
‡Debit carried forward 1921 £58,919.

REFERENCES

1. Summary in 'BRADSHAW'S RAILWAY MANUAL', (1906) p.298 omits detail but is useful simplified reference.
2. 'THE TIMES' (11th May, 1878).
3. 'THE MANCHESTER & MILFORD RAILWAY' (J.S. Holden) p.53–4, etc., 71–2.
4. 'RAILWAY MEN OF TODAY' ('Railway Press') 21st June 1889.
5. 'LONDONDERRY SENTINEL' (11th October, 1923).
6. MT58/282 (Public Record Office).
7. Copy of original kindly supplied by A.M. Hunt.
8. Abandoned Mines Plan No. 7063.
9. XM/623/328 (Caernarvon Record Office).
10. TOPOGRAPHICAL DICTIONARY OF WALES – 4th Edition (Samuel Lewis).
11. 'THE MINING JOURNAL' (1884) p.355 and 555.
12. 'ENGINEERING' Vol. 24 (23rd November, 1877).
13. Construction wrongly attributed to Brown, Marshalls & Co. in First Edition due to drawing in Metropolitan Carriage & Wagon Co. Ltd. archives being unmarked.
14. I am indebted to John L.H. Bate, Michael Seymour and A.J. Padley for suggestions in this respect.
15. 'RAILWAY & TRAVEL MONTHLY' (November 1917) p.284.
16. 'THE FESTINIOG RAILWAY' (J.I.C. Boyd) Vol. 2, p.335.
17. See also 'RAILWAY MAGAZINE' (1917) p.38.
18. Light Railway Investigation Committee Report, 1921.

PORTMADOC, BEDDGELERT & SOUTH SNOWDON RAILWAY
(Gauge 1 ft 11½ in.)

Incorporated by Act: 1 Edward VII chap. 262 of 17th August, 1901 (following Agreement of 18th March, 1901 with Portmadoc, Croesor & Beddgelert Tram Railway Co. for sale to new undertaking and dissolution of P.C.&B.T.R. Co.).
Act: 4 Edward VII Ed. Cap. 194 of 15th August, 1904. Arrangements with N.W.N.G. Railways and extensions in Caernarvon district.

The above two Acts to be treated as one in future.

Agreement: of 26th August, 1904 with N.W.N.G. Railways. Powers of the N.W.N.G. Railways Order of 3rd November, 1900 (Extension to Beddgelert) to pass to P.B.&S.S.R. by means of:
Light Railway Order: of 24th October, 1906. Beddgelert Light Railway Extension.
Light Railway Order: of 8th July, 1908. Extension to Caernarvon.
Light Railway Order: of 27th July, 1908. Extension to Bettws-y-Coed.

Opened: Partially constructed section built between 1906 and 1910 unofficially in use before 1911 for timber etc. purposes. Total length partially constructed at this time, 4 m. 60 ch.
  Never officially opened, nor extended in operational length.
Closed: Acquired by Welsh Highland Railway (Light Railway) Co. 1st January, 1922 as part of new system.
Registered Office: Llanberis (1914). 4 Broad Street Place, London, E.C.3 and Clark Street, Dolgarrog (1919) – offices of North Wales Power & Traction Co. Ltd.
Length: 12 m. 45 ch. authorised. 4 m. 60 ch. built.
Capital: See text.

The Official Returns of 1919 (last available) state that '4 m. 60 ch. is finished and being worked by horse traction: construction is at present in abeyance'.

Historical Summary

1901 Agreement with P.C.&B.T.R. Co. to sell to P.B.&S.S.R. for £10,000, when enacted (18th March). P.B.&S.S.R. incorporated by Act for line Beddgelert to Portmadoc along east bank of River Glaslyn (17th August).
1904 Act making arrangements with N.W.N.G.R. Co., and Extension to Caernarvon (15th August). Borrowing Powers of 1901, repealed but renewed. (Note: North Wales Power Act of same date transfers authority to build Power Stations to North Wales Power Co., thus leaving P.B.&S.S.R. Co. as but a railway undertaking.)

N.W.N.G.R. Co. (Beddgelert Light Railway Extension Order): these powers pass to P.B.&S.S.R. Co. (24th August).

Applications to work P.B.&S.S.R., both in this year and in 1905, as a Light Railway, prove unsuccessful (November).

1906 P.B.&S.S.R. Co. obtains Light Railway Order which also covers the former N.W.N.G. Co. Order for the Beddgelert Light Railway (24th October). Authority to abandon part of line then built under N.W.N.G. Rlys. Order of 1900 and build new line in lieu authorised by P.B.&S.S.R. Act of 1901, and to complete it by 24th October, 1909. (This date was not achieved.) Works begin north and south of Beddgelert but are abandoned due to shortage of capital.

P.B.&S.S.R. Co. press Board of Trade for Light Railway Order for section Snowdon–Bettws-y-Coed and lines in the Pass of Aberglaslyn (this would include a line linking the N.W.N.G. Rlys. and P.B.&S.S.R. termini in Beddgelert).

1907 Powers to build Beddgelert–Bettws-y-Coed line, lapse.

1908 Extension to Caernarvon: Order. Revival of lapsed powers extended to 7th July, 1913, with powers to extend and deviate (8th July).

Application to work as Light Railway given (27th July).

Authorisation to build a line connecting Beddgelert, Bettws-y-Coed and Capel Curig (originally possessed by the Snowdon & Bettws-y-Coed Light Railway) passes to P.B.&S.S.R. C. (27th July).

1909 Powers of 1906 Light Railway Order lost due to non-completion.

1913 All powers lapse; no lines completed.

[1914 See N.W.N.G.R. Co. summary for proposals for combined development].

Under the terms of the P.B.&S.S. Act of 17th August, 1901, it is convenient to deal with the position of the Portmadoc, Croesor & Beddgelert Tram Railway Co. first, as being the only portion of the scheme where some tangible evidence of railway (strictly, tramway) existed. The 18th March, 1901 Agreement between three parties, namely, the Tram Co., H.W.A. Littledale who had succeeded to the £8,000 mortgage) and Messrs. George Edward Heyl Dia and William John Glover (together) provided for the sale of the undertaking to the P.B.&S.S.R. for £10,000. Russell was not included in the arrangements as he was to be paid off. It was said that 'there had never been any passenger traffic over the railways of the Croesor Co. and the present condition and state of repair thereof are not such as to justify or allow the conveyance of passengers thereon and it is expedient that the said railway should be repaired and improved as by this Act provided'. Under sections 6, 7 and 8, the Croesor undertaking was acquired, dissolved and transferred in that order!

Working agreements between the P.B. & S.S. and N.W.N.G. Railways Co., Cambrian, Festiniog and Snowdon Mountain Tramroad Co. were envisaged.

The Agreement for the purchase of the Portmadoc, Croesor & Beddgelert Tram Railway Co. was to be completed within twelve months of the Act, and this being done, the Company would be dissolved. A Receiver was appointed to wind up its affairs – currently he was John Edward Jones. As to working over the Cambrian crossing, the Cambrian was to have control of this . . . an important factor in later years.

The new company was also given powers as a supplier of electrical power, a feature which was to link the later Welsh Highland Railway with some curious bed-fellows. This involved the building of dams and generating stations, and power to negotiate with local authorities for the supply of electric power.

George Edward Heyl Dia, William John Glover and Samuel Oppenheim were the first-named subscribers. Two railways were to be built;

Railway No. 1. 5 fur. 1 ch. long from the existing Portmadoc, Croesor & Beddgelert Tram Railway Co. at Penymount to a point on the bed of the old Gorseddau Railway 87 ft to the east of the frontage of the Queen's Hotel, Portmadoc.

Railway No. 2. 7 m. 1 fur. 4 ch. 15 yd. long commencing with junction of Portmadoc, Croesor & Beddgelert Tram Railway Co. at a point 3 m. 4 fur. from its commencement to terminate in a field at Bwlch Mwyalchen farm on the east bank of the Glaslyn river at the point of the Llyn Gwynant outlet.

The gauge was 1 ft 11½ in. with powers to increase to standard gauge. Powers for three years were obtained to purchase lands etc., and seven years for the completion of the line. As regards the one proposed tunnel in the Aberglaslyn Pass, this was to be restricted in length and no tipping of rubbish was to be allowed in the Pass or on the Glaslyn banks, though permission might be given for additional tunnels and tipping availability. Festiniog merchandise rates were to apply. If a junction was made with that Railway, a signal box, points etc., would be provided at the expense of the promoters.

Separate regulations applied to the electrical side of the business, and accounts were to be kept apart.

As to the Tram Co.'s powers to build an extension to Borth-y-gest (never exercised), the plans did in fact propose an electrified single line with three chain passing loops extending from Black Rock Sands, near Criccieth, extending through Morfa Bychan, round Borth Bay and, following the proposed extension of the Portmadoc & Croesor Railway (Act 1865) would have tunnelled through the headland to make end-on junction with the original Croesor Tramway. The line would have used the existing Croesor Tramway to the junction where a new line to Beddgelert via Aberglaslyn would have branched off. Then following almost exactly the abandoned route of the North Wales Narrow Gauge Railways General Undertaking it would, however, have reached Llyn Gwynant by keeping south of Llyn Dinas to its terminal on the east shore of Llyn Gwynant. There was to be an overhead power line thence to Nant Gwynant Generating Station.

Like the Portmadoc, Beddgelert & Rhyd-Ddu scheme of 1898, a branch from north of the Beddgelert Siding (Railway No. 1) to terminate on the course of the old Gorseddau Railway, was empowered.

The Engineers were Messrs. Bennett & Ward Thomas, and A.M. Fowler. Though it would have been advantageous to apply for a Light Railway Order, the inclusion of electrical works, for which an Act of Parliament was required, ruled this out.

The Festiniog Railway, fearful for the intrusion of the new line on their preserve at Portmadoc, was given little or no time to consider the proposition in full. To protect their interests, they lodged an objection which resulted in the clauses provided to protect them. This was fortunate, for the Festiniog was in no position to pay further expense at this time; even the Directors' salary cheques for the month of February 1901 had been sent out with the request that they be not presented for payment until the month end and so avoid over-drawing on the Bank!

The electrical work in connection with the Act was, over a period of time and with additional time permitted, carried out. Nothing was done about the railway, but the scheme has been presented in some detail because almost every aspect of it was part of the foundation for a later scheme. We may envisage the railway, if built, as similar in conception to the Manx Electric Railway.

On 15th August, 1904 (the same date as another Act affecting the Portmadoc, Beddgelert & South Snowdon Railway, about to be described) the North Wales Electric Power Act was passed. This transferred the authority to build Power Stations, dams, etc., from the railway to a new body, and left the Railway Company entirely as a transport undertaking.

To give additional time for the completion of the above work, the Company obtained another Act (15th August, 1904) with Harper Bros., Consultants, and Sir Douglas Fox & Partners as Engineers. Three new lines were to be built; all in the County of Caernarvon. A Bristol contractor (name unknown), was said to be at work in 1904.

Railway No. 1. 2 m. 3 fur. 9 ch. long, from a junction with the North Wales Narrow Gauge Railways 70 yards south of the Dinas Junction station Goods Shed to terminate on the west bank of the Afon Seiont (the river in Caernarvon town) approximately opposite the town Gas Works – which lay on the east bank of the river.

Railway No. 2. 3 fur. 5½ ch. long being an extension from the terminus of Railway No. 1, involving a crossing of the river and terminating on the quays northeast of the Seiont.

A 'Railway No. 3' is shown in the Plans but not covered by the Act, which would have continued along the west bank of the Seiont to a point opposite the east bank terminal.

The feature of this Act was the clearest intention of the promoters so far. It might be seen that to all intents and purposes, the North Wales Narrow Gauge Railways and the Portmadoc, Beddgelert & South Snowdon Railway were soon to merge (if not into one undertaking), under one management. How otherwise did the Snowdon Railway (which after all at this stage was a horse tramway between Portmadoc and Croesor) intend to reach Caernarvon? At this time one might only conjecture, for the North Wales Narrow Gauge Railways held the key to the section between Beddgelert and South Snowdon and there were no plans at all for a railway to cross the Glaslyn and link the Snowdon Railway with the North Wales Narrow Gauge Railways' Beddgelert Extension. The route between South Snowdon and Dinas Junction was the N.W.N.G. Railways' main line but clearly that Company was now willing to permit the Snowdon to extend on its behalf into Caernarvon itself. This was a desirable and positive goal, for its present terminus at Dinas Junction involved interchange of passengers and freight – not to mention being at the behest of the London & North Western Railway – and was seen to be but a temporary and embarrassing arrangement for which a speedy remedy was sought.

Railway No. 1 made much use of that section nearer Caernarvon of the former Nantlle Railway which, upon becoming part of the Carnarvonshire Railway had gone into the Euston Empire. Parts of its sinuous course were abandoned when an improved site was found. Even the old tunnel at Coed Helen would be put to use. There was a nominal junction between this line and Railway No. 2 in the woodlands on the steep west bank of the river; here Railway No. 2 branched off eastwards to cross the river on the same site of a bridge as had been used by the Nantlle Railway but which had by then been demolished. Railway No. 3 (shown on the Plans but not empowered in the Act) would have continued for about 3 furlongs along the west bank. Once across the river, Railway No. 2 would have passed the Gas Work's entrance, run up alongside the L.N.W.R.'s branch down on to the quays and passed to a terminus beneath the Castle walls.

Five years were allowed for the completion of the work and a considerable portion of the Act was given over to clauses protecting the L.N.W.R.'s line between Caernarvon and Dinas Junction – as would be expected! Section 24 permits the Snowdon and N.W.N.G. companies to enter into fully integral working agreements respecting the proposed and all existing lines. Although no work was done under this Act, it laid the foundations for closer relationships between the two companies, first to be revealed in the N.W.N.G. Railways Light Railway Order of 6th June, 1905.

Following an Agreement between the Railways Co. and the Snowdon Co. dated 26th August, 1904 – and so rapidly following on the Act just discussed – the powers given to the Railways Co. under a Light Railway Order of 3rd November, 1900 were given to the Snowdon Co. This Agreement was ratified by a Light Railway Order dated 24th October, 1906 which allowed three years for completion of the work specified. The project in question was the extension of the North Wales Narrow Gauge Railways' line from its unsatisfactory terminus at Rhyd-Ddu southwards to Beddgelert, where junction could be made with the new railway intended to be built northwards off the old Croesor Tramway from Portmadoc ending at Llyn Gwynant. This was known as the 'Beddgelert Extension'.

In the period between 3rd November, 1900 and 24th October, 1906 (owing to shortage of funds), very little had been done on the Extension by the N.W.N.G. but in view of the many schemes for railways in the area about which *nothing* was ever done, it is surprising to record that at least a minimal amount of work took place; this was mainly immediately north of Beddgelert. To the P.B.&S.S. Engineers (Sir Douglas Fox & Partners) it was clearly of unsuitable grade and curve*; the 24th October, 1906 Order permitted the Snowdon Co. to abandon this unfinished work. More of tactical importance was authority to make a new line from the Goat Hotel, Beddgelert (extending from the N.W.N.G. Extension 6 furlongs 1 chain) to pass behind the south-west corner of the Hotel, pass south of Gelert's Grave and make end-on junction with the P.B.&S.S.R. Act of 17th August, 1901, on the east bank of the River Glaslyn and 350 yards south of Sygun Terrace, Beddgelert. The Order gave full working agreement with the N.W.N.G.R. and to Caernarvonshire County Council the right to advance capital.

Though no work was being done under the P.B.&S.S. Act of 17th August, 1901, work was being done under the 24th October, 1906 Order. This was almost entirely based on Beddgelert, which became one centre for activities.

To the north the line was re-surveyed and a number of sharp curves on stiff gradients only suited to electric traction was eased to provide a better start for northbound trains from Beddgelert (under the later Welsh Highland Order, the same length of line was abandoned almost completely in favour of a longer and more sinuous course involving heavier earthworks but easing curves and grade still more). To the south, the cutting and tunnel behind the Goat Hotel was completed, and a stone overbridge crossing the Beddgelert – Portmadoc road was made. In the field between this bridge and the Glaslyn, the abutments for an occupation bridge beneath the line, and stone culverting to take the Glaslyn's flood water away, were built. Some of this work stood unfinished and unused for over sixty years.

The Light Railway Commissioners' Enquiry at Beddgelert on 3rd February, 1904 re the Extension (or 'Beddgelert Light Railway' as they refer to it) reveals that though Mr. W.A. Harper was dubbed

---

*and especially for the adoption of steam traction which seemed more likely than the proposed electrification!

'Engineer' to the scheme, he continued to rely on Randall Casson (solicitor of Breese, Jones & Casson, Portmadoc) to act for him. Harper and Fox both agreed the proposed course under the P.B. & S.S. Act of 17th August, 1901 was impossible and some work on the site, working far into the night, produced detail alterations in time for a February 1904 Enquiry. The Lord Lieutenant of the County (Greaves) was involved and the National Trust was concerned for conservation of the Aberglaslyn Pass. A revised idea was for a line '200 yd. from the Goat Hotel, Beddgelert, round a corner and out of sight of the hotel windows' which would forestall the proprietor's early opposition to the new railway (this idea would pave the way for the 24th October, 1906 Order). So little conception had some correspondents involved that they imagined the junction between a line from Beddgelert and a line up to Llyn Gwynant would meet (on paper at least) inside the Aberglaslyn Tunnel!!¹

A contractor's railway was laid from the road overbridge south of Beddgelert to a point on the formation at Tyn-y-Coed; some formation had been completed between there and Rhyd-Ddu when powers lapsed.

The contractor's track was the T-rail and chair used on the Croesor and elsewhere, and a clue as to the source might be found in the abandonment and lifting of the Gorseddau line during the 1890s, which would explain the availability of such material, possibly from a local scrap dealer. Certainly there were flooded sections of abandoned course with this track in them still to be seen during the 1960s.

[All the foregoing was done under the auspices of The Portmadoc, Beddgelert & South Snowdon Railway (Beddgelert Light Railway Extension) Order, 1906. North Wales Narrow Gauge Railways powers to build the Extension had lapsed on 3rd August, 1903; three years were now permitted to complete the intended new programme.]

As to the 1906 Order, the bridge south of Beddgelert was to be of stone and the surrounding embankments etc. were to be planted out with trees, shrubs etc. All this was duly done. An interesting clause was that no station was to be built within a mile of the Goat Hotel except for one which would have been near the junction with the proposed Llyn Dinas line on the *east* bank of the Glaslyn, where there might be 'a platform for passenger traffic only'. Objections from the hotel must have been completely overcome when the Welsh Highland scheme was prepared, for the Beddgelert station was only a little distance from the hotel yard!

The gauge was to be the usual 1 ft 11½ in and steam or electric power was permitted.

Work under the Order tended to be carried out in a desultory fashion and during this somewhat spasmodic progress, some more statutory advance was accomplished in the shape of two more Orders during 1908, neither of which was destined to make any visible difference to the actual construction or to be seen in the field!

It remains to look briefly at the Orders just mentioned, dated 8th and 27th July respectively, and the second gave authority to work the P.B. & S.S.R. schemes of its Acts of 1901 and 1904 as Light Railways; (it was only the second Order of that year, a matter of nineteen days, and as it concerns the immediately previous Orders, it may be taken out of date order). The real purpose was – once more – to give authority to the P.B. & S.S.R. to construct new railways which had earlier been granted to other undertakings within the same parentage. In this case the North Wales Power & Traction Co. Ltd. had in November 1903 applied for and obtained a Light Railway Order to build the Railways Nos. 1 & 2 about to be described. (Management, Secretariat and Registered Office was identical with that of the Snowdon Co.) They would have made junction with the empowered P.B. & S.S.R.'s new railways near Beddgelert and underline the extraordinary attractions of a narrow gauge line between Beddgelert and Bettws-y-Coed: such a line had first been part of the N.W.N.G.R. plan but had never materialised, even though it was part of something much longer. Now, thirty-six years later, a 'Bettws Application' (as it was called) still held its spell.

Snowdon and Bettws-y-Coed Light Railway

It is now desirable to insert another brick into the edifice now a-building! Though never a rail was laid it is part of an overall plan to sell electricity – and this lies at the back of most of this tale!

The North Wales Power & Traction Co. Ltd.'s powers of November 1903 lapsed on 3rd August, 1907 and by Order of 27th July, 1908 the P.B. & S.S.R. took them over. Though never built, the railway is well worth description.

Railway No. 1.   (7 m. 2 fur. 75 ch.) from an end-on junction with the terminus of the 1901 line, along the south-east shore of Llyn Gwynant in a northerly direction parallel to and on the west side of the Beddgelert road.

The line would have tunnelled under this road near the Pen-y-Gwryd Hotel, and then swung north-east, running south of the same road to enter Capel Curig from the north-west.

Railway No. 2.   (5 m. 6 fur. 5.95 ch.) from an end-on junction with Railway No. 1 and by tunnel under land behind the Royal Hotel, Capel Curig, the property of Lord Penrhyn (the tunnel not to exceed 350 yd. length). Thence over the Nant-y-gwryd river, south-east then north-east parallel to the Beddgelert road. Then crossing the same road and the Llugwy River to enter Bettws from the north-west and north of the same road.

Five years were given for completion, and an interesting feature in view of environmental awareness in the present day, is the new protection given to the National Trust (which appears for the first time) in that overhead structures etc. in the Aberglaslyn Pass should be of such colour as the Lord Lieutenant might direct, and that all insulators must be 'of a brown colour'. All walls etc. were to have broken tops and be planted out where possible, as must be crevices etc. in retaining walls. Lord Penrhyn's property around Capel Curig was similarly guarded and he had the right to have a station provided for his hotel there on its east side, and to have a private path between the two premises. The Earl of Ancaster too (owner of the Gwydr Estate) was to have a Goods Station built for him 1 m. 4 fur. from the commencement of Railway No. 2 and he too, had the right to plant trees, saplings etc. along with Lord Penrhyn. J.W. Wyatt's land alongside Llyn Gwynant was protected by having the line laid as near as possible to the public road; all boathouses destroyed had to be replaced. In short, public awareness of amenity values was extensively covered by the Order and showed very advanced thinking. The Swallow Falls, Miners' Bridge, banks of the Llugwy, position of stations not already mentioned, the design and construction of bridges, the penalties for erecting buildings of any kind between certain points on the line, the erection of rustic screen walls to hide trains passing from the eyes of those 'standing on the southern bank of the River Llugwy' were among the ordinary and extraordinary details . . . in fact, the Company were to be considerably restricted by the Order's conditions which alone might have been sufficient to deter the promoters! As if this was not enough, there was a financial penalty clause for failure to complete by date and for every day thereafter. Harper Bros. were again the Engineers: Sir Douglas Fox & Partners, Consulting Engineers.

A Historical Summary would show the following:

1901 N.W.P. & T.C.L.: Act to build S. & B.L.R.
1903 See N.W.P. & T.C.L. 'The Bettws Application'. Powers to build railways Beddgelert – Bettws-y-Coed with a junction at P.B. & S.S. terminal at Beddgelert. (N.B. This was not the same exact situation there as another proposal for a combined P.B. & S.S. and N.W.N.G. station.)
1904 Snowdon & Bettws-y-Coed Light Railway Order obtained to reconstruct and work their lines as a Light Railway.
1907 Powers to build, lapse.
1908 Authority to build now passes to P.B. & S.S. (27th July), with continuing status of Light Railway. (Board of Trade documents define the scheme as the 'Beddgelert, Capel Curig & Bettws line').

What were all these confusing plans about, with railways running hither and thither, extending to mileages over twice that of those already in existence? The force which was promoting this complex was not always in the forefront, and stemmed from the European development of hydro-electric current generation at the time; the central body in Caernarvonshire was the North Wales Power & Traction Co. Ltd.

with headquarters at Dolgarrog, and intending to build a number of water-powered generating stations . . . not all of which came into being. The Company was a businesslike enterprise; electricity in a district where the oil lamp and candle held sway was a desirable means of improving economic and social life in North Wales. Already some quarries had deserted water power for the new force, but to make the generation viable, large quantities of electricity had to be sold. Europe had already begun the construction of light railways, electrically driven, and a growing tourist trade gave extra impetus to their existence. The same could be done in Wales. The Isle of Man had done it on a small scale, with a rail gauge of 3 feet.

The Caernarvonshire dream was of a light railway complex extending from Caernarvon, down through Beddgelert into Portmadoc (with a branch to Borth-y-gest) and out again on the Festiniog Railway to Blaenau Festiniog; it could be (with the electrical work already being done by Kellow at Croesor Quarry) that with sufficient business to justify it, even the Croesor line would be worthy of conversion . . . horse to electrical power in one step!! The long 'branch' from Beddgelert to Bettws-y-Coed would have been a desirable link, passing on its way the Cwm Dyli Generating Station. All such would be in the hands of the Power Co. and amalgamated to that end: this is foreshadowed in a note accompanying the P.B. & S.S. application for the Order they obtained on 24th October, 1906 'If this Order goes through, the P.B. & S.S. will then desire to amalgamate the three Light Railway Orders'. By Orders of 8th July and 27th July, 1908, the P.B. & S.S. would find itself with ability to build the line Dinas–Caernarvon (powers were now revived), the Beddgelert–Bettws-y-Coed line (taking over the Bettws Co. rights), and overall, having the status of a Light Railway throughout. The time permitted to achieve all this seemed ample enough . . . they had until 7th July, 1913 – but they failed to carry out any of the work. It will be seen that the problems lay at the heart of the scheme rather than with the railways themselves: the electrical side of the business (so to speak) was to fail.

Some note of urgency is clear in the volume of paper created at the Board of Trade – at this time no less than David Lloyd George is President of the Board of Trade, and the promoters intended to press their cause whilst they may have felt they would be given a sympathetic Welsh-Ear.

[The North Wales Power & Traction Co. Ltd., formed for the purpose of generating and selling electricity will have later consideration. Apart from obtaining the original Order for the Beddgelert and Bettws-y-Coed line ('The Bettws Application') in November 1903, it has little further links with this narrative save in its removal from the scheme under the North Wales Electrical Power Act of 15th August, 1904 whereby powers to build generating stations were transferred to it. Until then, such powers had been held by the P.B. & S.S. itself under its Act of 1901; the Act gave that undertaking much more authority than a pure railway company – it might not only build generating stations, sell electricity throughout Caernarvonshire, but also impound the waters of Llyn Llydaw and Llyn Teryn and use the same. The main generating station was to be at Cwm Dyli, near the junction of the Afon Glaslyn and Nant Cynnyd. In the foregoing may be sensed the basis of the Beddgelert–Bettws-y-Coed promotion.]

A non-starter though it may have been, the notice of intention to build it which appeared in the newspapers raised a storm of protest such as would occur when a motorway was planned today. Even the Local Authorities opposed it '. . . it was not needed, . . . the navvies would camp out on the banks of the Llugwy and contaminate the water supply. Fever would break out . . .'. The promoters replied that they were spending £71,000 on an electrically-worked line which would overcome the earlier objections to the N.W.N.G. scheme over the same route, as the steep gradients could easily be overcome by electric trains. As noted earlier, the National Trust was loud in its objections, and was told 'exceptional steps would be taken to screen the line from public gaze by the erection of rustic walling of character to conform to the requirements of the Bettws U.D.C.' The route would involve gradients of 1 in 19; curves of 6 chains; 50 lb. rail would allow an axle loading of 10 tons; 35 lb. a loading of 8 tons. Speeds would be limited to 20 m.p.h. or even 15 m.p.h. in places.

Public awareness was never more strong than in Edwardian days; letters in 'THE TIMES' stressed this was not a matter for the Board of Trade to decide – it should go before Parliament. Local feeling was incensed by the recent building of the Snowdon Mountain Tramroad where it had been cheated when the promoters dodged officialdom . . . it seemed that anyone might now promote a railway by going direct to the Board of Trade for a Light Railway Order, thus circumventing the risk of a Parliamentary Enquiry. But in effect, the Light Railway Commissioners were also to prove they too had standards . . . Actually, it was not so much the Beddgelert–Bettws-y-Coed section which incensed, it was the passage of the line southward from there, through the Pass of Aberglaslyn even though the promoters had promised a tunnel. Now there were rumours that the tunnel would be shorter than agreed! So it went on. Would tunnels now be obviated and rustic screens put up instead? It was quite unclear to the objectors.

Such was the sudden growth of these feelings that the Board of Trade solicitor was bound to point out that when the N.W.N.G. proposed a railway along this course a few years before, it had not met with such opposition. The Board of Trade had complied with local requests and he could find no reason to withhold the Order for the line to Bettws-y-Coed. He noted that much of the opposition came from English people with houses in the district whilst many of the residents supported the idea; Prof. W.P. Kerr of University College, London had initiated such opposition. A curious denunciation from locals was that the train 'might carry tourists through Bettws without stopping'.

The Light Railway Commissioners themselves found objections in granting an Order to a Limited Company but on being re-assured that the P.B. & S.S. was prepared to 'take over the Order' on an alteration to the borrowing powers, and also that the same was anxious 'to work if not wholly acquire the Moel Tryfan Undertaking of the N.W.N.G. Rlys. Co.', they assented.

The last word must be left to the 'NORTH WALES CHRONICLE' for 21st April, 1905; 'Snowdon will almost be encircled by electric lines in a couple of years'. It need not have worried![2]

Though space has been allotted to 'The Bettws Application' at some length, it had so many features pertaining to present-day applications that extended reference is earned. Now to return to further P.B. & S.S. schemes.

The Order of 8th July, 1908 (Light Railway Extension at Caernarvon) began by giving power to abandon Railway No. 2 of the 15th August, 1904 Act regarding a railway in Caernarvon (crossing the Seiont and ending on the east quay) and of course, not built.

Instead, two lines were to be constructed viz:

Railway No. 1.   (3 fur. 4 ch.) from a junction with the proposed line between Dinas and Caernarvon (authorised by the 1904 Act) at a point 2 m. 58 ch. north of Dinas, thence north and west along St. Helen's Road, Caernarvon, to end 103 yds. north of the Harbour Office on the east quayside.

Railway No. 2.   (6 ch.) from an end-on junction with Railway No. 1, thence west and ending at a point 42 ft north-east of the Slate Quay at Aber Ferry, Caernarvon harbour.

Three years were permitted for completion. As the line would have been virtually a street tramway along St. Helen's Road and the Quays, a speed limit of 8 m.p.h. was imposed. Another curious imposition was that the Company must 'dig up and remove the pig market of the Corporation . . . and at their own expense . . . relay the same in such other part of the Borough. . . .' Eight pounds a year were to be charged for upkeep of St. Helen's Road.

The L.N.W.R.'s harbour lines would have to be crossed on the level and de Winton's works (the firm was by then in liquidation) would have had to have temporary road access made to them during the line's construction.

No work was done under the Order.

The Orders for 1908 were regarded as the consolidation of all that had gone before. They included alterations of alignment to meet criticism of damage to the Pass of Aberglaslyn and Llyn Dinas, the easing of fears expressed by the Goat Hotel, Beddgelert, the reduction of the severe gradients and curves posed by earlier routes, the failure of previous promotions to finish work on time – or even to begin at all – and so on. The N.W.N.G. was accused of allowing the extension of time for their Order of 1900 'to lapse by inadvertence'. Long lists of company titles, dates, share capital et al passed between the Board of Trade and the Light Railway Commissioners and dismay prevailed at the complexity of it all. Details of the overhead electrical equipment had been decided even down to colour 'such as the Lord Lieutenant of Caernarvonshire may direct' for the posts, 'but the insulators must be brown'. Tunnels must not be reduced in length, walls should have serrated tops (and portions where top soil had been removed must be replanted), Scotch Fir, Broom and Bracken must be planted in the screes of the Pass and where the Company was not owner of the land, it must 'endeavour to obtain permission to plant'.[3]

None or little evidence of such feverish activity could be found then or later in the county. Little disturbance to rock or soil – save around Beddgelert as noted – reflected these activities in the Metropolis. Even what was being done had come to a halt and with the coming of the First War minds were directed away from local schemes.

[With the coming of that War, the only working line in the district which had bearing on these schemes – the North Wales Narrow Gauge line – was hard hit; there was but little passenger traffic, the tourist traffic was greatly reduced, and the system was whittled down eventually to being a slate carrier of much diminished tonnages. Ultimately, under the provisional title of 'The Portmadoc, Beddgelert & South Snowdon Railway (Light Railway) and The North Wales Narrow Gauge Railways (Light Railways) Revival and Transfer of Powers Order', an application was made to the Light Railway Commissioners in 1914, but consideration had to be postponed. A Public Enquiry was held by the Commissioners in the County Hall, Caernarvon on 18th October, 1921. This event led to the marriage of the North Wales Narrow Gauge Railways to the Portmadoc, Beddgelert & South Snowdon Railway and the ultimate birth of their sole offspring, the Welsh Highland Railway.]

The capital status of the P.B. & S.S. changed continuously as a result of Orders giving powers previously owned by other companies. It is no small wonder that, bemused by their position, the Company wrote to the Commissioners on 26th May, 1909 for clarification. They stated that share capital and borrowing powers given by the Acts of 1901 and 1904, and the Order of 1906, were amended by the Order of 1908. This resulted in a share capital of £100,000 with borrowing powers for the same amount for a railway between Portmadoc and Rhyd-Ddu via Beddgelert and including a line between Dinas and Caernarvon. For the authorised railway between Beddgelert and Bettws-y-Coed additional amounts were sanctioned: viz.: Capital £90,000 and borrowing powers £30,000.

From the Commissioners' reply it was clear that to remedy their financial embarrassment, the Company was considering an application for a Treasury Grant, for which they were told they would have to enter into a contract for the completion and working of their lines with an existing railway. The Commissioners felt that in view of the impoverished state of the North Wales Narrow Gauge Railways, the Treasury would hardly accept that Company to be 'an existing railway', and a free grant would not necessarily guarantee that the N.W.N.G. could complete the unfinished portions of the authorised P.B. & S.S. Rather, the Commissioners felt, it would be preferable to make arrangements with the Cambrian or L.N.W.R. companies! It might too be acceptable if arrangements were made with the Power Co., who would take up share capital under a different section of the Light Railways Act. Under the Act of 1901 and the Order of 1906, local councils were permitted to advance money to a total of £32,000. Additionally, under the Order of 1908 the Caernarvon County Council was permitted to advance a further £10,000, but under a resolution of that Council this second advance was allocated to the proposed line from Beddgelert to Bettws-y-Coed! As the Snowdon Co. was only interested in completing its partially constructed Portmadoc–Rhyd-Ddu section, this was not the sort of reply to give them much-needed encouragement; worse, the final paragraph of the Commissioners' reply reminded them that five months hence, on 24th October, 1909, the period for completion of the Beddgelert–Rhyd-Ddu section would expire.

Very little is known about the origins of this 'Electrical Empire' with the N.W.P. & T. Company at its heart and railways (among other businesses) along its periphery, but a strong influence must have been the concept of Gethin Jones, and it may be to him alone that the source of the idea is due. Jones was, if nothing else, a man of imagination; he conceived two tramways to the top of Carnedd Llewelyn (one from Aber and one from Dolgarrog), a line from Llanberis to Roman Bridge and a link from the N.W.N.G. to the interchange of Cambrian and Festiniog Railways at Minffordd. The latter would have extended to Beddgelert from Rhyd-Ddu, passed north and east of the village, through the Pass of Aberglaslyn and thence via Llanfrothen. And all this at least a decade *before* the P.B. & S.S.R. came about: furthermore, when that Company received powers to build the Beddgelert – Bettws link, he urged them to extend the line to Corwen, much as the original N.W.N.G. intention: Penmachno might have been served by a branch.

In partnership with others, and known as Gwalia, he and they planned various enterprises ranging from the collection of water, the generating of electricity to the building of electric railways. It seems that when the Welsh partners' knowledge had been fully exploited, the other partners may have abandoned them for another and more promising connection. It was Gethin Jones' view that the P.B. & S.S.R. was simply the embodiment of Harper Bros. and Bruce Peebles & Co. Ltd. of Edinburgh, who dictated policy, especially in regards to the N.W.P. & T. Co.'s promotion of the Beddgelert–Bettws line.

The partnership called Gwalia produced a printed pamphlet in January 1901 dubbed 'The Cataract Park & Tramway Scheme' with which they tried to interest the L.N.W.R. Company (the site of this scheme is not precisely clear, but the L.N.W.R. was being encouraged

The following pictures were taken during the construction of the P.B.&S.S.R. Beddgelert-Nantmor section prior to the abandonment of the work c.1908; all the pictures are thought to be dated in 1906.

(Courtesy NEI Peebles Ltd.)

Contractor's temporary track at the southern end of the short tunnel on the south side of Beddgelert station site (note the stub points). Abandoned by 1909, the tunnel was later used by the Welsh Highland Railway.

The overbridge south of The Goat Hotel, Beddgelert, a feature which was completed. This portion of the civil engineering work was never incorporated into the Welsh Highland Railway. This view looks southwards.

Two short tunnels in the Pass of Aberglaslyn; formation work beyond the second tunnel has yet to be started. Conservationists had tried in vain to prevent a railway threading the Pass.

The mouth of the southernmost of the Aberglaslyn tunnels, showing the structure gauge frame mounted on a skip chassis. At this time it is probable that the bore had not penetrated to the northern mouth.

This embankment is built from excavations taken from the tunnel of the previous picture with the underbridge showing the skills of both bricklayer and mason. These bridges were built before the embnkment-work reached them.

The cutting north of Nantmor being worked from the southern end. Material obtained from here was used for embankment-work for some distance to the south.

The remaining scenes show civil engineering sites between the time of abandonment and the present day.

Pitt's Head road overbridge, looking north. This feature had been completed before work ceased. *J.I.C. Boyd*

The abandoned works at a distance south of Pitt's Head *c*.1920; this was the length worked for forestry during the First War. *C.R. Clinker*

Waterlogged cutting north of Beddgelert (not used by the Welsh Highland Railway) looking south in April 1971.   *J.I.C. Boyd*

Welsh Highland (*left*) and P.B.&S.S. (*right*) routes climb side-by-side northwards out of Beddgelert, the less-steeply-inclined W.H.R. on the west side of the cutting. The embankment route was never used. Photographed in April 1971.   *J.I.C. Boyd*

Contractor's track of Croesor Tramway-type materials still lay in a flooded, unfinished cutting
north of Beddgelert in March 1957. *J.M. Lloyd*

Reaching out from the south side of Beddgelert, the road bridge and unfinished embankment
were to carry the intended electric railway east to cross the Glaslyn, but these works never
carried rails; March 1969. *J.I.C. Boyd*

Bruce Peebles & Co. made an exhaustive photographic record of their products, including many components for the P.B.&S.S.R. locomotives. Here are portions of the vertical traction motor for the Three-Phase system which never came into existence. Photographs of a completed locomotive have not survived. *(per Dr John Manners)*

to build a station, suggesting it was near the site of the later Dolgarrog Halt). There is also mention of a 'Park & Carnedd Llewelyn Tramway Scheme' which was promoted after Gethin Jones' meteorological researches proved there was far less mist on that mountain compared with Snowdon – this was during 1902/3. There was, at the same time, a Power Scheme, and these enterprises were not to interfere with each other; reservoirs were to be constructed at Eigiau and Cedryn and the tramway was designed not to interfere with that work.

Transactions (of which no facts are given) led to 'the whole estate and the whole of our schemes pertaining to it are handed over exclusively to the Power Co. . . . although the Power Co. do not own the summit of Carnedd Llewelyn, everything pertaining to the tramway and the summit belongs to them and they have the right of Railway and Boat connection in the Vale' (of Conway), 'Old Tramway site to Cwm Eigiau' (the abandoned Eigiau Tramway) 'power for working all facilities connected with the Park-Tramway Scheme'.

Geographically, these schemes are connected with the Conway Valley; such documentary evidence as survives is not always supported by maps; the whole is only part of what might appear to be a complex intrigue, about which only one side of the picture is known, and much of it is bound up with the N.W.P.&T. Co.'s acquisition of land and competitors in order to obtain the sales monopoly of its output. Nor can it be overlooked that records of this period have always been said to have been destroyed by the Dolgarrog authorities, but more cannot be read into this. Certain it is however, that Gethin Jones allowed his schemes, during 1903, to be revealed to the N.W.P.&T. Co. in return for what he expected would be a gentlemanly arrangement, gave them details of mines etc. around the south of Snowdon, informed them on the current position of the unfinished schemes around Beddgelert, of the situation of the Festiniog Railway and district slate quarries: he took Harper's representatives wherever he (Jones) was instructed, on the assumption he would be recognised. Jones maintained that the original P.B.&S.S.R. idea simply to build a tramway from Beddgelert to Llyn Gwynant to serve their proposed Power Station, 'would never pay unless it was extended to Bettws-y-Coed, and if extended, would tapp (sic) the L.N.W.R. system and the north sea coast tourist district . . .'. He also advocated 'tapping the Great Western Railway by extending to Corwen'.[4]

Whether Gethin Jones' faith in mankind ever fully recovered seems doubtful; whether he was one among many who were perhaps victims of a confidence trick to obtain local information and acquire rights is almost certain. Forty years ago, such industrial concerns who came into this part of Wales seldom enjoyed an unsullied local reputation by those who recalled their arrival. Such is the way of things.

The skirmishing around by the Snowdon Co. and the enquiries it was making for assistance from various sources, did not reveal what had been happening in the background. To find out why work finally faltered and stopped, and how the remains of the construction work and the unused powers of the various companies interwoven in the affray were put to further use, an Investigation Committee was set up. It found that the position was:

1. The Portmadoc, Beddgelert & South Snowdon Railway was financed by the North Wales Power & Traction Co. The Power Co. was the only shareholder in the Railway Co. Preliminary enquiries to the Manager of the P.B.&S.S. in November 1907 by Johnathan Davies of Davies Bros., slate merchants, Portmadoc (destined to become the Chairman of the Investigation Committee), revealed that 'the P.B.&S.S. was trying to complete the line but the position of the money market . . . is a serious obstacle'.

2. The P.B.&S.S. was a 'front'; the Power Co. did in fact obtain its Acts, its Powers, made all its purchases and completed construction. All Railway expenses were met by the Power Co. until such time as the Board of Trade passed the Railway for traffic, when the Power Co. would receive payment in shares. A list of Power Co. expenses was tendered up to 18th February, 1909.

3. By early 1909 the Power Co. was unable to finance the Railway Co. any further. In the private opinion of Aitchison (Manager of the P.B.&S.S.) the Power Co. had used its assets wastefully, and it was no wonder there was a shortage of money.

4. The Power Co. was now looking round for means of financing the completion of the P.B.&S.S. without having to raise the money itself. It would however co-operate with others who might find the capital to finish the work.

5. The basic fact of inability to finance completion was then made known publicly by the power Co. but details were unknown, even to Aitchison. In 1909, several Local Authorities (among them the Caernarvon Harbour Trustees, the Caernarvon County Council, and other local bodies) had formed a Special Committee to investigate the matter which ultimately entitled itself the 'Portmadoc Beddgelert & Caernarvon Light Railway Committee' (or Joint or Investigation Committee) being made up of various representatives of all interested parties.

6. The first meeting was in Portmadoc during February 1909 to consider the unfinished work known as the 'Beddgelert Railway'. It was followed by a Conference on 25th February 'to consider the affairs of the Beddgelert Railway'. By now, 'the Railway' was understood by all to include not only the P.B.&S.S. link between Beddgelert and the Croesor tramway, but Beddgelert to Rhyd-Ddu and further, a line from Dinas Junction to Caernarvon.

7. The physical position of the P.B.&S.S. in the February was given by Aitchison:

Between Croesor Junction and the south end of the Aberglaslyn tunnel all work, fencing and drainage had been done. No rails or ballast had been laid. No bridges were in, but the latter had been delivered and were lying at Portmadoc. The south end of the long tunnel was finished. The north half required completion. From the north tunnel end to the east bank bridge abutment opposite Beddgelert the formation was complete. The other abutment was ready and the bridge also lay at Portmadoc. The link from there to Beddgelert station was done 'except for a big bank which will pass across the meadow, the material for which will have to come from a point between Beddgelert and Rhyd-Ddu'. The line could be opened 'at little cost as far as Nantmor'. A lot of materials lay on the site; a small amount had been sold to the Festiniog Railway.

8. Aitchison stressed, for the information of the Committee, that there was no connection between the P.B. & S.S. and N.W.N.G. concerns, save that agreement was there for the N.W.N.G. to work the P.B. & S.S. lines when open, with N.W.N.G. stock etc.

9. Aitchison's position was tenuous. He was acting for the N.W.N.G., P.B. & S.S. and Power Companies as Manager and Engineer. The Power Co. had asked him to negotiate a means to complete the P.B. & S.S. Aitchison's involvement had reached a stage where he was at odds with his employers, he was likely to lose his position with the Snowdon Co. as they were cutting down on expenses, and he might have to take the Power Co. to court on certain matters. Therefore if he attended the Committee by invitation, it would be in a private capacity as a Civil Engineer only.

The 1909–11 years were slow and painful: the Local Authorities were each hesitant to commit themselves and waited to see who would take initiative; each had an axe to grind, and it was not the same axe. Authorities interested in keeping full employment in slate quarries in the Croesor Valley, for instance, were not especially worried about the link to Beddgelert; the P.B. & S.S. had bought land in anticipation of opening the extension from Dinas to Caernarvon, but powers had lapsed – The Harbour Trustees were anxious to see this scheme revived and the land bought at the harbour-side put to use. This would not interest the ratepayers in Croesor. Davies' job as Chairman was unenviable.

By 1911 the preparations were as complete as they could be. There was an air of dis-interest, and it seemed impossible to find dates when all the local representatives could meet together and neither Portmadoc nor Caernarvon suited some as a venue. Prominent industrialists and landowners already had their hands full. However, in January 1912, a "Joint Committee" meeting made some progress. Noel Humphreys of Chester* was by then the 'Secretary pro tem' of the P.B. & S.S. and attended as the representative of that Railway and the Power Co. He had no connection with the Railways Co. He stated his principals were

*a participant in the Gwalia negotiations.

ready to sell their interests for cash and emphasised that Aitchison's earlier recommendation that they be sold for shares in a new concern was no longer acceptable. In order to qualify for a Treasury Loan under the Light Railway Act, they had got the L.N.W.R. to agree to construct, finish and work the line so long as it did not have to finance it. Consultations with Frank Ree, the L.N.W.R. General Manager, had dragged on owing to his ill health, hence delay in calling a meeting. The Snowdon Co. offered for sale:

1. Land at Caernarvon Harbour.
2. The Croesor Railway (cost £10,000) which had been 'relaid and remetalled and was now being worked by horse traffic'.
3. The work done on the line and fencing.
4. The unused Orders for a line Beddgelert–Rhyd-Ddu and Portmadoc–Beddgelert still in force (as they would be until 1913). [The Extension to Caernarvon powers had lapsed.]

At the meeting it was suggested that the G.W.R. should take over both Festiniog and North Wales Narrow Gauge lines and complete the link. The first step, however, was for the Committee to open negotiations with J.C. Russell who, as Receiver of the N.W.N.G., was virtually the only person who might decree one way or another. Meanwhile Humphreys added that rails and bridge materials on site in 1908 had subsequently been sold.

The stumbling block now proved to be Russell, who would not come to terms. This impasse was cleared by his death in late 1911, but the news that Aitchison would become Receiver from 15th January, 1912 was not available to the meeting of that month and Humphreys had to add from Old Bank Buildings, Chester that:

1. He could confirm the L.N.W.R. would construct and work the line as a Light Railway.
2. Russell's recent death afforded an opportunity . . . for a complete scheme for completion of the Light Railways.
3. Mr. Lake, the N.W.N.G. Railway's Chairman, was willing to bring his Company into the scheme. He was just waiting for Aitchison to come back from holiday. (August 1912.)
4. Success depended on all local authorities being prepared to come in and finance the venture (as they were permitted to do under the Light Railway Act). Finance depended on them.
5. He suggested their title should now be the 'Caernarvon–Portmadoc Light Railway Investigation Committee'.

He was able to add that the N.W.N.G. line was operating at a profit 'and earning sufficient to pay the Debenture Interest', and that the P.B. & S.S. was operating at a profit as between Portmadoc and Croesor. He and Aitchison were ready to attend the Committee on invitation.

Breese & George were made solicitors to the Committee. They were later to be closely involved in local railway matters.*

Davies, the Chairman, continued his investigations. For some reason the proposal of the L.N.W.R. was not entirely acceptable to the Committee. Davies approached the Cambrian to see if they would work and construct – and find one third of the Capital too if asked – but Williamson their Manager could get no real satisfaction from his Board, and before January 1915, when correspondence ceased, Davies had had to tell him they were now negotiating with Euston again. It was clear that the Cambrian's position north of Afon Wen was the old stumbling block; they certainly refused to work a narrow gauge link between Dinas and Caernarvon in a territory which seemed quite hostile! Instead, Davies hammered away at Euston and to overcome the problem of trans-shipment at Dinas, he suggested a mixed gauge railway into Caernarvon and an extension on narrow gauge on to the quays there. By now (October 1914) estimators for the work had decided to leave out the Caernarvon Extension altogether.

At this stage the Joint Committee recommended that the promoters of the scheme should be the Caernarvon County Council and it be proposed by individuals without using the title of the Council. The Light Railway Commissioners considered a draft Order in November 1914 for the 'Transfer & Revival of Powers' of both P.B. & S.S. and N.W.N.G. concerns.

By now it seemed the Cambrian Railways was on the point of answering proposals; the L.N.W.R. was apparently hooked but not landed. In the outcome a firm decision was made by neither, for both were becoming too heavily involved in wartime matters to consider the propositions from the Joint Committee for the time being. The Committee decided it must summarise its findings by a Report and then shelve the matter until the war's end. It was rejuvenated as the 'Portmadoc Beddgelert & Rhyddu Light Railway'† and met at the County Offices, Caernarvon on 24th September, 1921 to prepare for a Light Railway Commissioners' Local Enquiry at the same venue.

Summary of Joint Committee Report (undated but c. January 1915)

P.B.&S.S.R. Expenses to date:

Purchase of Croesor Railway	£11,518
Land at Cost	6,150
Cost of construction	73,000
Legal & Engineering expenses	12,000
	£102,668

N.W.N.G. 'This line worked at a disadvantage from the start. It depends on the L.N.W.R. at Dinas for passenger traffic and all goods traffic has to be trans-shipped. The terminus at Rhyddu is disadvantageously placed . . .' (Various efforts to link it with Portmadoc since 1901 are recited.)

---

*Formerly Lloyd George & George of Pwllheli. Name changed to Breese & George summer 1914 (William George: sole partner). Later Evan R. Davies and William George. (Evan R. Davies was later to be prominent with the Festiniog Railway).

†And practically any other permutation of names did duty at this time!

'All local industry has lacked efficient railway service especially mines and quarries where the effect of war has been to put many on short time and close other workings. Present cost per ton of coal or etc. to such workings averages 3s. 2d. to 15s. from Portmadoc or Caernarvon and would be reduced by three quarters if carried by rail.' (A list of local quarries and mines from the Report is appended.)

The owners of the two Railways were prepared to sell the same for £30,000 or £10,000 in cash and £30,000 in shares if any company could be formed to acquire them.

Estimated cost of the work is:

To completion of undertaking	£50,000
Land	1,500
Repair of N.W.N.G.	5,000
Legal & Engineering expenses	3,500
or £4,000 per mile.†	£60,000

†On the basis of a 12-mile line the cost was likely to be nearer £5,000 per mile.

The purchase price would be divisible as ⅔ to N.W.N.G. and ⅓ to P.B. & S.S.

The Report goes on to describe sources of capital and suggested amounts; these include the Development Commission, Treasury, Local Authorities. It concludes that the L.N.W.R. is ready to work the line, on terms to be arranged.

The Route described

Sufficient work was done on the civil engineering to enable a description of the railway as finally abandoned (unfinished) to be given. Briefly, work was accomplished from South Snowdon to a point just above the Welsh Highland's Hafod Ruffydd Halt, and on further short isolated sections a few chains to the south, and then became minimal or non-existent southward to Tyn-y-Coed. South of here and right into Beddgelert, earthworks were almost finished, and an abandoned stub earthwork remains south of Beddgelert. Further on, on the east bank of the Glaslyn, embankment, earthworks, tunnels and bridges were completed through the Aberglaslyn Pass, Nantmor and up to a point half a mile south of Nantmor Halt site, where the earthworks reached flood-plain level. The formation was done between here and the intended bridge over the Afon Dylif but from the east bank of this river, embankment was complete with track as far as a junction with the Croesor Tramway, a length of 45 chains. It also appears that the Croesor Tramway between Llanfrothen road crossing and the Cambrian crossing Portmadoc, was re-sleepered in 4 ft 6 in. × 9 in. × 4½ in. sleepers carrying Indian metre gauge standard 41¼ lb. flat bottomed rails. As much of the abandoned work can still be seen and is worthy of study, detail will now be given.

The contractors, Messrs. Bruce Peebles & Co. Ltd. of Edinburgh started work at South Snowdon, Beddgelert and the junction with the Croesor Tramway. Southwards from South Snowdon work proceeded

Quarries & Mines in district served by Croesor, P.B.&S.S. and N.W.N.G. lines in 1915, together with Parish and number of employees, from the Joint Committee Report.

Parish	Undertaking	Employees	Parish	Undertaking	Employees
Llandwrog	Alexandra	250	Llanfrothen	Croesor bach or	
	Moel Tryfan	250		Cynicht	25
	Braich	80		Aberglaslyn	
	Vron	100		(Copper)	12
	Brynfferam	60		Park	55
Beddgelert	Cwmllan	100		Brondanw	6
	Gerynt	60		Fron Boeth	50
	Cwmcloch	20		Hafodty	30
	Goat	5	Bettws	Ystrad (Iron)	30
	Meillionen	10	Garmon &	Hickman's (Iron)	80
	Cwmcath	10	Rhyd-Ddu	Garn & Cwm Trysgwl	
	Dinas Ddu	20		(Copper)	10
	Castell	15		Glanrafon	400
	Llyn Llagi	6		Victoria	120
	Lliwedd (Lead &	65		Dreflan	35
	Copper)			Garreg Fawr	30
	Lliwedd bach			Plas-y-nant	40
	(Lead & Copper)	26		Snowdon	50
	Braich yr Oen			Castell Cidwm	25
	(Lead & Copper)	24		West Snowdon	80
	Hafod y Porth			Ffridd	20
	(Lead & Copper)	5		Gader Wyallt	45
	Gwynant Lake			Llyn Gader	20
	(Lead & Copper)	6		Bwlch-y-ddeillior	35
	Perthi (Manganese)	?		Princess	30
	Sygun & Mynydd			Prince of Wales	100
	Mawr (Lead & Copper)	55		Quellyn	25
Llanfrothen	Croesor	300			
	Rhosydd	250			
	Pant Mawr	140			
	Tan Rhiw,				
	Nantmor (Ochre)	8			
	Brynfelin (Copper)	60			
	Bryndu (Copper)	4			

(All names used are spelt as in the Report and may not agree with the text.)
Unless otherwise stated, slate or slab is obtained.
(Some listed concerns had long been out of business.)

fairly rapidly and easily along a slightly undulating course involving gradients of 1 in 80–95 but maintaining a gradual climb all the way until with a slight curve to the west and by building up the Beddgelert road to avoid a railway cutting of size, the track passed under the road by means of a segmental skew stone arch of 11 ft span of rather larger loading gauge than those on the N.W.N.G. section to the north. (See structure diagram.) Immediately beyond the road bridge, stone abutments were built for a cattle overbridge of 18 ft span, but this was never completed. The course then entered a somewhat turbarish area at the summit of the Pass, with mountain on either hand, and there was a shallow cutting to the summit. At the summit (650 ft) the P.B. & S.S. works were 1 m. 10 ch. from South Snowdon. This locality is known as Pitt's Head, a nickname taken from a mass of boulders standing near the road overbridge, one of which was said to resemble the profile of that statesman.

On the foregoing section, Harper's Section Drawings for what is headed 'N.W.N.G. Rly. Beddgelert Extension' involve intended gradients of Level, up 80, down 95, Level, up 81, Level (ending with Pitt's Head bridge), up 50, Level (Summit). [Significantly, the originals are signed 'G.C. Aitchison' and dated 8th April, 1904 at Llanberis. Due to delays, Harper's copies therefrom are over-stamped 12th September, 1907. At this date the P.B. & S.S.R. Registered Office is that of the Snowdon Mountain Tramway at Llanberis.] As the works were never fined-down, these precise figures may not have been achieved, but on the summit section where no rock-work was involved, the finished formation was completed.

This summit length was one of the few places on the whole (ultimate) new railway where there was no sound foundation for the track. Even the P.B. & S.S. work mentioned here, had sunk and lost stability by the time of refurbishment by the Welsh Highland Railway. Hundreds of tons of stone were tipped in by Fox & Partners to improve the track-bed, but enginemen always took the length at reduced speed to counteract the roll of the engine. The Welsh Highland's 'Baldwin' locomotive was in particular, a rough performer here.

South from the summit, the line dropped at 1 in 50, 66 and (at 1 m. 9 ch. from Snowdon) began a long fall at 1 in 40, immediately below a level crossing of the road leading to Gader Slate Quarry, which would take it to 1 m. 68 ch. where the downgrade would have eased to 1 in 41. From the level crossing, a considerable cutting, followed by a long embankment on a high clockwise horse-shoe curve, was to be built. The cutting was never fully deepened, but the ensuing embankments were almost finished.

By taking the line westward round the horse-shoe, the formation was able to follow the hill contours and so avoid a steep drop down the valley of the Afon Colwyn into Beddgelert. So as the railway swung away from its intended destination, road and river veered away to its left hand and fell steeply down the valley. In a fashion almost without parallel since the Festiniog Railway was built in the 1830s, the Snowdon Co.'s course presented a traditional narrow gauge route, of a type which had become a feature of overseas railways, but for which British terrain never seemed to call in great measure.

After a short run south-westward along this embankment, another curve took the line north-west briefly and then, by a complete half circle, it passed anti-clockwise through a cutting and then over an embankment to cross the Afon Cwm-ddu, a tributary of the Colwyn. It was intended here to place a girder bridge and, on its further side, to reduce the gradient slightly to 1 in 41 as previously mentioned. However, the contractors never tipped in sufficient fill to complete the embankments up to the bridge abutments, and a temporary bridge involving a steep inclination each side, was utilised until, in the early 1920s, the Welsh Highland contractors completed the work and used a comparatively small ferro-concrete culvert to take the river through the embankment.

At this point, the northern section of Snowdon Co.'s work came to a halt. It was sufficiently far advanced for Parry, the timber contractor with his mill at South Snowdon station, to use a locomotive and gain admittance to the forestry at this point. Immediately south of the unfinished Cwm-ddu bridge, a loop was installed and, a few yards south of here, the metals laid by the contractor ended in a shallow cutting. It has not been possible to determine how much of the foregoing was laid with permanent way; it would seem that most if not all of it received 'Leeds Forge 1904' 41¼ lb./yard flat bottomed rails and again, most if not all the ballasting was done. There is also evidence that T-bulb rails were used, possibly firstly as contractor's line and additionally as temporary forestry tracks, a use for the uncompleted work to which the First War gave birth, and which the promoters could not have anticipated!★

Beyond here, desultory earthworks were carried out. Most of the embankment (now running almost due south) to the Hafod Ruffydd road crossing was finished, as was the low short embankment beyond. This was exactly 2 m. from South Snowdon. A shallow cutting beside Hafod Ruffydd house was begun and 30 chains further on, there was to be a magnificent double horseshoe curve through Coed Mawr, bringing the railway alongside the Afon Colwyn again. Part of the southern extremity of earthwork (an embankment beside the Afon Meillionen) was finished, but work ceased abruptly on this at a point where today a modern forestry road comes up beside the abandoned formation. To visit the spot today does not even entail leaving the seat of the car! Nothing at all was attempted on the remainder of the horseshoe, where the later contractor met with much heavy work. There was the beginning of a bridge over the Afon Meillionen and a small isolated cutting built opposite Beudy Tan-y-llwyn-isaf, but nothing again until 3 m.

★According to C.R. Clinker, local information suggested that earth and track work was being done in winter/spring 1912–13. Perhaps this was only on the length worked by Parry, to put the section into some sort of runnable condition?

43 ch. the work which had come northwards from Beddgelert was met. Here again, the ultimate purpose proved to be a horse-worked forestry line which though temporary, found its way onto large scale Plans. On Harper's sections, the intention was to increase the fall following the double horseshoe, and below Afon Meillionen bridge, to drop at 1 in 37 from 3 m. 50 ch.

[The forestry line was taken straight off the contractor's railway just beyond what became a cutting behind Tyn-y-Coed. Here it had been intended to carry the small Afon Glochig stream over the line on an aqueduct, but for temporary purposes it was bridged south of the house and a steep line carried away up and northwestwards into Parc Tyn-y-Coed forest. This timber line curved west and west-south-west and ended just below the sheepfold south of Beudy Ysgubor. There is virtually nothing to be seen on the site today, save for the most primitive and light earthworks near the top. The line was 27 chains long from the main route and very steep indeed. Horse power and gravity were sufficient for its needs.]

South of Tyn-y-Coed the railway was on a very different course to that adopted by the Welsh Highland. For the first few yards, the earthworks have been destroyed by Welsh Highland building. Then, below and to the east of the W.H.R. formation, there opens up a quite remarkable rock cutting of ever-increasing depth and curve, resulting finally in a left-hand horseshoe in part rock cutting and then embankment immediately north of Cwm-cloch-isaf. The works are remarkably preserved and even in their overgrown and waterlogged state remain a monument to the strength of purpose and confirmed optimism of the promoters. When it is also considered that from the point behind Tyn-y-Coed where the civil engineering work re-commenced (3 m. 43 ch. from South Snowdon) the gradient was to be an unbroken 1 in 28 to within a few yards of Beddgelert station, the confidence of the builders is evident.

Emerging on to open ground beside Cwm-cloch-isaf, the contractor's track in T-bulb rail with chairs and sleepers, lay intact but under water; some chairs were rudely fashioned in wood at this point.

Curving now west and then south, the embankment falls to merge with the later Welsh Highland cutting which comes in on its right hand and then, by embankment used also by the W.H.R., into Beddgelert. There is an interesting place where the Snowdon Co. crossed an occupation road by overbridge, the W.H.R. by level crossing. Beyond, a stone P.B. & S.S. road overbridge was completed in concrete by the W.H.R. and shortly afterwards, there is a fine Snowdon Co. stone bridge crossing the Afon Cwm-cloch.

The site of Beddgelert station was cleared. The grade eased to 1 in 42 on entering, but the site was level. Of the work north from here to Tyn-y-Coed, most embankment was complete, but the cuttings in rock were not all fully opened out and some not finally deepened. They were sufficient for the timber trains, however. Falling at 1 in 29, the track entered a rock cutting south of Beddgelert and at 3 m. 30 ch. there was a 132 ft tunnel in bare rock from whence the course swung south-east and, emerging from the cutting crossed the Beddgelert–Portmadoc road by a stone bridge. The embankment continued for a few yards beyond and then petered out. Further on still, stood the isolated abutments for an underbridge to connect the lands divided by the new embankment. Unsupported by earth filling, they made a bizarre monument. Until recently there was also the stonework for a flood water culvert. Beyond this point, the Afon Glaslyn would have been crossed, but the records give no clue as to the form of bridge.

It is significant that the drawings for the route from here to the Croesor Tramway are headed 'Croesor, Beddgelert section' (no company being stated), dated 21st June, 1904, and probably originated from Aitchison at Llanberis. Harper's copies are again dated 12th September, 1907.

The 'Beddgelert Extension' survey only takes the Extension to the Glaslyn river bank just mentioned (but beyond its authorised terminal). These Records, therefore, embody the link from the authorised junction on the east side of the Glaslyn with the 1901 proposals for a line up the Gwynant valley. One detail is worth mentioning. In view of the ultimate abandonment of the works south and east of Beddgelert station tunnel, and the new course to Bryn-y-felin adopted by the Welsh Highland, it is ironic that a short railway was in fact built by the Snowdon Co. along this later-adopted course. It led along the west side of the Portmadoc road, at a point south of the Beddgelert tunnel mouth, for about five chains. Steeply inclined, it ended at the roadside and enabled equipment to be loaded there for building this isolated section which otherwise had no convenient link with a road.

To take up the next section of work, the Glaslyn had to be crossed. The point where the bridge was to be built is still visible, and from here, down through Aberglaslyn all civil engineering work was finished. It begins with rubble embankment on the riverside, and entering the canyon-like Pass of Aberglaslyn* with its river and rapids falling below on the right, takes up a shelf position on the craggy side of the gorge. Tunnels were required where shoulders of mountain stood in the way. The first is 132 ft long and is followed almost immediately by a second of 99 ft. The third pierces the side of Craig-y-llan and is 957 ft in length with a slight curve at the north end. All are unlined and no ornamentation has been attempted. The reason for their generous bore is a matter for speculation. It could be that an eventual standard gauge loading-gauge was envisaged, but perhaps (more likely) there was optimism that the overhead electrical equipment would be installed from the start. The fall from the Glaslyn bridge was 1 in 105, 266, then level; then came a short 1 in 57 rise, then level, and through the tunnels, 1 in 114 and throughout the third, 1 in 40. At the south mouth

---

*The name *Aber Glaslyn* ('The confluence of the Blue Pool') was probably derived from copper deposits in the water. There were several mines in the vicinity.

it was intended to steepen the fall to 1 in 32, and the rubble embankment with a stone overbridge carrying the road to the Cwm Bychan mine, was completed: transport at the mine was by a wire ropeway supplied by R. White & Sons, Widnes. The tunnels just mentioned, however, were not fully opened out by the contractor. Certainly Fox & Partners survey for the Welsh Highland allowed for opening out the Aberglaslyn tunnels to their present dimensions. What does survive is an interesting letter from Harper's to the Festiniog Manager dated 18th July, 1904:

> 13, St. Helens Place,
> London, E.C.
>
> *Size of Tunnel.* If it is not troubling you too much, we should be glad if you would let us know the height and width of the tunnels on the Festiniog line. Also the maximum height and width of your locomotives.
>
> We are thinking of making the Aberglaslyn Tunnel 11 ft 6 ins. high by 11 ft wide. In case at any time your Rolling Stock should come on to our line, would it pass through our tunnel?
>
> Yours faithfully,

Of course at this juncture, it was thought that *one* tunnel in the Pass would suffice (*three* were part-finished on abandonment). The envisaged possibility of through running might be wishful thinking, careful forethought or sudden inspiration. There was no special link between the N.W.N.G. and Festiniog at this time.

The long tunnel was provided with three refuges at each side, mainly at its southernmost end. A fourth on the west side was to be found nearer the north end whilst the W.H.R. contractors added two more at equal distances along the east wall at the north end. Although the tunnel was opened out later to standard gauge dimensions, Welsh Highland rolling stock never really necessitated this lavish provision, and when Festiniog coaches came over the line, the recesses were even more of a luxury! Far-sighted though the large bores may have been, they added immensely to costs (height 14 ft (centre of arch), width 11 ft). The long tunnel varied in width throughout, caused by differing rock; it was widest at the south end but in the middle increased momentarily to 12 ft 9 in. A letter from Aitchison to Robert Casson of 30th November, 1903 claimed that the line had to be in tunnel through the Aberglaslyn Pass for aesthetic reasons, but that this was impossible from the engineering standpoint.

The civil engineering south of the long tunnel was heavy and not finally completed by the Snowdon Co. The tunnel had provided much material for the ensuing embankment over the mine road and the bridge over the Afon Bychan, but this had not been brought to formation level when work stopped. Just beyond was a formidable cutting in rock which was not completely pierced either. It was not possible to run between the Aberglaslyn section of the work and the remainder further south for this reason.

As previously mentioned, south from the tunnel the intended grade was 1 in 32, but at the Nantmor road, reached at the end of the rock cutting, the grade was to ease to 1 in 70. Second thoughts about making a Halt on level track beside the road crossing prevailed, and a fresh section was drawn providing for this, but altering the fall from the tunnel mouth to 1 in 40 with a short level section for the Halt. When the Welsh Highland completed these works, the Halt had to do without its level, and the grade remained consistent at 1 in 40.

The Snowdon Co. diverted the Nantmor road, and the Halt was to stand just south of a new road crossing on the level. From here the work had been finished, in part rubble embankment and less formidable cuttings to a point where the Llanfrothen road was to be crossed and for which it was diverted. The bridge was not begun. South again, (and below the Nantmor Halt site falling at 1 in 36 and 250) not only had the formation been brought up to the required standard, but the fences had been erected too. The fall was completed down to the Glaslyn flood plain by a long embankment of 1 in 67 ending at 6½ miles from South Snowdon, and then, by earthworks and fencing ready to receive the permanent way, a fall of 1 in 2,200 ended before the 7th milepost, so bringing the finished works on to the flood plain. Just beyond here was the Welsh Highland Halt at Hafod-y-llyn, not of course even considered at this time.

The P.B. & S.S. formation – mainly on level ground – to the point where the Afon Dylif was to be crossed (a grade of 118 up and 152 down was required to climb up and over the bridge which was not built) – and included in this finished length was a crossing of the Afon Nant-y-mor on which work was not started.

East of the site of the Dylif bridge, some old Croesor rails had been laid over what was to be level railway as far as the point of junction with the Croesor Tramway. Formation work on this length was almost complete.[10]

With the cessation of powers in 1909, and with all construction ceased, but it would seem that on the scale of what had been achieved (probably over two years rather than the whole three-year term permitted by the Act) another twelve months – and sufficient funds – would have been ample to bring the line to operating condition.

Electrification and Electric Locomotives

So much of what has gone before falls into the might-have-been category, that further extension along the same lines seems pointless: however, there is much that is worth recording and some of what follows carries that certain 'mystique' which characterises the whole scene.

It was intended that power supplies should come from the existing Nantlle route around Llyn Quellyn rather than from Cwm Dyli to Beddgelert. By this circuitous way the number of poles was reduced, as

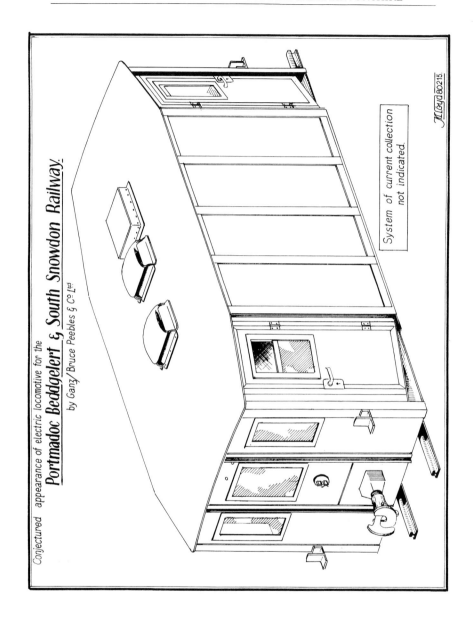

Conjectured appearance of electric locomotive for the
Portmadoc Beddgelert & South Snowdon Railway.
by Ganz/Bruce Peebles & Co Ltd

System of current collection not indicated.

JLloyd 80215.

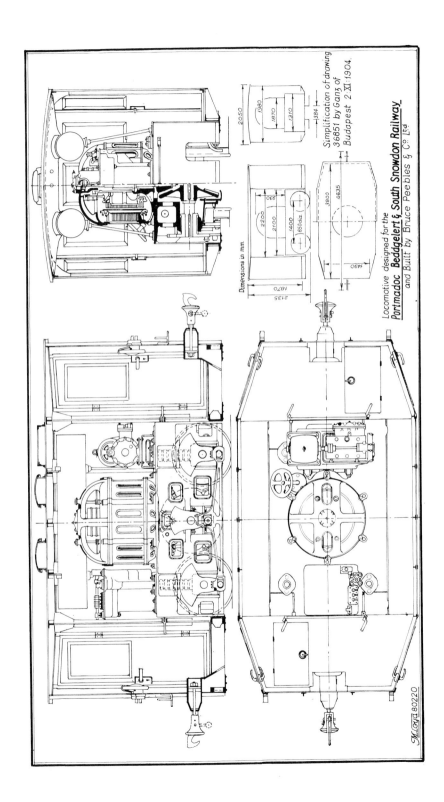

Dimensions in mm.

Simplification of drawing
36851 by Ganz of
Budapest 2·XI·1904.

Locomotive designed for the
Portmadoc Beddgelert & South Snowdon Railway
and Built by Bruce Peebles & Cº Ltd

HLGrd 80220

the line also fed Dinorwic and Pen-yr-Orsedd Quarries. Alongside the railway would have run a 10,000 volt feeder, two pole-lengths away from the trolley wires over the track; the latter would be fed with 500 volts by nine transformers along the length of the railway. A branch intended to link the South Snowdon Quarry up from Gwynant, had apparently been dropped.[5] The feeders were distanced at the insistence of the Board of Trade, who were fearful that should a high-tension feeder break, passengers in the train would be endangered; Bruce Peebles were sceptical of this, quoting the Valtellina Railway where there were 20,000 volts on the same poles as the trolley wire. (The Valtellina Railway used Ganz of Budapest locomotives.)

Although there is evidence that railway construction was still in hand in 1908, it is suggested that the amount by then was small. J.C. Russell had told N.W.N.G. shareholders in early 1906 that there were delays in arrangements between their Company and the P.B. & S.S.R., and electrification of their line.[6] Periodicals referred to the problems besetting the N.W.P. & T. Co.'s power scheme. Nonetheless, the Power Co. was still trying to enlarge its grip and promote its basic intent, so that economy on the railway side of the business in order to use funds for other developments, would be logical. 'Back-pedalling' may have been the order of the day! Photographs of construction work suggest the years up to 1906, and none appear thereafter. Bruce Peebles' men, Vincent Waite (d. c.1955) and George Paton (d. c.1978) were both back in Edinburgh by 1907 and although they were mainly concerned with the power station, it tends to show their employers had largely pulled out by 1907. [Paton went back to North Wales as Chief Engineer in May 1907, staying with the N.W.P. & T. Company and its successors until retirement.][7]

In this uncertain climate did the purchase of steam locomotive *Russell* imply the P.B. & S.S.R. was hedging its bets, so that whether all or part of its line, or all or part of the N.W.N.G. was electrified or not, a locomotive suitable for the terrain was on hand?

The problems of the day were not confined to the N.W.P. & T. Co., for in February 1908 Bruce Peebles went into voluntary liquidation. The building of the P.B. & S.S.R. has been given as the cause of this failure:

> . . . Ten electric locomotives were built for the Portmadoc, Beddgelert and South Snowdon narrow gauge railway. The abandonment of the railway in 1908 because of the high cost of cutting the track through dense rock formations resulted in financial difficulties which seriously affected the Company at that time.[8]

This leads the tale conveniently into the matter of the electric locomotives (assuming there was ever more than one finally completed). Between 1947 and 1962, 'B.P. News' was the house magazine of Bruce Peebles & Co. and in January 1949 it wrote:

> Some of our readers may still remember the imposing row of ten electric locomotives which lined the side of the Works' pond for many years and were eventually

broken up for scrap around 1916. Many a tale has been told about (them) . . . they were ordered by the (P.B. & S.S. Railway). The narrow gauge – it was only two feet – made it necessary to use vertical motors driving the wheels by bevel gearing and connecting rods. The railway was abandoned in 1908 . . . It was at this time that Portheim* was in Moscow negotiating a £1,000,000 electrification scheme. He came very near to success, but manufacturing commitments at home, coupled with the Portmadoc fiasco, were running ahead of available resources and the contract was never signed.

W.V. Waite had joined Bruce Peebles at the Tay Works in 1898 and years later he recalled: 'At this date' (apparently 1904) 'I took over the construction of the N.W.P. & T. Co.'s new E.H.T. Power Station . . . and electrification of the three main quarries in North Wales'. (These were given as Oakeley, Dinorwic and Pen-y-Orsedd.) 'Simultaneously, we spent a considerable sum of money (£180,000) on the North Wales narrow gauge railway, which was abandoned . . . at an early date in 1907 I returned to Edinburgh.' (He later returned to North Wales to complete the electrification of the Llandudno & Colwyn Bay Electric Railway.) The contract for the Cwm Dyli (or Nant Gwynant) scheme was signed in 1904.

The Incorporated Municipal Electrical Association visited Peebles' East Pilton Works in June 1905 and four items of interest were on display. One of these was a three-phase locomotive, which was described in the seven-page leaflet given to delegates from the annual convention in Edinburgh. It said:

> The Three-phase locomotive shown in the shops is one of ten which have been ordered by the P.B. & S.S.R., all of which are to be built at East Pilton Works . . . The 100 horsepower motor . . . is capable of hauling fifty tons up gradients of 1 in 40, which represents the maximum service that will be required of it . . . It will be seen that the arrangement of such high power on so narrow a gauge . . . (is remarkable).

Another source maintains that five were bought from Budapest in 1905 and the remainder built in Edinburgh the next year.

Although the aforementioned reference to the 'row of ten' implies a formidable loss of business, doubts have been expressed that more than one was ever completed, and the remainder were simply shells or similar. Was any attempt made to dispose of them? Did the makers feel that after the First War, the railway would be revived and the material taken off their hands? In the numerous photographs which the firm had taken to advertise its products, no picture of the type has survived. The scrap drive of World War I saw the end of them. What would the units have looked like? Presumably they would have had a strong resemblance to the Ganz drawing labelled 'Portmadoc Railway' (p.293) which in itself leaves something to the imagination. The motors in practice were rated at 90/180 H.P., and 250 H.P. could be sustained for a short period only, perhaps only for a few minutes. By using one locomotive between Portmadoc and Beddgelert and then double-

---

*Roland S. Portheim, director in charge of the London Office who left the firm after the 1908 collapse.

heading north of there to Rhyd-Ddu, thence onward, one again, the little engines would have coped with the loads and gradients. Probably either one double or two single trolley pole collectors mounted on the roof for the two overhead wires would have been employed and with the all-over roof, driving positions at each end, 'cased-in' appearance of sheeting which would be taken down to track level, they might be taken for steam-trams at first sight! 25 m.p.h. was allegedly achieved on the level.* The drawings are dated 1904; was the extension to the N.W.N.G. at Rhyd-Ddu envisaged in the original specification, bearing in mind that construction had proved – at that date – to involve a gradient of 1 in 28?

The makers installed a test track at the Works, incorporating a loop to determine the position of the trolley wires above it (April 1905) and of the many drawings (each having a Ganz number additionally) none seem to have survived; there were about one hundred concerning the 'Portmadoc loco'.

Clearly Bruce Peebles envisaged a wider market for the locomotive than the North Wales potential offered. The first finished engine, after being shown to the I.M.E.A. Conference delegates in June, was taken next month to the Agricultural Hall, Islington, for the 3rd International Electric Tramway & Railway Exhibition held during the first fortnight of July 1905. (Earlier exhibitions were held in 1900 and 1902 – all were promoted by 'THE TRAMWAY & RAILWAY WORLD' periodical.) During the Exhibition the magazine printed pictures which showed glimpses of Bruce Peebles' stand with the P.B. & S.S. locomotive on it . . . but never a full view. It was not unlike the Ganz drawings and the panelling was painted in traditional manner with the upper in a light, and the lower a darker, colour. The issue of July, p. 152 had:–

> 'The first three-phase electric locomotive built for the United Kingdom is also on view. This is built for the P.B. & S.S. Rly. and nine other locomotives of similar construction are in hand. This locomotive presented special difficulties in design owing to the fact that it was necessary to haul loads of 50 Tons up grades of 1 in 18.† Owing to the narrow gauge (1 ft 11 ins.) it was found impossible to arrange the motor horizontally: the motor therefore has a vertical shaft. It is a 100 H.P. machine but capable of exciting 250 if required for short periods.'

Considering all the facts it would seem that the locomotive weighed about 10 Tons, which would make it capable of lifting about 27 Tons on a grade of 1 in 27 without loss of adhesion. On an upgrade of 1 in 28 – such as would be encountered on leaving Beddgelert – an approximate five minute overloading of 160 H.P. would have started and accelerated the train hauled by one locomotive. By the top of the 1 in 28 the engine would have been on overload for about 12 minutes . . . thus giving a reasonable margin of safety.

A short reference to Bruce Peebles will not be out of place – David

---

*There may have been an error in winding the motors, as a photograph of the wound stator suggests that only 12½ m.p.h. would be reached!

†a printing error?

Bruce Peebles (1826–1899) was a gas engineer whose 1866 company, D. Bruce Peebles & Co. of Fountainbridge, became wellknown in the gas industry; seeing that electricity would soon compete with gas, Peebles began to transfer his interests and opened an electrical department which soon gained status alongside the gas business. After negotiating a licence to manufacture three-phase electrical equipment pioneered by the Hungarian firm of Ganz & Co. of Budapest, the organisation was changed and in December 1902 it became Bruce Peebles & Co. Ltd. ready to supply complete electrical installations and carry out themselves the civil and mechanical engineering which went alongside.* The N.W.P. & T. Co. together with the P.B. & S.S.R. schemes were among their first contracts. It is suggested that they embarked on the construction of the locomotives, confident that all the outdoor work was proceeding well, without formal orders being placed: when by 1908 the N.W.P. & T. Company stopped work on railway projects, not only locomotives (completed or otherwise) but other equipment was left on their hands. This was to bring about the virtual collapse of the business as then constituted.[9] Tradition has it that a quantity of poles to carry the overhead wiring was delivered to Beddgelert, only to find its way in due course as poles for urban usages in various local communities. The existence of 'iron telegraph poles' along the Welsh Highland near Pont Croesor in 1929 may also be linked with this source: is it too incredible that they may have been erected by the Snowdon Co. to carry the overhead wiring?!

Steam Locomotive

Name	Type	Builder	No.	Date	Withdrawn
RUSSELL	2–6–2T	Hunslet Engine Co. Ltd.	901	1906	Extant

Cylinders	10¾ in. × 15 in.†	Total Heat Surface	381 sq. ft
Driving wheels	2 ft 4 in.	Fuel capacity	14½ cwt.
Pony wheels	1 ft 6 in.	Tank capacity	440 galls.
Wheelbase	15 ft 6 in.	Weight Working Order	20 tons
Pressure	160 lb. sq. in.	Tractive Effort at	
		75 per cent b.p.	7425 lb.

In the face of the fact that the railway was incomplete, it would seem reckless for the Company to order a locomotive – the only one in its own name – before the railway was nearly ready. The reason lay in the close liaison with the N.W.N.G.R., whose own engines were by then over thirty years old and were out-dated, if not unsuited to working a railway which would include some of the most remarkable gradients in the British Isles. The directors therefore felt justified in ordering something for the Beddgelert Extension which could be relied upon to

*In May 1903 had acquired the sole rights for ten years in the 3-phase A.C. electrical patents of Ganz & Co.: in 1904 opened the new East Pilton Works, Granton, Edinburgh, alongside the Caledonian Railway. The Company was closely associated with street tramway work world-wide. The Company was absorbed by the Reyrolle Parsons Group in 1969 and has undergone subsequent changes.

†Boston Lodge records (Festiniog Railway) of 1921 give 9½ in. × 14 in.

operate south of South Snowdon with a margin of power. The N.W.N.G. line already owned one engine by the Hunslet Engine Co. of Leeds, and to them went the order.

Hunslet had sent a specification on 31st January and G.C. Aitchison, A.M.I.C.E., F.C.I.S., Manager of the P.B. & S.S.R., placed the order on 13th February, 1906, so there was little delay. Drawings were prepared between 20th March and 14th May and by 26th May the engine was already undergoing steam trials; it left Leeds for North Wales on 29th May.

The remarkably short time in which the engine was built has produced several theories, the most recent being that as the engine was urgently required, priority was given. This seems a most unlikely tale, unless it could be supported by some surcharge on cost; there seldom was a manufacturer whose customers did not want their goods as a matter of urgency! More probably – though there is no supporting evidence – by using certain standard parts and existing designs where available, expedition was possible. The new engine was larger than anything used before on the N.W.N.G. The design was based on a class of 2–6–2T engines built in 1898 for the Sierra Leone Government Railway. Details differed, and it was larger than the Sierra Leone class, though of a narrower gauge. It was carried on outside frames to the driving wheels, with inside frames to the pony trucks, whilst Walschaert's Valve Gear was employed, only for the third time by the makers.

There was a curious feature about the gauge as ordered. The P.B. & S.S.R. returned its official gauge as 1 ft 11½ in. The N.W.N.G. Railways' returned 1 ft 11¼ in., 1 ft 11½ in. and 2 ft! Hunslet's records show the engine to have been ordered for 1 ft. 11¼ in. Apparently the original order was given for a gauge of 1 ft 11⅞ in. but amended before completion of the engine.

Among the items common to the Sierra Leone engines and *Russell* were the coupled wheels, reversing gear, springs, axleboxes and outside motion generally. A special design was made up for the frames and cylinders and the engine above, so that a number of drawings were necessary where departure from Sierra Leone standards was made. The boiler was larger and based on one supplied on an engine for Leeds Corporation Waterworks (0–6–2T No. 865 of 1905). The minimum radius curve for the N.W.N.G. was 198 feet radius (as against 120 feet for Sierra Leone) and it was not necessary to cut away the side frames to allow the pony trucks to swing; these had inside bearings.

Behind the outside main frames, compensating beams linked the coupled axle-boxes. There was a spark-arrester, Ramsbottom safety valves, sand reservoir in a dome fitting between chimney and steam dome (later moved) for forward direction only; the other sand reservoir was a saddle over the firebox. Westinghouse Class F. Pump on the leading end of the right-hand tank with a reservoir between the main-frames, centre buffer-couplers with side chains, bunker over and

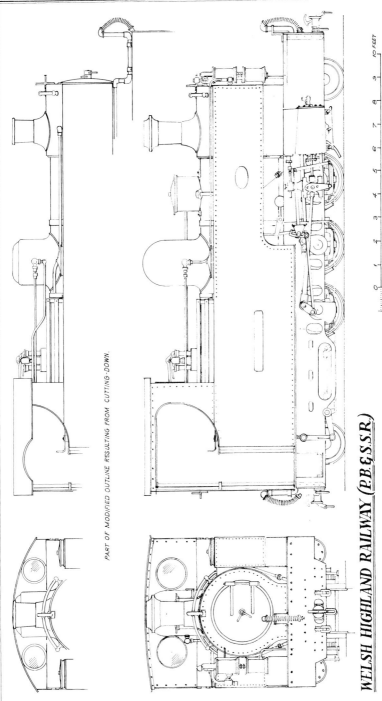

PART OF MODIFIED OUTLINE RESULTING FROM CUTTING-DOWN.

WELSH HIGHLAND RAILWAY (P.B.&S.S.R.)

"RUSSELL" BY HUNSLET, MAKER'S NUMBER 901 OF 1906 IN ORIGINAL FORM. MANY MODIFICATIONS WERE MADE OVER THE YEARS CULMINATING IN THE DRASTIC CUTTING-DOWN OF 1923-24. BASED ON MAKER'S DRAWINGS UNDER № 28900 DATED MAY 14 1906.

0 1 2 3 4 5 6 7 8 9 10 FEET

alongside the firebox top with access on the left hand through the cab weathersheet featured, and the side tanks ran the full length of the engine. The coupled wheelbase was 5 ft 6 in. (the original overall wheelbase was reduced from 15 ft 8 in. to keep it as short as possible).

Painting was in N.W.N.G. colours, the principal being a red-brown (some sources state brown – similar to North British Railway, and others 'Midland Red') lined in black, the black having a thin yellow line each side of it. The Hall cranks and buffer beams were vermilion, as was the ground of the brass nameplate on the tank sides. There was no lettering or number.

Of course, *Russell* never went into service on the actual P.B.& S.S.R., as even the track immediately south of South Snowdon was unready for use. She was delivered to Dinas Junction and took up duties as if just another member of the N.W.N.G.R. locomotive stock.

The statistical returns for locomotives were part of the Statutory Returns required under s.9 Regulation of Railways Act 1871 as amended by s.32 Railway and Canal Traffic Act 1888. There is no reference in them or in the instructions on completing the forms issued by the Board of Trade as to the question of whether a locomotive was owned or not. As leasing of locomotives was common and the lessor was not usually another railway company it must have been assumed at the time that the railway company was expected to return the number of locomotives that it used rather than the number it owned. The behaviour of the N.W.N.G. and P.B.&S.S.R. over *Russell* was therefore neither ploy nor accountancy fiddle but a pragmatic approach adopted by all railway companies in complying with the requirement to fill in the Board of Trade forms.

No other locos or rolling stock were ordered by the Company, whose expenditure by 1920 was £47,791, and visible assets on abandonment were an unfinished railway between South Snowdon and Croesor Junction, and a new locomotive at work only on an associate railway.

Directors

		Other directorships included
1911	Col. Henry PLATT, Llanfairfechan	Liverpool & N. Wales Steamship Co.
	Joseph BEECHING, Huyton	Lancs. United Tramways Co.
	Henry R. HOGG, Kensington	Canadian Electric Traction Co. N. Wales Power & Traction Co. Sunderland Dist. Elec. Tramways Co.
	E. Noel HUMPHREYS, Chester (Chartered Accountant)	East Halkyn Mining Co.
1919	Arthur Francis BOTT, Stevenage	Cleobury Mortimer & Ditton Priors Light Rly.* Aluminium Corp. Ltd.
	Joseph Walker CASSELLS, Orford	Aluminium Corp. Ltd.

*Seat on Board given to contractors, Bott & Stennett, who held shares under terms of construction contract.

Directors	Other directorships included
Capt. Samuel G. BIBBY, Sutton (Chartered Accountant)	N. Wales Power & Traction Co. (Deputy Chairman) Aluminium Corp. Ltd.
*Henry Joseph JACK, Maenan Manor, Llanrwst	Aluminium Corp. Ltd. (Managing Director) N. Wales Power & Traction Co. (numerous othe coys. in aluminium business)
Kenneth McKenzie CLARK, Sudbourne	N. Wales Power & Traction Co. (Chairman) Aluminium Corp. Ltd.

*1922 Board unchanged but JACK Managing Director.
By 1925 his other directorships included:

Bauxite Refining Co. Ltd.
(Managing Director)
Gwalia Ltd.
Gwynedd Trust Ltd.
Snowdon Mountain Tramroad &
Hotels Co.
Unity Investment Trust Ltd.
Welsh Highland Railway
Festiniog Railway

REFERENCES

1. Public Record Office. MT 6-1529/2: MT 58/282.
2. Public Record Office. MT 6-1485/1: MT 58/316.
   Caernarvon Record Office, Box 12, Breese, Jones & Casson Collection.
   University College of North Wales (Bangor). Cynhaiarn Collection 556–562.
3. Public Record Office. MT 6-1721.
4. Gethin Jones' Papers. (Courtesy David Gwyn.)
5. 'Electrical Review' (1906) p.911–9: p.955–9.
   'Electrician' (1906) p.578–80: p.622–5: p.660–3.
6. 'Electrical Review' (1906) p.636.
7. George K. Paton: from a Curriculum Vitae of about 1909 formerly in possession of Bruce Peebles.
8. 'THE STORY OF BRUCE PEEBLES 1866–1954' p.55. (Published 1955.)
9. Courtesy Dr. J. Manners: Snowdon Mountain Railway: Rodney Weaver. Also 'The Narrow Gauge' No.94 p.10–15. [Some sources give conflicting information.]
10. Drawings and official information concerning the foregoing supplied courtesy Freeman, Fox & Partners.

EXPENDITURE

(Up to 1901 see Portmadoc, Croesor & Beddgelert Tram Railway Co.)

	1902	1903	1904[5]	1905	1906[4]	1907	1908	1909	1910[6]	1911	1912	1913	1920	1921
Maintenance Works and Way			83	64	78	69	60	63	62	72	51	56	N.R.	N.R.
Loco Power Cost			242	203	172	176	185	195	181	191	175	154	N.R.	N.R.
Repairs and Renewals Carr. and Wagons			10	10	11	10	10	9	15	–	–	3	N.R.	N.R.
Traffic Expenses			73	71	60	60	51	53	58	56	52	52	N.R.	N.R.
Profit/Loss on Working			81	(96)	(76)	(66)	16	107	151	204	183	86	(51)	(17)
Merchandise Tons			698[2]	311	308	Nil	259	530	314	359	230	★	★	★
Minerals Tons			9035[2]	8005	6553	7195	7299	7841	7290	7637	7112	★	★	★
Train miles (Goods)[1]			x	x	x	x	x	2772	2772	2772	2772	2772	1173	1311
Wagons for merchandise[3]			Nil	4	4	4	4	4	4	4	4	4	4	4

Given as 1½ ton capacity (slate)

★ Tonnages for

	1913	1919	1920	1921
General Merchandise	244	906	161	256
Coal, Coke, etc.	467	282	315	282
Other Minerals (slate, etc.)	5820	N.R.	1510	1730
Livestock	N.R.	N.R.	5	6

Notes on Returns

x No mileage returned for these years 'cannot be given: haulage by horses only'.

1 Figures for 1909–1919 (no other figures for 1919 available) clearly fictitious – all same.

2 'Partly estimated'.

3 Predecessors' Returns showed nil return for all types of Rolling Stock. From 1913 the four were returned as 'Mineral' not 'Merchandise'

4 'The Croesor Section (a horse tramroad) was the only section of the Coy.'s line open for traffic in 1906.' (This repeated each year thereafter.)

5 'The Line is being constructed under an arrangement by the North Wales Power & Traction Coy. Ltd., that Coy. taking the shares and debentures on payment.'

6 'The actual construction was in abeyance at the end of the year 1910' (this repeated for ensuing years).

Notes not shown by above

1901 Authorised Capital £270,000.
1904   £294,000.
1909   £318,000.
1904 Issued Shares £13,535.
1905   £50,000 – to 1921.

Authorised Loan £60,000 + £15,000 from Local Authority
£98,000.
£106,000 – to 1921.

ACKNOWLEDGEMENTS
(Second Edition)

In some previous publications within the Series, the Author's task has been eased by the existence of those who had made a special study of certain of their contents. Caernarvonshire, whilst enjoying the well-earned interest it deserves from railway historians, has produced no such specialists. Worse than this, past accounts have been sketchy and repetitive so that the task of collecting material apart, the manuscript has involved many years of work.

The demanding job of unearthing and collating archive material is a time-consuming and extremely expensive pursuit; material is not always available without prior notice and is often not on the premises. I am convinced that the collection and treatment of available material is now beyond the time and means of the average historian, unless he is professionally involved, subsidised – or his objects are limited. The cost of publication, too, is more than most publishing houses is prepared to risk.

My thanks therefore to two loyal friends: Jeremy S. Wilkinson who has sifted through masses of often-irrelevant material in North Wales, Manchester and London which enabled the Author to take a smaller share of this part of the work and saved an enormous amount of time, and John M. Lloyd. He and I have covered the fieldwork not once but many many times and this groundwork on many occasions proved that what may be found in the archives is not necessarily what actually happened! Such matters make up the love of the chase! John Lloyd's drawing and maps are drawn and redrawn with loving care and patience.

I recall with gratitude the companies who have come to my assistance, including Messrs. R.Y. Pickering & Co. Ltd., The Hunslet Engine Co. Ltd., The Metropolitan Cammell Railway Carriage & Wagon Co. Ltd., Messrs. Beyer Peacock & Co. Ltd., The Vulcan Foundry Ltd., Messrs. Freeman Fox & Partners and many others too numerous to mention.

Groundwork for this book began in Portmadoc in 1944; throughout my wife has been my constant assistant as we plotted together to give the neglected narrow gauge railways of Caernarvonshire the calibre of book we thought they deserved.

I also acknowledge:

The County Record Offices at Caernarvon and Dolgellau.
The Archivist, University College Library, Bangor.
The National Library of Wales.
The Librarian, Manchester Central Reference Library.
The Librarian, Manchester Law Society Library.
E. Boydell & Co. Ltd.
The Baldwin Locomotive Co.
Trustees of The Narrow Gauge Railway Museum
Welsh Highland Light Railway (1964) Ltd.

A.C. Baker
J.L.H. Bate
D.E. Bick
J.F. Bolton
C.R. Clinker
B.E. Crompton
R.W. Chaney
Thomas Davies
J.M. Dunn
A. Michael Davies
P. Vaughan Davies
Robert Evans
M.D. Greville
A.G.W. Garraway

F.M. Gates
C.C. Green
David Gwyn
S.H.P. Higgins
Frank Hewitt
W.E. Hayward
G.E. Hughes
Robert Hudson Ltd.
R.Y. Honychurch
R.W. Kidner
Dr. Jean Lindsay
T.S. Lascelles
Charles E. Lee
David M. Lee

Dr. John Manners
W.J. Milner
E. Mellowes
Graham Morris
Professor C.L. Mowat
Donald Mackereth
Gerry Nicholas
Professor G.H. Platt
R.R.J. Plummer
G. Parker
L.T.C. Rolt

A.E. Rimmer
Douglas Rendell
Bernard Roberts
Michael Seymour
R.E. Tustin
Rodney Weaver
Colin Wilson
Colonel Dudley West
P.B. Whitehouse
H.F. Wheeller
W.H. Whitworth

The Author is also indebted for the loan and use of illustrations duly credited individually.

BIBLIOGRAPHY
(Dates recent unless given otherwise where known)

General

Madocks and the Wonder of Wales: E. Beazley, Faber 1957.
History of Caernarvonshire: A.H. Dodd, Caerns. Hist. Soc. 1968
Slate Quarrying in Wales: Morgan Richards, 1876
Snowdonia: Various, Collins 1949
Cambrian Travellers' Guide (2 Edn.): George Nicholson, 1813
Topographical Dictionary of Wales (4 Edn.): S. Lewis, 1850
Mines, Mills and Furnaces: Morgan Rees, H.M.S.O. 1969
British Mining: R. Hunt, 1887
Steamers of North Wales: Frank C. Thornley, Stephenson 1968
Industrial Revolution in N. Wales: A.H. Dodd, University of Wales 1950
Tours in Wales: Pennant, Humphreys 1883
Anglesey and North Wales Pilot: Henry Glazebrook, Yachting Monthly 1961

Railway

Chester Division of the Great Western Railway (official): G.W.R. 1924
Great Western Railway – Running Powers (official): G.W.R. 1924
Industrial & Independent Locomotives & Railways of N. Wales:
    Bradley & Hindley, Birmingham Locomotive Club 1968
The Chester & Holyhead Railway: J.M. Dunn, Oakwood Press 1968
Light Railways: Mackay, Crosby Lockwood 1896
Etude Technique sur le chemin de fer Festiniog & quelques autres chemins de fer a voie
    etroite de l'Angleterre: M.E. Vignes, 1878
The Festiniog Railway: J.I.C. Boyd, Oakwood Press 1975
Report of Investigation Committee on Light Railways: 1921

Among other sources consulted:

Index to Parliamentary Papers on Railways, The Electrical Review, The Mining Journal, The Engineer, Engineering, The Locomotive Magazine, Railway Magazine, Bradshaw's Railway Manual, Journal of Transport History, Stock Exchange Year Book, Skinner's Register of Defunct Companies, Universal Directory of Railway Officials, Directory of Directors, Official Returns – Ministry of Transport, British Transport Commission Historical Records, House of Commons Sessional Papers, House of Lords Record Office, Registrar of Companies, National Library of Wales (especially collections; Longueville, Glynllifon, Henry Robertson and Davies Brothers), County Record Offices, Caernarvon (especially Collections; Breese Jones & Casson, W.A. Madocks and J.W. Greaves), Dolgellau, (especially Collection; Taylor & Francis re. Croesor United), Library of University College North Wales (especially Collections; Carter Vincent, Searell and Cynhaiarn), Manchester Law Society Library, Narrow Gauge Railway Society, L.N.W.R. Earlstown records, G.W.R. Swindon records, Liverpool Museum, Ordnance Survey, *The Times*, Geological Survey & Mineral Statistics of Great Britain, Archaelogia Cambrensis for 1968 (D.M. Rees: 'Copper Mining in North Wales'), Quarry Managers' Journal, Archives of the Narrow Gauge Railway Museum Trust. The house journals and private publications of about one dozen enthusiast and professional bodies have been searched, together with surviving copies of short-lived monthly publications now defunct.

INDEX

To simplify this Index, certain collective headings have been used under which each subject – where appropriate – is listed. These are:

Geographical references and especially place names (stations in particular) where not indexed separately, may be found under 'Route' (see above).

MAPS, PLANS & DIAGRAMS

ROLLING STOCK DRAWINGS

Symbols:

are standard throughout the series. Where a symbol is peculiar to one map a suitable note is made thereon. In the interest of clarity special symbols may be used in some areas, e.g. the Nantlle Valley and Gilfach-Ddu where different 'narrow gauge' trackage co-existed.

RAILWAYS:

	Standard Gauge	Narrow Gauge
Railways built:		
- projected:		
- closed/abandoned:		
Snowdon Mountain Railway-'Abt' System built:		
Snowdon-Rhyd-Ddu: 'Rigi' System proposed:		
Padarn Railway· 4-foot gauge:		
Nantlle Railway· 3ft 6ins. gauge:		
"2-foot" gauge quarry lines where appropriate:		
Mixed gauge:		
Course doubtful or existence questionable:		
Tunnels:		
Inclines: Position of drum shown conventionally:		

OTHER SYMBOLS:

Waiting Shed or Station: ▰ s	Stop Board: S.B•	Signal Box: ⊠
Goods Shed: ▰ G.S.	Altitude Board:	Ground Frame: ◳
Locomotive Shed: ▰ L.S.	Gradien Post:	Signal Post: •S.P.
" Shelter: ⬓	Mile Post: •M.P.	Semaphore Signals:
Carriage Shed: ▰ C.S.	Crane:	Branch subsidiary Signals:
Weigh Bridge: ▰ W.B.	Water Crane: ○—	Point Disc Signals-F.R-type:
Level Crossing- ungated: ⟋ L.C.	Water Tank: ▰ W.T.	F.R-type Home Signal controlling movement in both directions by separate arms.
" gated:	Turntable-loco: ⊘	
Loading Pier:	" -wagon: ◇	
Wharf or Platform Edge. Higher level shown feathered:	Turning Plate:	Catch Point or Trap: C.P.
	Canal:	Locked Scotch:
	Aerial Ropeway: ◇—·—·—◇	

SYMBOLS PECULIAR TO FESTINIOG RAILWAY DIAGRAMS:

Original Signalling:	Semi-modern Signalling by McKenzie & Holland:	Signalling additionally in use 1974-on:
Main Line: 'Home' controlling movement in both directions by separate arms:	Semaphores in various arrangements, branch and subsidiary arms shown ringed:	Single and multiple aspect colour light signals:
Distant or auxiliary:		Upper-quadrant semaphores:
Subsid. Point Indicator:		Banner (Disc) Signals:
Point Disc:	Electric Staff Apparatus: ◇	Somersault semaphores:
Specials: Stop Signal for Moelwyn Tunnel:	Locking or Fouling Bar: —	Original slate mileposts with indication of marking shown nearby: ■ ▲ ⚠
Stop Signal for 'Down' trains to Penrhyn Crossing:	Gate Lock:	

ABBREVIATIONS:

Tramway:	Tᵞ	Slate Wharf:	} see also	S.W.	Quarry:	Qᵞ
Railway:	Rᵞ	Goods Platform:	above	G.P.	Works:	Wks.
Footpath:	f.p.					

Other than for titles and a limited number of early drawings, natural features are indicated by *Italic writing*, 'man-made' ones by sanserif type as this.

M.Lloyd 80218